Practical Utopia

Dartington Hall was a social experiment of kaleidoscopic vitality, set up in Devon in 1925 by a fabulously wealthy American heiress, Dorothy Elmhirst (née Whitney), and her Yorkshire-born husband, Leonard. It quickly achieved international fame with its progressive school, craft production and wide-ranging artistic endeavours. Dartington was a residential community of students, teachers, farmers, artists and craftsmen committed to revivifying life in the countryside. It was also a socio-cultural laboratory, where many of the most brilliant interwar minds came to test out their ideas about art, society, spirituality and rural regeneration. To this day, Dartington Hall remains a symbol of countercultural experimentation and a centre for arts, ecology and social justice. *Practical Utopia* presents a compelling portrait of a group of people trying to live out their ideals, set within an international framework, and demonstrates Dartington's tangled affinities with other unity-seeking projects across Britain and in India and America.

Anna Neima completed her doctorate in history at the University of Cambridge and is now a Leverhulme Early Career Fellow. Her first book, *The Utopians* (2021), tells the story of six communities started around the globe after the First World War.

T0382272

Modern British Histories

Series Editors:

Deborah Cohen, *Northwestern University*
Margot Finn, *University College London*
Peter Mandler, *University of Cambridge*

'Modern British Histories' publishes original research monographs drawn from the full spectrum of a large and lively community of modern historians of Britain. Its goal is to keep metropolitan and national histories of Britain fresh and vital in an intellectual atmosphere increasingly attuned to, and enriched by, the transnational, the international and the comparative. It will include books that focus on British histories within the UK and that tackle the subject of Britain and the world inside and outside the boundaries of formal empire from 1750 to the present. An indicative – not exclusive – list of approaches and topics that the series welcomes includes material culture studies, modern intellectual history, gender, race and class histories, histories of modern science and histories of British capitalism within a global framework. Open and wide-ranging, the series will publish books by authoritative scholars, at all stages of their career, with something genuinely new to say.

A complete list of titles in the series can be found at:
www.cambridge.org/modernbritishhistories

Practical Utopia

The Many Lives of Dartington Hall

Anna Neima

CAMBRIDGE
UNIVERSITY PRESS

Shaftesbury Road, Cambridge CB2 8EA, United Kingdom

One Liberty Plaza, 20th Floor, New York, NY 10006, USA

477 Williamstown Road, Port Melbourne, VIC 3207, Australia

314–321, 3rd Floor, Plot 3, Splendor Forum, Jasola District Centre, New Delhi – 110025, India

103 Penang Road, #05–06/07, Visioncrest Commercial, Singapore 238467

Cambridge University Press is part of Cambridge University Press & Assessment, a department of the University of Cambridge.

We share the University's mission to contribute to society through the pursuit of education, learning and research at the highest international levels of excellence.

www.cambridge.org
Information on this title: www.cambridge.org/9781009048729

DOI: 10.1017/9781009049269

First published 2022
First paperback edition 2024

A catalogue record for this publication is available from the British Library

ISBN   978-1-316-51797-0   Hardback
ISBN   978-1-009-04872-9   Paperback

Contents

Illustrations

Acknowledgements

I would like to thank, in no particular order, the editors of the Modern British Histories series – in particular Peter Mandler, who nurtured this project from its inception with characteristic wisdom and generosity; Liz Friend-Smith and everyone at Cambridge University Press who helped this book on its way; Alexandra Harris, Lucy Delap and the anonymous reviewers of Cambridge University Press for providing thoughtful and inspiring responses to early drafts; the University of Cambridge, Selwyn College and the Arts and Humanities Research Council for funding the doctorate on which this book is based; the New York–Cambridge Training Collaboration participants from 2015 to 2018, whose warm collegiality buoyed my research; the efficient and welcoming staff of the Dartington Hall archives in Exeter and of the Humanities Reading Rooms in the British Library; Yvonne Widger and Kevin Mount, who kindly shared their deep knowledge of Dartington with me; Ivor Stolliday, who read carefully through my manuscript and helped me understand both Dartington's labyrinthine finances and the intense love and fury the community evokes; Leina Schiffrin, Etain Kabraji and Mary Bride Nicholson for their vivid memories of their time at Dartington; Rhodri Samuel, Jonathan Cooper and Mark Kidel, who assisted me with my research; Lise Butler and Dave Anderson for their help in accessing books and journals; and my parents Rachel Watson and John Sanderson, my husband Luke and son James, who provided welcome encouragement, discussion and distraction along the way.

Introduction
An Experiment in the Art of Living

In 1920, a Yorkshire-born agricultural economist, Leonard Elmhirst, wrote a letter to Dorothy Straight (née Whitney), a wealthy New York philanthropist and the woman he loved, about the 'complete breakdown' he had suffered a short time before.[1] For most of his life, he told her, he had expected to become a priest. Then came the 'great deluge' of the First World War. 'I found that the bottom of life had dropped out,' he wrote, 'and that the old beliefs could not stand the test'. The war had destroyed his faith in orthodox Christianity. It had made him question the self-oriented, market-driven doctrine of laissez-faire liberalism that underpinned the Western world. But he had recovered his sense of optimism and purpose, he told Dorothy, and he now wanted to dedicate himself to serving humanity – working to build a more harmonious world: 'what Graham Wallas calls "The Great Society"' and 'someone else called "The Kingdom of Heaven"'. He intended to create a community apart from mainstream society where a new way of living could be pioneered.

Dorothy was enthusiastically supportive. Since the age of nineteen, she had ploughed her great fortune and abundant energies into social reform. The First World War and her husband Willard's death from influenza in 1918 had made her all the more determined to contribute to the public good in a fundamental way – now she, too, hoped to reshape society from the ground up. 'I am filled with that terribly absorbing desire to work, and help and carry through something useful,' she wrote, 'I can't help realizing every night how much more I might have done.'[2] In 1924, Dorothy and Leonard married – drawn together by a shared dream of shaping an alternative, more holistically fulfilling and communitarian model for living. They agreed that if they truly believed in the 'principles which we talk so easily about', they must not 'sit down idly under a

---

[1] Leonard to Dorothy, 27 October 1920, LKE/DWE/10/A, Dartington Hall Archives (unless specified otherwise, all archival references in this book are to this collection).
[2] W. A. Swanberg, *Whitney Father, Whitney Heiress* (New York, 1980), 250.

system which defies them' but must make 'some attempt however feeble to pursue our ideal'.[3] In 1925, they bought Dartington Hall in South Devon and began a social, cultural and educational experiment that they hoped would 'set the pace' for Britain and the rest of the world.[4] They devoted the rest of their lives to this project, which became one of the best-known and most influential of the many small-scale interwar utopian experiments.

When the Elmhirsts arrived, Dartington was a run-down estate supporting only a handful of people. Within a few years it housed a school, departments of dance-drama, crafts and textiles, and numerous industrial and agricultural enterprises. Dorothy and Leonard's ambition for this multifaceted community was twofold. All participants should have an existence that allowed them to be more than just economic units: they would contribute to a revived rural economy, but their days would also incorporate learning, creativity and a sense of spiritual communion, resulting in a life of complete fulfilment. The second hope was that participants would be fully involved in running the estate, creating a thriving social democracy that would perfect them as individuals and bring about the unified progress of the community as a whole. Dartington was not, in the Elmhirsts' eyes, an exercise in escapism: they hoped that this 'abundant' experiment in integrated, democratic living would function both as a test bed for ideas – inspiring people well beyond its physical boundaries – and as an imitable model, 'an ideal for all groups to work to'.[5]

Beyond the overarching desire to be an 'ideal spiral of all feeding in', Dartington's objectives were never prescriptively spelled out.[6] This was, to a degree, intentional: the Elmhirsts wanted their community to be 'built by people and not on paper', growing up organically rather than outlined out in a manifesto.[7] It was also because Dorothy and Leonard were not clear conceptual thinkers, finding it difficult – even impossible – fully to articulate their ideals. Instead, they tried to live by them. The Elmhirsts' ambitions were implied by those they invited to join them and by the enterprises they instigated. The looseness of their hopes for Dartington allowed a range of idealists and reformers, sometimes with

---

[3] Leonard Elmhirst to Eduard Lindeman, 7 January 1924, box 2, Eduard Lindeman Archives, Columbia University, DWE/G/7/C. Leonard tended to be the mouthpiece for and executor of the couple's shared ideas, while Dorothy's influence on the shape of Dartington was often tacit. To give voice to her role, the term 'the Elmhirsts' will sometimes be used in this book where it was Leonard who was doing the actual articulation, but of a joint position.

[4] Leonard to Dorothy, 19 May 1923, LKE/DWE/11/C.   [5] Ibid.

[6] Leonard Elmhirst, untitled note, 27 January 1936, LKE/G/S9/A.

[7] Leonard Elmhirst to Eduard Lindeman, 7 January 1924, box 2, Eduard Lindeman Archives.

I.1 Rex Gardner's drawing for the 500th edition of Dartington's daily news sheet, *News of the Day*, 1934 (© Dartington Hall Trust and the Elmgrant Trust)

conflicting agendas, to work at the same time towards their particular iteration of a better life in the 'perfect playground' of the estate.[8]

Capacious vagueness of ideology was not the only aspect of the Elmhirsts' community-building that was unusual. In a period of

---

[8] Leonard, 'Note for talk', 16 May 1936, LKE/G/S8/F. This concept of Dartington echoes Michael Saler's characterisation of the fantasy worlds proliferating in this period as 'playgrounds'; both the Elmhirsts' estate and these fictional worlds were sites for experimenting with new ideas about how to live. *As If: Modern Enchantment and the Literary Prehistory of Virtual Reality* (Oxford, 2012), 7.

economic uncertainty, Dartington was well financed, Dorothy's fortune – estimated at $35 million in 1925 – allowing the translation of ideals into reality at a rate beyond most reformers' wildest dreams.[9] In addition, both the Elmhirsts, but Leonard especially, had a particular gift for friendship, maintaining networks of reform-minded acquaintances around the globe. This quality, along with the Elmhirsts' ideological openness and wealth, meant that Dartington became a nexus of international idealism. It impacted and was influenced by reforming projects in Europe, Asia and America, including the Bauhaus, Rabindranath Tagore's Sriniketan and the New Deal. Like the loci of late-nineteenth-century utopian socialism delineated by Leela Gandhi, it developed into a 'hybrid and eclectic' scene, fuelled by friendship, which brought together disparate radical subcultures from across the world.[10]

At its best, Dartington's inchoate inclusiveness generated an atmosphere that was inventive, inspiring, rich in possibility and hope; at its worst, it produced muddled thinking, inconsistency and hypocrisy, and left a few participants with a permanent sense of grievance. The enterprise alternately impressed and perplexed observers. 'I can see many aims and objects desperately tangled', wrote one visitor in 1931.[11] But to another, Dartington was 'the image of the future, all our utopic ideas having become realities. It is encouraging, it is consoling to know such a place exists in the world.'[12]

This book avoids framing Dartington in terms of either a 'failed' or 'successful' utopian experiment; all utopias are reactions to a particular historical moment and, as that moment changes, so do visions of the 'good place', with old ideas inevitably falling by the wayside. For me, the wonder and interest in revisiting the Elmhirsts' project – in telling this small-scale story about very big ideas – does not come from the question of whether or not Dartington demonstrated an ideal social blueprint. Rather, it comes from the humane and imaginative ways in which those involved in the community responded to the perceived problems of their

---

[9] Between 1925 and 1936, Dorothy spent about $8 million in America, and the same sum in England, mainly on Dartington. Despite this, and the effects of the Depression, strategically diverse holdings meant her fortune was valued at $45 million in 1936. Michael Young, *The Elmhirsts of Dartington: The Creation of a Utopian Community* (London, 1982), 299.

[10] Leela Gandhi, *Affective Communities: Anticolonial Thought, Fin-de-Siècle Radicalism, and the Politics of Friendship* (Durham and London, 2006), 177–8 and passim.

[11] William St John Pym, response to 1931 Dartington questionnaire, T/PP/P/1/E.

[12] Andrée Karpelès to the Elmhirsts, 3 June 1935, LKE/G/21/F. Andrée Karpelès, a painter, illustrator and translator, worked for a time at Sriniketan with Leonard. She later ran the Indian edition of the magazine *Messages d'Orient*, published in French in Alexandria.

time, dedicating the very material of their lives to mastering what Dartington habitué Aldous Huxley called 'that most difficult and most important of all the arts – the art of living together in harmony and with benefit for all concerned'.[13] It comes, equally, from the window that the Elmhirsts' activities open onto larger histories.

Dartington can be read in a dizzying number of ways. In the British context, it can be framed as a case study in rural regeneration or in the dethroning of elite patronage and philanthropy by state-sponsored intervention.[14] With an eye to the United States, it can be interpreted as part of the history of transatlantic progressivism or of the globalisation of American philanthropy.[15] From the viewpoint of India, it can be understood as a demonstration of the 'religious revival' of which Rabindranath Tagore was a part.[16] Situated in a wider field, the experiment can be seen as an episode in the worldwide history of utopianism or in the centuries-long endeavour to make capitalism moral.[17] The Elmhirsts' project gives a vivid illustration, too, of two important twentieth-century developments: the attempt to marry local attachments with international horizons – what the philosopher Kwame Appiah calls 'rooted cosmopolitanism';[18] and the emphasis on the significance of everyday lived experience in forging a 'common culture'.[19] This book will consider all these frameworks, and more, to make sense of the various elements that made up the Elmhirsts' estate. But, overall, it interprets Dartington

---

[13] Aldous Huxley, 'Ozymandias', in *Adonis and the Alphabet, and Other Essays* (London, 1956), 100.

[14] Paul Brassley, Jeremy Burchardt and Lynne Thompson, *The English Countryside*; David Matless, *Landscape and Englishness* (London, 1998); Brian Foss, 'Message and Medium: Government Patronage, National Identity and National Culture in Britain, 1939–45', *Oxford Art Journal* 14 (1991), 52–7.

[15] Daniel T. Rodgers, *Atlantic Crossings: Social Politics in a Progressive Age* (Cambridge, 1998); Inderjeet Parmar, 'Foundation Networks and America Hegemony', *European Journal of American Studies* 7 (2012), 2–25.

[16] Ruth Harris, 'Rolland, Gandhi and Madeleine Slade: Spiritual Politics, France and the Wider World', *French History* 27 (2013), 579–99.

[17] Dennis Hardy, *Utopian England: Community Experiments 1900–1945* (London, 2000); Jay Winter, *Dreams of Peace and Freedom: Utopian Moments in the Twentieth Century* (New Haven and London, 2006); Stefan Berger and Alexandra Przyrembel (eds), *Moralizing Capitalism: Agents, Discourses and Practices of Capitalism and Anti-Capitalism in the Modern Age* (Cham, 2019).

[18] Kwame Anthony Appiah, 'Cosmopolitan Patriots', *Critical Inquiry* 23 (1997), 617–39, at 633. See also *The Ethics of Identity* (Princeton, 2005).

[19] Leela Gandhi, *The Common Cause: Postcolonial Ethics and the Practice of Democracy, 1900–1955* (Chicago, 2014); Raymond Williams, *Culture and Society* (London: Vintage, [1958], 2017) and *The Country and the City* (London, [1973] 2017). See also, Marc Stears, *Out of the Ordinary: How Everyday Life Inspired a Nation and How it Can Again* (Cambridge, MA, 2021).

as a series of responses, sometimes overlapping, sometimes clashing, that sought to grapple with the inadequacies of laissez-faire liberalism.

What did laissez-faire liberalism mean for the Elmhirsts? The word 'liberal' was deployed very loosely in the years between the wars: Julia Stapleton suggests that there were so many forms of liberalism that it is best to think of the variants not as part of one ideology, but as 'sensibilities – articulating a style of political action appropriate to the English political world they characterized'.[20] Dorothy and Leonard used 'liberalism' more vaguely than most. By and large, they saw laissez-faire liberalism as a set of destructive tendencies: individualistic competition; a way of life shorn of any meaning beyond getting and keeping; an atomised society, rather than one that emphasised humankind's inter-connection; the loss of a higher, transcendent meaning that gave a unifying altruistic or spiritual purpose to individual existence and to society as a whole. Sometimes they viewed themselves as rejecting all forms of liberalism; more frequently, their aim was to reconfigure liberalism in a more socialised, holistically fulfilling form: they believed it should be a means of building a satisfying individual way of life that also involved contributing to the collective good.

With the emergence of totalitarianism in the 1930s, the picture was further muddied as those at Dartington began defining their ideas against authoritarianism – which often involved a new enthusiasm for 'English' liberal individualism. At the heart of this idea was an association of the English national character with the countryside, whose varied landscape and culture was seen to underpin a diverse individuality that acted as a bulwark against the scourge of totalitarian ideas.[21] The Elmhirsts enthusiastically subscribed to this view of the distinctiveness of English liberalism, and it was one of the original reasons that they situated their experiment in the deep countryside. 'Liberal-reforming' is therefore used in this book to imply both condemnation of laissez-faire liberal tendencies and an embrace of the idea of a distinctive, individualistic 'English' liberalism.

Alongside 'liberal-reforming', I frequently characterise Dartington and its participants as 'progressive', a term also sufficiently contested and ambiguous to need early definition. As Emily Robinson finds, in the interwar period the word's centre of gravity tended towards the political left, but it was also deployed by conservatives opposed to socialist and

---

[20] Julia Stapleton, 'Resisting the Centre at the Extremes: "English" Liberalism in the Political Thought of Interwar Britain', *The British Journal of Politics & International Relations* 1 (1999), 270–92, at 273.

[21] Ibid, 276.

revolutionary action.[22] It was associated with active citizenship but was used in a range of non-political settings as well – to characterise efficient business practice, for example, or cultural experimentation.[23] The word's meaning is further complicated by the Atlantic context that informed politics in Britain: in the United States, 'progressive' tended to be a less inclusive term, more clearly identified with a political movement and the Progressive Party that grew out of it – a movement with which Dorothy was involved.[24] The label 'progressive' is a useful one for Dartington exactly because it is so vague and diffuse, encompassing – as the estate did – political aspirations, loosely framed desires for the shape of future society, and narrower meanings, as in the case of child-oriented 'progressive' educational reform. This book unpacks alternate senses where they arise, but generally when it uses 'progressive' it is gesturing, as the Elmhirsts were when they used it, to a capacious socio-political ideology – implying left-leaning (but not revolutionary) ideas about promoting social change and revolving around the ideals of individual fulfilment and active social participation; and also a mentality focused on moving beyond the present. As Robinson writes, 'to be progressive is to anticipate the future and, in doing so, it is to bring that future into being'.[25]

Dartington's history in the first half of the twentieth century fell into three phases, which were shaped by the community's internal dynamics, by Britain's domestic politics, and by the rise of fascist regimes in Europe. Beginning in 1925, the Elmhirsts concentrated on reform at a local level, and here they came closest to achieving their goal of demonstrating a holistically fulfilling community life. Dorothy funded the project generously. Participants' expectations were high. The community succeeded in merging its educational, spiritual and practical aims and activities and in attracting interest from progressives in Britain and across the world. The years after the First World War saw widespread disenchantment with conventional methods of achieving change – with 'politicians, governments, treaties, and conferences' as Leonard put it – and Dartington's radical approach proved attractive to many.[26]

The second phase, beginning in the early 1930s, was triggered by the totalitarian dystopias that were threatening abroad and the seeming lack of political response to these in Britain. Dartington took in an influx of

---

[22] Emily Robinson, *The Language of Progressive Politics in Modern Britain* (London, 2017), chapter 2. See also, David Blaazer, *The Popular Front and the Progressive Tradition* (Cambridge, 2009), 18–19.
[23] Robinson, *Progressive Politics*, chapters 4 and 5.   [24] Rodgers, *Atlantic Crossings*.
[25] Robinson, *Progressive Politics*, 4, 49.
[26] Leonard to Dorothy, 3 February 1922, LKE/DWE/10/F.

European refugees. At the same time, the Elmhirsts began to feel that their enterprise should be offering a more immediate, realistically costed and widely replicable model of community. Their drive became less towards local organic integration and more towards efficient administration and outside impact. Over the course of the 1930s, echoing the trajectory of other elites in Britain, they gradually moved away from a vision of society as perfected through autonomous local groups to one in which reform was led from the centre. For Christopher Lawrence and Anna-K Mayer, this shift in the locus of responsibility for regeneration in the 1930s was 'the road to the welfare state'.[27]

The Second World War precipitated Dartington's third stage. It brought to the fore a 'social-democratic' notion of democracy, led by an organised working class, which undermined the concept of independent, elite-led social experiments.[28] The war also brought about the extension and centralisation of government. From this point onward, the Elmhirsts began working mainly to turn Dartington into an outpost of research and development for the government – and they succeeded in making significant contributions to the construction of the welfare state. This shift did not mean that the notion of change being achieved through small communities fell entirely by the wayside. Dorothy and Leonard went on, in the 1950s and 1960s, to be involved in supporting the community development movement in Britain and abroad. Meanwhile, others at Dartington took a different route during and after the Second World War, withdrawing from democratic engagement in favour of more individualistic self-exploration.

The Elmhirsts and their supporters sometimes used the term 'utopia' to describe what they were building at Dartington – denoting the effort to turn a radical social vision into a real place that might inspire wider change. But they also used the word in a negative sense – implying impractical, unrealistic social dreaming – when describing the 'innumerable social experiments', past and present, from which they wanted to distinguish Dartington.[29] Robert Owen's New Harmony, for example, was 'not based on sound economics, or sound psychology';[30] the

---

[27] Christopher Lawrence and Anna-K Mayer, 'Regenerating England: An Introduction', in Christopher Lawrence and Anna-K Mayer (eds.), *Regenerating England: Science, Medicine and Culture in Interwar Britain* (Amsterdam, 2000), 1–24 at 2.

[28] Ross McKibbin, *Classes and Cultures: England 1918–1951* (Oxford, 1998), 533.

[29] Leonard Elmhirst to Eduard Lindeman, 7 January 1924, box 2, Eduard Lindeman Archives.

[30] Leonard to A. W. Ashby, 4 June 1934, LKE/LAND/1/B. The Welsh industrialist and social reformer Robert Owen set up the community of New Harmony on socialist principles in America in 1825. By 1827 it had been torn asunder by disputes over its governance. Ian L. Donnachie, *Robert Owen: Owen of New Lanark and New Harmony* (East Linton, 2000).

late-nineteenth-century model villages of Bournville and Port Sunlight were too paternalistic;[31] the Cotswold Bruderhof Community and Welwyn Garden City had ambitions that were too narrow.[32] Early on, Soviet Russia was deemed by some at Dartington to be utopian in the positive sense, with one employee demanding a '"Five Years Plan"'.[33] But as the totalitarian regimes grew stronger through the 1930s, more emphasis was placed on Dartington's being different from any others. While the Russians had revolutionary group socialism, Leonard argued that what America and Britain needed was the gradual evolution of 'socialised individualism'.[34] The term 'utopian' is deployed in this book in the same ambivalent sense that it had for Dartington's participants: it describes an impulse to turn high ideals into a lived reality that verges on the impractical and quixotic – which is a very good way of encapsulating the Elmhirsts' project as a whole.

Dartington's multiple experiments – while too easily written off as marginal and eccentric by contemporaries and historians – had effects and consequences in a variety of fields.[35] Its pioneering work in soil surveys and its championing of access to the arts influenced post-war government policy. It contributed significantly to moulding twentieth-century traditions of handcraft, modernism, learning-by-doing, countercultural spirituality and communitarianism. While it is a moot question whether these disparate activities could have happened without the Elmhirsts' initial utopian and holistic inspiration, one certainly cannot understand them individually without tracing them back to those roots – which is part of what this book does. Dartington merits close study as an intellectually-linked constellation of experiments in education, the arts, spiritualism, agriculture and social organisation that has rarely been looked at in the round.[36]

---

[31] John Wales to W. B. Curry, 4 March 1936, C/DHL/1/B. Port Sunlight was a model village built by the Lever Brothers in 1888 to house their workers. Bournville was a similar endeavour begun by George Cadbury in 1893.

[32] J. J. Findlay, *The Dartington Community: A Story of Social Achievement*, unfinished manuscript written 1937–9, LKE/G/13/B. The Bruderhof, started in Germany in 1920, promoted communitarian Christian living. In the 1930s, under pressure from the Nazis, it moved to England, setting up in the Cotswolds. Welwyn Garden City, also founded in 1920, by Ebenezer Howard, was one of several garden cities intended as radical vehicles for social and environmental reform.

[33] Anonymous response to 1931 questionnaire, LKE/G/13/B.

[34] Leonard to Arthur Geddes, 24 February 1923, LKE/IN/6/D.

[35] For such criticism, see, for instance, William St John Pym, response to 1931 questionnaire, T/PP/P/1/E and Hardy, *Utopian England*, 157.

[36] Victor Bonham-Carter's *Dartington Hall: The History of an Experiment* (London, 1958) and Michael Young's *The Elmhirsts* are the only books that offer a full survey of the estate. Both authors were prejudiced in the community's favour: Bonham-Carter because he was appointed Dartington's official historian by the Elmhirsts, his role being to document the estate's activities in great detail rather than to analyse them in the wider

This book also illuminates a wider landscape of holistic reformism. The ideal of promoting wholeness, integration, unity or syncretism cropped up in a huge range of forms and places in the interwar years, in Britain and further afield. Progressive educators tried to address the needs of the whole child, rather than dividing learning up into narrow subjects.[37] Artists seized on the project of unifying the various media, or the process of creation, or life with art.[38] Those who had lost their Christian faith sought syncretic alternatives that amalgamated spirituality with the findings of modern science.[39] Idealist philosophers argued that society was not an 'atomistic' aggregate, but a single organism with a shared purpose that was embodied in a general will.[40] An abundance of projects were set up to encourage more integrated living, including the Brynmawr Experiment in Wales, Ditchling in Sussex and Rolf Gardiner's Springhead estate in Dorset.[41] British post-war social democracy itself owes some of its zeal and efficacy to such holistic origins (which of course it combined with others). In all of these fields of thought and action, there were different panaceas offered for different sorts of ills, but the basic problem distinguished was the same: the need to uncover an underlying essence that would restore unity and meaning. Dartington mirrored and cross-pollinated with many of these unity-seeking projects, and a study of the community draws attention to the broader holistic moment that they constituted.

There are pluses and minuses to looking at one utopian experiment as representative of a reforming milieu. Dartington bears the peculiar imprint of its founders. Dorothy retained unusually close connections with America and Leonard with India. Leonard was idiosyncratically preoccupied with the application of scientific techniques, Dorothy with her own spiritual journey and with the professional arts. Both of them were interested in the fate of the countryside, almost to the exclusion of the town. Dorothy's wealth removed Dartington from the average run of

---

context; Young because he was a pupil at Dartington School, then a protégé of the Elmhirsts and a trustee of the estate, signalling his commitment to the project by taking the title 'Baron Young of Dartington' when he was given a life peerage in 1978.

[37] William Boyd and Wyatt Rawson, *The Story of the New Education* (London, 1965).

[38] Michael Saler, *The Avant-Garde in Interwar England: Medieval Modernism and the London Underground* (New York and Oxford, 1999).

[39] Jenny Hazelgrove, *Spiritualism and British Society Between the Wars* (Manchester, 2000); *John Warne Monroe, Laboratories of Faith: Mesmerism, Spiritualism, and Occultism in Modern France* (Ithaca and London, 2008).

[40] Jose Harris, *Private Lives, Public Spirit: A Social History of Britain, 1870–1914* (London, 1993), 228. See also Sandra den Otter, '"Thinking in Communities": Late Nineteenth-Century Liberals, Idealists and the Retrieval of Community', *Parliamentary History* 16 (1997), 67–84.

[41] Dennis Hardy surveys the communities of this period in *Utopian England*.

social reform projects. In spite of these specificities, their estate offers an overview of responses to uneasiness about laissez-faire liberalism across specific fields, projects and groups that have already been studied discretely but lack connection to the larger span. While allowing Dartington its peculiarities, this account will show that the enterprise was not, as historian Dennis Hardy would have it, insular and unrepresentative – 'a community of indulgence, a place of privilege, rather than an important social experiment'.[42] Rather, it was a significant nexus in a wider realm of people trying urgently to conceptualise and put into practice what it meant to live a good life in the wake of the First World War and in the run-up to the Second.

This book begins by introducing Dorothy and Leonard Elmhirst and giving an overview of Dartington's development between 1925 and 1945. Each subsequent chapter focuses on a particular aspect of the estate. Chapter 2 is about the various approaches taken to reorganising and reunifying the affective, spiritual or social framework of society. Chapter 3 looks at how progressive education was used as a tool to create citizens who were fulfilled and socially responsible. Chapter 4 is about how Dartington approached the arts as a means of synthesis in an age of specialisation and division. Chapter 5 explores efforts to regenerate the countryside by reforming local agriculture and industry, and above all, by promoting democratic social participation. The book concludes with an examination of Dartington's fortunes through the second half of the twentieth century and into the twenty-first.

Each of these chapters builds outwards into its own specific historical field but also emphasises the Elmhirsts' constant efforts to keep the various segments of their enterprise woven together: the sum meaning of Dartington was more than its parts – it was the effort to join them together 'in one organic whole', and the connection to the wider politics of holistic idealism.[43] 'I really don't know what appealed to us the most', wrote a visiting couple who later decided to leave a legacy to the estate, '– the whole, I suppose, without any possibility to analyse one thing separately'.[44]

I.1   A Note on Archives

The main archive that this book relies on is that of the Dartington Hall Trust, a collection started by the Elmhirsts in 1925 and maintained by

---

[42] Ibid, 157.   [43] Leonard, 'Situation', September 1927, DWE/DHS/1/F.
[44] Andrée Karpelès to the Elmhirsts, 3 June 1935; C. A. Hogman, Karpelès' husband, to Leonard, [n.d.], LKE/G/21/F.

the estate's staff and trustees to the present day. This was housed on the Dartington estate until March 2012, when it was moved to the Devon Heritage Centre in Exeter. Its contents range from the correspondence and notebooks of Leonard, Dorothy and several other key participants of their experiment to agricultural and sociological surveys; from programmes and photographs left over from plays and exhibitions to departmental accounts, memoranda and the minutes of meetings. These papers were not systematically amassed, particularly in the 1920s. There are missing or multiple copies of documents; documents that are undated or unattributed; documents that have been scrawled on tentatively in hindsight – often by Leonard, who had a keen interest in history and record-keeping – in an attempt to provide them with some context. Early on, this collection seems to have been kept simply because there was the space to do so; later, it came to be seen as a crucial educational resource, for the estate's participants and for outsiders. Producing an account of their work so that others could learn from it became, for the Elmhirsts, an essential part of their experiment, and in the 1950s they commissioned ruralist and historian Victor Bonham-Carter to complete this task.[45] Over the next twenty years, Bonham-Carter and archivist Robin Johnson organised Dartington's records into broad categories, relating to the commercial departments; to the non-commercial work of the Dartington Trust; and to Dorothy and Leonard's correspondence and documents. The present-day archive retains this form.

Like all official archives, whether national, colonial or parochial, the Dartington Hall Trust collection must be approached with caution – as something produced by people with influence, 'as a symbol or form of power'.[46] In what it preserves and in how it is arranged, it presents a story sanctioned by the Elmhirsts, and at the same time, often inadvertently, it silences other stories. Although Dorothy and Leonard saw theirs as a democratic project – a 'common enterprise' – the lives of the workers who made up the majority of the Dartington community are marginalised in the archives.[47] When their voices do appear – answering surveys about their level of satisfaction, quoted in the minutes of an estate

---

[45] Victor Bonham-Carter ended up writing several books on Dartington, including *Dartington Hall: The History of an Experiment* and *Dartington Hall: The Formative Years, 1925–1957* (Dulverton, Somerset, 1970).

[46] Carolyn Steedman, *Dust* (Manchester, 2001), 2; Helen Freshwater, 'The Allure of the Archive: Performance and Censorship', *Moveable Type* 3 (2007), 5–24; Ann Laura Stoler, 'Colonial Archives and the Arts of Governance: On the Content in the Form', in Francis X. Blouin and William Rosenberg (eds.) *Archives, Documentation, and Institutions of Social Memory: Essays from the Sawyer Seminar* (Ann Arbor, MI, 2006), 267–79.

[47] Dorothy to Reverend Drake-Brockman, 9 February 1932, DWE/A/7/B.

meeting or in Dartington's daily newspaper, setting down a short memoir – their opinions are usually framed by someone else: the compiler of questionnaire responses, the meeting's secretary, the paper's editor, the archivist. Dissent among Dartington's workers and other local people, of which there was clearly a substantial amount, is muted by the gloss of official commentary.

Other voices are muted too. Men feature more prominently than women, indicating that gender politics were more conventional than the progressive agenda of Dartington might suggest. The most significant written statements, opinions and directives in the archive come from Leonard rather than Dorothy. A self-effacing character, Dorothy encouraged her husband to be the public front of their project. Leonard himself recognised that while he was occupied with highly visible 'cow, bull, field and tree activities', Dorothy's chief contribution to their experiment was dealing with 'the intimate problems and difficulties in personal relationships that no-one measures, that few notice, and that – when the story of Dartington is written, will largely go unrecorded'.[48] Since it is clear that Dorothy's money, ideals, tastes and gift for friendship were vital to shaping Dartington, the historian must search for her influence in the silences.

There are few mentions of sex and sexuality in the archive or in the officially sanctioned accounts of the estate. Reading against the grain – drawing together scribbled asides, participants' memoirs, the comments of outsiders – it is clear that this was a deliberate act of suppression, that sex was on the minds of many involved in the Elmhirsts' project. This took the form of dissident sexual desire, disputes over sex education, extra-marital affairs, the guarding or stretching of gender norms, libidinal currents in the arts, spiritual questing and radical visions of an international society. As Matt Houlbrook, Lucy Bland and other historians find, in the interwar period sex and sexuality figured importantly in the reconfiguration of ideas about selfhood and society.[49] Since this development obviously influenced Dartington, and since the Elmhirsts themselves appear to have been at least moderately supportive of it, why is sex so elusive in the archive? One of the reasons seems to be that Dorothy, Leonard and other participants worried that if the estate gained a

---

[48] Leonard, 'Time Budget 1934–5', 8 November 1934, LKE/G/S8/1.

[49] Matt Houlbrook, 'Thinking Queer: The Social and the Sexual in Interwar Britain', in Brian Lewis (ed.) *British Queer History: New Approaches and Perspectives* (Manchester, 2013), 134–164; Lucy Bland, *Modern Women on Trial: Sexual Transgression in the Age of the Flapper* (Manchester, 2016); Laura Doan, 'Topsy-Turvydom: Gender Inversion, Sapphism, and the Great War', *GLQ: A Journal of Lesbian and Gay Studies* 12 (2006) 517–42.

reputation for radical sexual politics, it would lose its appeal for more conventional people who might otherwise have supported it.[50] Another is that experimentation with sex and sexuality proved to be an angst-ridden and fractious business – our 'ingrowing toenail', Leonard called it – interrupting the harmony of the community without yielding obvious dividends by way of social improvement.[51] The Elmhirsts did not, perhaps, want this messy and unresolved side of their project preserved for posterity.[52]

The lacunae in the Dartington archive can be filled to an extent by triangulating the estate's records with other sources: local newspapers, the published and unpublished memoirs of participants, oral history, collections of letters held elsewhere.[53] Even so, as Carolyn Steedman writes of archival work generally, there will still be gaps, and historians must be alert to 'how the emptiness indicates how once it was filled'.[54]

---

[50] Group meeting, Sunday 25 June 1933, T/AE/4/F.
[51] Notebook, Leonard to Gerald Heard, 26 December 1934, LKE/G/17. See also Wyatt Rawson to Eduard Lindeman, July 1927, DWE/G/7/C.
[52] A rare attempt to recover and celebrate Dartington's history as an oasis of queer culture is Jonathan Cooper's 'Friends of Dorothy' (unpublished talk given at Dartington's first queer arts festival, 'A Dartington Outing', held in 2017).
[53] This book draws, in particular, on the Eduard Lindeman Archives at Columbia University, the Leach Archives at the University Centre for the Creative Arts, the Nancy Wilson Ross Archives at the Harry Ransom Center and the British Library Newspaper Archive.
[54] Steedman, *Dust*, 11.

1　Overview

> You happen to be the only woman in the world today who has shared so many of my own experiences; vital loss in the war, an attitude of pacifism, a real knowledge and sympathetic understanding of problems and countries the world around, a driving power to spend in causes and for people.　　　　　　　　Leonard to Dorothy (unsent letter, 1924)[1]

Dartington Hall was built on a strong, companionate relationship between two complex, contradictory people who were, on the face of it, an unlikely match: a very rich American who yearned for spiritual meaning and a world of equals, yet would renounce none of her personal privilege, and a Yorkshire-born would-be vicar who lost his faith in Christianity and embraced a 'scientific' approach to helping humanity instead – but whose romantic passion for new ideas and projects impeded him from ever using truly empirical methods.[2] Dorothy was a realist and could be ruthless in her treatment of people, while Leonard was an eternal optimist who 'did not think in terms of contractions, dilemmas and insoluble problems' and whose trust in others often turned out to be misplaced.[3] What united them was their idealism and sense of social mission: the desire to help people, and in particular to model a better way of living. The paths that led them to marry and start Dartington illuminate a rich early-twentieth-century landscape of philanthropy, humanitarianism, spirituality and international exchange, and show how affective relationships, whether based on friendship or love, fuelled far-reaching collaborative reformism.[4]

---

[1] Leonard to Dorothy, July/August 1924, quoted in Michael Young, *The Elmhirsts of Dartington: The Creation of a Utopian Community* (London, 1982), 95.
[2] Michael Young quoted in Anthea Williams, 'First Draft of C7', March 1979, T/HIS/21/A, Dartington Hall Archives (unless specified otherwise, all the following archival references are to this collection).
[3] Ibid.
[4] For the wider landscape of affective reformism, see Eric Rauchway, *The Refuge of Affections: Family and American Reform Politics, 1900–1920* (New York, 2001); and Leela Gandhi, *Affective Communities: Anticolonial Thought, Fin-de-Siècle Radicalism, and the Politics of Friendship* (Durham, SC and London, 2006).

1.1   The American Heiress and the Yorkshire Squire

Dorothy Payne Whitney was born in 1887, the youngest daughter of William Collins Whitney – a wealthy industrialist who had been secretary to the US Navy and was described by Henry Adams as the man who had 'satiated every taste, gorged every appetite, won every object until New York knew no longer what most to envy, his houses or his horses'.[5] She had an emotionally isolated childhood in 'a beautiful house in New York – a kind of Renaissance palace, with great salons and long galleries': there was a ten-year gap between her and her three elder siblings; her forceful, socialite mother, Flora (née Payne), died when she was six, and her stepmother then died when she was twelve.[6] In 1904, her father died as well, leaving Dorothy three-tenths of his fortune. When she came of age four years later, aged twenty-one, she was worth around $8 million.[7] She knew that some of her money derived from monopolies her father had held over public franchises, since a scandal had broken about this the year she came of age – part of a campaign for political reform that was sweeping through America.[8] Dorothy had had a 'penchant for doing her own thinking' since childhood, and she had a strong sense of social responsibility that derived, in large part, from her Protestant upbringing.[9] These characteristics, combined with her guilt over the source of her wealth, meant that she was not content to settle down to the conventional debutante round of sociability and husband-seeking. Instead, she embarked on a series of philanthropic causes – this marked the beginning of a lifelong search for better ways of being, for both herself and others.

In the rich New York social set in which Dorothy moved, it was common for people to engage in philanthropy, but Dorothy's efforts went far beyond what was usual. She started by volunteering at settlement houses, and then she moved on to thinking about how she could improve the organisation of the houses themselves.[10] One of her major projects was to establish the Junior League House, an apartment house

---

[5] Henry Adams, *The Education of Henry Adams* (Boston and New York, 1918), 268. See also W. A. Swanberg, *Whitney Father, Whitney Heiress* (New York, 1980).

[6] Dorothy, 'Background and Foreground – A Personal Pattern', [n.d.], DWE/S/1/E.

[7] Young, *Elmhirsts*, 41.

[8] Swanberg, *Whitney Father*, 198–201. Michael Sandel discusses progressive 'trust-busting' in *Democracy's Discontent: America in Search of a Public Philosophy* (London, 1996), 211–21. See also Marc Stears, *Demanding Democracy* (Princeton and Oxford, 2010).

[9] William Collins Whitney quoted in Jane Brown, *Angel Dorothy: How an American Progressive Came to Devon* (London, 2017), 19.

[10] Ibid., 28–30; Karolyn R. Gould, 'The Modest Benefactor', *Cornell Alumni News* 3 (1975), 19–21.

1.1 Dorothy and Leonard outside Dartington Hall, 1925
(© Dartington Hall Trust and the Elmgrant Trust)

for working women, which she insisted should be structured as a self-supporting organisation rather than one permanently reliant on donations – foreshadowing her hopes for Dartington.[11] She found some of the companionship she had lacked as a child in the bonds she forged with other female reformers, including Jane Addams and Lillian Wald. Like the Victorian slum visitors studied by Seth Koven, her philanthropy was fuelled by a desire to belong – to find 'communities of loving solidarity' – as well as to help the poor.[12] Such affective sentiments would be a strong force at Dartington, too, with the Elmhirsts hoping to create a community 'where people are <u>friends</u>' (emphasis in the original).[13]

A number of Dorothy's co-reformers concentrated their forces on campaigning to expand women's social and political rights.[14] Dorothy also supported the Women's Trade Union League and campaigns for women's suffrage, but feminism was not a central motivation in her

[11] Rauchway, *Refuge*, 32.
[12] Seth Koven, *Slumming: Sexual and Social Politics in Victorian London* (Princeton, 2004), 184.
[13] Leonard Elmhirst to Eduard Lindeman, 7 January 1924, box 2, Eduard Lindeman Archives.
[14] Johanna Neuman, *Gilded Suffragists: The New York Socialites Who Fought for Women's Right to Vote* (New York, 2017).

reforming activities. In her private life, too, she was diffident about asserting women's equality: rather than directly challenging gender conventions, she wrote in her diary that she wanted to find a husband of large ambition so that she could be 'part of his work' – in this way she could exercise influence beyond the limited, domestic realm of action expected of a woman without inciting controversy.[15] In 1911, Dorothy met and married Willard Straight, a charming, dashing diplomat and businessman who appeared to fit her requirements.[16] Straight's driving hope was to create an 'American empire' – taking political influence in Asia away from Britain, Russia and Japan and ensuring it was held instead by those who were enlightened, liberal and allies of the United States.[17] The couple lived in Peking (Beijing) for six months until the revolution of 1911, and then they returned to New York. In China, Dorothy had discovered she did not particularly share her husband's vision of an American empire and that, anyway, he was more inclined to dreamy idealism than to the ambitious, practical action in which she had hoped he would assist her. Once back in America, she persuaded Willard that he should channel his energies, instead, into helping her confront the country's domestic ills.[18]

A book suggested to the couple a novel way of approaching this challenge: journalist and political theorist Herbert Croly's *The Promise of American Life*.[19] Poignantly for Dorothy, Croly attacked capitalists like her father, who exploited the weak for their own gain. He argued that the elite needed to become more socially responsible and to devote themselves to turning America into a more united and democratic nation. Under the influence of this book, Dorothy and Willard financed the setting up of a journal, *The New Republic*, which was co-founded by Croly, Walter Lippmann and Walter Weyl. The journal was ostensibly run as a 'gentlemen's club' headed by Willard, but, successfully extending her power across the normative gender divide, Dorothy's guiding hand was firm in the background – as it would be at Dartington.[20] *The New Republic* became the influential mouthpiece of a

[15] Dorothy quoted in Swanberg, *Whitney Father*, 224.
[16] After attending Cornell University, Willard Straight worked as a Reuters correspondent and then joined the diplomatic service before becoming the representative of the interests of J. P. Morgan and E. H. Harriman in China. Herbert Croly, *Willard Straight* (New York, 1925).
[17] Dorothy Whitney Straight quoted in Eric Rauchway, 'A Gentleman's Club in a Woman's Sphere: How Dorothy Whitney Straight Created *The New Republic*', *The Journal of Women's History* 11 (1999), 60–85 at 79.
[18] Croly, *Willard Straight*, 459.
[19] Herbert Croly, *The Promise of American Life* (Cambridge, MA, 1965 [1909]), 207.
[20] Rauchway, 'A Gentleman's Club in a Woman's Sphere'.

group Marc Stears terms the 'nationalist progressives'.[21] This would be the strand of American progressivism that exerted the most direct influence on Dartington.

The nationalist progressives opposed competitive individualism and promoted social unity in the form of a state-centred 'new nationalism'. They saw the extension of democratic mechanisms and the development of an educated, participative electorate as the necessary preconditions of a truly democratic polity. Doubting the immediate capacities of the mass of the population, however, they, like the British Fabians with whom they exchanged ideas, were prepared to allow significant political power to an elite dedicated to bringing about such social progress.[22] 'Democracy does not mean merely government by the people, or majority rule, or universal suffrage,' as Croly put it.[23] Dorothy instinctively supported this view. Throughout her life, she would combine egalitarian rhetoric and gestures of self-abnegating humility with the automatic assumption that she had the right to lead: as a friend and fellow reformer wrote, 'Dorothy always takes the hard chair and the drumstick – with which she conducts the meeting.'[24]

Dorothy and Willard's collaboration on *The New Republic* was short-lived. In 1917, Willard enlisted in the US army, seeing a chance to advance his dream of expanding America's liberal influence. The next year he died of influenza while attending the Paris Peace Conference, leaving Dorothy, aged thirty-one, a widow with three young children.[25] It was, she remembered, 'the hardest period in my life'.[26]

In spite of her unhappiness over her husband's death and her horror at the destruction wrought by the war, Dorothy pushed on with her social reform projects. She continued to support *The New Republic* and helped found the New School for Social Research, a university (still running today) that aimed to offer ordinary labourers a high level of education and to investigate how the social sciences could be harnessed to social reform.[27] She worked closely with the Young Men's Christian

[21] Marc Stears, *Progressives, Pluralists, and the Problems of the State: Ideologies of Reform in the United States and Britain, 1909–1926* (Oxford, 2006).
[22] Ibid., 79.   [23] Croly, *Promise*, 207.
[24] Ruth Morgan quoted in Swanberg, *Whitney Father*, 250.
[25] Their children together were Whitney Willard Straight (1912–1979), who became a racing driver and industrialist; Beatrice Whitney Straight (1914–2001), who was a successful actress; and Michael Whitney Straight (1916–2004), who was recruited at Cambridge by Anthony Blunt and worked as a Soviet spy and as editor of *The New Republic*.
[26] Dorothy, 'Background and Foreground – A Personal Pattern', [n.d.], DWE/S/1/E.
[27] Dorothy pledged $10,000 a year to the New School for ten years. Peter M. Rutkoff and William B. Scott, *New School: A History of the New School for Social Research* (New York, 1986), 10–13.

Association, the Junior League and other reform organisations.[28] She was one of six leaders chosen by a coalition of a hundred women's organisations to attend the Disarmament Conference in Washington in 1922.[29] She took courses in economics, sociology and psychology. She read Thorstein Veblen's *Theory of the Leisure Class* (1899), Bertrand Russell's *Why Men Fight* (1916) and R. H. Tawney's *The Sickness of an Acquisitive Society* (1920) – all indictments of liberal individualism's damaging consequences.[30] She had gradually lost her Christian faith in her twenties, but she longed for spiritual meaning, a desire manifested in experimentation with séances and Christian Science.[31] None of these myriad activities, however, gave Dorothy the sense she craved of living 'the life of ideals in action', and so she continued to seek.[32]

*

Leonard Knight Elmhirst, six years Dorothy's junior, was the second of the nine children of a Yorkshire squire and parson – a man whose estate, though not large, was sufficient to give him financial independence and whose family had tilled the same land since the fourteenth century. Leonard was raised in a hierarchical country society of philanthropic parish visits, and he went to a conventional public school, Repton, and then to Cambridge, intending to become a parson like his father.[33] At Cambridge, his tutor was the humanist Goldsworthy Lowes Dickinson, a philosopher and political scientist whose main preoccupation was world unity – rooted, Gabriel Hankins argues, in his homosexual disidentification with imperialist, heterosexual masculinity.[34] Leonard embraced Dickinson's desire to promote international fellowship. Under the influence of his tutor's freethinking, he also began to have doubts about his

[28] Dorothy became the first president of the Junior League in 1921 after its various branches had been amalgamated into a national organisation. She was instrumental in shifting it away from amateur philanthropy into more heavy-duty reform work. Brown, *Angel Dorothy*; Gould, 'The Modest Benefactor'.
[29] Gould, 'The Modest Benefactor', 20.   [30] Ibid.
[31] Anthea Williams notes, 'Dorothy's séances after Willard's death', [n.d.], T/HIS/S22.
[32] Dorothy to Leonard, 24 October 1921, LKE/DWE/10/D.
[33] Young, *Elmhirsts*, 10–15.
[34] Gabriel Hankins, *Interwar Modernism and the Liberal World Order: Offices, Institutions, and Aesthetics after 1919* (Cambridge, 2019), 35. The son of a prominent Christian socialist, Goldsworthy Lowes Dickinson was a fellow of King's College, Cambridge and was heavily involved in the University Extension Scheme. He was driven to political activism by the outbreak of the First World War, playing a central role in the international pacifist Bryce Group. D. E. Martin, 'Dickinson, Goldsworthy Lowes (1862–1932)', in *Oxford Dictionary of National Biography* (Oxford University Press, first published 23 September 2004, revised 27 May 2010), www.oxforddnb.com/view/article/32815.

Christian faith. This did not affect his 'knight erranty' sense of social responsibility: as with Dorothy, all through his life, the desire to help humanity would be a defining characteristic.[35]

Leonard's younger brother Ernest died at Gallipoli in 1915, and then his eldest brother William at the Somme the following year. This made the war very personal for Leonard and also made him the heir to his father's estate. After failing to meet the health standard for fighting in the First World War, he worked for two years for the Young Men's Christian Association in India and then in the army education corps in Dublin. He spent five months as secretary to Sam Higginbottom, a missionary and agriculturalist at Allahabad, who advised him that if he wanted to contribute usefully to the sum of human happiness, he should go to America and study agriculture.[36] Leonard followed this advice. He had lost his Christian faith in the war and could no longer enter the Church, yet, above all, he wanted to find a way to help others. He characterised himself at this time as an 'idealist, socialist, anarchist, reformer, cutter down of privilege and surplus income, giver of support to all'.[37] But, like Dorothy, he struggled through his early years to work out how to turn the wish to do good into effective practical action.

In this period, Leonard began to dream of 'innumerable small experiments ... out of whose walls the city of Jerusalem will have to be built' – a very different dream to *The New Republic*'s vision of state-centred, elite-led social reform.[38] His ideals were akin to a group of British theorists that Marc Stears terms 'socialist pluralists', who included Harold Laski, G. D. H. Cole and R. H. Tawney. Although this group shared with the national progressives the dream of democratic social unity and a belief in the necessity of an informed, engaged citizenry to achieve this end, it was fiercely opposed to the centralised, bureaucratic state and to elite initiatives. Both out of distrust of the central state and out of a conviction that good citizens could only be made through early and direct community political participation, it saw 'small, localized, and democratised associations as the agents and units of meaningful reform'.[39] (Both the national

---

[35] Leonard was thus characterised by a friend – Gerald Heard to Leonard, 11 November 1924, LKE/G/17/E.

[36] First arriving in India as part of a Presbyterian mission, Sam Higginbottom went on to study farming at Ohio State University and then to found the Allahabad Agricultural Institute in 1919. Funded by a consortium of churches based in New York, the institute's purpose was Christianity-infused research and training in agriculture and veterinary sciences. Sam Higginbottom, *The Gospel and the Plow, or the Old Gospel and Modern Farming in Ancient India* (London, 1921).

[37] Leonard, notebook, 1917, LKE/G/S17/C.

[38] Leonard to Eduard Lindeman, 7 January 1924, box 2, Eduard Lindeman Archives.

[39] Stears, *Progressives*, 2.

progressive and socialist pluralist positions are contained within the term 'progressive' as defined in this book.) Leonard began to feel that social improvement could only be brought about by small, independent enterprises. The progress of civilisation lay not with conventional politics but with 'schemes outside all the orthodox tracks'.[40]

Leonard met Dorothy in 1920 when he was studying agricultural economics at Cornell, developing his passion for scientific methods. He had been appointed president of the Cosmopolitan Club for foreign students and had been advised to approach Dorothy to ask for funds.[41] She agreed to help. From this point on, the two kept up a correspondence, Leonard moving swiftly from thinking of Dorothy as a 'Fairy Godmother' to falling for her romantically.[42] Dorothy was mourning Willard, raising her children, and deeply embroiled in her philanthropic and social-reform ventures. At first, she showed little interest in Leonard – but gradually she warmed to him as he persisted in his writing and she began to see how closely their experiences and ideals aligned.[43] 'We're both in a hole over the war, we're both out on a search', was how Leonard put it.[44] They agreed that society was headed in the wrong direction and wanted to replace national competition and personal gain with a more collective, holistic philosophy of living that would allow the whole person to flourish.

In 1921, Leonard went to Bengal to help the poet and reformer Rabindranath Tagore set up his Institute for Rural Reconstruction (usually known as Sriniketan). Tagore had approached Dorothy to support this project while he was in New York on a fundraising tour. Dorothy was put off by the 'woolliness' of Tagore's ideas and was not willing to give money to him directly, but she agreed to sponsor Leonard's involvement instead.[45] It was, in part, a test of his worth. Dorothy was fundamentally more in sympathy with Leonard's aspirations to promote the international fellowship of all humankind than with Willard's liberal imperialism. She wanted to see whether, unlike Willard, he could convert his zeal into practical action.

---

[40] Leonard to Dorothy, 19 May 1923, LKE/DWE/11/C.
[41] Willard Straight had left a bequest to make his college a more welcoming place for students, and Dorothy used this to build a union building called the Willard Straight Hall. Leonard K. Elmhirst, *The Straight and Its Origin* (Ithaca, NY, 1975).
[42] Young, *Elmhirsts*, 62.
[43] Leonard, '16 August 1923', notebook, LKE/G/S17/C. Dorothy and Leonard's courtship was conducted chiefly by letter while Dorothy was in New York and Leonard was in Bengal. See LKE/DWE.
[44] Leonard to Dorothy, 13 July 1921, LKE/DWE/10/B.
[45] Her reaction was recalled in a letter from Leonard to Dorothy, 22 August 1955, quoted in Young, *Elmhirsts*, 75.

Sriniketan was one of a constellation of reforming projects set up by Tagore, most of them, including a school and a university, based at the nearby campus of Santiniketan.[46] Its focus was bringing back to the villages what Tagore called 'life in its completeness', the life of economic, social, creative and spiritual vibrancy that he deemed to have atrophied since the British arrived in India.[47] Tagore aimed to liberate Indians from below: through Sriniketan, protected from 'out and out nationalists on one hand and orthodox officialdom on the other', citizens would achieve self-realisation, social unity and the capacity to stand free of their colonial rulers.[48] Leonard spent two years in Bengal and felt that he had finally found his place there, using his training at Cornell to help others live a fulfilling life. The First World War, he told Tagore, had forced on his generation 'beastliness we would never have chosen for ourselves', but Sriniketan offered the kind of work he had 'always longed to take a shot at'.[49]

Leela Gandhi uses the term 'affective communities' to evoke how, in the late nineteenth and early twentieth centuries, Westerners and colonial subjects, united in their rejection of imperialism and their embrace of radical social thinking, forged cross-cultural friendships.[50] At Sriniketan, Leonard entered into such a transnational 'politics of friendship', building close bonds with some of the idealists he met in Bengal and on his travels in Japan, China and South America as Tagore's private secretary, and celebrating his discovery of 'the true spirit of international brotherhood'.[51] This affective mode of reformism would shape Dartington. The estate became a place of international friendships that brought together marginalised and othered cultures and ideas – including anticolonialism, homosexuality, modernism, Eastern spirituality, socialism and educational progressivism – and amalgamated them in an inchoately oppositional community that set itself apart from mainstream society. After his time at Sriniketan, Leonard would always cherish the ethic of friendship – 'the ideal

---

[46] For an overview of Tagore's life, see Krishna Dutta and Andrew Robinson, *Rabindranath Tagore: The Myriad-Minded Man* (London, 1995); on his community-building work, see Anna Neima, *The Utopians: Six Attempts to Build the Perfect Society* (London, 2021), chapter 1.

[47] Rabindranath Tagore's phrase is quoted in Uma Das Gupta, 'Tagore's Ideas of Social Action and the Sriniketan Experiment of Rural Reconstruction, 1922–41', *University of Toronto Quarterly* 77 (2008), 992–1004 at 992.

[48] Leonard to C. G. Stevens, 14 March 1929, LKE/IN/21/B.

[49] Leonard K. Elmhirst, *Poet and Plowman* (Calcutta, 1975), 81.

[50] Gandhi, *Affective Communities*.

[51] Ibid., 26; Leonard to Dorothy, 3 February 1922, LKE/DWE/10/F.

human relationship', he called it – as the basic building block of a good society.[52]

Dorothy and Leonard's own friendship tipped definitively into romance, and in 1924 they married in the garden of Dorothy's house on Long Island. Dorothy was thirty-eight and Leonard was thirty-two. From the beginning, theirs was a relationship of shared mission: rather than being 'a slackening off, a loosing of armour,' Leonard wrote, their love was 'a tightening up ... a dashing off into the fray'.[53] Throughout their forty-four years together, each would have their own interests – for Dorothy, the arts and spirituality; for Leonard, agriculture and science – but their relationship remained strongly companionate. 'I think of the world like a great Rolls,' Leonard wrote to Dorothy after six years of marriage, '– and you and I sometimes riding in it, but more often struggling to patch up the gear box and lying on the muddy road getting properly "messed", but getting a bit of a kick out of it all – n'est-ce pas?' He relied on his wife to check him if he got 'too carried away' with ideas.[54] He cherished her reflective, spiritually minded introspection and her sensitivity about human relations, as he found himself constantly distracted by 'bricks and mortar things'.[55] Dorothy, in turn, admired Leonard's optimism, his 'creative, pioneering spirit' and his 'power to stir people to something beyond themselves' because she herself was shy and often found people 'paralyzing'.[56]

Susan Kent argues that the upheaval of the First World War brought about a renewed emphasis in Britain on the idea that men and women should have separate spheres – the former public, the latter domestic.[57] The Elmhirsts' marriage was, to a degree, inflected by such gender conservatism: just as Dorothy had used Willard as a front for her involvement in *The New Republic*, she called Dartington 'Leonard's plan' and treated him in public as the head of their project.[58] Behind the scenes, however, the dynamics of their relationship were less conventional. Dorothy was older, had been married before, and was experienced in encouraging men to help her enact her ambitions for social reform. She also held the purse strings, paying ab lib for Dartington during its first

[52] Leonard to Eduard Lindeman, 7 January 192[4?], box 3, Eduard Lindeman Archives.
[53] Young, *Elmhirsts*, 86.   [54] Leonard to Dorothy, 26 October 1930, LKE/DWE/12/E.
[55] Leonard to Dorothy, 26 August 1931, LKE/DWE/12/E.
[56] Dorothy to Leonard, 4 September 1921, LKE/DWE/10C; 25 April 1926, LKE/DWE/12/D; 1 October 1932, LKE/DWE/13A.
[57] Susan Kingsley Kent, *Making Peace: The Reconstruction of Gender in Interwar Britain* (Princeton, 1993). See also Alison Light, *Forever England: Femininity, Literature and Conservatism between the Wars* (London, 1991).
[58] Dorothy to Eduard Lindeman, 14 May [1925?], box 2, Eduard Lindeman Archives.

four years, then settling on it a generous endowment that she sometimes supplemented.[59] While Leonard was the official face of Dartington, Dorothy was just as central to the project, shaping it to her vision. Throughout their marriage, Dorothy also ran a grant-giving organisation in New York, the Committee on Commitments, which supported diverse pacifist, educational, artistic and social reform causes to the tune of around $100,000 a year.[60] Far from objecting to his wife's independence of action, Leonard celebrated it, seeing it as a complement to his own character. 'If I was 100% man she'd be too masculine for me,' he wrote to his brother: 'capable, vigorous, farsighted, a statesman in her way and one of those thoroughly international women that only America produces. But I'm not, and she sweeps me off my feet.'[61]

1.2   An Overview of Dartington Hall

> Sometimes Dartington seemed to me a synthesis of the whole universe, something that gave peace and happiness to my international mind. Sometimes, I liked to see in it just a symbol of "old England".   *Andrée Karpelès to the Elmhirsts (1935)*[62]

By the time the Elmhirsts married, Dorothy had lived in China, had houses in several locations in America and had toured extensively around Europe and Asia, while Leonard had travelled in the Middle East, studied in America and worked in India and Ireland. They were globe-trotters with international outlooks: they had 'crossed the boundaries of nationalism', as Leonard put it.[63] Despite – or perhaps because of – their cosmopolitanism worldview, they idealised the rooted community, the local place and the particular. It was a perspective they shared with progressives on both sides of the Atlantic: the organic rural community was widely seen as a bulwark against the socially atomising effects of capitalist modernity.[64]

The Elmhirsts decided that their own particular rooted community should be in England. Leonard wanted to prove that Tagore's ideals were

---

[59] Brown, *Angel Dorothy*, 112.

[60] Its members included, at various times, Eduard Lindeman, Herbert Croly, the reformer Ruth Morgan, and Dorothy's American private secretary, Anna Bogue. It ran until 1936, when it was reorganised and renamed the William C. Whitney Foundation. File DWE/US.

[61] Leonard to Richard Elmhirst, 25 June 1923, quoted in Young, *Elmhirsts*, 95.

[62] Andrée Karpelès to the Elmhirsts, 3 June 1935, LKE/G/21/F.

[63] Leonard to Dorothy, 13 October 1924, LKE/DWE/11/C.

[64] David Matless, 'Topographic Culture: Nikolaus Pevsner and the Buildings of England', *History Workshop Journal* 54 (2002), 73–99; Doreen Massey, 'Places and their Pasts', *History Workshop Journal* 39 (1995), 182–92, at 191; Rodgers, *Atlantic Crossings*, 326 and passim.

'workable in other than a purely rural country'; and, with the Labour Party coming to the fore, he deemed England to be a nation more likely than America to be influenced by example.[65] Dorothy agreed. She had been to England several times and compared her liking of it to that of Henry James' Anglophile heroes: 'There's no doubt James subtly understood what it means for a certain type of American to be returning, as it were, to his home – England!'[66] She celebrated the country as a place 'where an underlying freedom exists and where life itself and the quality of living count above other things'.[67]

In spite of the Elmhirsts' vision of Dartington as a place with deep local roots, Dorothy continued for several months to imagine that their move to England would only be temporary. 'We aren't leaving for good, you know,' she told friends. The plan was 'to get something going over there – and then to return here'.[68] Her concept of supporting Dartington from afar, as one of several reform projects around the world, echoed the strategy of big American philanthropic organisations like the Rockefeller Foundation, and aligned with Dorothy and Leonard's international orientation.[69] These two visions of Dartington – as part of an international philanthropic regime and as an organic local community – would co-exist throughout the experiment's early decades and never be fully reconciled. Together they point towards the kind of 'rooted' or 'partial' cosmopolitan identity that Kwame Appiah writes about. It is possible, Appiah argues, to combine loyalty to one local society (or several) with a celebration of, and sense of obligation towards, the wide variety of human cultures and humanity as a whole.[70] While this form of hybrid identity sounds appealing in theory, Dartington's history demonstrates the contradictions and tensions that can intervene in the process of living it out.

The Elmhirsts decided to look for a place to start their experiment in the West Country: Leonard wanted to put space between himself and his Yorkshire family, and Rabindranath Tagore, who had been there as a young man, revered the region for its beauty.[71] While Dorothy wound up

[65] Leonard to Dorothy, 19 May 1923, LKE/DWE/11/C.
[66] Dorothy to Leonard, 24 October 1924, T/HIS/S20/A.
[67] Dorothy to Leonard, 14 September 1934, LKE/DWE/13A.
[68] Dorothy to Eduard Lindeman, 14 May 1925 [?], box 2, Eduard Lindeman Archives.
[69] Emily Rosenberg, 'Missions to the World: Philanthropy Abroad', in Lawrence J. Friedman and Mark D. MacGarvie (eds.), *Charity, Philanthropy and Civility in American History* (Cambridge, 2003), 241–57.
[70] Kwame Anthony Appiah, 'Cosmopolitan Patriots', *Critical Inquiry* 23 (1997), 617–39, at 633. See also *The Ethics of Identity* (Princeton, 2005), chapter 6.
[71] Rabindranath Tagore stayed at his sister-in-law's house at Torquay. Krishna Dutta and Andrew Robinson (eds.), *Selected Letters of Rabindranath Tagore* (Cambridge, 1997), 11.

her affairs in America, Leonard asked a land agent for a list of properties with good soil, 'woods, forest, orchards etc.' and, if possible, 'historical associations thrown in'.[72] He then took the first driving lesson of his life, bought a car and set off with a list of forty-eight estates in hand. The first property on the list, a Georgian mansion, he judged too dull; the second was Dartington Hall. It was made up of some 800 acres, looped round on two sides by the River Dart.[73] The hall itself had once been given by Richard II to his half-brother and had later remained in the Champernowne family for three hundred years until financial pressures in the 1920s forced them to sell.[74] The nearest big towns were Plymouth and Exeter. Totnes, a smaller town with a train that ran directly to London, was right next to the property. There were only seventeen people living on the estate, and it was dilapidated.[75] Leonard did not mind this – it merely confirmed his view, widely held in the interwar years, that the British countryside was 'depressed and broken' and ripe for reform.[76] Dartington's gentle, undulating landscape, close to Dartmoor, and its rich history seemed to him to offer an ideal setting. Writing to Dorothy that he had discovered 'a veritable fairy land' where 'the handiwork of nature joined with the reverent hand of generations of men', he immediately opened negotiations to buy.[77]

The Elmhirsts idealised the medieval village as a place of communitarian harmony, a view common among interwar social reformers.[78] They arrived at Dartington determined to turn it into something of a modern equivalent. Yet the setting – an ancient manor that had belonged to an owner with royal blood – presented a very different social ideal: almost immediately, Leonard began referring to himself as 'lord of the manor' and Dorothy as 'the squire's wife'.[79] Dorothy's son Michael Straight (a dedicated member of the Communist Party, therefore not without prejudice) later judged that by placing themselves in a 'wholly

---

[72] Young, *Elmhirsts*, 103–4.
[73] Over the next two decades they would add 3,000 acres to it, much of it woodland. Victor Bonham-Carter gives a detailed overview of the estate's geography in *Dartington Hall*.
[74] Nikolaus Pevsner, *Devon* (Harmondsworth, 1989 [1952]), 311.
[75] Leonard to S. K. Ratcliffe, 4 March 1929, LKE/G/26/A.
[76] Howkins, Alun, 'Death and Rebirth? English Rural Society, 1920–1940', in Paul Brassley, Jeremy Burchardt and Lynne Thompson (eds.), *The English Countryside between the Wars: Regeneration or Decline?* (New York, 2006), 10–25, at 24.
[77] Leonard to Dorothy, 6 March 1925, LKE/DWE/12/A.
[78] See, for example, Angela Bartie, Linda Fleming, Mark Freeman, Tom Hulme, Alexandra Hutton and Paul Readman, 'Historical Pageants and the Medieval Past in Twentieth-Century England', *The English Historical Review* 133 (2018), 866–902; Saler, *The Avant-Garde*.
[79] Leonard to Edgar Fowles, 9 August 1927, LKE/DCC/6/A; Leonard to Dorothy, 6 March 1925, LKE/DWE/12/A.

1.2 Dartington's courtyard being re-modelled to Beatrix Farrand's design in the 1930s (© Dartington Hall Trust and the Elmgrant Trust)

feudal' setting, the Elmhirsts were 'negating the concept of a democratic community from the start'.[80] Tensions between ideals of egalitarian collectivity and patrician stewardship would thread unresolved through Dartington's history.

The Elmhirsts' vision was also inflected by the politics of Devon. The county had a traditional, agrarian economy.[81] This reinforced Dorothy and Leonard's conception of society as encapsulated in the village community and their tendency to ignore the urban problems which preoccupied many reformers of the period – unsurprisingly, as around eighty per cent of the English population lived in towns.[82] Leonard's attitude to

---

[80] Michael Straight to Michael Young, 11 September 1980, T/HIS/S22/D; Roland Perry, *Last of the Cold War Spies: The Life of Michael Straight, the Only American in Britain's Cambridge Spy Ring* (Cambridge, MA, 2005).

[81] John Sheail, *Rural Conservation in Interwar Britain* (Oxford, 1981), 25–6.

[82] Approximately nine million out of a population of forty-five million lived in the countryside in 1931. Brassley et al. 'Introduction', in Brassley et al. (eds.), *The English Countryside*, 3.

cities was that they were 'no place to live in'[83]: they had, he wrote, 'a devastating effect upon human nature', inducing acquisitiveness and competition[84]; the 'conditioning process of conscious communal life' was only possible in the countryside.[85] Such anti-urban feelings were shared by agrarian revivalists globally but were particularly significant in England, one of the most industrialised countries in the world.[86] Devon, while increasingly altered by tourism, attracted those who prized traditional agrarian values, such as the author Henry Williamson.[87] Although the Elmhirsts sometimes framed Dartington as 'not a rural experiment as such but an attempt to set up a new balance between city and country', their concerns were predominantly with reforming society by reforming the countryside.[88] This, in a sense, defined the edges of their project – their experiment could only work on a small scale and in a rural setting. It did not mean that it could not be scaled up, only that its configuration would then have to change significantly.

Dartington, the Elmhirsts insisted, 'has no politics'; party politics was 'barren' and obstructed the long-term search for social solutions.[89] This non-partisan approach was reminiscent of a broader interwar trend whereby politicians toned down party rhetoric in favour of an emphasis on unity and harmony.[90] It also echoed a long-standing mode of ethical democracy – illustrated, for example, by Edward Carpenter – that rejected the compromised world of formal politics in favour of a focus

---

[83] Leonard to Arthur Geddes, 24 February 1923, LKE/IN/6/D.
[84] Leonard to Dorothy, 13 March 1923, LKE/DWE/11/C.
[85] Leonard to Frederic Bartlett, 2 January 1934, LKE/G/S8/D.
[86] For explorations of interwar agrarianism in Germany and America, for example, see John Alexander Williams, *Turning to Nature in Germany: Hiking, Nudism, and Conservation, 1900–1940* (Stanford, 2007); Rogers, *Atlantic Crossings*.
[87] Henry Williamson, who wrote *Tarka the Otter* (1945), withdrew from London to Devon after being deeply scarred by his experiences in the First World War. Sam Smiles gives an overview of interwar Devon in 'Refuge or Regeneration: Devon's Twentieth Century Identity', in Sam Smiles (ed.), *Going Modern and Being British: Art, Architecture and Design in Devon c. 1910–1960* (Exeter, 1998), 1–14. For contemporary celebration of 'traditional' Devon, see John Betjeman, *Devon: Shell Guide* (London, [1936]) and Stephen Reynolds, *A Poor Man's House* (London, 1911).
[88] Leonard, transcription of Sunday evening meeting, 23 September 1928, LKE/G/31/A. For the wider identification of 'Englishness' with the rural landscape in the interwar years, see Peter Mandler, 'Politics and the English Landscape since the First World War', *Huntingdon Library Quarterly* 55 (1992), 459–76; and for an equivalent American tendency, T. J. Jackson Lears, *No Place of Grace: Antimodernism and the Transformation of American Culture 1880–1920* (Chicago; London, 1981), 74–83.
[89] Leonard in the Dartington Hall news sheet, *News of the Day*, 30 March 1928, T/PP/EST/ 1–8; Leonard to J. S. Martin, 15 August 1927, LKE/DCC/6/A.
[90] Jon Lawrence, 'The Transformation of British Public Politics after the First World War', *Past and Present* 190 (2006), 185–216; Helen McCarthy, *The British People and the League of Nations: Democracy, Citizenship and Internationalism, c.1918–45* ([n.p.], 2013), chapter 2.

on lived practice.[91] For all their apolitical talk, however, the Elmhirsts consistently viewed Labour as 'the most balanced and the most idealistic' political party, voting for it, making donations to its politicians and hoping Dartington would 'lend a hand to the Labour group'.[92]

Dorothy and Leonard's left-wing politics put them at odds with their locality. It was one of the reasons that instead of influencing their neighbours, the Elmhirsts found that they were cold-shouldered by them. The Totnes constituency of which Dartington was a part comfortably returned a Conservative candidate in the five elections between 1924 and 1945, with Labour never garnering more than thirteen per cent of the vote until the Second World War.[93] Socially, Devon was conservative and hierarchical, which impeded Dorothy and Leonard's early ambitions to create a community democracy, and drew them towards a more paternalistic approach and then to the idea of contributing to centralised socialism instead. John Benson, a historian whom the Elmhirsts invited to write the 'folk-history' of the Dartington parish, found that 'the folk never had a history independent of the Hall' – the community had always been in the 'hands of the lords of the manor'.[94] The parish, he wrote, was 'still hungering for the old patriarchal regime' and the 'demand at Dartington for self-expression, self-determination and "help yourself"' was asking it 'to walk before it has ever learnt to crawl'.[95] Devon's traditionalism was in contrast to Essex, another county that attracted social experimentation. Close to London and with substantial Labour support, it was a hotbed of reforming schemes, including the modernist workers' estate at Silver End, Henry Ford's experimental farm on the Fordson Estate and the Bata Shoe Company's industrial settlement at East Tilbury.[96] If the Elmhirsts had chosen such a location – rather than

[91] Leela Gandhi, *The Common Cause: Postcolonial Ethics and the Practice of Democracy, 1900–1955* (Chicago, 2014), 12–13.
[92] Leonard to Dorothy, 19 May 1923, LKE/DWE/11/C. Politicians the Elmhirsts assisted included Labour MP Ellen Wilkinson and the unsuccessful Independent Labour Party candidate for Totnes, Kate Spurrell. Leonard to Ellen Wilkinson, 15 October 1931, LKE/G/33/I; Elmhirsts to Kate Spurrell, 1 November 1935, DWE/G/S2/D.
[93] F. W. S. Craig, *British Parliamentary Election Results, 1918–1949* (Chichester, 1983 [1969]), 333.
[94] John Benson, who briefly taught at Dartington School in the 1920s, to Leonard, 1932, T/HIS/5/B. The Elmhirsts' desire for a 'folk history' echoes a broader interest in the history of everyday life among the interwar liberal middle class whose aim was to foster participatory democracy. Laura Carter, 'The Quennells and the "History of Everyday Life" in England, c. 1918–69', *History Workshop Journal* 81 (2016), 106–34.
[95] John Benson to Leonard, 1932, T/HIS/5/B.
[96] Craig, *British Parliamentary Election Results*, 349–53; Louise Campbell, 'Patrons of the Modern House', *Journal of the Twentieth Century Society* 2 (1996), 41–50; Joanna Smith '"Work Collectively and Live Individually": The Bata Housing Estate at East Tilbury', *Twentieth Century Architecture* 9 (2008), 52–68; Kit Kowol, 'An Experiment in

assuming that the populace of any place would rally enthusiastically to their ideals – their efforts to engage the surrounding countryside might have been more successful.

Dorothy and Leonard's first model for Dartington was a self-governing socialist–pluralist community. The project began, as the Elmhirsts had planned, as a small, informal community, oriented around a school: a Sriniketan in England. It gradually expanded its activities as the holistic, connecting-it-all impulse reached towards the logical conclusion. As well as the school, the estate comprised of the dilapidated medieval manor, a clutch of hamlets, extensive forestry and several farms.[97] These facilities were initially developed to broaden students' horizons, but soon they supported flourishing projects in their own right. Within five years, there were departments of dance-drama, crafts, textiles, forestry, building, farms, poultry, gardens, orchards and research. There were also sporadic efforts to fuse these elements together through the creation of a common philosophy or mode of living, using principles derived from a combination of religion, spirituality and the social sciences. The Elmhirsts aimed to create a community in which the creative, spiritual and practical parts of life would be linked.

Dartington drew two kinds of participant. The first – who are not the main focus of this book – were the ordinary workers, locals such as Frank Crook, a tenant farmer under the Champernownes who stayed on when the Elmhirsts bought the estate, or Herbert Mills, who first worked as a beater on the Champernowne estate and later joined the Elmhirsts as an odd-jobs man.[98] Both sent their children to Dartington School but were relatively little involved in the ideological life of the estate.[99] For many in this group, Dartington mainly represented a welcome job in a time of high unemployment. They were uninterested in the philosophical commitments or 'found the object too large'.[100] The enterprise's idealistic nature could even make it a more difficult place to work: as one employee complained, 'the lack of a feeling of stability – a constant change of policy, change of people to work with, change of conditions to work under – produces a feeling of unrest and insecurity'.[101]

Conservative Modernity: Interwar Conservatism and Henry Ford's English Farms', *Journal of British Studies* 55 (2016), 781–805.
[97] Young, *Elmhirsts*, 102.
[98] Michael Young's interview with Mrs Crook, 23 August 1977, T/HIS/S20/D; Herbert Mills, reminiscences, 21 January 1970, LKE/G/31/E.
[99] Frank Crook was so opposed to the Elmhirsts' social ideas that in 1946 he stood for the Conservatives against Leonard as county councillor. Leonard won the contest by 200 votes. Leonard, notebook, LKE/DCC/3/F; Young, *Elmhirsts*, 278–9.
[100] Herbert Mills, reminiscences, 21 January 1970, LKE/G/31/E.
[101] Marjorie Wise, response to 1929 questionnaire, T/PP/P/1/D.

The second type of participant – more central to this account – was the non-locals who were drawn to Dartington by its ideals and were more actively involved in shaping the community. Their nature is less easily summarised, but they might be termed 'practical idealists'.[102] They were progressive in their social views, in the broad sense of hoping to shape a better future based on individual satisfaction and communal unity. They were not, for the most part, intellectuals – although many were passionate about ideas. Nor were they purely technocratic – although some had leanings that way. They felt uncomfortable with the modern world but wanted to reform it rather than escape from it – an impulse that resembled Victorian philanthropic or missionary zeal, although many of them had departed from orthodox Christianity.[103] They were equivocal, even hostile, towards the state, but nonetheless remained close to it, part of the interrelated circle of the professional and ruling elite delineated by Noel Annan in fact and Anthony Powell in fiction – men and women who would often go on to become involved in state-building during and after the Second World War.[104]

Many early participants of this type were acquaintances of Leonard. Three of his brothers and several friends from his university days were among the first to arrive on the estate; this fairly conventional masculine social network was, perhaps, one of the reasons why progressive gender politics did not feature prominently at Dartington in the first few years.[105] This group included people like Wyatt Rawson, who had been at Cambridge with Leonard, and was relieved to be saved from schoolmastering at his brother's conventional prep school by the chance of joining 'a community of sentiment and of purpose'.[106] Gradually, as Dartington's reputation spread, more people arrived from further afield. As their numbers increased, this elite group became more and more

[102] The term 'practical idealists' was used by Eleanor M. Elder to describe the Elmhirsts (letter to Dorothy, 26 February 1933, DWE/G/S1/F).

[103] Ross McKibbin explores elites' sense of disenfranchisement in *Classes and Cultures: England 1918–1951* (Oxford, 1998), 52–5.

[104] Noel Annan, 'The Intellectual Aristocracy', in J. H. Plumb (ed.), *Studies in Social History: A Tribute to G.M. Trevelyan* (London, 1955), 241–87 and *Our Age: The Generation that Made Post-War Britain* (London, 1990); Anthony Powell, *A Dance to the Music of Time* (London, 1991 [series of novels, originally published between 1951 and 75]); Richard Weight, 'State, Intelligentsia and the Promotion of National Culture in Britain, 1939–45', *Historical Research* 69 (1996), 83–101.

[105] The three brothers were Pom, a lawyer, who became a legal advisor and trustee for Dartington and also ran the Elmhirst family estate in Yorkshire, which Leonard gave to him when he inherited it in 1948; Richard, who followed Leonard to Cornell, then returned to run the Dartington poultry unit; and Vic, who also studied at Cornell, and became an informal deputy for Dorothy and Leonard.

[106] Wyatt Rawson to Eduard Lindeman, July 1927, box 2, Eduard Lindeman Archives.

distinct from the local workers, giving rise to a feeling, uncomfortable both for them and for the locals, that the estate's 'social functions are now definitely "upper-middle-class"'.[107] This did not mean a total loss of the sense of the estate's being more egalitarian than the world outside it: for Yvonne Markham, a Welsh miner's daughter who worked as a nursery maid in London before joining Dartington's domestic staff in 1934, the 'lack of division between people was the main thing, that was absolutely the main thing. I didn't realise there was such a life'.[108] It is notable, however, that Markham came from Wales rather than Devon: the Elmhirsts were always more successful in attracting non-locals who were already invested in the social transformation they were trying to bring about than they were in converting locals to their ideas.

Dartington's staff was small enough to be housed in two buildings in 1925, but by 1933, there were 846 employees and 124 tenants.[109] Despite the growth and some tensions between different types of partici-pants, there remained early on a vigorous sense of shared idealism. Many people were simultaneously involved in education and the arts, agricul-ture and industry. Estate meetings were held every Sunday to discuss progress and direction. A daily news sheet, *News of the Day*, was issued to nurture a sense of shared ownership.[110] These activities represented an attempt to forge the kind of 'common culture' that Raymond Williams (who grew up in this period) would later delineate – defining culture as the collective work of an entire society, uniting all its members in a shared project.[111] Yet, undermining these gestures towards unity and self-government, the estate was being run from the top, Dorothy's nationalist-progressive faith in elite guidance winning out over Leonard's socialist–pluralist ideas of group direction.

The Elmhirsts' immediate hope of uncovering 'in the people a deep faith in themselves, wherewith to set their own house in order, by their own effort' shifted into a future register – democratic responsibility would first have to be learned.[112] They, like the national progressives,

---

[107] John Wales to W. B. Curry, 4 March 1936, C/DHL/1/B.
[108] Maria Elena de la Iglesia (ed.), *Dartington Hall School: Staff Memories of the Early Years* (Exeter, 1996), 36.
[109] Leonard to John Mountford, 11 December 1933, LKE/LAND/2/B.
[110] *News of the Day* was first published in December 1927 and was distributed to all the 'feeding centres' on the estate so that it could be read at mealtimes. It was also sent to some of Dartington's external supporters. T/PP/EST/1/001.
[111] Raymond Williams, *Culture and Society*, 436.
[112] Leonard to Ellen Wilkinson, 19 April 1927, LKE/G/33/I. This shift was similar to the diminishing fierceness of Leonard's desire to promote self-government in the British colonies, especially in India: it remained on his agenda but became a more far-off ambition than it was in the early 1920s, requiring untold levels of preparation.

wished that 'the common folk could have the chance to play their own hand and run their own show' but feared they would 'make a mess' unless sufficiently prepared for their role.[113] This echoed a shift in interwar progressive education, whereby the hope that children, freed from adult norms, could forge a better way of living in the immediate was gradually superseded by the belief that children were limited in their capacity and must be carefully prepared by adults to become responsible citizens in the future.[114] In the early period, the estate remained informal in its configuration, and most participants accepted it was still in 'the planning phase', which helped conceal brewing tensions over control and between the disparate personnel and ideologies that were influencing it. It did not immediately matter that the Elmhirsts were constantly losing money; or that, as Dorothy wrote, 'we haven't yet as a group become conscious of our spiritual needs, nor have we yet developed any common philosophy or religious ideas which gives meaning to the whole enterprise'.[115]

As Dartington became more established, its participants were supplemented by a growing penumbra of non-resident supporters – politicians, social reformers, intellectuals, artists and society figures who motored or came down on the train to stay for the weekend. Some of them were invited by the Elmhirsts since it was key to their reforming mission that Dartington's activities be broadcast widely. With time, though, increasing numbers of people wrote asking to visit or simply turned up unannounced. Their names are a 'who's who' of the progressive left of the interwar years: Ellen Wilkinson, Aldous Huxley, Bertrand Russell, John Maynard Keynes, Stephen Spender, W. H. Auden, Barbara Wootton, among many others.[116]

Most visitors were excited by what they saw, particularly in the 1920s, when the embryonic nature of the estate's development allowed the widest range of readings of its purpose. A few, like William St John Pym, later Director of Staffing and Administration at the BBC, diagnosed muddled thinking and hypocrisy. Pym warned the Elmhirsts that their efforts 'to square communistic theories with the possession and enjoyment of great

---

[113] Leonard to Dorothy, 29 March 1926, LKE/DWE/12/D.

[114] Laura Tisdall, *A Progressive Education: How Childhood Changed in Mid-Twentieth-Century English and Welsh Schools* (Manchester, 2019); Laura King, 'Future Citizens: Cultural and Political Conceptions of Children in Britain, 1930–1950s', *Twentieth Century British History* 27 (2016), 389–411.

[115] Dorothy to Ruth Morgan, May 1928, quoted in Rachel Esther Harrison, 'Dorothy Elmhirst and the Visual Arts at Dartington Hall 1925–1945', unpublished PhD, University of Plymouth, 2002, 126.

[116] Records of Sunday evening meetings, T/AE/3 and 4.

wealth' was 'eating your cake and having it'. They should, he suggested, stop purporting to be 'something "special"' and 'make a fresh start and a bold bid for normality' – hunting, paying calls, going to church, and hosting 'normal unfreaky uncranky good old Tory men of the world'.[117] By the mid-1930s, amid national and international political and economic tensions, criticism of Dartington's wealth, its rarefied atmosphere and its lack of replicability were more common. By this point too, however, the Elmhirsts' reform focus was shifting away from the local and towards the national so that imperfections in the community itself were of less significance to them, or at least easier to ignore.

From the beginning, the estate cross-pollinated vigorously with an immense array of other reforming enterprises, including pedagogic experiments in America and Europe; rural regeneration schemes in England such as Henry Morris' village colleges; groups of idealistic artists from institutions like the Cornish School in the United States and the Bauhaus in Germany. The Elmhirsts remained particularly closely connected with America, returning there every summer and receiving a drip-feed of newspaper clippings, books and letters from their friends.[118] A glimpse of their engagement with American progressive politics is given by a dinner they attended at the White House at the invitation of Eleanor and F. D. Roosevelt in 1933.[119] Other guests included Frances Perkins, Secretary for Labour, and Henry Wallace, Secretary of Agriculture, and the talk turned to Dartington and a community development experiment the Roosevelts were planning in West Virginia.[120] In the 1930s, Dorothy and Leonard found, in the New Deal, a practical model for how grassroots democratic endeavour might be combined with enlightened central leadership without sacrificing the benefits of either.[121] Dartington itself bore a striking resemblance to

---

[117] William St John Pym, response to 1931 questionnaire, T/PP/P/1/E.

[118] A particularly busy conduit was between Dorothy and Anna Bogue, the private secretary who ran her American households in New York and Long Island. DWE/US/1/A.

[119] Dorothy worked closely with Eleanor Roosevelt in New York on various social schemes, including organising a welfare centre during the First World War. The two were life-long friends. Brown, *Angel Dorothy*, 90 and passim.

[120] The dinner is discussed by Joseph P. Lash in a letter to the Elmhirsts, 27 September 1968, LKE/USA/4/A, and is recounted in his book, *Eleanor and Franklin* (London, 1972), 396. The West Virginia project, led by Eleanor Roosevelt, was called Arthurdale – a de-centralised, de-industrialised subsistence homestead that was intended to provide for unemployed coal miners, but was not a great economic success. C. J. Maloney, *Back to the Land: Arthurdale, FDR's New Deal, and the Costs of Economic Planning* (Hoboken, NJ, 2011).

[121] Jess Gilbert, *Planning Democracy: Agrarian Intellectuals and the Intended New Deal* (New Haven; London, 2015).

the New Deal – which Daniel Rodgers calls 'a great, explosive release of the pent-up agenda of the progressive past' – in that it was messily inclusive, with even its progenitors not quite knowing what it was that they were creating.[122]

The rise of totalitarian dystopias abroad intensified the desire of Dartington's participants to demonstrate the viability of their own social model. But, as the number and variety of participants grew, so did the tensions. Many incomers, especially in the 1930s, were more preoccupied with outward-facing, professional agendas – making an impact in the world of modern dance, progressive education or agrarian science – than with subsuming their vocational ambition to a unified collective. There was antagonism between those who wanted to prioritise the profit-making of their department and those who were interested in Dartington as a place of education, a source of artistic patronage or an integrated mode of life beyond 'the cash nexus'.[123] One observer, the organicist Rolf Gardiner, complained that the estate 'constituted a sum of addition instead of a sum of multiplication', its innumerable departments and experts having little in common and surrounding 'a vacuum, a hollowness' rather than a definite centre.[124] It was not just the absence of a clear, unifying philosophy that was the problem. Like other reforming projects, the Elmhirsts' integrative vision was hampered by the challenge of combining abstract ideals with commercial realities and by the day-to-day frictions of group living. Leonard compared the estate to a biological organism 'which grows and in so doing differentiates itself', losing its 'original ("naïve") unity' as each department undergoes 'a gradual "extraversion", a growing adaptation to the needs and standards of the world'.[125]

The Elmhirsts had hoped Dartington could succeed 'without resorting to a great deal of organization', but it became increasingly clear that it could not.[126] This was not only because of the conflicting priorities of those involved but because Leonard was determined to prove the estate's economic viability so that it could provide a blueprint for others – and poor management and endless changes of tack meant it was haemorrhaging money.[127]

To resolve these problems, after a series of unsuccessful experiments with management by committee, Dartington Hall Ltd was formed in

---

[122] Rodgers, *Atlantic Crossings*, 415–6.
[123] John Wales, *News of the Day*, 4 March 1936, C/DHL/1/B.
[124] Rolf Gardiner to Leonard, 16 June 1933, LKE/G/15/B.
[125] Leonard Elmhirst, untitled note, [n.d.], LKE/G/S8/B.
[126] Dorothy to Ruth Morgan, May 1928, quoted in Harrison, 'Dorothy Elmhirst', 126.
[127] Leonard, untitled note, [n.d.], LKE/G/S8/A.

1929, its board of directors controlling the commercial departments. This was a private limited company with an initial capital of £65,000, later raised to £125,000.[128] Leonard had 64,999 shares and Fred Gwatkin, one of the Elmhirsts' lawyers, had one. Continuing to exercise her influence unofficially, Dorothy had none. Two years later, Dartington Hall Trust was set up, an educational foundation with charitable status, governed by trustees and intended to foster the wider ideas behind Dartington by overseeing the running of the non-commercial branches – the arts, education and research.[129] With these developments came a central office to increase efficiency and profitability; a more formal accounting system; a restructuring of the departments; and a managing director, scientist W. K. Slater. Dorothy and Leonard hoped the company-and-trust formation would offer a model that could be replicated by others and would ensure the continuity of their enterprise after their deaths.[130] The innovation can be read as part of the Elmhirsts' wider experiments with promoting community autonomy: the trust was a touchstone for English interwar intellectuals, including F. W. Maitland, wishing to defend group rights against the scrutiny or encroachment of the state.[131] Alongside this consideration, however, it was important to the Elmhirsts that the trust was a charitable one, offering exemption from income tax. Leonard was chairman of both company and trust, and he and Dorothy were trustees, but day-to-day guidance of the estate was increasingly devolved to managers, breaking down the early sense of democratic collaboration.

In spite of a growing formal apparatus, there remained at Dartington's heart the hope of transforming the nature of personal relationships: to 'strike at the roots of the present system' of capitalist individualism, as Leonard put it, by building a community of 'loving friendship'.[132] Christianity did not feature overtly at Dartington, but this idea of friendship was often couched in the language of late-Victorian Christian socialism with which Leonard and other participants had been raised – the desire to promote 'mutual giving, the love that casteth out fear, mutual

---

[128] Victor Bonham-Carter, *Land and Environment: The Survival of the English Countryside* (Rutherford, NJ, 1971), 141; Young, *Elmhirsts*, 298.

[129] The trust began in 1931 as three trusts – one holding the land, one managing the school, one promoting research and holding shares in the company. In 1932, they were merged into one, the Dartington Hall Trust, of which Leonard was chairman until 1972. Bonham-Carter, *Land and Environment*, 141.

[130] Leonard, 'Summary of Dartington Constitution', April 1931, LKE/G/SG.

[131] Julia Stapleton, 'Introduction', in Julia Stapleton (ed.), *Group Rights* ([n.p.], 1995), ix–xxxix and 'Localism Versus Centralism in the Webbs' Political Thought', *History of Political Thought* 12 (1991), 147–65 at 162.

[132] Leonard to Eduard Lindeman, 7 January 192[4?], box 3, Eduard Lindeman Archives.

sacrifice and mutual aim and endeavour'.[133] The careful monitoring of daily interpersonal interactions at Dartington in the project's early years – with participants 'trying to hold up the mirror to each other with love in our hearts' – echoed the minutely scrutinised modes of interaction that shaped the lives of those in the Christian community of Kingsley Hall in East London, where residents lived as if every tiny domestic detail 'resonated through the cosmos'.[134]

Sue Morgan argues that in the interwar years religious and sexual discourses often worked symbiotically rather than in opposition in the process of 'self-making'.[135] This is borne out at Dartington, where quasi-religious efforts to remodel affective relationships intertwined with the testing out of new ideas about sex and sexuality. John Piper, who visited the estate in 1943, judged 'every path in the garden' to have been 'the scene of 100 illicit and very unhappy affairs'.[136] While he, as many visitors were prone to, was indulging in a degree of sensationalism, the community certainly had more than an average share of liaisons between unmarried couples, adultery, divorce and homosexual relationships.[137] Dorothy's eldest son, Michael, aged fifteen, had an affair with dancer Margaret Barr, a decade his senior, creeping into her cottage after school – and he was not alone among the students in taking advantage of the sexual licence that Dartington offered.[138] There was no single, coherent ideology driving this sexual experimentation. Unlike other prominent progressives – Dora and Bertrand Russell, for example, or Jack and Molly Pritchard – the Elmhirsts themselves lived domestically conventional lives and did not publicly embrace contemporary theories connecting sexual liberation and social reform.[139] Nonetheless, they seem tacitly to have accepted the unconventional behaviour that went

---

[133] Thomas Dixon, *The Invention of Altruism: Making Moral Meanings in Victorian Britain* (Oxford, 2008), 239–44 and passim; Leonard to Dorothy, 12 December 1924, LKE/DWE/12/A.

[134] Wyatt to Eduard Lindeman, 16 May 1927, DWE/G/7/C; Seth Koven, 'The "Sticky Sediment" of Daily Life: Radical Domesticity, Revolutionary Christianity, and the Problem of Wealth in Britain from the 1880s to the 1930s', *Representations* 120 (2012), 39–82, at 39.

[135] Sue Morgan, '"The Word Made Flesh": Women, Religion and Sexual Cultures', in Sue Morgan and Jacqueline de Vries (eds.), *Women, Gender and Religious Cultures in Britain, 1800–1940* (New York, 2010), 159–87, at 159.

[136] Frances Spalding, *John Piper, Myfanwy Piper: Lives in Art* (Oxford, 2009), 228.

[137] See, for example, Notes from meeting on 3 or 4 November [1935] between Leonard, Felix Green and Gerald Heard, LKE/G/17/E.

[138] Perry, *Last of the Cold War Spies*, 30.

[139] Stephen Brooke, 'The Body and Socialism: Dora Russell in the 1920s', *Past & Present* 189 (2005), 147–77; Jack Pritchard, *View from a Long Chair: The Memoirs of Jack Pritchard* (London, Boston, Melbourne and Henley, 1984).

on around them as part of their experiment in living. This breaking away from norms at Dartington echoed a national transformation in discourses surrounding sex and sexuality after the First World War, a transformation that formed part of a wider reconfiguration in modes of self-understanding and self-fashioning.[140]

Dorothy had written that the fact that Dartington was 'a community of ordinary people' was 'really the most important fact about it'.[141] But the paradox at the heart of this supposedly egalitarian community of loving friendship was the Elmhirsts themselves, who remained apart from the others, their lifestyle never anything other than upper class. The household at the Hall was run along the same aristocratic lines as Dorothy's previous establishments in America, albeit rather less grandly.[142] To begin with it had twenty staff: a butler, Walter Thomas, previously employed by the Marquess of Bute, along with a 'footman, cook, odd man, four housemaids and two kitchen maids; a head gardener with several assistants; a nurse and nursery maid; two chauffeurs and a car man'.[143] Dorothy laid out the garden in grand style with the assistance of American landscape architect Beatrix Farrand, creating what was one of England's largest private garden projects of the period.[144] Dorothy's children, as was customary among the elite, spent much time away from their parents; the children Dorothy and Leonard later had together – Ruth, born in 1926 (Dorothy had a miscarriage the year after) and Bill, born in 1929, when Dorothy was forty-two – were left chiefly to a nanny in a nursery at the top of the house.[145] It was unsurprising that many employees, even with a more formal machinery of government in place, saw the Elmhirsts, rather than the managing director or trustees, as the ultimate authority at Dartington. The local vicar told Dorothy and Leonard that in 'one of the most conservative rural areas of England', people could not conceive of them as anything other than the traditional 'big-house-centre'.[146]

---

[140] Laura Doan, *Disturbing Practices: History, Sexuality, and Women's Experiences of Modern War* (Chicago, 2013); Lucy Bland and Laura Doan, *Sexology in Culture: Labelling Bodies and Desires* (Chicago, 1998); Virginia Nicholson, *Among the Bohemians: Experiments in Living 1900–1939* (London, 2003).

[141] Dorothy to Ruth Morgan, May 1928, quoted in Harrison, 'Dorothy Elmhirst', 126.

[142] Michael Young's interview with Paula Morel, 23 August 1976, T/HIS/S22.

[143] Michael Young's interview with Marjorie Fogden, 15 September 1976, T/HIS/S22.

[144] The estate's garden, which was one of Dorothy's great passions, was designed in consultation, first, with Harry Tipping, an English designer and a journalist for *Country Life*, and, later, with Beatrix Farrand.

[145] Michael Young's interview with Richard Elmhirst, December 1977, T/HIS/S20/D. Young himself, informally adopted into the Elmhirst family, thought Dorothy and Leonard were 'more at home with other people's children than their own'. *The Elmhirsts*, 119.

[146] R. A. Edwards to Leonard, May 1945, LKE/DEV/1/K.

The middle-class idealists who joined the enterprise found it particularly difficult to reconcile themselves to the Elmhirsts' being in part their friends, in part their employers. There was an 'awkwardness of situation – being both of, and not of, your house parties', the teacher Wyatt Rawson complained to Dorothy – of being 'as it were, at your beck and call' and not 'able to live a life that is really my own'.[147] Musician Imogen Holst, brought up in more thoroughgoing socialist circles, was 'worried by the richness of Dartington' and only agreed to work there because she felt that the arts needed money to thrive.[148] Leonard's elite rural background made it relatively easy for him to get on with people and to seem to ignore the social hierarchy he was so familiar with. 'He used his acute sense of class to keep class in its place,' according to his friend Max Nicholson.[149] He nonetheless was seen to have the rich person's characteristics of expecting '"to buy the answer"' to problems, by hiring an expert rather than letting solutions evolve slowly, and of suspecting his staff of complacency about the need to turn a profit.[150]

Dorothy, negotiating both a foreign country and a new class system, fared less easily in the erratically egalitarian, experimental environment of Dartington. The English 'rarely ask questions and don't seem to care what one feels', she wrote on her arrival in Devon, 'it is going to take me some time to get on to them'.[151] She continued to find her position awkward, even after twenty years in England – refusing to play the benevolent squire's wife but being 'frightened of the too personal relationships' that seemed to be the alternative.[152] She developed a small number of close friendships with artists and spiritual seekers, but most staff and visitors found her a difficult companion. She never gave up trying to overcome her shyness, but 'her wealth was a barrier', remembered the pianist Roland Anderson. 'It was like talking to royalty'.[153] Dorothy's wealth could also blind her to the reality of employees' financial situations: she gave a bicycle to her secretary one day and then re-gifted it

---

[147] Wyatt Rawson to Dorothy, [1927?], DWE/DHS/2/F.
[148] Imogen Holst's father, the composer and adult educator Gustav Holst, was a follower of William Morris and a conductor in the Hammersmith Socialist Choir as well as a teacher at St Paul's Girls' School. Michael Young's interview with Imogen Holst, 21 March 1977, T/HIS/S22/A.
[149] Michael Young's interview with Max Nicholson, 6 April 1978, T/HIS/S22.
[150] Victor Bonham-Carter to Michael Young, 7 September 1980 [copy], LKE/PEP/1/A; Leonard to Fred Gwatkin, 28 September 1934, LKE/LF/16/A.
[151] Dorothy to Eduard Lindeman, 9 June [1925?], box 2, Eduard Lindeman Archives.
[152] Dorothy to Leonard, 16 August 1942, LKE/DWE/13/F; Dorothy, response to 1929 questionnaire, T/PP/P/1/D.
[153] Ronald Anderson interviewed by Michael Young, 8 October 1977, T/HIS/S20/D.

to a visitor the next – not realising the significance of the loss.[154] These everyday, granular tensions that accompanied the effort to live the good life echo the friction and unease surrounding the domestic experiences of many of the progressive elite across England. Supporting democracy but not reconciled to being 'ordinary people', they grappled with what Virginia Woolf termed – with mixed feelings of horror and exhilaration – 'Our Transition Age'.[155]

How did the Elmhirsts knotty, multi-faceted, somewhat chaotic project appear from the outside? While it was their intention to influence society at large, Dorothy and Leonard disliked enterprises that 'spread their religion in an organized way', and they refused to write about Dartington themselves.[156] They also tried at first to control articles written about the estate by others. Nonetheless, Dartington did appear frequently in the press, first locally, and then nationally and internationally, and also in books – and the commentary was near-unanimous in its enthusiasm (although often inaccurate).[157] In part, this positivity may have been a sign of the Elmhirsts' influence in progressive circles: when, for instance, Professor J. A. Scott Watson wrote an unauthorised and mildly critical article on Dartington for *The Listener*, suggesting its farms were over-capitalised, Leonard used his contacts to make known his displeasure and soon received an apology.[158] Positive press coverage also reflected a widespread desire for an alternative rural 'design for living' – and how, in the absence of 'written charters, creeds, constitutions', people were free to project their hopes for this on the Elmhirsts' estate.[159]

[154] Young, *Elmhirsts*, 302.
[155] Virginia Woolf quoted in Alison Light, *Mrs Woolf and the Servants*, 207. Seth Koven also explores this realm in the context of philanthropy in the East End of London, with an emphasis on changing notions of Christian behaviour ('Radical Domesticity, Revolutionary Christianity').
[156] Leonard to Eduard Lindeman, 7 January 192[4?], box 3, Eduard Lindeman Archives. The Elmhirsts considered then set aside the idea of setting up an evangelising printing press (Leonard to Sir Henry Lopes, 14 February 1928, LKE/DEV/3/D).
[157] Dartington's activities were regularly reported in the *Western Morning News, Exeter and Plymouth Gazette, Western Times* and *Western Daily Press*, and appeared in national publications including *The Listener* and *Country Life* (British Library Newspaper Archives). The estate also featured in the *New York Herald Tribune*, among other American newspapers, and in H. J. Massingham's book, *Country* – Dartington was 'recapturing the art of living as a self-dependent local community' (London, 1934), 132.
[158] Exchange of letters between Leonard, agricultural economist John Maxton and Professor J. A. Scott Watson, 1933 (LKE/LAND/3/F); J. A. Scott Watson, 'Rural Britain Today and Tomorrow – vii: Tradition and Experiment in the West', *The Listener*, 22 November 1933, 797.
[159] *Nottingham Journal*, 16 August 1935, British Library Newspaper Archives; Dorothy to R. A. Edwards, 2 August 1942, DWE/G/S3/G.

The conservative local press reviewed Dartington positively as 'a revival of the old patriarchal system when the country squires were the natural leaders'.[160] In spite of their democratic ideals, the Elmhirsts took on some of the traditional duties of big landowners – and appeared in such papers as *The Western Morning News* in the guise of squire and lady, opening fetes and village halls and supporting worthy causes, while their employees participated in intra-parish sports and livestock shows. Conversely, for the intellectual Gerald Heard, writing for the progressive London-based journal *The Architectural Review*, the Elmhirsts' estate was the very opposite of backward-looking and squirearchical – it was uncovering a new, egalitarian social format, the 'brick out of which the reconstructed national house can be built'.[161] In later decades, as Dartington's activities took on a more settled form, its ability to be all things to all men declined. Inevitably, the result was disenchantment. Rolf Gardiner, an early supporter, launched a scathing attack in 1941: Dartington was 'a supreme warning' of 'how not to do' rural reconstruction; it had given its 'soul to the ungodly trinity of "planning", chemistry and cost-accountancy', overthrowing its early commitment to self-sufficiency and spiritual unity.[162] His disapproval may have, in part, stemmed from envy; the Elmhirsts had far more influence as a result of this 'selling out' than he ever did with his own experiments with rural reform.

Outside print media, gossip gives a sense of high levels of local hostility towards Dartington from the start. Criticism reported from within a forty-mile radius included that it was a nudist colony, 'an American firm, with American money and Communistic ideas', that it was 'not a genuine business' and was undermining those that were.[163] Dartington church and village hall, both on the doorstep of the estate, became rallying points for a local community life that defiantly resisted being annexed to the Hall. With a few exceptions, like the Liberal MP for Cornwall Francis Acland, the Westcountry gentry were similarly unenthused by the Elmhirsts' vision. Their number included Conservative MP for Plymouth, Nancy Astor – an American transplant to the Westcountry who, with her philanthropic activities and spiritual

---

[160] *Western Morning News*, 16 June 1932, British Library Newspaper Archives.
[161] Gerald Heard, 'The Dartington Experiment'.
[162] Rolf Gardiner, 'Rural Reconstruction', in H. J. Massingham (ed.), *England and the Farmer* (London, 1941), 91–107, at 91.
[163] Robert Cowan gathered the gossip he had heard locally in a report for Dartington's sales manager James Harrison, 27 January 1936, T/PP/P/1/G.

bent, bore a strong resemblance to Dorothy.[164] Astor visited Dartington several times but was 'so full of her own ideas' that the Elmhirsts found it impossible to 'get through to her anything of what we are really after'.[165] Hostility extended to London, particularly in the 1930s as international politics became more fraught. Captain Arthur Rogers, a leading member of the far-right Liberty Restoration League, spoke against the estate in Parliament and spread rumours about the Elmhirsts that ended in their bringing a court case against him.[166] Relations between Dartington and the surrounding countryside improved in the late 1930s, by which time many local families had at least one member in the Elmhirsts' employ, but it was only the travails of the Second World War and the nationwide social-democratic utopia-building moment during and after it that brought Dartington and its surrounds significantly closer together.

In spite of local resistance, by the mid-1930s Dartington was fêted nationally and internationally: it offered a timely alternative to the totalitarian dystopias looming on the Continent; and it was heralded as 'The New Rural England', an antidote to the 'present low state of English agricultural and of rural life'.[167] Yet, while its external impact grew, the original hope of the estate itself modelling the fully integrated, rural 'good life' receded. The different elements – the school, the arts, the spiritual seeking and the commercial departments – failed to combine. Organic social unity – the kind of decentralised, holistic, bottom-up autonomy Tagore had hoped to achieve in India, or the socialist pluralists in Britain – drifted further and further from the estate's grasp. The Second World War was in a way a timely *deus ex machina*: its economic demands made Dartington profitable for the first time and the ascendance of a new social-democratic politics meant that the Elmhirsts could comfortably repurpose their vision of Dartington as a pre-figurative example of 'life in its completeness' into one of the estate as a research

---

[164] Alongside her political activities as MP for Plymouth from 1919 to 1945, Nancy Astor was a passionate convert to Christian Science. Martin Pugh, 'Astor, Nancy Witcher, Viscountess Astor (1879–1964)', *Oxford Dictionary of National Biography* (Oxford University Press, first published 23 September 2004, revised 1 September 2017) [www.oxforddnb.com/view/article/30489].

[165] Leonard to Gerald Heard, 8 November 1929, LKE/G/17/E. Nancy Astor visited Dartington several times but never warmed to it.

[166] [n.a.], 'Report of a Speech by Captain Arthur Rogers, OBE, Honorary Secretary, Liberty Restoration League, at a Private Meeting of Members of both Houses of Parliament', June 1938, LKE/LF/18/C; Arthur Rogers, *The Real Crisis* (London, [1938]); Richard Griffiths, *Patriotism Perverted: Captain Ramsay, the Right Club, and British Anti-Semitism, 1938–40* (London, 2015 [1998]); Valentine Holmes, legal opinion, 28 November 1936, LKE/LF/18/C.

[167] [n.a.], 'The New Rural England', *The Architect and Building News*, 30 June, 14 July, 21 July 1933.

and development station in the national effort to construct a welfare state. For the head of Dartington's research department, J. R. Currie, by 1950, the estate's activities were 'congregated here mainly for administrative and practical purposes, and not as part of a prototype for the structure of society'; it was the 'synthesis of Dartington's experience that is the valuable product as far as the outside world is concerned'.[168]

By the mid-1930s, Dartington was also already starting to make the transition, completed in the second half of the century, from a centre of community reform to a tourist stopping-off point. To its stream of reform-minded visitors, it added a more dispassionate species – the touring motorist.[169] A semi-formal permit system was introduced, accompanied by an estate map.[170] 'Seldom a day passes when an estate worker is not disturbed by a party, large or small, peering at or passing by his particular piece of work,' ran the estate newsletter in 1934. But it cautioned against irritation – visitors paid sixpence, bought estate products and spread the idea of Dartington 'in fields wider by far than any advertisement department'.[171] Dartington was included in John Betjeman's *Shell Guide To Devon* in 1936.[172] A 1937 Mass Observation survey entry recorded a stop-in at Dartington on a 'short motoring holiday', which included a tour of the departments, a visit to the estate showroom and 'devonshire tea in apple garden attached' and made no mention of social ideals.[173] While the Elmhirsts and various specialists based at Dartington contributed to national reconstruction in the decades that succeeded the war, the estate itself was becoming a product to be consumed rather than a locus for experimental living. This was part of a wider shift towards viewing traditional, rustic 'Deep England' as a place to be carefully preserved for the pleasure of town-dwellers, rather than a dynamic social and economic unit in its own right.[174]

Mass Observation, another expansive, connecting-it-all project, followed a trajectory notably similar to Dartington's through this period:

---

[168] J. R. Currie to Leonard, 22 December 1950, LKE/G/S13/B.

[169] For the interwar rise of the 'motoring pastoral', see David Matless, *Landscape and Englishness* (London, 1998), 95–101 and David Jeremiah, 'Motoring and the British Countryside', *Rural History* 21 (2010), 233–50.

[170] David Jeremiah, 'Dartington Hall – A Landscape of an Experiment in Rural Reconstruction', in Paul Brassley et al. (eds.), *The English Countryside*, 116–31, at 119.

[171] *News of the Day*, 28 September 1934, T/PP/EST/1–8.

[172] Dartington was described as 'a unique scheme for combining rural life with industrial, which, though sounding Utopian, is made possible'. Betjeman, *Devon: Shell Guide*, 27.

[173] Leslie Ernest Charles Hughes, Day survey, 12 August 1937, S49, Mass Observation Archive, University of Sussex.

[174] David Matless, 'Definitions of England, 1928–89: Preservation, Modernism and the Nature of the Nation', *Built Environment* 16 (1990), 179–91, at 187.

an independent reforming endeavour in the 1930s, it successfully collaborated with the state during the Second World War, but struggled to find a role for itself afterwards. The programme began in 1937, combining democratically minded social research with a surrealist manifesto that tried to 'discern "the unconscious fears and wishes of the mass" and to draw out its poetic dimension in a scientific manner'.[175] The Second World War gave it tighter focus, since it was commissioned by the government to provide reports on morale, but afterwards it lost impetus, ultimately becoming a company devoted to market research.[176] Its founders nonetheless continued independently to pursue their ideals of observing and improving society: Charles Madge, for example, as a member of United Nations and UNESCO missions in Asia and Africa, and Tom Harrisson as an ethnographer and museum curator in Sarawak.

The Elmhirsts, similarly, found an outlet for their enthusiasm for grassroots, communitarian social reform abroad after the war, even as Dartington transmogrified into a tourist attraction and retail venue. Until their deaths – Dorothy's in 1968 and Leonard's in 1974 – they gave extensive support to the community development movement, particularly in India. They also supported community development in Britain, helping fund Michael Young's Institute of Community Studies. Some of Dartington's other interwar participants, meanwhile, had more radical responses to the rise of social democracy, withdrawing from efforts at democratic engagement in favour of a more individualistic self-exploration that fed into the American post-war counterculture.[177]

---

[175] Jeremy MacClancy, 'Brief Encounter: The Meeting, in Mass-Observation, of British Surrealism and Popular Anthropology', *The Journal of the Royal Anthropological Institute* 1 (1995), 495–512, at 509.

[176] Nick Hubble, *Mass-Observation and Everyday Life: Culture, History, Theory* (Basingstoke, 2006), 8–9 and passim.

[177] For instance, the public intellectual Gerald Heard, for several years closely involved with Dartington, moved to California to found a meditational 'missionary college'. See Chapter 2.

2   Social and Spiritual Questing

> Dartington is a religion, but unlike the religions we are accustomed to, which are centred round a performance held at specified times, it is a religion which goes on continuously and has done so from its inception.   John Drummond (194(5?))[1]

Like many elites born into the late nineteenth century, the founders of Dartington were raised to believe that the highest good was the 'selfless service to others that Christ so insistently proclaimed'.[2] In this period in Britain and America, Christianity and the ideal of social service twined together, structuring both private belief and public behaviour in what Seth Koven terms a '"practical" or "lived" theology'.[3] The First World War – along with the gradual atrophy of faith brought about by scientific discovery – shook this socio-spiritual edifice. Looking back, Leonard wrote that 'how we tried in those years before the war to turn Christ into a religion, to check action and situation against him' was 'not a real escape from the challenge that science and psychology and the war were to make to us, to know our own minds, to mature our own thought ... to link devotion and religious purpose to the new situation of today'.[4] The Church, it seemed to Leonard, and to many like him, had been complicit in the war; Christianity could therefore neither explain nor mitigate the conflict's brutality.[5] The Elmhirsts emerged from the war feeling that orthodox faith was no longer adequate as a guide either to belief or to

---

[1] John Drummond, [194(5?)], draft chapters for a book later published as *A Candle in England* (London, 1947), LKE/DEV/3/C, Dartington Hall Archives (unless specified otherwise, all the following archival references are to this collection).

[2] Dorothy to the secretary of the Dartington Parochial Church Council, 16 July 1948, DWE/G/S3/B. For analysis of Christian altruism, see Frank Prochaska, *The Voluntary Impulse: Philanthropy in Modern Britain* (London, 1998) and *Christianity and Social Service in Modern Britain: The Disinherited Spirit* (Oxford and New York, 2006).

[3] Seth Koven, *The Match Girl and the Heiress* (Oxford, 2015), 18.

[4] Leonard to Gerald Heard, 26 December 1934, LKE/G/17.

[5] Philip Jenkins, *The Great and Holy War: How World War I Became a Religious Crusade* (Oxford, 2014).

conduct. They were unmoored from the 'safe anchorage' that had framed their lives so far.[6]

Historians discussing the fate of Christianity in the twentieth century debate the position it occupied in people's lives: whether it was an official structure; a set of behaviours, like church going or prayer; a force shaping a shared cultural and social life; or an internal experience of transcendence.[7] For the Elmhirsts, Christianity constituted some element of all of these things. When they 'lost faith', they did not simply give up on everything Christianity had signified for them. They (mostly) stopped going to church, and they jettisoned what Dorothy called the 'forms and dogmas' of Christianity.[8] They refused to teach Christianity in their school at Dartington.[9] But, partly intentionally and partly inadvertently, they held onto some of the language and ideas that had constituted their Christian worldview. One of the most significant vestiges was an ethos of public service: the belief that they, and others, were 'burdened with a sense of universal social responsibility which must find channel and expression'.[10] A second important remnant was a vision of humanity as spiritually interconnected – and the view that this connection between individuals should be honoured in a social philosophy that emphasised ties of 'direct relationship and responsibility', rather than in the atomistic individualism of laissez-faire liberalism.[11]

The Elmhirsts' experience was far from unique. As historians including Alex Owen find, there were numerous elites in the Western world whose Christian faith was altered or destroyed by the First World War.[12] Many of these men and women channelled their desire for a continued spiritualised or ethical understanding of life – what Owen terms their 'religious sense' – into searching for new, transformative visions of what to think and how to behave.[13] Just as pre-war Christianity operated on several levels, feeding into private belief and public behaviour, so did efforts to replace it. People looked – variously, or all at once – for new

---

[6] Leonard to Gerald Heard, 26 December 1934, LKE/G/17.

[7] Jeremy Morris, 'Secularization and Religious Experience: Arguments in the Historiography of Modern British Religion', *The Historical Journal* 55 (2012), 195–219, at 211–17.

[8] Dorothy to the secretary of the Dartington Parochial Church Council, 16 July 1948, DWE/G/S3/B.

[9] Dorothy to Leonard, 30 October 1927, LKE/DWE/12/E.

[10] Leonard to Dorothy, 1 February 1945, LKE/DWE/14/B.

[11] Leonard to Eduard Lindeman, 7 January 1924[?], box 2, Eduard Lindeman Papers, Columbia University Archives.

[12] Alex Owen, 'The "Religious Sense" in a Post-War Secular Age', *Past and Present* 1 (2006), 159–77; Jenny Hazelgrove, *Spiritualism and British Society Between the Wars* (Manchester, 2000).

[13] Owen, 'The "Religious Sense"'.

forms of spiritual meaning; for a new guide to moral behaviour; for replacements for Christianity that promoted affective or social fulfilment – dealing with happiness, love, self-realisation; and for different frameworks for understanding the nature of society as a whole. Collectively, this chapter terms these searches 'socio-spiritual questing'. Emily Robinson and Keith Gildart frame this esoteric realm of seeking as a form of progressivism: critical of the limitations of materialism, emphasising the unity of humankind and promoting radical social transformation, it was also closely bound up with more usually recognised forms of progressivism – for instance in the form of interwar Labour Party politicians enthusiastically engaging with séances, ghost hunting and theosophy.[14]

One approach in this diverse realm of questing was to experiment with new forms of religiosity: by reforming Christianity; adopting Eastern faiths such as Buddhism or the Bahá'í Faith; or replacing traditional religion with more elastic sorts of spiritualism that perpetuated ideas of transcendence and telos but rejected orthodox rituals and doctrines.[15] Another approach was the effort to use the social sciences to promote affective or spiritual fulfilment – 'social sciences' being a term used very loosely here, as it was at the time, to encompass psychology, sociology and anthropology, disciplines whose boundaries were all under negotiation.[16] The search also included more disparate projects, like pacifism, exploring 'spiritualised' art, or syncretic combinations of several of the above.[17] In all of these areas of seeking, the legacy of nineteenth-century

---

[14] Keith Gildart, 'Séance Sitters, Ghost Hunters, Spiritualists, and Theosophists: Esoteric Belief and Practice in the Parliamentary Labour Party, c.1929–51', *Twentieth Century British History* 29 (2018), 357–87; Robinson, *Progressive Politics*, 110–11.

[15] On reforming the Church, see Matthew Grimley, *Citizenship, Community, and the Church of England: Liberal Anglican Theories of the State between the Wars* (Oxford, 2004). On Eastern spirituality, Sumita Mukherjee, 'The Reception Given to Sadhu Sundar Singh, the Itinerant Indian Christian "Mystic", in Interwar Britain', *Interwar Britain, Immigrants & Minorities* 35 (2017), 21–39. On alternative spiritualities, John Warne Monroe, *Laboratories of Faith: Mesmerism, Spiritualism, and Occultism in Modern France* (Ithaca and London, 2008); T. J. Jackson Lears, *No Place of Grace: Antimodernism and the Transformation of American Culture 1880–1920* (Chicago and London, 1981); and Martin Green, *Mountain of Truth: The Counterculture Begins, Ascona, 1900–1920* (Hanover and London, 1989); Alex Owen, *The Place of Enchantment: British Occultism and the Culture of the Modern* (Chicago and London, 2004).

[16] Stefan Collini, 'Sociology and Idealism in Britain 1880–1920', *Archives Européennes de Sociologie* 19 (1978), 3–50, at 34.

[17] Martin Ceadel, *Pacifism in Britain 1914–1945: The Defining of a Faith* (Oxford, 1980) and *Semi-Detached Idealists: The British Peace Movement and International Relations, 1854–1945* (Oxford and New York, 2000); Michael Saler, *The Avant-Garde in Interwar England: Medieval Modernism and the London Underground* (New York and Oxford, 1999).

Christianity was felt in the way people expressed and navigated the new ideas that were coming to the fore.

Historians have, understandably, often studied these various approaches separately. Some scholars concentrate on the fate of orthodox Christianity: whether by looking at quantitative measures like church attendance, at how the faith continued to structure social discourse, or at efforts to reform the Church.[18] A second strand of research focuses on spiritualism, emphasising how the vogue for spiritualism in the Victorian period – the popularity of séances, the occult and theosophy – gained renewed vigour in consequence of the First World War. Jenny Hazelgrove, for example, emphasises the diversity of popular spiritual modes in the interwar years, while Michael Saler looks at more diffuse efforts to 'spiritualise' or 're-enchant' the modern world through art and literature.[19] A third strand of historiography is devoted to pacifism, which, as Martin Ceadel and others find, amounted to a faith in its own right in the years between the wars.[20] A fourth strand of historiography – though by no means the last – focuses on the rise of the social sciences by looking either at the emergence of a particular discipline or at the field as a whole.[21]

Historians have drawn attention to overlaps between some of these forms of interwar socio-spiritual questing. The development of psychological thought and practice was informed by spiritualist ideas, as Mathew Thomson highlights.[22] Georgina Byrne notes that some members of the Church of England were eager to adopt elements of spiritualist teaching in order to fit Anglicanism for modern times.[23] Several accounts of the evolution of specific social scientific disciplines in Britain show the intermixing of science and quasi-religious ideas of

---

[18] Callum G. Brown, *The Death of Christian Britain* (London and New York, 2001); Jeremy Morris, 'The Strange Death of Christian Britain: Another Look at the Secularization Debate', *The Historical Journal* 46 (2003), 963–76; Grimley, *Citizenship, Community, and the Church of England.*

[19] Hazelgrove, *Spiritualism and British Society*; Saler, *The Avant-Garde*, viii and '"Clap If You Believe in Sherlock Holmes": Mass Culture and the Re-enchantment of Modernity, c. 1890–c. 1940', *The Historical Journal* 46 (2003), 599–622. See also Joy Dixon, *Divine Feminine: Theosophy and Feminism in England* (Baltimore and London, 2001).

[20] Ceadel, *Pacifism in Britain* and *Semi-Detached Idealists.* See also Peter Brock and Thomas Socknat (eds.), *Challenge to Mars: Essays on Pacifism from 1918–1945* (Toronto and London, 1999).

[21] See, for example, Dorothy Ross (ed.), *Modernist Impulses in the Human Sciences, 1870–1930* (Baltimore and London, 1994).

[22] Mathew Thomson, *Psychological Subjects: Ideas, Culture and Health in Twentieth-Century Britain* (Oxford, 2006).

[23] Georgina Byrne, *Modern Spiritualism and the Church of England, 1850–1939* (Woodbridge, 2010).

transcendence, holism and telos.[24] More comprehensive surveys of social science in America illuminate the way in which pioneering practitioners in the fields of sociology, anthropology and psychology struggled to define their social role: debating, in particular, over whether they ought to be objective – confining themselves to empirical fact-finding – or purposively, even spiritually, involved in helping to create a better society.[25] In the minds of some purposive scientists (although not the majority), the way in which social science could improve the lot of mankind was construed as part of the search for a 'new religion'.[26]

This chapter adds to these individual instances of overlap. It draws attention to how, in one sense, all these different strands of historiography are looking at the same phenomenon: the effort to find ways to (re)infuse life with a structure, meaning and purpose that had previously been provided by orthodox Christianity. It is fruitful to consider the different forms of socio-spiritual questing together because, often, it was not a single one of them that was adopted but several, the languages and frameworks indiscriminately intertwined in the search for spiritual fulfilment and social harmony in the aftermath of the wars.[27] Between the certainty of Victorian Christianity and the secular scientific modes

---

[24] A wide-ranging survey of efforts to revise the human sciences across Western society in this period is given in Ross, *Modernist Impulses*. Specifically British studies include Christopher Lawrence and George Weisz (eds.), *Greater Than the Parts: Holism in Biomedicine, 1920–1950* (Oxford, 1998); Thomson, *Psychological Subjects*; Roger Smith, 'Biology and Values in Interwar Britain: C.S. Sherrington, Julian Huxley and the Vision of Progress', *Past and Present* 178 (2003), 210–42. Mike Savage offers some cross-disciplinary analysis of the social sciences in the interwar period in Britain in *Identities and Social Change in Britain Since 1940: The Politics of Method* (Oxford, 2010).

[25] Mark Smith delineates the conflict between 'objectivist' and 'purposive' social scientists in America (*Social Science in the Crucible* (Durham and London, 1994)). Andrew Jewett explores the persistence of the belief in American universities that science carried with it a set of ethical or quasi-religious values capable of providing a direction for a democratic culture (*Science, Democracy, and the American University: From the Civil War to the Cold War* (Cambridge, 2012)). Anne Harrington tracks the rise of 're-enchanted science' in interwar Germany, focusing in particular on the holistic approach of Gestalt psychology (*Reenchanted Science: Holism in German Culture from Wilhelm to Hitler* (Princeton, 1996)).

[26] Social scientists who took this view include Carl Jung, who interwove spiritualism and psychiatry, and the anthropologist Geoffrey Gorer, who had a brief flirtation with mysticism before reverting to more orthodox academia. Alex Owen, 'Occultism and the "Modern" Self in *Fin-de-Siècle* Britain', in Martin Daunton and Bernhard Rieger (eds.), *Meanings of Modernity: Britain from the Late-Victorian Era to World War II* (Oxford, 2001), 71–96, at 86.

[27] The apparently 'wrong-headed' turns towards mysticism of otherwise 'respectable' intellectuals such as A. R. Orage and Aldous Huxley are less puzzling in the context of a widespread, restless and ecumenical quest for meaning, which often took individuals beyond the range of any single framework. Thomson, *Psychological Subjects*, 80; Jerome Meckier, 'Mysticism or Misty Schism? Huxley Studies Since World War II', *The British Studies Monitor* 5 (1974), 165–77.

that came to dominate after the Second World War, there was a fleeting moment of ideological and methodological syncretism. Interwar socio-spiritual questing was so wide-ranging and amorphous that it defies comprehensive survey. Dartington Hall provides an alternative way of drawing together its various strands: an unusual convergence in a diffuse landscape of seeking.

The Elmhirsts occasionally discussed their plans to start a social experiment in overtly Christian terms – for instance, as an attempt to build 'The Kingdom of Heaven' – but mostly they saw themselves as replacing rather than adapting a Christian framework.[28] They hoped, as Dorothy wrote, to find 'a new synthesis of faith and works', creating a community that modelled a way to live a spiritually satisfying life that also contributed to the social good.[29] Not every part of Dartington reflected this conjoined ambition. It proved difficult to knit spiritual and social-reforming aims together, and individual projects often became predominantly about one or the other. Nonetheless, the desire to repurpose Victorian Christian ideals of public service and a spiritually united society was a vital force shaping Dartington.

Since Dorothy and Leonard were willing to engage with practically all theories, their estate became a magnet for many different types of socio-spiritual seeker, both from Britain and further afield.[30] It attracted spiritually minded artists, reforming vicars and those who saw salvation in Eastern religions or in social science. As well as offering an unusual microcosm of interwar attempts to find alternative socio-spiritual frameworks, Dartington is a rare example of this search intersecting with a large-scale practical reform project. A study of the community adds to the work of historians including Susan Pedersen, Peter Mandler, Frank Prochaska and Eve Colpus, who emphasise continuities between elites' shared sense of Christian public duty in the nineteenth century and a more fragmented field of religious, spiritual and moral ideals and forms of public behaviour in the twentieth century.[31] As Colpus writes, for a

---

[28] Leonard to Dorothy, 27 October 1920, LKE/DWE/10/A.
[29] Dorothy to Waldo Frank, 28 June 1938, DWE/G/4/C; Dorothy and Leonard, *Faith and Works at Dartington*, re-printed from *The Countryman* (Totnes, 1937), 8–11.
[30] Steven J. Sutcliffe uses the term 'seeker' to describe those who used alternative spirituality to pursue an ideology of radical personal transformation in the counterculture of the 1960s, but it can be applied as appositely to the interwar fraternity of more socially minded questers. *Children of the New Age: A History of Spiritual Practices* (London, 2003), 37.
[31] Susan Pedersen and Peter Mandler (eds.), *After the Victorians: Private Conscience and Public Duty in Modern Britain: Essays in Memory of John Clive* (London and New York, 1994); Prochaska, *The Voluntary Impulse* and *Christianity and Social Service*; Eve Colpus, *Female Philanthropy in the Interwar World: Between Self and Other* (London, 2019).

generation that 'spanned the Victorian, Edwardian, wartime and post-war worlds, the notion that there were distinct ages, each with its own ethical and social character, made little sense'.[32]

This chapter begins by considering the loss of faith in the Church experienced by Dorothy, Leonard and a third figure closely connected to Dartington's socio-spiritual life, the public intellectual Gerald Heard. It then turns to four of the more spiritually oriented approaches to filling the gap left by the lived theology of Christianity at Dartington (later chapters focus on projects in which social considerations were to the fore). The Elmhirsts tried re-shaping the role of the Church with the help of the arts; explored the possibilities of Eastern spirituality; worked to advance humankind's unity, with Heard's help, through group spiritual exploration; and experimented with a planned regime of 'psycho-physical hygiene' to be deduced on the basis of science.[33] In these approaches there were recurring tensions, which echoed debates in wider society: between private spiritual exploration and contributing practically to the social good; between the ideals of group spirit and individual freedom; between paternalism, expert guidance and egalitarian democracy.

By comparison with the other main areas of Dartington – education, the arts and rural regeneration – socio-spiritual questing yielded little obvious fruit. No one, coherent alternative to organised Christianity emerged. Dorothy and Leonard's vague open-mindedness, combined with the intangibility of the problem they were attempting to solve, resulted in much woolliness of thinking. Yet this questing was what drove the Elmhirsts to set up Dartington in the first place, and it shaped many of the projects on the estate. Individuals visiting or participating in the community were inspired by the juxtaposition and diversity of approaches about how to live in a moral, spiritual or psychologically fulfilling way. As will be shown, such interwar experimentation fed into the deployment of social science in the building of the post-Second-World-War welfare state, into the syncretic spiritualism of the New Age, and into a commoditised culture of self-improvement in the second half of the twentieth century.

2.1   Beyond Christian Orthodoxy

The paths taken by Leonard, Dorothy and Gerald Heard beyond ortho-dox belief and into socio-spiritual questing serve as a paradigm for those

---

[32] Eve Colpus, 'Women, Service and Self-Actualization in Inter-War Britain', *Past & Present* 238 (2018), 197–232, at 200.
[33] Leonard, note on setting up a community council, 14 March 1939, LKE/G/S8/A.

of many other elites who were drawn to participate in Dartington. Leonard and Heard, although they did not meet one another until the 1920s, followed very similar trajectories. Both were sons of clergymen who expected to follow their fathers' vocation. At Repton School, Leonard was particularly influenced by his headmaster, William Temple (later to become Archbishop of Canterbury), in whose activities he would remain interested until Temple's death in 1944.[34] Temple was driven by the desire to serve the public in the spirit of Christ and also to ensure – in the face of signs of its seeming decline – that Christianity remained at the centre of Western culture.[35]

Leonard and Heard came under the sway of a second charismatic man who was striving to discover a suitable modern mode of religiosity when they took the Historical Tripos at Cambridge. Their tutor G. L. Dickinson's unresolved search for spiritual meaning, which was mystic rather than Christian, catalysed in each of his students an incipient religious doubt. At the same time, the young men were impressed by Dickinson's high-minded sense of service and passion for the improvement of mankind, which later manifested in his involvement in developing the idea of the League of Nations.[36] In spite of Leonard and Heard's dwindling confidence in orthodox Christian faith, they both went on to begin the Divinity Testimonium needed for ordination, not yet prepared to abandon their intended paths.[37]

Leonard worked for the Young Men's Christian Association in India during the First World War – a war in which he lost two brothers, and Heard one.[38] Both Leonard and Heard found that the conflict, coming on top of the influence of Dickinson and other sceptics at Cambridge, 'shattered many of [their] inherited beliefs'.[39] Anglican clerics often

---

[34] LKE/G/32/C; LKE/G/S14/B.

[35] William Temple's activities included helping in the formation of the British Council of Churches (1942) and the World Council of Churches (voted into existence in 1937, but officially inaugurated in 1948); convening the Malvern Conference in 1941 to promote the Church's role in society; and writing a Penguin Special on *Christianity and Social Order* (1942). John Kent, *William Temple: Church, State, and Society in Britain, 1880–1950* (Cambridge, 1992); Edward Loane, 'William Temple and the World Council of Churches: Church Unity "Lite"', in *William Temple and Church Unity: The Politics and Practice of Ecumenical Theology* (New York, 2016), 153–77.

[36] D. E. Martin, 'Dickinson, Goldsworthy Lowes (1862–1932)', in *Oxford Dictionary of National Biography* (Oxford University Press, first published 23 September 2004, revised 27 May 2010) [www.oxforddnb.com/view/article/32815].

[37] Michael Young, *The Elmhirsts of Dartington: The Creation of a Utopian Community* (London, 1982), 22; Paul Eros, '"One of the Most Penetrating Minds in England": Gerald Heard and the British Intelligentsia of the Interwar Period', unpublished PhD thesis, University of Oxford, 2011, 3–4.

[38] Alison Falby, *Between the Pigeonholes: Gerald Heard, 1889–1971* (Newcastle, 2008), 9.

[39] Leonard, 'A moment of assurance', 1971, LKE/DWE/18/A.

identified Britain's national cause with God's during the war, a patriotism strengthened by the fact that the head of state was the head of the Church.[40] For Leonard and Heard, the Church's support for what they saw as an unnecessary and horrifyingly brutal conflict meant that they could no longer look to it as a guide to life: 'its authority had gone', wrote Leonard.[41] Yet both men continued to long 'to sacrifice the self in a positive endeavour' – to find an alternative, spiritually infused form of social service.[42] This echoed a common urge among elites to re-theorise the Victorian Christian notion of public duty in a new form: what the reformer Beatrice Webb called 'the transference of the emotion of self-sacrificing service from God to man'.[43]

Heard and Leonard channelled their impulse to serve into promoting rural regeneration. Heard became the private secretary of Sir Horace Plunkett, a pioneer of Irish agricultural cooperation and an influence on Tagore.[44] Leonard worked for a time with English missionary Sam Higginbottom on rural community development in India and then went to study agricultural economics at Cornell – an institution whose pioneering work in agricultural extension had, since the 1890s, emphasised not just scientific farming but also the moral or even spiritual awakening of farmers as good citizens.[45] Leonard was drawn to this agenda since his

---

[40] Although the war drew enthusiasm from many religious leaders in Britain, there were also those who saw it as diametrically opposed to their faith. The pacifist Fellowship of Reconciliation, for example, set up in 1914 to promote international harmony, had attracted over 7,000 members by the end of the war. Jenkins, *The Great and Holy War*; Aimee E. Barbeau, 'Christian Empire and National Crusade: The Rhetoric of Anglican Clergy in the First World War', *Anglican and Episcopal History* 85 (2016), 24–62.

[41] Leonard to Dorothy, 12 September 1921, LKE/DWE/10/C.

[42] Leonard to Aldous Huxley, 27 July 1935, LKE/G/18/A.

[43] Beatrice Webb, *My Apprenticeship*, vol. 1 (London, 1926), 153. See Pedersen and Mandler, *After the Victorians*. Thomas Dixon also explores how altruism as an ethical doctrine came to be adopted by the non-religiously orthodox (*The Invention of Altruism: Making Moral Meanings in Victorian Britain* (Oxford, 2008), 113). It should be noted that philanthropy based on Christian belief had already begun being supplemented by 'quasi-religious' social service based on a 'Religion of Humanity' in the previous century (Gertrude Himmelfarb, 'The Age of Philanthropy', *The Wilson Quarterly* 21 (1997), 48–55).

[44] Philip Bull, 'Plunkett, Sir Horace Curzon (1854–1932)', *Oxford Dictionary of National Biography* (Oxford University Press, first published 23 September 2004, revised 3 January 2008) [www.oxforddnb.com/view/article/35549]. Rabindranath Tagore read Horace Plunkett and A.E.'s [a pseudonym used by George William Russell] *The National Being* (1916) on Irish cooperative living (Louise Blakeney Williams, 'Overcoming the 'Contagion of Mimicry': The Cosmopolitan Nationalism and Modernist History of Rabindranath Tagore and W. B. Yeats', *American Historical Review* 112 (2007), 69–100, at 97).

[45] J. Peters Scott, '"Every Farmer Should be Awakened": Liberty Hyde Bailey's Vision of Agricultural Extension Work', *Agricultural History* 80 (2006), 190–219.

desire to contribute to society retained an element of spirituality, even if that spirituality was now loose and undefined.

During a two-year course in agricultural economics, Leonard absorbed a peculiarly American faith in science – and in particular in the social sciences – as an alluring new catch-all discipline that might bring about social progress in place of the Church.[46] Since the Church was 'dying throughout England', he wrote to Dorothy, 'Can the scientists and psychologists show us the way?'[47] Later he expanded on this idea: whilst science had, 'up to the present, done so much to upset the balance of things', it could be 'harnessed and used for the benefit of the community, bringing new life to the group'.[48] Leonard's view reflected the widespread faith among early-twentieth-century American progressives that the human sciences could remake American culture, creating the conditions for democratic self-government – and sometimes also promoting spiritual unity.[49] By the early 1920s, he had decided that the best way to explore this possibility was through 'innumerable small experiments' into how to live – experiments, like Dartington, which he compared to 'the early monasteries and missionary settlements across Europe'.[50] While Leonard had abandoned Christian orthodoxy, its language, doctrines and historical structures would continue to figure large in his mental landscape.

Heard, who had been exposed to both anthropology and psychic research at Cambridge, began a career as a writer, taking as his main theme the quest for a new belief system that would combine science and spirituality in a 'third morality'.[51] Like Aldous and Julian Huxley, who were his friends and frequent visitors to Dartington, Heard saw reconciling spirituality with science as a vital part of rebuilding a world shattered by war.[52] Late-nineteenth-century ideals – modelling behaviour on Christ and trying to build 'a kingdom of heaven on earth' – needed

---

[46] Andrew Jewett surveys the efforts of interwar progressive scientists in American universities to promote scientific democracy in *Science, Democracy, and the American University*. Dorothy Ross concentrates on progressive social scientists' contribution to the evolution of ideas of American exceptionalism, with science offering an accelerated path to a golden future. *The Origins of American Social Sciences* (Cambridge, 1991).

[47] Leonard to Dorothy, 12 September 1921, LKE/DWE/10/C.

[48] Leonard, Sunday evening meeting, 23 September 1928, LKE/G/31/A.

[49] Andrew Jewett, *Science, Democracy, and the American University*, 109–37.

[50] Leonard to Eduard Lindeman, 7 January 1924[?], box 2, Eduard Lindeman Archives, Columbia University Archives.

[51] Eros, 'Gerald Heard'; Falby, *Between the Pigeonholes*.

[52] Aldous Huxley, *Ends and Means: An Inquiry into the Nature of Ideals* (London, 1937); Paul T. Phillips, 'One World, One Faith: The Quest for Unity in Julian Huxley's Religion of Evolutionary Humanism', *Journal of the History of Ideas* 268 (2007), 613–33.

incorporating with science in order to forge a new faith and pattern of behaviour for a new age. Efforts to combine syncretic religious experimentation with science had been a prominent feature of the previous century, as J. Jeffrey Franklin and other historians find – but Heard and many of those who were involved with Dartington felt that they were starting this process from scratch, or that it had at least taken on a new urgency after the war.[53]

Dorothy Elmhirst, like Leonard and Heard, was raised in a tradition of liberal Protestantism and embraced the concomitant practical theology that a good Christian must live in the service of others. Before she married, like numerous middle- and upper-class women on both sides of the Atlantic, she spent much energy, time and money on philanthropy and social reform.[54] She attended church regularly, meeting and often forming strong friendships with other female reformers inspired by Christ's self-renouncing love, including the devout social activist Ruth Morgan.[55]

Dorothy had been gradually deviating from conventional Protestantism into a more all-embracing religiosity before the First World War, and she lost her Christian faith entirely during it.[56] Her response to this was different from Leonard's – a demonstration of the varied reactions to doubts about Christianity in this period and also of the gender politics that shaped these reactions. Leonard mostly channelled his post-Christian 'religious sense' into social work. While he had some interest in the more interior question of spiritual life, he was often distracted from this by what he called the 'escape mechanism of a multitude of exterior activities' – by the Edwardian, outward-facing concept of Christian manly public duty.[57] Dorothy, too, dedicated a huge amount of energy to social work after she lost faith, but she also embarked on a lifetime of intense spiritual

[53] J. Jeffrey Franklin, *Spirit Matters: Occult Beliefs, Alternative Religions, and the Crisis of Faith in Victorian Britain* (Ithaca and London, 2018).
[54] Frank Prochaska, *Women and Philanthropy in Nineteenth-Century England* (Oxford, 1980); Sarah Ruffing Robbins, 'Sustaining Gendered Philanthropy through Transatlantic Friendship: Jane Addams, Henrietta Barnett, and Writing for Reciprocal Mentoring', in Frank Q. Christianson and Leslee Thorne-Murphy (eds.) *Philanthropic Discourse in Anglo-American Literature, 1850–1920* (Bloomington, IN, 2017), 211–35.
[55] Jane Brown, *Angel Dorothy: How an American Progressive Came to Devon* (London, 2017), 29, 34.
[56] W. A. Swanberg, *Whitney Father, Whitney Heiress* (New York, 1980), 235.
[57] Leonard, 'Time Budget 1934–5', 8 November 1934, LKE/G/S8/1; Michael Roper, 'Between Manliness and Masculinity: The "War Generation" and the Psychology of Fear in Britain, 1914–1950', *Journal of British Studies* 44 (2005), 343–62.

exploration, starting with dabbling in séances and Christian Science on the death of her first husband.[58]

Dorothy's inner journey – framed by the ecumenical idea that 'the spirit of man is connected with a larger spirit that infuses all life' – can be followed in the Dartington archive through numerous notebooks filled with poems, biblical extracts, hymns, prayers, cuttings on theology, the arts, psychology, philosophy and education, as well as with her own thoughts and feelings.[59] She placed a strong emphasis on correct daily conduct, and particularly on the everyday struggle to treat others generously and as equals. Her efforts to be 'inconspicuous and unnoticed' – by going last through doors, taking the worst chair and the worst cut of meat – made even her own children uneasy.[60] Her sense of the importance of daily conduct in making the spiritual self echoes the ethos of Kingsley Hall, the 'people's house' set up by Muriel Lester and her sister Doris in 1915 to promote revolutionary Christianity, and also of the Panacea Society, a millenarian community founded in 1919 by Mabel Barltrop.[61] Kingsley Hall, the Panacea Society and Dartington were led by influential, independent-minded women. Yet their founders' preoccupation with humble, modest and moral behaviour carried with it a flavour of the Victorian Christian myth of the woman as the 'angel in the house', in which women's pious personal conduct was deemed necessary to keep husbands and children on the straight and narrow, indirectly safeguarding the faith of society as a whole.[62] Alex Owen finds that spiritualism could provide an arena for stretching gender norms – the public authority of female mediums disrupting the idea of 'separate

[58] Anthea Williams notes, 'Dorothy's séances after Willard's death', [n.d.], T/HIS/S22. Dorothy appears to have remained interested in séances for several decades, attending one in 1933 where she asked about connecting with the 'subconscious mind' and the 'universal spirit'. Typescript record of 'Sitting with Mrs Eileen Garrett', 25 July 1933, DWE/G/8/B.

[59] Dorothy to R. A. Edwards, 2 August 1942, DWE/G/S3/G; for example, Dorothy, 'Form of Meditation for Daily Use', [n.d.], DWE/G/S3/A.

[60] Beatrice Straight to Nancy Wilson Ross, 7 June 1936, 156/2, Nancy Wilson Ross Archives.

[61] Seth Koven, 'The "Sticky Sediment" of Daily Life: Radical Domesticity, Revolutionary Christianity, and the Problem of Wealth in Britain from the 1880s to the 1930s', *Representations* 120 (2012), 39–82, at 39. Dorothy stayed several times with the Lester sisters, donating to their charitable work and being introduced by them to various figures in the pacifist movement (Muriel Lester to Dorothy, 28 April 1936 and 5 September 1936, DWE/G/S2/A; Doris Lester to Dorothy, 22 May 1933, LKE/G/22/A). Jane Shaw, *Octavia, Daughter of God: The Story of a Female Messiah and her Followers* (London, 2011).

[62] Anne Hogan and Andrew Bradstock (eds.), *Women of Faith in Victorian Culture: Reassessing the Angel in the House* (Basingstoke, 1998).

spheres' – but it could also, as these communities show, function as a way of reinforcing traditional expectations of female behaviour.[63]

Dorothy was as fervent in her interest in social science as she was in spirituality. As a young woman engaged in philanthropic work in New York, she had given increasing attention to the theories underlying social reform, attending lectures in economics, sociology and psychology at Columbia University.[64] Through her friendships with reformers such as Eduard Lindeman and Herbert Croly, she kept abreast of American purposive social science even once living in Devon. Since social science in America was considerably in advance of that in Britain, the Elmhirsts' precocious faith that psychologists and sociologists could promote individual fulfilment and social – or even spiritual – harmony is in part explained by this transatlantic connection. When social scientists began to visit Dartington, Dorothy folded their guidance into her everyday practice of self-development, writing, for example, that the psychologist William Sheldon had 'shown me what an underlying tenderness can be – I have always been so harsh – so unable to feel compassion … I hope this hard icy core is beginning to thaw out'.[65] Evidently, social science satisfied more than spiritual and social aspirations – it touched affective ones, too.

Alongside social science and spirituality, pacifism formed a central strand in the Elmhirsts' and Heard's quest to replace the nineteenth-century framework that had intertwined Christianity and the social good.[66] As with many contemporaries, they viewed the pacifist cause as being not just about promoting political harmony but about cultivating social and spiritual unity; it was as much a matter of faith as of diplomatic relations.[67] Dorothy and Leonard donated significant amounts to peace-seeking organisations, including the Peace Pledge Union (PPU), the League of Nations Union and the British Anti-War Council.[68] For a short time in the 1930s, Heard worked directly with the PPU. But the three of them were less concerned with supporting

---

[63] Alex Owen, *The Darkened Room: Women, Power and Spiritualism in Late Victorian England* (London, 1989).

[64] Brown, *Angel Dorothy*, 28–30; Karolyn Gould, 'The Modest Benefactor', *Cornell Alumni News* 3 (1975), 19–21.

[65] Dorothy, 'Notes on Talk by Bill Sheldon', [n.d.], DWE/G/S7/E/7.

[66] When, in 1934, the Elmhirsts came to drawing up a list of their priorities, they put 'world peace' at the top of the list. Leonard, 'Time Budget 1934–5', 8 November 1934, LKE/G/S8/1.

[67] Ceadel, *Pacifism in Britain*; Daniel Gorman, 'Ecumenical Internationalism: Willoughby Dickinson, the League of Nations and the World Alliance for Promoting International Friendship through the Churches', *Journal of Contemporary History* 45 (2010), 51–73.

[68] DWE/G/S2/B; LKE/G/S5/I; John Strachey, treasurer of the British Anti-War Council, to Dorothy, 8 December [1933?], DWE/G/S2/A; Dorothy to Canon Morris, 29 May 1940, DWE/G/S2/C.

the formal pacifist movement than they were with discovering a 'common philosophic basis' by which people around the world could live together harmoniously.[69] This was where Dartington came in. '[I]f people can once really learn to live and work in an understanding relationship with one another and not in a fear relationship, in social groupings of the size of Dartington,' Leonard wrote, combining the language of psychology with the language of Christianity, 'why not in larger groupings still – until the world is at peace through the casting out of fear by comprehension and love'.[70] The Elmhirsts and Heard saw Dartington as a test bed for socio-spiritual modes that would bring peace to all of humankind: producing 'a pattern which will be worth handing to the macrocosm outside as a way of life, good in all its parts, inner and outer'.[71]

In 1935, Aldous Huxley, representative extraordinaire of the interwar intellectual zeitgeist, gave a talk at Dartington. He announced that society needed 'a practical mystical religion acceptable to all scientists, logical in thought and yet embodying a kind of mysticism that is not apart from life but that combines self-fulfilment and self-sacrifice'.[72] The Elmhirsts hoped that Dartington would contribute to the creation of this religion, joining spirituality with the promotion of the social good to provide a practical theology for everyday life.[73] As in the wider sphere of socio-spiritual questing, there was little consensus among Dartington's participants about the shape this new religion should take. Should they reform the Church; adopt a religion from abroad; or make one up from scratch? Should they focus on inner belief or on outer social structures? Should each person be free to find their own religion – an idea that harmonised with the Deweyan democratic agenda of freeing the individual to think and act – or should they be led by experts?[74] As will be seen in the following examples of socio-spiritual questing on the estate, none of these queries was ever comprehensively answered. But, in the loosest sense, participation in the community did offer a replacement for Christianity and its conjoined ideal of public service, since living and working there was a way for people to dedicate themselves to what Leonard called 'the search for the highest good'.[75]

---

[69] Leonard, 'Time Budget 1934–5', 8 November 1934, LKE/G/S8/1.   [70] Ibid.
[71] Margaret Isherwood to Leonard, [n.d.], DWE/6/C2.
[72] Sunday evening talk by Aldous Huxley, 10 February 1935, LKE/G/18/A.
[73] Leonard, untitled note, [n.d.], T/DHS/A/3/A.
[74] Leonard, 'The Long View', 27 June 1936, LKE/G/S8/A. John Dewey wrote, 'my own life of thought has been a struggle to get liberation – freedom from a tradition inherited and still embodied at least in the formulae of civilization'. Quoted in Mark Smith, *Social Science*, 37.
[75] Leonard, Sunday evening meeting, 23 September 1928, LKE/G/31/A.

2.1.1   The Model of the Medieval Church

In spite of their loss of orthodox belief, the Elmhirsts viewed churches as offering one possible focal point in their search for a new socio-spiritual framework. A church already stood at the physical centre of most villages and, while Dorothy and Leonard judged the institution of Anglicanism to be 'dying' under the weight of fossilised forms, they thought that its churches could still function as hubs for local community.[76] Since, for the Elmhirsts, the project of promoting community unity had a spiritual dimension, their concept of churches being community centres also carried spiritual overtones – but they saw that spirituality as being of an inclusive kind that extended well beyond the bounds of the Anglican faith.

In re-envisioning the role of churches, the Elmhirsts were inspired by the Middle Ages. Like Arts and Crafts figures such as William Morris, they saw medieval churches as having been vital meeting points for the local community: alongside being centres of religion, wrote Leonard, they were linked to 'all the acts of ordinary daily life'.[77] In particular, the Elmhirsts were enthused by the idea of making churches into centres of artistic performance by and for the community – bringing back 'medieval days, when the church or churchyard served as the national theatre'.[78] It was several years before Dorothy and Leonard found a way to turn this notion of repurposing churches along medieval lines into a practical experiment.

Despite a passion for architectural restoration, the Elmhirsts made no effort to rebuild the thirteenth-century church that stood on Dartington Hall's grounds, marked by a tower and a scattering of gravestones – although they did occasionally use this ruin for putting on plays.[79] The next closest church was St Mary's, which stood just beyond the boundaries of the estate. Leonard, more absolute in his abandonment of Anglicanism, did not engage with this church closely, but Dorothy attended Sunday services there early on. As well as viewing it as a possible social centre, she thought that the church might have something to offer those on the estate, including herself, in need of direct spiritual guidance, and she also hoped to avoid creating 'unnecessary barriers

---

[76] Leonard to Dorothy, 12 September 1921, LKE/DWE/10/C.
[77] Leonard, 'Plymouth Playgoers' Circle', 10 March 1935, LKE/G/S8/A; Anna Vaninskaya, *William Morris and the Idea of Community: Romance, History and Propaganda, 1880–1914* (Edinburgh, 2010).
[78] Leonard, 'Plymouth Playgoers' Circle', 10 March 1935, LKE/G/S8/A.
[79] Little survives of these performances in the archives, except for a couple of photos (see TPH/12/I).

between myself and the village'.[80] But St Mary's vicar, J. S. Martin, was deeply conservative, and he did his best to make his church a rallying point for opposition to the Elmhirsts and their progressive enterprise from the start. He preached sermons against them and obstructed their efforts to work with local institutions like the village hall and school.[81] Such hostility ruled out the possibility of turning St Mary's into a medieval-style church of the arts.

A better prospect for exploring the community-building potential of churches arose in 1931, when Edward Drake-Brockman, rector of St Paul de Leon Church in the village of Staverton, close to Dartington, asked the Elmhirsts for help in putting on a nativity.[82] His request was inspired by seeing one of the mystery plays commissioned by George Bell, Dean of Canterbury from 1925 to 1929.[83] Bell was the leader of a constellation of Anglicans who hoped to return the Church to the centre of the community via local religious art. The group's work was part of a wider effort by interwar Anglicans to revivify the Church by identifying it with the entire nation – in effect, making the Anglo-Christian community and England synonymous.[84] In 1928 Bell invited John Masefield and Gustav Holst to write a nativity, *The Coming of Christ*, the first original drama to be put on in an English cathedral since the Reformation.[85] The next year, along with his director of religious drama, E. Martin Browne, Bell set up the Canterbury Festival as a showcase for religious plays.[86]

Dartington lent its music director and head of dance-drama to help with preparations for 'A Mystery of the Nativity' at St Paul de Leon. Elizabeth was played by Dorothy, the Holy Child by her daughter, Angel

[80] Dorothy to R. A. Edwards, 2 August 1942, DWE/G/S3/G; R. A. Edwards, 'Dartington: A Report for the Bishop of the Diocese', January 1948, DWE/G/S3/G; Anthea Williams' interview with Margaret Isherwood, 18 April and 11 May 1977, T/HIS/S22.
[81] Leonard to Edgar Fowles, 9 August 1927, LKE/DCC/6/A; Dorothy, note, 1928[?], DWE/DHS/1.
[82] For the place of this performance in the wider socially reforming dramatic landscape, see Anna Neima, 'The Politics of Community Drama in Inter-War England', *Twentieth Century British History* (2019), 170–96.
[83] 'Nativity Play, Staverton', 17 December 1931, *Western Morning News*, British Library Newspaper Archives.
[84] Grimley, *Citizenship, Community, and the Church of England*, 12.
[85] E. Martin Browne, 'T. S. Eliot in the Theatre: The Director's Memories', *The Sewanee Review* 74 (1966), 136–52, at 137.
[86] Heather Wiebe, 'Benjamin Britten, the "National Faith", and the Animation of History in 1950s England', *Representations* 93 (2006), 76–105, at 78; E. Martin Browne, *The Production of Religious Plays* (London, 1932). One of the plays commissioned by Bell and Browne was T. S. Eliot's *The Rock*, part of which Dorothy quoted in her notebook of spiritual contemplation – a reflection on the spiritual nature of communities: 'What life have you if you have no life together?/There is no life that is not in community,/And no community not lived in praise of God' (DWE/G/S7).

2.1 'A Mystery of the Nativity' in St Paul de Leon Church, Staverton, 1932 (© Dartington Hall Trust and the Elmgrant Trust)

Gabriel by her son and Joseph by Mark Tobey.[87] About sixty villagers were involved, although they were not allotted central roles; as with Dartington as a whole, although this project was clothed in democratic rhetoric, its reality was paternalistic. The nativity was performed on 16 and 17 December, and Drake-Brockman recorded how both nights 'the church was packed with people, sitting and standing. Many stood outside peering through the windows.'[88] The crowd included not just parishioners and residents of Dartington Hall but Lady Florence Cecil, married to the Bishop of Exeter, and Geoffrey Whitworth, founder of the British Drama League. A review in the *Western Morning News* dwelt on the cooperation between 'all sections of the community' and on how the nativity was 'not merely an interesting resurrection of a relic' but a successful 'modernisation', forging a language to fit contemporary times – a 'modern mystery play'.[89]

---

[87] 'Nativity Play, Staverton', *Western Morning News*, 17 December 1931, British Library Newspaper Archives.

[88] E. D. Drake-Brockman, *Staverton on the Dart: From Records of Church and Parish* (Exeter, 1946), 66.

[89] 'Nativity Play, Staverton', *Western Morning News*, 16 and 17 December 1931, British Library Newspaper Archives.

The Elmhirsts had succeeded in using art and the church to draw together the local community – and also to revivify that community by attracting visitors from further afield. But this success did not turn out to help much in their effort to create a sustainable new social-spiritual framework for Dartington. Drake-Brockman, who had initially wanted the play to be an annual event, reported to the Elmhirsts that their efforts had 'stirred a bitterness in one or two, pitiable to think of' – and, perhaps for this reason, he never suggested a repeat.[90] If Devon had not been so conservative a county, or if the Elmhirsts and Drake-Brockman – as with George Bell and the cathedral community of Chichester – had had a more coherent and well-disposed demographic to appeal to, their hope of using churches as hubs to reinvigorate the community might have been longer-lived.

It was only when J. S. Martin was replaced by the more open-minded, left-leaning R. A. Edwards in 1940 that the Elmhirsts found a progressive clergyman willing to engage closely with their estate. Edwards often lectured at Dartington – struggling valiantly to apply Christian doctrine to questions about 'surrealism, Federal Union, birth-control, modern psychologists, anything'.[91] He was also involved in helping with the estate's post-Second-World-War planning. He advised the Elmhirsts that Dartington, lacking 'a firm point of view', had degenerated into 'mere living' and was alienating the surrounding countryside with its bohemianism. It could recover from this disoriented, insular state, he wrote hopefully, by becoming 'church-conscious'.[92] Dorothy, in particular, welcomed the rector's interest, but neither she nor Leonard showed any desire to make organised Christianity central to their experiment.

As early as the 1920s, the idea that art in itself could act as a medium for promoting socio-spiritual unity – without being moored to the Church – also began to take hold at Dartington. Creative expression was seen as a way of bringing together the community and a means by which 'everyone everywhere, could transcend the boundaries of self and enter into a communion with what lies behind the surface'.[93] This concept of art's role, which is elaborated on in Chapter 4, gained considerable purchase among the estate's participants and was echoed more widely in Britain.[94] In spite of the success of this idea, people on the

[90] E.D. Drake-Brockman to Dorothy, 10 February 1932, DWE/A/7/B.
[91] R.A. Edwards, 'Dartington: A Report for the Bishop of the Diocese', January 1948, DWE/G/S3/G.
[92] R.A. Edwards to Leonard, 26 July 1942, DWE/G/S3/G.   [93] Young, *Elmhirsts*, 216.
[94] See, for example, Christine Iglesias, 'Modernist Unselfing: Religious Experience and British Literature 1900–1945', unpublished PhD thesis, Columbia University, 2018; Saler, *The Avant-Garde*.

estate continued to crave – and to demand the Elmhirsts' help in finding – a more definite socio-spiritual framework.

2.1.2   Eastern Spirituality

After the First World War, as Priya Satia finds, many European intellectuals and reformers felt that the East offered 'the chance for redemption from the decadence that had led Europe to the destructive end of the world war'.[95] French intellectual Romain Rolland, for example, saw 'the West representing science and materialism' and moral decline, and 'the East spirituality and the search for transcendence'.[96] In this wave of enthusiasm for the East, different religious traditions were often bundled together imprecisely in what Sumita Mukherjee terms a 'homogenous export-friendly' religious cosmopolitanism.[97] The resulting amorphous vision of 'Eastern spirituality', with its wise gurus in robes and sandals and everyday life suffused with spiritual meaning, was a construct created not only by Orientalist Europeans but also by spiritual teachers from Asia, including Rabindranath Tagore, who sculpted their message in a way that they hoped would gain traction in the West.[98] It was in this rather vague form that many at Dartington looked to Eastern religion as an alternative spiritual framework – an inspiration that fuelled both private spirituality and group efforts to find enlightenment.

Tagore was one of the key figures influencing this view. A leading advocate of Indo-Asian spirituality, he argued that the individualistic, materialistic West needed to learn from the higher, more transcendent wisdom of the East, 'the mother of spiritual Humanity'.[99] When Leonard worked with Tagore at Sriniketan, he encountered a vision of a 'life in its completeness' that made the spiritual part of the day-to-day.[100] For him, Eastern spirituality represented the opposite pole to the formal institutions of modern Western Christianity. 'Unlike the West, the East has

---

[95] Priya Satia, 'Byron, Gandhi and the Thompsons: The Making of British Social History and Unmaking of Indian History', *History Workshop Journal* 18 (2016), 135–70, at 138; J. J. Clarke, *Oriental Enlightenment: The Encounter Between Asian and Western Thought* (London, 1997), 95–103.

[96] Ruth Harris, 'Rolland, Gandhi and Madeleine Slade: Spiritual Politics, France and the Wider World', *French History* 27 (2013), 579–99, at 584.

[97] Mukherjee, 'The Reception Given to Sadhu Sundar Singh', 22.

[98] Krishna Dutta and Andrew Robinson, *Rabindranath Tagore: The Myriad-Minded Man* (London, 1995); Richard King, *Orientalism and Religion: Postcolonial Theory, India, and the 'Mystic East'* (London, 1999).

[99] Fakrul Alam and Radha Chakravarty (eds.), *The Essential Tagore* (Cambridge, MA, 2011), 186.

[100] Leonard Elmhirst, *Rabindranath Tagore: Pioneer in Education. Essays and Exchanges Between Rabindranath Tagore and L.K. Elmhirst* (London, 1961).

2.2 Rabindranath Tagore and Rani Mahalanobis visiting Dartington in 1930 (© Dartington Hall Trust and the Elmgrant Trust)

avoided drawing any decided line between what is secular and what is religious', he wrote. 'Both Hindu and Buddhistic tradition – and their counterparts, Taoism and Zenism' had succeeded in creating a life where there was 'no Sunday and weekday, song and hymn, sacred and profane, but a thread of inner meaning seems to run through so much of all they think or do'.[101] Leonard hoped that Dartington would achieve this blending of the sacred with the everyday, although his interest in grasping the details of any specific Eastern religion was limited.

[101] Leonard, 'Talk for Plymouth Playgoers' Circle', 10 March 1935, LKE/G/S8/A.

Dorothy, too, was fascinated by the East, both aesthetically and spiritually. She lived briefly in China during her marriage to Willard Straight, and, together with her first husband, founded *Asia* magazine to further Western knowledge of the East.[102] She was close friends with Nancy Wilson Ross, a bohemian American novelist whose diverse passions included Eastern religions, and who eventually converted to Buddhism.[103] Dorothy read many books by or about South Asian spiritual teachers and incorporated their ideas into her private spiritual practice.[104] Before they began Dartington, she wrote to Leonard about 'a possible religious synthesis of East and West', a synthesis which 'perhaps can be lived'.[105] She also lent her fortune to the development and promotion of Eastern spirituality. Tagore, who visited Dartington in 1930, dedicated his collection of lectures on spirituality, *The Religion of Man*, to her in gratitude for her underwriting of Sriniketan.[106] Dorothy encouraged the scholarship of Arthur Waley, a translator of Chinese and Japanese texts who stayed at Dartington frequently and who dedicated his book, *The Way and its Power: A Study of the Tao Tê Ching and its Place in Chinese Thought*, to both the Elmhirsts.[107]

The most palpable contribution that Eastern spirituality made to day-to-day life at Dartington was to inspire two groups that met regularly to discuss spiritual belief and how best to live on the basis of that belief. One was Gerald Heard's 'generating cell', which is examined in the following section. The second was a Bahá'í Faith group led by the artist Mark Tobey. The Bahá'í Faith originated in nineteenth-century Persia (in a sign of the transatlantic scope of interest in Eastern spirituality, Tobey had first encountered it in Greenwich Village).[108] It emphasised three unities: that there is only one God, the source of all creation; that all

[102] *Asia* magazine, begun in 1917, ran articles on Eastern policy, commerce, culture and religion. After Straight's death, Dorothy continued to support it until 1941, when its editor Richard Walsh and his wife, writer Pearl S. Buck, bought it from her.
[103] Nancy Wilson Ross, an authority on Eastern religions, was connected to several progressive hubs in the interwar years: she studied at the Bauhaus with her husband and became friends with many of the artists, actors, dancers and musicians associated with Dartington and with the Cornish School in Seattle. She lived in Dorothy's Long Island house during the Second World War.
[104] See, for instance, Gerald Heard to Dorothy, [n.d.], DWE/6/F1; Dorothy to Leonard, 19 November 1924 and 19 February 1934, LKE/DWE/6/B.
[105] Dorothy to Leonard, 19 November 1924.
[106] Rabindranath Tagore, *The Religion of Man* (New York, 1931).
[107] Arthur Waley, *The Way and its Power: A Study of the Tao Tê Ching and its Place in Chinese Thought* (London, 1934).
[108] Christopher Reed, 'Sublimation and Eccentricity in the Art of Mark Tobey: Seattle at Midcentury', in *Bachelor Japanists: Japanese Aesthetics and Western Masculinities* (New York, 2017), 201–90, at 204–5.

religions have the same source and come from that God; and that all humans are equal, unified in their diversity. Its unity-seeking and inclusiveness meant that it fitted well into the community at Dartington. Tobey – 'so devoted to Bahai' that he was 'nearly like a priest' – quickly gathered a number of followers into his group, sharing his ideas and books with them.[109] The potter Bernard Leach immersed himself in study and grew a beard in imitation of his teacher.[110] Dorothy, much taken by the Bahá'í idea of merging the individual self with the universal, kept a copy of a pamphlet on the faith folded into one of her books of spiritual reflections.[111]

Many of those who engaged with Eastern spirituality at Dartington, whether through the Bahá'í Faith, Heard's 'generating cell' or otherwise, were gay, bisexual, single or in some other way did not entirely conform to conventional sexual or gender expectations.[112] Spirituality became a realm where people could explore identities outside the dominant mould of straight and male – a pattern that Lucy Delap, Sue Morgan and other scholars find echoed across the twentieth century.[113] The pursuit of the spiritual could be parsed as a deep commitment to a form of sexuality, albeit through renouncing physical sex: Heard, for example, took a vow of celibacy in the mid-1930s and dedicated an entire book to explaining how, by re-channelling their lustful energies into the spiritual search, men could achieve connection with the 'universal reality'.[114] It could, alternately, be understood as a way of sublimating unacceptable desires: of submerging 'animal qualities', as Tobey put it, 'by becoming "completely integrated with the mass spirit".[115] Differently again, the spiritual search could be seen as offering the possibility of complete annihilation of the problematic self: a system in which the 'partial and incomplete self is united with all others in a unity, sanity, self-forgetfulness and

---

[109] Beatrice Straight to Nancy Wilson Ross, 1 January 1937, 156/2, Nancy Wilson Ross Archives; Michael Young's interview with Willi Soukop, 1 April 1979, T/HIS/S22.

[110] Emmanuel Cooper, *Bernard Leach: Life & Work* (New Haven, CT and London, 2003), 180.

[111] Horace Holley, *The Baha'i Faith*, DWE/G/S7/E/7.

[112] Mark Tobey and Gerald Heard were gay; Arthur Waley was bisexual; Bernard Leach was married but questioning about his sexuality; the schoolteacher Margaret Isherwood and the artist Jane Fox-Strangways – both companions with Dorothy in her spiritual questing – were single; while Dorothy was powerful, wealthy and independent, but performed 'feminine' submissiveness.

[113] Lucy Delap and Sue Morgan (eds.), *Men, Masculinities and Religious Change in Twentieth-Century Britain* (Basingstoke, 2013); Sue Morgan, '"Sex and Common-Sense": Maude Royden, Religion, and Modern Sexuality', *Journal of British Studies* 52 (2013), 153–78.

[114] Gerald Heard, *Pain, Sex and Time: A New Hypothesis of Evolution* (London, 1939).

[115] Reed, 'Sublimation and Eccentricity', 205–6.

communion'.[116] As often was the case in the Elmhirsts' community, these different notions existed side by side, without being clearly theorised or reconciled to one another.

The alliance of Eastern spirituality with non-heteronormative desire and radical social reformism at Dartington echoes Leela Gandhi's work on the international 'affective communities' formed between various types of othered affiliation, including homosexuality and anti-colonialism, at the end of the nineteenth century – characterised, she writes, by 'a mystical-democratic apprehension of inter-connectedness'.[117] Like *fin de siècle* socialist utopianism, Dartington bridged India and the West, joined together eclectic causes, and emphasised the importance of day-to-day conduct and of affective relationships; several Dartington participants, including Heard, also took inspiration from the gay poet and social reformer Edward Carpenter, who was a key figure in the movement Gandhi describes.[118]

The Bahá'í Faith had a profound impact on the lives of a few at Dartington – an impact reflected in the transatlantic world of early-twentieth-century questing. (Notable Bahá'í converts included Richard St Barbe Baker, English conservationist and founder of the reforestation organisation Men of the Trees, and American feminist and pacifist Martha Root.[119]) Some of the idealists in Dartington's orbit gave themselves over to Eastern spirituality entirely. A. R. Orage, respected editor of the progressive *New Age* journal, left his position to follow the Greek-Armenian mystic G. I. Gurdjieff in the 1920s, much to the puzzlement of his friends.[120] Dorothy's friend Herbert Croly, founding editor of *The New Republic*, also turned away from political progressivism in the 1920s to seek enlightenment through Eastern mysticism, including by following Gurdjieff's spiritual 'exercises'.[121] But while Dorothy, and to a lesser extent Leonard, remained open to the possibilities that Eastern spirituality offered, they did not commit their estate to it wholeheartedly. In

---

[116] Gerald Heard to Leonard Elmhirst, 6 December 1934, LKE/G/17/E.

[117] Leela Gandhi, 'Other(s) Worlds: Mysticism and Radicalism at the Fin de Siècle', *Critical Horizons* 2 (2001), 227–53, at 243; *Affective Communities: Anticolonial Thought, Fin-de-Siècle Radicalism, and the Politics of Friendship* (Durham and London, 2006).

[118] 'Group readings', T/AE/4/F.

[119] Jiling Yang, 'In Search of Martha Root: An American Baha'i Feminist and Peace Advocate in the Early Twentieth Century', unpublished PhD thesis, Georgia State University, 2005.

[120] Paul Beekman Taylor, *Gurdjieff and Orage: Brothers in Elysium* (York Beach, ME; [Great Britain], 2001).

[121] David W. Levy, *Herbert Croly of the New Republic: The Life and Thought of an American Progressive* (Princeton and Guildford, 1985), 296; Professor E. A. Stettner interview with Leonard, 7 June 1973, DWE/G/2/B.

addition to their congenital urge to keep experimenting with new approaches rather than committing to a single one, this was because – at least in the form that it arrived at Dartington – Eastern spirituality was mostly about individual enlightenment. Since the Elmhirsts sought a framework that, like Victorian Christianity, also generated community unity and fuelled an ethic of public service, Eastern spirituality fell short. Eastern religious traditions, Buddhism in particular, would nonetheless continue to weave through Dartington's history, resurfacing as part of the 1960s and 1970s counterculture and again in the 1990s as a component of the spiritual ecology movement.

2.1.3   The Generating Cell

> This then is the answer to those who ask "What holds you together at Dart[ingto]n? What is your substitute for religion?" No substitute, but a "religion" which is at once more abstract and more concrete than the partial religions of the organized churches; more abstract in that its only dogma is assertion of the underlying unity of all men and all things; more concrete in that it has its roots in a shared experience of that unity.   Margaret Isherwood (a member of the generating cell, *c*.1935)[122]

Rather than accepting the promotion of communal unity as a spiritual end in itself, or focusing solely on Eastern spirituality, Gerald Heard saw in Dartington the possibility of forging a totally new faith. Like nineteenth-century Christianity, he hoped that this faith would be a source of spiritual meaning, self-sacrificing purpose and social unity, helping him to understand the world as having 'a complete meaning as a whole of which I am a cooperating part'.[123] Reflecting the syncretism of the wider realm of social-spiritual questing, Heard's work to create a new faith at Dartington – what he sometimes called 'the third morality' – drew together social science, Christianity and Eastern mysticism. It was also, as with much interwar questing, driven by the urgent desire to prevent another world war. Heard dedicated himself entirely to the spiritual quest, first in Britain and then in America. In doing so, he joined a disparate constellation of early-twentieth-century men and women – including the 'simple-life vagabonds' Martin Green finds passing through the countercultural Swiss community of Monte Verita, and the 'antimodern' American 'seekers' T. J. Jackson Lears writes about – whose spiritual approaches were 'diverse in origin, and indeed in direction and final purpose', but who formed a loosely configured

---

[122] Margaret Isherwood to Leonard, [*c*.1935], DWE/6/C2.
[123] Gerald Heard to Margaret Isherwood, 26 March 1934, DWE/G/6A.

international network.[124] This network laid the foundations for the New
Age counterculture that blossomed around the world in the second half
of the twentieth century.

Heard first met the Elmhirsts in the early 1920s in his capacity as
private secretary to Sir Horace Plunkett, who was advising Leonard on
agricultural cooperation.[125] Soon after this, he re-channelled his impulse
to serve society into working as a public intellectual – a mediator between
specialist forms of knowledge and the general public.[126] As the BBC's
first science reporter, he delivered a fortnightly talk, 'This Surprising
World', a round-up of scientific advances. At the same time, he lectured
on social ideas, including at the South Place Ethical Society, and published in such progressive forums as *Time and Tide*. Heard also read
widely and voraciously across the humanities and sciences. Underlying
all this activity was the desire to discover a new framework to replace both
Christianity and competitive, individualistic laissez-faire liberalism – to
serve the general good by drawing people together into spiritual and
social unity.

In 1929, Heard set out his vision of a new socio-spiritual framework in
a book, *The Ascent of Humanity: An Essay on the Evolution of Civilization
from Group Consciousness through Individuality to Super-Consciousness*.[127]
This argued that various ideas from social science, biology, philosophical
idealism, history and religion could be woven together to offer a method
for advancing social harmony. Human consciousness, Heard believed,
had evolved over millennia. Tribal man had no sense of individual self
but shared a common, harmonious 'co-consciousness'.[128] Gradually this
social unit had atrophied, until humankind reached its present state – the
'Hobbesian outlook' of man competing against man, nation against
nation for material gain – an outlook that had been responsible for the
First World War.[129] Harnessing the philosophical idealist notion of
intentional corporate advance towards teleological perfection and

[124] Green, *Mountain of Truth*, 14, 122, 156; Jackson Lears, *No Place of Grace*. One of
Green's subjects, the choreographer Rudolf Laban, moved from Monte Verita, via
Germany, to Dartington, which Green calls 'a genteel and protected version of
Monte Verita'.
[125] Gerald Heard and Leonard were in correspondence from at least 1923. Gerald Heard
to Leonard, 20 June 1923, LKE/G/17/E.
[126] For the details of Heard's career, see Eros, 'Gerald Heard' and Falby, *Between the
Pigeonholes*.
[127] Gerald Heard, *The Ascent of Humanity* (London, 1929). He published three other books
elaborating on his socio-spiritual ideas: *The Emergence of Man* (London and Toronto,
1931); *The Social Substance of Religion* (London, 1931); and *The Source of Civilization*
(London, 1935).
[128] Gerald Heard, *Ascent*, 15.
[129] Gerald Heard, 'Men and Books', *Time and Tide*, 26 October 1935, 1545–6.

extending the evolutionary mechanism into the psychological sphere, Heard suggested that humankind needed to work out the next evolutionary step, both spiritually and psychologically, to a life beyond individualism. People needed to be reconnected to the modern version of the tribal co-consciousness, which he termed the 'superconsciousness', and then all social competition would be eradicated.[130]

It was an eccentric, hybrid ideology. Heard has with justice been called a 'one-man Committee of Fuzzy Thinking' and a cuttlefish 'which emits its ink not to enlighten but to confuse its pursuers'.[131] Yet his efforts to combine Christian and idealist concepts of telos with evolution were not exceptional in Britain; such an approach was evident in fields as different as biology, city planning and political thought.[132] Heard's notion of multiple consciousnesses linked into a single, collective consciousness was also not unique. The psychologist William McDougall, for example, who influenced Heard, envisioned good democracy in terms of an organically unified society where each individual forms part of a 'national mind'.[133] The idea was evident, too, in science fiction. H. G. Wells' *The First Men in the Moon* (1901) depicted an alien society in which individuals are connected by a hive mind, and the interwar writer Olaf Stapledon, who corresponded with Heard, conjured a human society joined by a group mind in *Last and First Men* (1930).[134] Such speculation about future possibilities, Stapledon said, assisted social evolution by preparing 'for *long-range* planning'.[135]

Heard's imaginative, questing spirituality proved attractive to many in the disoriented post-war years, with admirers including Winifred Holtby, E. M. Forster and Harold Nicholson. The novelist Naomi Mitchison wrote that Heard was struggling towards some insight 'which was at the back of all our minds, of extreme importance but so far unexpressed. In fact he was our prophet.'[136] His allure reflected the interwar popularity of

---

[130] Gerald Heard, *Ascent*, 6.
[131] Stefan Collini, *Common Reading: Critics, Historians, Publics* (Oxford, 2008), 38; Ronald Knox, *Broadcast Minds* (London, 1932), 34.
[132] Patrick Geddes, for example, 'incorporated both evolutionary biology and Hellenistic idealism into his designs for a rational, organic, cosmopolitan "Eutopia"'. Jose Harris, *Private Lives, Public Spirit: A Social History of Britain, 1870–1914* (London, 1993), 230.
[133] William McDougall, *The Group Mind* (London, 1920), 187.
[134] *Last and First Men* also inspired Arthur C. Clarke to write *Childhood's End* (1953), one of most popular post-war depictions of the group mind. Arthur C. Clarke, 'Of Sand and Stars', in Arthur C. Clarke, *Spring: A Choice of Futures* (New York, 1984), 151–7.
[135] Robert Crossley, 'Olaf Stapledon and the Idea of Science Fiction', *Modern Fiction Studies* 32 (1986), 21–42, at 30.
[136] Naomi Mitchison, *You May Well Ask: A Memoir, 1920–1940* (London, 1979), 107.

the figure of the guru, venerated for their wisdom and charisma.[137] Heard was described in such terms by one Dartington participant: 'this unutterably strong drive towards the infinite, it shines in his eyes and makes him able to help others by his enthusiasm, whilst his range of subject is so great as to leave one gasping'.[138]

But Heard was impatient with merely offering theories.[139] He longed for action – to 'take some part in the social life of the world and not be merely a writer living detached in another country'.[140] By the early 1930s, he decided that he would turn the ideas he had laid out in *The Ascent of Humanity* into a lifestyle – what amounted to a practical theology, which he would embrace himself and encourage others to adopt. People should aim to live 'in co-operation with the purpose of life', he wrote, in order to realise their 'unity with all life and being'.[141] In an indication of the syncretic nature of interwar spiritual seeking, the methods he suggested for achieving this unity included asceticism, meditation, birth control and euthanasia. They also included individuals grouping together to form 'generating cells', whose meetings, based around meditation and spiritual reflection, would form the foundation of their efforts to achieve self-transcendence and connection with the superconsciousness.[142] Heard hoped that these generating cells would multiply and encircle the globe, creating a source of international 'telepathic' connection that would contribute to world peace.[143]

Dartington seemed to Heard the ideal place to try out this practical theology: the Elmhirsts, he wrote approvingly, were 'striving to build up a complete, purposive, fully conscious social organism (a thing which has never existed before)'.[144] His work tied him to London during the week, but between 1932 and 1935 he took the train to Devon at weekends to

[137] See, for example, Rom Landau, *God Is My Adventure: A Book on Modern Mystics, Masters and Teachers* (London, 1935).
[138] Richard Elmhirst to Nancy Wilson Ross, 27 May 1937, 125/10, Nancy Wilson Ross Archives.
[139] In *The Auden Generation: Literature and Politics in England in the 1930s* (London, 1976), Samuel Hynes presents the intellectual who wanted to make himself 'strong and effective in the public world' instead of 'the introspective neurotic' as belonging to the post-war 'Auden Generation', but the phenomenon was prevalent even in the war generation, as is evident in men like Heard's eagerness to transfer their spiritual quest to the sphere of practical social reform. Aldous Huxley, for example, moved from being a detached, cynical observer of society in the 1920s to being a socially engaged pacifist and mystic in the 1930s. His novel *Eyeless in Gaza* (1936) describes this shift.
[140] Gerald Heard to Margaret Isherwood, 8 June 1934, DWE/G/6A.
[141] Gerald Heard, *The Third Morality* (London, 1937), 186–7.
[142] Gerald Heard to Dorothy, 15 June 1932, DWE/G/5/D.
[143] Gerald Heard to Margaret Isherwood, 21 November 1932, DWE/6/F1.
[144] Gerald Heard, 'The Dartington Experiment', *Architectural Review* 449 (1934), 119–22.

lead a generating cell meeting in an oak-panelled room beside Dartington's main hall. These meetings, whilst more wide-ranging in scope, bore a resemblance to the 'psychosynthesis' group set up by A. R. Orage in London in the 1910s in order to work out how to integrate mysticism and social science.[145] Heard guided members through different unifying theories and techniques – taken from the world religions, 'from early Benedictinism to late Quakerism'; from the 'advanced Inner Life' of the East, dwelling especially on Buddhism; and from the social sciences, including the psychology of Carl Jung, Sigmund Freud and William James.[146] The group listened to American jazz and African folk music on the record player, such art being deemed likely to be a link back to the tribal 'co-consciousness'.[147] In between meetings, members exchanged letters of spiritual advice and confession – stretching to many pages in the Dartington Hall archive – and followed a catholic reading list prescribed by Heard, which included Dewey, Tagore, Kahlil Gibran and Edward Carpenter.[148]

The generating cell was eagerly embraced by Dorothy and by the intimates with whom she shared her spiritual journey. These were often people, like Heard himself, who – whether because of their sexual orientation, discomfort with their position in life or sense of spiritual unmooring – felt in some way at odds with the world. Others were critical of Heard's project. These tended to be men with more conventional social identities who felt little need for introspective spiritualism – men who, as Heard observed, were 'extrovert' and found it easy to engage in 'practical social service ... planning definite policies to be carried out in the outside world'.[149] For the school's headmaster, W. B. Curry, a self-confident individualist and agnostic, Heard's promotion of spiritual group-think was dangerously akin to the 'semi-mystical ideas of fascists'.[150] Bertrand Russell, a frequent visitor to the estate, warned that, because of Heard, 'Dartington was in danger of some sort of theosophical superstition tarnishing its bright rationality'.[151] Leonard complained

---

[145] James Webb, *Harmonious Circle: The Lives and Works of G.I. Gurdjieff, P.D. Ouspensky and their Followers* (London, 1980), 200–31.

[146] Notes from 17 November 1934 meeting, LKE/G/S9/A; Gerald Heard to Dorothy, 9 August 1934, DWE/G/6A.

[147] Notes from 17 November 1934 meeting, LKE/G/S9/A.

[148] See file DWE/G/6A and Gerald Heard, 'Group Readings', [n.d], T/AE/4/F.

[149] Gerald Heard to Dorothy, 7 November 1932, DWE/6/F1.

[150] [n.a.], notes from Sunday evening meeting, 25 February, LKE/G/9/A.

[151] These comments were discussed in letter from Gerald Heard to Margaret Isherwood, 29 October 1934, DWE/6/F2.

that Heard's system was 'running away from social duties' and that the generating cell was 'too empty and too much like uplift'.[152]

Many of these critics put the search for spiritual meaning second to contributing practically to the social good. Often they also considered it more important to safeguard individual freedom, which they saw as a special 'English' characteristic, than to promote group unity, which they associated with Continental totalitarianism.[153] The survival of the generating cell for several years is a testimony to Dorothy's strong, if often tacit, influence on Dartington. In an indication of Dartington's tendency towards a patriarchal mode, however, in spite of the intense spiritual experimentation that occurred there, it was Leonard's bluffer, more practical and outward-looking style of socio-spiritual questing that set the dominant tone of the estate. This public face was what prompted some observers, like the organicist Rolf Gardiner, to complain that Dartington lacked a spiritual centre – what Gardiner called the 'flame of whole (holy) belief'.[154]

For a time, Heard delighted in his group's progress. He felt that he was at last being of practical service to the world rather than indulging in disembodied theorising.[155] He wrote that the generating cell was achieving 'a sociological advance which will be as remarkable and far more useful than the great physical inventions of the 19th century'.[156] By the mid-1930s, however, things were going less smoothly. With the gathering threat of another war, Heard began to feel he should commit himself more fully to living out and promoting his pacifist system. 'Perhaps', he wrote, 'it will be necessary to take to a completely new way of life – a new way of earning one's living, of associating with others, of eating, sleeping, marrying, before the new and juster world can come.'[157] He was also worried by rumours about sexual promiscuity among Dartington's pupils and by W. B. Curry having an affair and divorcing his wife.[158] To Heard, these were examples of failures to sacrifice individual desire (including sexual desire) to the all-important quest for social and spiritual unity: people should let go of 'property, ties, possessions of private rights', he

---

[152] Leonard quoted by Gerald Heard in a letter to Margaret Isherwood, 8 October 1934, DWE/6/F2; Gerald Heard to Dorothy, 30 September 1932, DWE/G/5/D.

[153] This was a common view in the 1930s. Julia Stapleton, 'Resisting the Centre at the Extremes: "English" Liberalism in the Political Thought of Interwar Britain', *The British Journal of Politics & International Relations* 1 (1999), 270–92.

[154] Rolf Gardiner to Leonard, 16 June 1933, LKE/G/15/B.

[155] Gerald Heard to Margaret Isherwood, 26 March 1934, DWE/G/6A.

[156] Gerald Heard to Dorothy, 30 September 1932, DWE/G/5/D.

[157] Gerald Heard to Margaret Isherwood, 8 February 1935, DWE/G/6A.

[158] [n.a.], notes from a meeting at 42 Upper Brook Street with Leonard, Gerald Heard and Felix Green, 3–4 November 1935, LKE/G/17/E.

wrote, and become 'the completely publicised servants of the whole'.[159] Deciding that the Elmhirsts' estate had become 'a society without agreed moral principles', he disbanded the generating cell.[160]

In 1936, Heard began to work more directly for world harmony by joining the ranks of the Peace Pledge Union (PPU), set up by the popular Anglican priest H. R. L. Sheppard in 1934. By the time Heard joined the organisation it had over 100,000 members, who marched, petitioned, lobbied Parliament and organised lectures and meetings.[161] His efforts to promote 'pacifist mind exercises' and to establish hundreds of generating cells worldwide were ill-received since more immediate, practical measures were wanted by most members in light of the growing threat of war.[162] Disappointed with his failure to make an impact, terrified that the next conflict would destroy Europe entirely, Heard moved to America in the late 1930s – a step taken by a number of other pacifist intellectuals, including Aldous Huxley, Christopher Isherwood and W. H. Auden.[163]

In 1942, in the hills outside Los Angeles, Heard set up the pacifist community of Trabuco College. He had planned for this to be agriculturally self-sufficient – something akin to Dartington – but in reality, led by Heard, its participants devoted themselves mostly to seeking spiritual enlightenment.[164] During the war, the community drew the interest of British and Americans alike. Visitors included Aldous and Maria Huxley, Christopher Isherwood, Bloomsbury poet Iris Tree, Alan Watts – who went on to help popularise Buddhism across the United States after the Second World War – and Bill Wilson, the spiritually minded co-founder of Alcoholics Anonymous.[165] Ena Curry, the Dartington School headmaster's ex-wife, crossed the Atlantic to live nearby and was later joined by her sister, Dorothy's confidante Margaret Isherwood.[166]

Trabuco closed in 1949, the building donated to the Vedanta Society, but Heard – along with Aldous Huxley – became an influential New Age

---

[159] Gerald Heard to Margaret Isherwood, 18 October 1934, DWE/G/6/F2.

[160] Gerald Heard to Margaret Isherwood, 17 May 1935, DWE/G/6A.

[161] Andrew Rigby, *Challenge to Mars: Pacifism from 1918 to 1945* (Toronto, 1999), 179.

[162] Gerald Heard, 'The Significance of the New Pacifism', in Gerald K. Hibbert (ed.), *The New Pacifism* (London, 1936), 17; Eros, 'Gerald Heard', 115.

[163] W. H. Auden to Dorothy, 3 April 1932, DWE/G/1/A/3. David Robb gives an account of these seekers after a 'new, modern, syncretic spiritualism' in 'Brahmins from Abroad: English Expatriates and Spiritual Consciousness in Modern America', *American Studies* 26 (1985), 45–60.

[164] Gerald Heard, Trabuco pamphlet, September 1942, LKE/G/17/E.

[165] Anna Neima, *The Utopians: Six Attempts to Build the Perfect Society* (London, 2021), chapter 6.

[166] Margaret Isherwood's spiritual explorations at Dartington and then in America led to her writing *The Root of the Matter: A Study in the Connections Between Religion, Psychology and Education* (London, 1954).

guru. These 'Mystical Expatriates of Southern California', as they were called by Alan Watts, published extensively and lectured on college campuses, on the radio and at the growing number of centres for alternative spirituality in California.[167] Huxley's last novel, *Island* (1962), was a popular handbook among those starting communes across America. Inspired by Huxley's experiences at Dartington in the 1920s as well as at Trabuco in the 1940s, the book describes a utopia where the population lives in non-materialistic, cooperative harmony.[168] Conversation with Heard catalysed two young Americans, Michael Murphy and Dick Price, to start a residential retreat, the Esalen Institute, on the Californian coast.[169] This became the world headquarters of the 'human potentiality movement', promoting a blend of psychology and Eastern spiritualism that captivated the sixties generation.[170] There were many continuities between earlier centres of socio-spiritual seeking like Dartington and Trabuco and New Age network hubs like the Esalen. People embraced communitarian ideals and melded Western psychology, Christianity, Eastern spirituality, vegetarianism and meditation. But the seekers of the later period, although they lived in the shadow of the Cold War and Vietnam, had not experienced the realities of a full-blown international conflict like the First World War. Rather than searching for alternative social models that would promote pacifism and international unity, they tended to focus more on achieving self-liberation and self-actualisation.[171]

2.1.4   Purposive Social Science

> I sometimes would like to call a halt to the work of all laboratories and tell the scientists to busy themselves on taking social responsibility for their discoveries. So few of them do this, and ... there are very few demonstrations of the kind of channels along which scientific discovery should flow easily towards the increase of human welfare.   Leonard Elmhirst (1937)[172]

In trying to synthesise spirituality and science into a faith for the modern day, Gerald Heard and Dorothy Elmhirst focused mainly on the former.

---

[167] Alan Watts, *In My Own Way: An Autobiography 1915–1965* (London, 1973), 208.
[168] Aldous Huxley, *Island* (London: Vintage, 2005 [1962]); David Bradshaw, 'Huxley and Progressive Education: Daltonism and the Dartington Hall Débâcle', *Aldous Huxley Annual* 15 (2015), 1–20.
[169] Walter Truett Anderson, *The Upstart Spring: Esalen and the American Awakening* (Reading, MA, 1983), 12–13.
[170] Don Lattin, *Distilled Spirits* (Berkeley and London, 2012), 2; Jeffrey J. Kripal, *Esalen: America and the Religion of No Religion* (Chicago, 2007).
[171] Benjamin Zablocki, *Alienation and Charisma* (New York, 1980); Wallmeier, 'Exit as Critique: Communes and Intentional Communities in the 1960s and Today', *Historical Social Research* 42 (2017), 147–71.
[172] Leonard to Rathi Tagore, 28 June 1937, LKE/IN/21/D.

Leonard Elmhirst, attempting the same synthesis, placed more emphasis on science, and in particular on psychology. He was also less preoccupied than Dorothy and Heard with his own private journey away from Christianity, concentrating instead on developing a practical socio-spiritual framework for Dartington and the world – what he called a 'hygiene of the soul'.[173]

The desire to combine a 'modern' empiricist, scientific understanding of the world with a 'traditional' spiritual or animistic one was common in the early twentieth century – Michael Saler, who terms this the 're-enchantment of modernity', finds it evidenced in the popularity of Sherlock Holmes' joining of 'animistic reason' with rigorous observation and logic.[174] The way Leonard wanted to go about re-enchanting the world, however, was unusual unusual. In interwar Britain, as Mathew Thomson finds, psychology was often a 'theoretical, philosophical, humanistic, and outward-looking project' with 'a mystical dimension' – but lacking practical application; in America, it was commonly thought that social progress lay in science, which was used practically – but was not integrated with the spiritual realm.[175] By contrast, Leonard hoped his framework would join all these approaches: uniting social science and spirituality, theory and practice, 'research and laboratory, specialist, general practitioner and intelligent layman' to find 'the best modern approach to human problems'.[176]

The first social science expert he looked to was Eduard Lindeman, an American academic specialising in sociology, adult education and community development. Lindeman crossed the Atlantic to advise on Dartington's early stages.[177] Taking inspiration from G. D. H. Cole's decentralised guild socialism, his strategy for socio-spiritual reform – at Dartington and in general – revolved around 'the resurrection of the

---

[173] Leonard to Israel Sieff, 23 August 1948, LKE/PEP/5/B; Leonard, note on neo-psychology, July 1932, LKE/G/S17/C.
[174] Michael Saler, '"Clap If You Believe in Sherlock Holmes": Mass Culture and the Re-enchantment of Modernity, c. 1890–c.1940', *The Historical Journal* 46 (2003), 599–622, at 603.
[175] Thomson, *Psychological Subjects*, 57, 68 and 72.
[176] Leonard, note on setting up a community council, 14 March 1939, LKE/G/S8/A.
[177] Eduard C. Lindeman had a career that encompassed practical work as a community organiser, academic teaching and writing. He was sufficiently close to Dorothy to dedicate a book to her and possibly had romantic hopes that were blighted when she met Leonard. Lindeman's daughter Betty attended Dartington School and he continued to correspond with the Elmhirsts until his death in 1953. Wyatt Rawson to Eduard Lindeman, 16 May 1927, DWE/G/7/C; Joan C. Tonn, *Mary P. Follett: Creating Democracy, Transforming Management* (New Haven, CT and London, 2003), 350–4.

autonomy and the social responsibility of local community units'.[178] He thought that in social groups there should be no leaders, but 'a conscious effort on the part of the community to control its affairs democratically'; no religion but 'a system of morality supported by the organized community'.[179] Leonard and many other participants at Dartington seized eagerly on the idea of being 'amateur adventurers' sharing equally in building a community.[180] Yet Lindeman's vision did not have a clear spiritual component, and once he had returned to America, Leonard continued to feel that at Dartington there was 'a big gap somewhere – represented by the word religion – an aspect that is blank'.[181]

He decided that the answer was to recruit a socio-spiritual guide for the community in the form of a resident psychologist. Others on the estate also called for such an expert, 'what amounts to a parish priest': 'a person with a wide experience of humanity, a fair knowledge of psychology, unlimited patience and some philosophy of his own, someone who might perhaps help create some kind of religion'.[182] But Leonard found that the 'one amateur, one specialist children's and two professional' psychologists the estate employed in its first decade caused 'all kinds of trouble'.[183] None of the candidates tried out in the late 1930s was a success either, although several of them went on to have a significant influence in the wider field of psychology.[184]

One difficulty with the idea of having a psychologist embedded at Dartington was participants' resistance to anyone observing, or even leading, a community whose 'purpose was to be a group working together'.[185] Sir Frederic Bartlett, Cambridge's first professor of experimental psychology, wrote after visiting Dartington that there was danger in 'introducing into the group anybody whose predominant interests

---

[178] Eduard Lindeman, 'The Place of the Local Community in Organized Society', [n.d.], DWE/G/7/C. See also *Social Discovery: An Approach to the Study of Functional Groups* (New York, 1924).
[179] Eduard Lindeman, *The Community: An Introduction to the Study of Community Leadership and Organization* (New York, 1921), 14–15, 129.
[180] Leonard to Rabindranath Tagore, 10 November 1925, LKE/TAG/9/A.
[181] Leonard, response to 1929 questionnaire, T/PP/P/1/D.
[182] Richard Elmhirst to Dorothy, [1936?], DWE/S/1/C.
[183] Leonard to Frederic Bartlett, 20 July 1936, LKE/G/13/B.
[184] They included Karl Duncker, a German Gestalt psychologist who suffered a breakdown at Dartington and had to be sent for psychiatric treatment himself; a South African social psychologist, Dr O. A. Oeser, who taught at Dartington School for a time before becoming Professor of Psychology at Melbourne University; and German refugee Heinrich Jacoby, whose later work on self-development would be an inspiration for the Esalen Institute.
[185] Transcription of Sunday evening meeting, 23 September 1928, LKE/G/31/A; see also Margaret Isherwood to Leonard, [n.d.], DWE/6/C2.

were in social and comparative values, unless in some more apparent and practical manner he could pull his weight in the community plan'.[186] This danger had not arisen in Heard's case since he had presented himself not as an expert or observer but as one among equals, all of them striving for enlightenment.[187] The tension over expert input echoed interwar debates among philosophers and politicians about whether democracy was best served by having a strong elite guiding the less advanced majority, or whether a more egalitarian approach was preferable.[188] While the Elmhirsts paid lip service to the latter position, their actions tended to support the former – which, of course, justified their own continued leadership of Dartington.

A second difficulty was finding a truly purposive social scientist. For Leonard, this meant someone who was able to offer a socio-spiritual plan for the community: who was willing to 'initiate for us some positive synthesis and offer us some clue to a source of power through which we may achieve a wider horizon of consciousness and the vision of a new world'.[189] Most specialists did not think in terms of a higher consciousness aimed at advancing connectedness and spiritual telos – although the Elmhirsts' hope of finding such a scientist was fuelled by their friendship with Dr Basiswar 'Boshi' Sen, an Indian plant physiologist and founder of the Vivekananda Laboratory in Calcutta.[190] Sen's interest in the psychological and spiritual took him to visit Carl Jung, Romain Rolland and Albert Einstein, and fuelled his long friendship with Rabindranath Tagore. The whole Elmhirst family delighted in him as 'a rare combination – a scientist with a deep religious sense'.[191] This was exactly what they hoped to find for Dartington.

Since Leonard was unable to recruit a satisfactory resident guide for the estate, he tried asking for advice from his wide network of

---

[186] Frederic Bartlett to Leonard, 16 July 1936, LKE/G/13/B. Bartlett's contributions to experimental psychology were widely recognised. He was elected Fellow of the Royal Society in 1932, and later created C. B. E. and knighted. D. E. Broadbent, 'Bartlett, Sir Frederic Charles (1886–1969)', *Oxford Dictionary of National Biography* (Oxford University Press, 23 September 2004) [www.oxforddnb.com/view/article/30628].

[187] This egalitarian view changed after Heard left Dartington. He saw his community at Trabuco College as 'an echelon of visionaries whose role it was to transmit spiritual meaning to a secular society'. Eros, 'Gerald Heard', 11.

[188] Julia Stapleton, 'Historiographical Review: Political Thought, Elites, and the State in Modern Britain', *The Historical Journal* 24 (1999), 251–68; Marc Stears, *Progressives, Pluralists, and the Problems of the State: Ideologies of Reform in the United States and Britain, 1909–1926* (Oxford, 2006), 79; Tom Arnold-Forster, 'Democracy and Expertise in the Lippmann-Terman Controversy', *Modern Intellectual History* 1 (2017), 1–32.

[189] Leonard, note, [n.d.], LKE/G/S8/F.   [190] LKE/IN/16.

[191] Beatrice Straight to Nancy Wilson Ross, 11 October 1935, 156/2, Nancy Wilson Ross Archives.

acquaintances – from Cambridge, from America, and from from Europe – about the estate's socio-spiritual development. Dartington offered a rare opportunity to try out theories outside the laboratory, and a number of scientists showed an interest in helping.[192] Their suggestions, delivered in person or by letter, were aired at the Sunday evening meetings that the Elmhirsts encouraged all estate members to attend – replacing church-going with communal gathering. Two psychologists were particularly influential, Bartlett and an American called William Sheldon. Their ideas – some of them impractical, eugenically deterministic or imbued with spirituality – look, like British psychology generally in this period, to be an 'aberration' or outright failure if they are examined against the social sciences as they developed after the Second World War.[193] Yet, their willingness to cross from the theoretical and scientific to the practical and even spiritual establishes these psychologists – like the Elmhirsts themselves – firmly within an interwar landscape of syncretic socio-spiritual seeking.

Bartlett visited Dartington in 1934, after which Leonard sent him the results of a questionnaire that he and Dorothy had conducted in 1931 to assess participants' feelings about the estate.[194] Leonard asked for the professor's comments on the responses, for his advice on how to create a good community, and, more specifically, on how a man could be offered 'a oneness of life as he leaves the family and an ever increasing boundary to that oneness until it includes the whole of mankind, not in a woolly kind of upliftedness but in an ascending acuteness of consciousness'.[195] The distance between Leonard's belief in spiritual telos and the way social scientists tended to think was clear in Bartlett's bemused reply. 'I am afraid that the definite questions that you put there are so phrased that, with my perhaps deplorably empirical habit of mind, I find the greatest difficulty in envisaging them clearly.'[196] He nonetheless wrote that he found Dartington 'by long odds the most valuable and hopeful social experiment that I have ever seen', offering a series of observations that gave the Elmhirsts 'a feeling that there could be a meaning to all our struggles'.[197]

---

[192] Frederic Bartlett saw the 'bane' of British psychology as 'the too complete removal of theory from practice'. Bartlett to Leonard, 22 February 1935 LKE/G/13/B.

[193] Thomson, *Psychological Subjects*, 75; see also Collini, 'Sociology and Idealism', 22–3.

[194] Leonard conducted the questionnaire with the help of Margaret Isherwood. 'Questionnaire, January 1931, Dartington Hall, Totnes: papers and answers', LKE/G/13/B.

[195] Leonard to Frederic Bartlett, 2 January 1934, LKE/G/S8/D.

[196] Frederic Bartlett to Leonard, 22 February 1935, LKE/G/13/B.

[197] Frederic Bartlett to Dorothy, 11 November 1933, DWE/G/S1/F; Leonard to Frederic Bartlett, 10 February 1934, LKE/G/9/A.

Dorothy and Leonard wanted their findings at Dartington to be applicable to any other part of the globe.[198] Yet, especially as totalitarian regimes gained strength in the mid-1930s, their socio-spiritual ideas and those of their advisors became tinged with national specificity. Bartlett wrote to Leonard that 'you can't successfully impose a Viennese psychology on an English group without running for a fall'.[199] Leonard doubted that the German Gestalt psychologist Karl Duncker would be able to comprehend the 'anarchic habits' of England, and of Dartington in particular.[200] These views align with Mathew Thomson's findings that the introspective Freudian-type model popular on the Continent was seen as problematic in early-twentieth-century England.[201] To Bartlett, Freud's premise that 'everyone who is sound and normal' would talk about everything to everyone would not suit Englishmen's 'locked lips'.[202] Instead, he suggested 'English' solutions to Leonard: to maintain vigour, Dartington ought to make more contact with neighbouring communities through 'games contacts, aesthetic contacts, discussion contacts, administrative contacts'.[203]

From Leonard's point of view, the trouble with Bartlett and with other English social scientists was that they were not sufficiently purposive: that is, they did not seek to contribute directly to the improvement of the individual and of society – a process which Leonard sometimes framed in terms of increased unity and integration, and sometimes in terms of spiritual development. Bartlett saw in Dartington a source of anthropological data rather than the prospect of participating in the creation of a new socio-spiritual framework. Visiting it, he wrote, gave him 'something of the same excitement I had when I was sitting in the kraal of the queen-mother in Swaziland', and he encouraged Leonard to 'work up the data' into a paper for the *British Journal of Psychology*, of which he was editor.[204] Leonard, who wanted Dartington to be advanced by scientific methods, not used as a goldfish bowl by scientists, turned to American

---

[198] Leonard, 'Time Budget 1934–5', 8 November 1934, LKE/G/S8/1.

[199] Frederic Bartlett to Leonard, 22 February 1935 LKE/G/13/B.

[200] Karl Duncker worked at the Psychological Institute at the University of Berlin until he was exiled from Germany. It is possible that Bartlett had felt a Gestalt psychologist would be easier for Dartington to engage with (because both had a holistic outlook) than would a Freudian. Gregory A. Kimble and Michael Wertheimer (eds.), *Portraits of Pioneers in Psychology*, vol. 3 (New York and London, 1998), 165–9; Frederic Bartlett to Leonard, 16 July 1936, LKE/G/13/B; Karl Duncker to Leonard, 31 January 1937, LKE/G/9/A.

[201] Thomson, *Psychological Subjects*, 77.

[202] Frederic Bartlett to Leonard, 22 February 1935, LKE/G/13/B.   [203] Ibid.

[204] Frederic Bartlett to Leonard, 7 February 1934, LKE/G/S8/D and 22 February 1935, LKE/G/13/B.

academic William Sheldon to find a more complete commitment to progressively intentioned science.

Sheldon stayed at Dartington for six weeks in 1934 as part of a European tour during which he met Sigmund Freud and the German psychiatrist Ernst Kretschmer and studied with Carl Jung.[205] He advised the Elmhirsts that neither religion nor academic psychology could provide society with the 'vision of purpose and order' that they sought.[206] What was needed was a practical psychological enterprise run by a new breed of 'Promethean' psychologists who would categorise people on the basis of 'orientation panels' relating to their economic, social, sexual, religious and aesthetic balance, ensuring that they developed according to their 'best native possibilities'.[207] Shedding light on the difficult-to-access subject of sex and sexuality at Dartington, he admonished the Elmhirsts that 'the sex business' had 'got altogether out of hand' in their community: it was no longer 'good fun' – as he thought it should be – but had become 'a necessitous thing of heavy import'.[208] From his comments, it sounds as if long, painful discussions about how people ought to behave were more the order of the day than the hedonistic pleasure seeking that Dartington was often accused of by outside observers. This difficulty was not, Sheldon argued, sexual as such but stemmed from 'a problem of the general organization of character' – the result of Dartington's lack of a psycho-religious system.[209] His view speaks to Sue Morgan's argument that, in the interwar period, spiritual discourses continued to play an important role in the construction of sexual identity, working symbiotically with scientific approaches, including sexology and psychology, but not being completely eclipsed by them.[210]

For Sheldon, Dartington was the ideal 'psychological nursery' in which to experiment with this way of promoting socio-spiritual progress

[205] William Sheldon wrote his PhD at the University of Chicago and then worked at various other American universities. After his visit to Europe, the Elmhirsts, along with the Rockefeller Foundation, supported him on and off for several years, including during a stint researching 'Promethean psychology' at the Chicago Theological Seminary. Patricia Vertinsky, 'Physique as Destiny: William H. Sheldon, Barbara Honeyman Heath and the Struggle for Hegemony in the Science of Somatotyping', *Criminal Behaviour and Mental Health* 24 (2007), 291–316, at 295.

[206] William Sheldon to the Elmhirsts, 28 January 1935; William Sheldon to Dorothy, 3 November 1934, DWE/G/9/E.

[207] William Sheldon to the Elmhirsts, 1 and 28 February 1935, DWE/G/9/E. William Sheldon's worldview was delineated in his first book, some of which he wrote while at Dartington, *Psychology and the Promethean Will: A Constructive Study of the Acute Common Problem of Education, Medicine and Religion* (New York and London, 1936).

[208] William Sheldon, 'Panel pictures', 1 February 1935. DWE/G/9/E.   [209] Ibid.

[210] Sue Morgan, '"Sex and Common-Sense": Maude Royden, Religion, and Modern Sexuality', *Journal of British Studies* 52 (2013), 153–78.

since it offered a 'real life' rather than a laboratory setting.[211] The
Elmhirsts were initially enthusiastic too. Dorothy quoted his ideas in
her notebooks of spiritual reflections.[212] Leonard puzzled over how to
combine Sheldon's abstruse ideas with the bluffer advice of Bartlett.[213]
Ultimately, however, Sheldon's suggestions gained little purchase at
Dartington. In large part this was because, in the Elmhirsts' vision of a
group of people living together, gradually perfecting themselves and their
community, there was little room for biological determinism.[214] It would
later become clear that Dorothy and Leonard were wise in distancing
themselves from Sheldon. He went on to develop his ideas into a controversial system of 'somatotyping' – a classification system that associated
physiology and psychology – and to argue that delinquency could be
predicted from people's physiology.[215] Leonard had, like a number of
progressives, briefly dabbled in eugenics: wondering about the benefits of
'a little score card measuring' to prevent 'unfitted, unexplored, un-
understood personalities' from imperilling Dartington.[216] But he, along
with most of the scientific community, rejected Sheldon's eugenicist
schema, the devastating consequences of which were revealed by the
Nazi programme of 'racial hygiene'.[217]

Lack of success at discovering a 'hygiene of the soul' at Dartington did
not deter Leonard, who never stopped hoping that a '"citizen's guide to
psycho-hygiene"' would be forthcoming, helping people to live harmoniously with one another and to achieve spiritual fulfilment.[218] His ambition would, perhaps, have met with a warmer welcome in America, where

---

[211] William Sheldon to the Elmhirsts, 1 February 1935, DWE/G/9/E; William Sheldon to
the Elmhirsts, 28 January 1935, DWE/G/9/E.

[212] Dorothy, notebook, [n.d.], DWE/G/9/E.

[213] Leonard, notes, 17 May 1936, LKE/G/S9/A.

[214] William Sheldon, 'Panel-Picture', 1 February 1935, DWE/G/9/E.

[215] [n.a.], 'Memorandum to the Elmhirst Committee concerning the Ruth Morgan
Memorial experiment in psychology, 19 January 1937', DWE/G/9/E. Sheldon's work,
although largely forgotten now, was influential both within psychology and more
generally. Figures as well-respected as the anthropologist Margaret Mead were
intrigued by his somatotyping. Vertinsky, 'Physique as Destiny', 306.

[216] Michael Freeden, *Liberal Languages: Ideological Imaginations and Twentieth-Century
Progressive Thought* (Princeton, 2005), 145–72; Chris Renwick, *Lost Biological Roots:
A History of Futures Past* (Basingstoke, 2012), chapter 2; Leonard, 'On character',
13 January 1935, LKE/G/17.

[217] Sarah W. Tracy, 'An Evolving Science of Man: The Transformation and Demise of
American Constitutional Medicine, 1900–1950', in Lawrence and Weisz (eds.), *Greater
Than the Parts*, 161–88. Sheldon went on to compile a guide to his somatotypes in an
Atlas of Men (New York, 1954), illustrated with nude photos of undergraduates, and to
begin an *Atlas of Women*, which was abandoned due to the growing unpopularity of the
subject matter. Vertinsky, 'Physique as Destiny', 310.

[218] Leonard to Dr C. P. Blacker of the Ministry of Health, 31 August 1943, LKE/PEP/1/A.

a key aspect of the New Deal was the ideal of a purposive social science that could assist, though not direct, social-democratic transformation.[219]

2.2   The Therapeutic Ethos and the Social Scientific State

Leonard had to wait until after the Second World War for his vision of science as a tool for promoting social progress to take wider hold. The 1950s and 1960s were, as Mike Savage writes, a time 'in which social science became vested with unprecedented hopes and aspirations'.[220] Expertise in social science became part of the renewed armoury of the elite: in place of an inherited gentlemanly identity, it offered them a 'natural' leadership role in the welfare state as experts and advisors based on 'technique, skill, and expertise'.[221] The discipline did not, however, provide what Leonard, Dorothy and Heard had sought between the wars: a complete 'religion' that was a source of spiritual meaning, individual purpose and community unity. Rather, its influence separated into two strands.

As the Elmhirsts' generation died out, a lot of the drive to incorporate experimental spiritualities with social reform died with it. The vestiges of the nineteenth-century Christian ethos of self-sacrificing public service yielded to one that prioritised self-fulfilment, self-discovery and self-actualisation.[222] One strand of social science – psychology in particular – fed into the therapeutic culture of self-improvement. This culture was also fuelled by Eastern-influenced New-Age spirituality of the type that Gerald Heard helped shape, and by international hubs of alternative living like the Esalen Institute and Dartington Hall.[223]

A second strand of social science threaded into post-war state social planning. For the most part, this project lacked the streak of religious mission, the yearning to promote transcendental unity and moral purpose, which characterised the hopes of the Elmhirsts and their contemporaries. As Jose Harris writes, visions of a moral citizenry advancing society towards a teleological good had fallen out of favour by the 1940s, 'deposed by various forms of positivism' – in particular the benchmarks

---

[219] Jess Gilbert, *Planning Democracy: Agrarian Intellectuals and the Intended New Deal* (New Haven, CT, 2015), 179.

[220] Savage, *Identities and Social Change*, 20.   [221] Ibid, 78–9, 216.

[222] An interest in self-realisation was present earlier in the century, but the Second World War brought it to the fore. Nikolas Rose, *Inventing Ourselves: Psychology, Power and Personhood* (Cambridge and New York, 1996), 3; Thomson, *Psychological Subjects*; Roger Foster, 'The Therapeutic Spirit of Neoliberalism', *Political Theory* 44 (2016), 82–105, at 85–7.

[223] Srinivas Aravamudan, 'New Age Enchantments', in *Guru English: South Asian Religion in a Cosmopolitan Language* (Princeton, 2006), 220–64, at 223.

of economics.[224] The danger of the purposive mobilisation of scientists had been demonstrated during the Second World War, not least by the nuclear bomb. Most practitioners had retreated to the safety of a more objectivist, empirical definition of their subject.[225]

Nonetheless, a significant contingent of socialists in the 1950s continued to be concerned with the nebulous questions of 'happiness, well-being, fellowship, and community', and even with spiritual fulfilment – including the Socialist Union, an ethical socialist group within the Labour Party, and the New Left.[226] Echoing Leonard's interwar ambitions, some in this contingent drew on social science to promote organic spiritual community and ethical citizenship. This reprise of method and objective was not coincidental: Michael Young, a pupil at Dartington School from 1929 to 1933, a protégé of the Elmhirsts and later a trustee of the estate, was a key figure in the project – overlapping with the New Left and the Socialist Union, although he mostly remained independent from both groups.

As a student, and then on his frequent visits from London, Young witnessed the struggle at Dartington to find a socio-spiritual model that would balance community and individual, science and faith, and hold up against the social fragmentation that seemed to be the chief threat of modernity. He was close to Dorothy, on her persistent spiritual quest, and to Leonard, whose enthusiasm for social science Young enlarged into an influential career in sociology and social entrepreneurship.[227] As Leonard had conducted several sociological surveys of community feeling among Dartington's members, so Young, in 1953, formed the Institute of Community Studies with Peter Willmott as a base for research into the social factors that influenced individual and community well-being in East London.[228] Even before this, Young had used the Elmhirst-funded think-tank Political and Economic Planning (PEP) – he was its secretary from 1941 to 1945 – as a vehicle for analysing the conditions for political participation and good community life using

[224] Jose Harris, 'Political Thought and the Welfare State 1870–1940: An Intellectual Framework for British Social Policy', *Past and Present* 135 (1992), 116–41, at 136. See also Jeremy Nuttall, *Psychological Socialism: The Labour Party and Qualities of Mind and Character, 1931 to the Present* (Manchester, 2006).

[225] Smith, *Social Science in the Crucible*, 261.

[226] Lise Butler, *Michael Young, Social Science, and the British Left, 1945–1970* (Oxford, 2020), 6; Lawrence Black, 'Social Democracy as a Way of Life: Fellowship and the Socialist Union, 1951–9', *Twentieth Century British History* 10 (1999), 499–539.

[227] Many of the letters between Young and the Elmhirsts are in the Dartington Hall archive, chiefly in files DWE/G and LKE/G. See also Asa Briggs, *Michael Young: Social Entrepreneur* (London, 2001).

[228] Butler, *Michael Young*, chapter 4.

social science.[229] It was an approach he elaborated on further when he left PEP to direct the Labour Party's research department, continuing to link social science to holistic moral and ethical issues.

While socio-spiritual questing at Dartington had some impact on wider society, it was a common complaint among participants that the community lacked 'a nucleus, a centre, an agreed symbol of what it all stands for'[230]; that the 'spiritual links which kept the original venture together had not grown apace with the different sections of the state'.[231] The Elmhirsts themselves lamented being 'haphazard in our devotion of time, effort, or endowment' to what they considered the most vital of their objectives: 'the search for a basic philosophy of human existence that satisfies the two sides of human nature ... the intellectual and the religious'.[232] Their difficulties in formulating a definite socio-spiritual framework were partly because this was a huge and intangible ambition. It was also because they were so uncoordinated in their approach: they admired aspects of Christianity, of Eastern spirituality, of alternative spiritual forms and of the social sciences, but did not strive consistently to synthesise them in a clear, reproducible form. Dorothy focused on her private spiritual journey, while Leonard concentrated on social-scientific planning; these were not easy pre-occupations to amalgamate. The Elmhirsts' difficulties in finding a clear lived theology also reflected the wider fragmentation of ethics and morality in the twentieth century. Raymond O'Malley, who taught at Dartington in the 1930s, wrote in 1983, 'If not a church, then what? The humiliating fact is that, in our century, there is, so far as I can see, *no* acceptable focus, no agreed place or institution or symbol that gives meaning or coherence to the whole.'[233]

Social-spiritual questing was nonetheless of vital importance to Dartington. It was Dorothy and Leonard's search for a way to live well and to contribute to the social good that inspired the entire venture. The desire to serve society, rooted in a Christian ethos, drove many of the people who joined the community. Dartington represented – albeit organically rather than systematically – a philosophy of living that did, in a sense, replace the nineteenth-century socio-spiritual framework of

---

[229] Butler, *Michael Young*, chapter 2; Daniel Ritschel, *The Politics of Planning: The Debate on Economic Planning in Britain in the 1930s* (Oxford, 1997), 145–83; Abigail Beach, 'Forging a "Nation of Participants": Political and Economic planning in Labour's Britain', in Richard Weight and Abigail Beach (eds.), *The Right to Belong: Citizenship and National Identity in Britain, 1930-1930* (London, 1998), 89–115.

[230] Raymond O'Malley, Dartington School teacher, to Michael Young, 5 January 1983, T/HIS/S20/D.

[231] [n.a.], 'How can Dartington become more of a community?', 8 July 1945, DWE/S/1/E.

[232] Leonard, 'Time Budget 1934–5', 8 November 1934, LKE/G/S8/1.

[233] Raymond O'Malley to Michael Young, 5 January 1983, T/HIS/S20/D.

Christianity: it was a negotiation with 'how to be' in the modern world. This negotiation involved melding Christian ideals of public service and a Christian or idealistic vision of people as interconnected and responsible for one another together with an interest in promoting personal affective and spiritual fulfilment. The personnel sent out by the estate – whether Gerald Heard to California or Michael Young to London to lobby for the holistic use of social science in politics – were missionaries of the faith. Many people who visited the Elmhirsts' experiment saw it as offering something more transcendent than a template for social reform. For the refugee German philosopher Professor Hugo Fischer, Dartington realised 'ultimate values'.[234]

---

[234] Professor Hugo Fischer, a refugee from the Nazi regime, to Dorothy, 1953, DWE/G/4/D. Fischer's combination of rationalism, mysticism and interest in India fitted him well to appreciate the wider scope of the Elmhirsts' socio-spiritual questing. Elliot Y. Neaman, *A Dubious Past: Ernst Jünger and the Politics of Literature After Nazism* (Berkeley, CA, 1999), 83–4.

3   Education for Change

> "Politics" is not the cure, – the young men and women, and the educational systems of the world, on these the whole burden rests. Either youth must win through or the world will perish.   Leonard to Dorothy, 1922[1]

For the Elmhirsts, conventional education, underpinned by a competitive, laissez-faire belief system, had failed to teach people 'citizenship and its responsibilities' or how to 'work out a definite purpose or ideal of life either for themselves, their own nation, society as a whole or the world'.[2] In the aftermath of the First World War, they saw reforming education as a key to a more harmonious future – a view that was widely shared.[3] Dorothy and Leonard were vague in their definition of the 'conventional education' that they wished to reform, but their disapproval encompassed the rigid regimes of public schools, the state sector's focus on results, rote-learning, strict discipline, competitive examinations and a set curriculum divided into narrow subjects. Like other reformers, they tended to characterise conventional education as coherent, organised ideology (which it was not). This 'invented opponent', as Laura Tisdall terms it, was what allowed educational reformers to present themselves as thorough-going 'progressives', moving away from the flawed practices of the past and towards a better future.[4]

---

[1] Leonard to Dorothy, 3 February 1922, LKE/DWE/10/F.
[2] Leonard to Michael Sadler, 11 December 1917, LKE/G/28/A.
[3] The literature on the progressive education movement is extensive. Key surveys are R. J. W. Selleck, *The New Education, 1870–1914* (London, 1968); *English Primary Education and the Progressives, 1914–1939* (London, 1972); W. A. C. Stewart and W. P. McCann, *The Educational Innovators, vol. 2: Progressive Schools 1881–1967* (London, 1968); and Laura Tisdall, *A Progressive Education: How Childhood Changed in Mid-Twentieth-Century English and Welsh Schools* (Manchester, 2019).
[4] Tisdall, *Progressive Education*, 45. The term 'progressive education' was coined in the 1960s and applied retrospectively to the interwar period to a phenomenon that contemporaries often called 'new education' (Shaul Bar-Haim, 'The Liberal Playground: Susan Isaacs, Psychoanalysis and Progressive Education in the Interwar Era', *History of the Human Sciences* 30 (2017), 94–117). While it is a useful term for educational reformers, it does not denote a homogeneous ideology, nor does it map directly onto to social or political progressivism.

The Elmhirsts' vision of an ideal education system was one that promoted learners' freedom and holistic fulfilment; that was integrated with its rural surroundings; and that extended from the cradle to the grave. The idea that children must have the freedom of self-directed learning was common among progressive educators – appearing frequently, for example, in the journal of the New Education Fellowship, the main forum for educational reform in England.[5] As Tisdall finds, however, this concept was construed in two very different ways. 'Non-utopian progressive educationalists', as she terms them, championed children's freedom to develop into psychologically healthy adults through a mode of education that was designed and controlled by grown-ups.[6] These pedagogues were child-centred, in the sense that they wanted education to be tailored to suit the individual child – but they viewed children as limited in capacity, and in need of guidance in order to grow into responsible citizens. 'Utopian progressive educationalists', conversely, believed that children were distorted by exposure to adult norms; they must be completely freed from these norms so that a new, ideal generation (and a new ideal society) could be forged. The non-utopian progressive view gained wide traction in the state sector in the interwar period, while the utopian view was less common.[7] Utopian progressives included A. S. Neill, founder of Summerhill school, Dora and Bertrand Russell, founders of Beacon Hill school, and the educational reformer Edmond Holmes, who put the group's viewpoint succinctly: 'the child's outlook on life, before it has been perverted by education, is fundamentally right, while the adult's is fundamentally wrong'.[8]

The Elmhirsts, at least in the 1920s, were whole-hearted utopian progressives, believing in the society-redeeming possibilities of children freed from adult convention. 'Over and over again,' Leonard wrote in 1927, two years after the opening of Dartington School, pupils 'have forced our hand along what I think of now as the right lines'.[9] In the interwar years, this view of children was shared by a wide variety of people who were not directly involved in education, including artists,

---

[5] Celia M. Jenkins, 'New Education and its Emancipatory Interests (1920–1950)', *History of Education* 29 (2000), 139–51.

[6] Tisdall, *Progressive Education*, chapter 1.

[7] Laura Tisdall finds that progressive ideas of child-centred education had already come close to 'state orthodoxy' by 1939, but that practical educational change before the Second World War was 'stymied by limited funds' ('Teachers, Teaching Practice and Conceptions of Childhood in England and Wales, 1931–1967', unpublished PhD, University of Cambridge, 2014, 20).

[8] Edmond Holmes, *The Tragedy of Education* (London, 1913), 5.

[9] Leonard to Michael Sadler, 17 March 1927, LKE/G/28/A.

psychologists, philosophers and social planners.[10] The science fiction writer Olaf Stapledon, for example, wrote several novels featuring children who promise social salvation – including *Odd John* (1935), in which a child succeeds in founding a utopian colony, which is then destroyed by adults.[11] Dartington attracted wide interest because it constituted something of a practical test of this belief in children's promise.

Dorothy and Leonard's second pedagogical ideal was to combine educational reform with rural regeneration. For many educators in Britain, the country childhood was a distant, reified symbol of 'a traditional way of life that ought to be retained at all costs' – part of the central importance of the countryside to national identity.[12] For the Elmhirsts, however, the country childhood was not an abstract or nostalgic concept deserving of such veneration: Leonard, raised in rural Yorkshire, thought the countryside could 'in itself be just as much of a prison to a child as a home in a city slum'.[13] Rather, he and Dorothy saw giving rural children a good education as a way to revive a countryside in decline. Leonard explained to the politician Ellen Wilkinson that behind Dartington lay 'a conviction that the villages of England, as also of India ... have yet to come into their own. That is why, for us, it is our relation to the Village School which is to be the crux of the problem, and through it, to the parent and the labourer.'[14] As in Denmark, whose folk high schools the Elmhirsts looked to as a model, Dartington School was intended to be 'the spiritual adjunct to, if not the spiritual motor for' a larger project of rural regeneration.[15]

---

[10] Even the Boy Scouts could be viewed in this 'utopian progressive' fashion. 'It was youth's rendezvous, with new hopes, a new vision of life, a great promise ahead,' wrote the journalist Sir Philipp Gibbs, on observing the 1933 World Jamboree. 'We older men who remember the past had no place here.' (Mischa Honeck, 'The Power of Innocence: Anglo-American Scouting and the Boyification of Empire', *Geschichte und Gesellschaft* 42 (2016), 441–66, at 454.) Richard Overy discusses how closely educational reform was bound up with wider hopes for social progress in *The Morbid Age: Britain Between the Wars* (London, 2009).

[11] Olaf Stapledon, *Odd John: A Story Between Jest and Earnest* (London, 1935); Laura Tisdall, 'The Psychologist, the Psychoanalyst and the "Extraordinary Child" in Postwar British Science Fiction', *Medical Humanities* Special Issue, 'Science Fiction and the Medical Humanities' 43 (2016), 4–9.

[12] Tisdall, 'Teachers', 186–7.

[13] Leonard, 'Situation', September 1927, DWE/DHS/1/F.

[14] Leonard to Ellen Wilkinson, 19 April 1927, LKE/G/33/I.

[15] Daniel T. Rodgers, *Atlantic Crossings: Social Politics in a Progressive Age* (Cambridge, 1998), 357. Inspired by nineteenth-century reformer N. F. Grundtvig, the Danish folk high schools were (and are) institutes for adult education, intended to enlighten the people democratically and spiritually, rather than to promote academic achievement or training for a career.

While most progressive educators concentrated on children, the Elmhirsts thought that education should be 'not just for the young': it must 'touch every individual within range', resulting in a 'continuous widening field of consc[iousness] from cradle to grave'.[16] This idea was partly inspired by the importance given to continuing education by American social progressives, and partly by Leonard's experiences working with the Young Men's Christian Association and the Workers' Education Association (WEA) in Britain.[17] The Elmhirsts' hope was 'to educate heads, foremen and every individual worker, so that every department becomes a school', and to find a more 'vivid', participative educational style to replace the 'academic approach and the lecture habit' of the WEA.[18] Their efforts to build a model of democratic, life-long learning attracted the approbation of leading community educators, including Henry Morris, secretary of education for Cambridgeshire; Sir Michael Sadler, vice-chancellor of the University of Leeds and a pioneer in the university extension movement; and the American adult educator Eduard Lindeman.

The few existing studies on education at Dartington have focused solely on the school, and have done so in the context of the history of the progressive education movement.[19] In that regard, the Elmhirsts' experiment was interesting but not enormously original since it was driven more by social ideals than by new educational techniques. It was, as one of the first teachers, John Wales, wrote, 'less an educational than a social experiment, an experiment in the art of living'.[20] Potentially innovative plans, such as a laboratory-cum-nursery, never took off. Nor did the school have a significant impact on the direction of progressive education in the state system, although it did foreshadow a national move in the same direction – so much so that Dartington's trustees in the late 1960s worried that the school no longer seemed progressive enough in an era of radical de-schooling.

It is when the Elmhirsts' educational project is looked at in the round, as part of a move to promote rural reform, life-long learning

---

[16] Leonard, 'Aims of Dartington', 3 November 1935, LKE/G/S8/F.

[17] John Wales, 'A letter from Dartington', January 1927, T/DHS/A/2/F. Eduard Lindeman's *The Meaning of Adult Education* gives an example of the American progressive ideas that influenced Dartington's continuing education (New York, 1926).

[18] Leonard to John Wales, 21 March 1930, T/DHS/A/2/F; Leonard, 'Extension at Dartington', 1940, LKE/EDU/7/B.

[19] Mark Kidel, *Beyond the Classroom: Dartington's Experiments in Education* (Devon, 1990); Maurice Punch, *Progressive Retreat: A Sociological Study of Dartington Hall School and Some of its Former Pupils* (Cambridge, 1977).

[20] John Wales, 'A letter from Dartington', January 1927, T/DHS/A/2/F.

and international harmony that it holds most interest. Ideologically plastic, unfettered by economic necessity and well-connected, it was the only progressive educational scheme begun in interwar England as part of a larger social experiment. As such, it offers a singular demonstration of the intense cross-fertilisation of progressive education with other holistically minded programmes that sought to re-think the competitive liberal philosophy of the previous century. This cross-fertilisation yielded a place where ruralists, socialists, eugenicists, pacifists and internationalists (among many others) could imagine, and sometimes see put into action, their hope that reformed education would be a fast-track to utopia.

Dartington's first educational phase, from 1926 to 1931, was inchoate but steered closest to the Elmhirsts' vision of putting learning for all at the heart of their experiment. Dorothy and Leonard concentrated on building up the school in symbiosis with the estate – Leonard, in particular, wanting life and education so intertwined in the lives of all Dartington's participants that he pledged 'never to mention the word school from the start'.[21] This stage came to a halt between 1929 and 1931, in the face of several reports criticising welfare and teaching standards, and complaints from the estate's commercial branch that the school was impeding their profitability. In the 1930s, Dartington School was run as a more discrete venture. Under the control of a new headmaster, W. B. Curry, it increased in size, acquired a more coherent shape and direction, and gained more traction in the wider progressive educational community – but it also became detached from the rest of the Dartington project. The Elmhirsts channelled their aspirations to use education to promote social regeneration into other areas instead: supporting the village school; setting up schemes for school leavers; planning a new state school; and piloting innovative adult education schemes in collaboration with the WEA and the University College of the South West. This chapter will consider the phases in Dartington's educational project chronologically, but it begins by looking at the influences that inspired the Elmhirsts – a wide array that illustrates how interwar progressive education was shaped by an environment of humanitarian international exchange.[22]

---

[21] Leonard to Wyatt Rawson, 8 February 1925, T/HIS/S22/B.

[22] For this international cross-pollination see, for example, Ann Taylor Allen, *The Transatlantic Kindergarten: Education and the Woman's Movement in Germany and the United States* (New York, 2017) and Eckhardt Fuchs, 'Educational Sciences, Morality and Politics: International Educational Congresses in the Early Twentieth Century', *Paedagogica Historica* 40 (2004), 757–84.

3.1   Inspiration

> [A] school such as has not happened yet, drawing on India, America, China, – again a concentration, again education, again the fellowship of a few men of ideals and spirit, – not politics, or press, or even adult education, not public schools nor panaceas nor 'isms', but fellowship, children, service, and a hoping for results after 25 years.   Leonard Elmhirst (1924)[23]

The main influence on Leonard's pedagogical thinking was the period he spent helping Rabindranath Tagore establish the Institute for Rural Reconstruction (Sriniketan) in Bengal, a project intended both to educate villagers in economic self-reliance and to create a more holistically fulfilling daily life.[24] A key component of the institute was the system of education for children from the surrounding villages, later called Siksha-Satra ('multi-purpose school'), which drew on inspiration as diverse as Robert Baden-Powell's English Scout movement and the American 4-H movement, and would go on to influence M. K. Gandhi's nationalist scheme of 'Basic Education' in the 1930s.[25] Siksha-Satra had two main elements. Children had an individually chosen 'home project' – such as poultry-raising or food preserving – intended to fuel their desire to learn naturally and in their own way. Alongside this, they were part of a scout organisation that did welfare work in the community, from administering quinine against malaria to marshalling fetes.[26] Students were, to a degree, self-governing, with emphasis put on the 'cooperative principles which will unite the teachers and students in a living and active bond'.[27] Instead of 'moulding them into one pattern', wrote Leonard, each child

---

[23] Leonard to Dorothy, [29 July 1924], LKE/DWE/11/E.

[24] Leonard K. Elmhirst, 'Siksha-Satra', *Visva-Bharati Bulletin* 9 (1928) 23–39; *Poet and Plowman* (Calcutta, 1975); and *Rabindranath Tagore: Pioneer in Education. Essays and Exchanges between Rabindranath Tagore and L.K. Elmhirst* (London, 1961). See also Uma Das Gupta, 'Tagore's Ideas of Social Action and the Sriniketan Experiment of Rural Reconstruction, 1922–41', *University of Toronto Quarterly* 77 (2008), 992–1004.

[25] Following Tagore, Gandhi's 'Basic Education' promoted Indian self-sufficiency by making the practical crafts, usually the preserve of the lower castes, central to the teaching programme in place of such 'colonial' or 'elite' skills as literacy and academic learning. Unlike Tagore, however, Gandhi did not prize creative self-expression or knowledge about Western science, and omitted these from his curriculum. Krishna Dutta and Andrew Robinson (eds.), *Selected Letters of Rabindranath Tagore* (Cambridge, 1997), 490; Krishna Kripalani, *Rabindranath Tagore: A Biography* (London, 1962), 8.

[26] Santidev Ghosh, 'Sikshasatra and Naitalimi Education', in Santosh Chandra Sengupta (ed.), *Rabindranath Tagore: Homage from Visva-Bharati* (Santiniketan, 1962), 121–37, at 121. See also Stewart and McCann, *Educational Innovators*, 130, and Leonard Elmhirst, 'Siksha-Satra'.

[27] Rabindranath Tagore quoted in Ghosh, 'Sikshasatra', 121.

was allowed to 'develop along his own line within certain social bounds' – a principle of 'socialised individualism' that would also be central to Dartington.[28]

For Tagore, the aim of Sriniketan was to liberate Indians from below. Through education, disenfranchised rural citizens would achieve self-realisation and social unity. The subsequent cooperation between races, castes and religions would give them the capacity to stand free of their colonial rulers. Tagore was not driven by overt nationalism; he opposed Gandhi's *Swaraj* campaign and anything else that strengthened the 'hungry self of the Nation'.[29] His utopian ideal, held in common with many other interwar reformers, was to unite mankind in global fellowship, and he saw grass-roots education as an important place to start.[30] It was 'chiefly because of the international ideal' that Leonard was drawn to Sriniketan.[31] There he received a practical grounding in how to start a school that was integrated with the surrounding villages but also looked out globally – a bottom-up project in international community building.[32]

In the early 1920s, Leonard found his hopes for internationalist, democratic education echoed in many quarters. It was, as Sir Michael Sadler remarked to him, part of a global phenomenon – a 'new temper of mind towards education, especially in its relation to life'.[33] World unity had been the main preoccupation of Leonard's Cambridge tutor Goldsworthy Lowes Dickinson; it was central to the work of another of Leonard's acquaintances, Peter Manniche, who founded the International People's College at Elsinore in Denmark in 1921, an institution that was intended to strengthen local community life and to build bridges between nations.[34] The pioneering city planner Patrick Geddes,

[28] Leonard Elmhirst, 'The Robbery of the Soil and Rural Reconstruction', in Sengupta (ed.), *Rabindranath Tagore*, 12–4; Leonard to Arthur Geddes, 24 February 1923, LKE/IN/6/D.
[29] Rabindranath Tagore, *Nationalism* (London, 1976 [1916]), 80.
[30] Mohammad A. Quayum, 'Imagining "One World": Rabindranath Tagore's Critique of Nationalism', *Interdisciplinary Literary Studies* 7 (2006), 33–52. For a range of internationalist models put forward as alternatives to nationalism, see Jeanne Morefield, *Covenants Without Swords: Idealist Liberalism and the Spirit of Empire* (Princeton, 2005).
[31] Leonard to Rabindranath Tagore, 3 April 1921, [transcript], LKE/TAG/9/A.
[32] Leonard to Dorothy, 3 February 1922, LKE/DWE/10/F.
[33] Michael Sadler to Leonard, 21 December 1921, LKE/G/28/A.
[34] The Elmhirsts corresponded with Peter Manniche through the 1920s, made donations to his projects and were influenced by his book, *The Folk High Schools of Denmark and the Development of a Farming Community*, written with Holger Begtrup and Hans Lund (London, 1929). The folk college movement in Denmark was primarily inspired by nineteenth-century Danish writer Nikolai Frederick Grundtvig, who was also an important influence on Eduard Lindeman. Grundtvig had visited utopia-builder Robert Owen at New Lanark and brought back Owen's ideas about the importance of

whom Leonard met during his time in India, set up the Collège des Ecossais in Montpellier as an 'international hall of residence whose occupants would promote world citizenship'.[35] Tagore was made president of a subsidiary institution of Geddes' school, the Collège des Indiens, which aimed to 'realise in common fellowship of study the meeting of East and West'.[36] Leonard was surrounded by people who believed that education could bring about a better world, and that a better world meant a more democratic and unified one. For many of them, including Tagore and Manniche, self-directing local communities were the key building blocks in this pacifist, democratic, internationalist vision.

Pedagogical ambitions at Dartington were also strongly influenced by Dorothy's experiences in America, where education, adult education in particular, was part of a series of Progressive-Age experiments intended to tame industrial capitalism.[37] When living in New York, Dorothy became an admirer of John Dewey, whose philosophical ambition revolved around replacing the individualistic psychology of laissez-faire liberalism with a recognition that individuals were part of an interrelated whole – and for whom education was an important way to 'get the social organism thinking'.[38] She attended Dewey's lectures, published him in *The New Republic*, and absorbed his views that progress towards democracy came from the active adaptation of the individual to his environment, a process that education must advance by promoting critical, inquisitive thinking and participative behaviour.[39] As with Tagore's

community schooling. He advocated a network of self-governing folk high schools, a 'common centre ... to gather and unite all the energies of society'. Max Lawson, 'N.F.S. Grundtvig', *Prospects: The Quarterly Review of Comparative Education* 23 (1993), 613–23.

[35] Hugh Clout and Iain Stevenson, 'Jules Sion, Alan Grant Ogilvie and the Collège des Ecossais in Montpellier: A Network of Geographers', *Scottish Geographical Journal* 120 (2004), 181–98, at 182. The college was based on the Collège des Ecossais that had provided a base for Scottish Catholics in Paris in the seventeenth and eighteenth centuries. It foundered in the Second World War and was converted into a training centre for educational administrators. Leonard kept up a correspondence with Patrick Geddes, admiring 'the way in which you launch forward into all kinds of fields' – an approach which he saw as similar to his and Dorothy's ambition of meeting 'problems on every side, social, economic, agricultural'. Leonard to Patrick Geddes, 25 May 1926, LKE/IN/6/E.

[36] Prospectus of Collège des Indiens, [n.d.], LKE/IN/6/E.

[37] Andrew Jewett, *Science, Democracy, and the American University: From the Civil War to the Cold War* (Cambridge, 2012), 196–223. There was a strong transatlantic tie in a grant from the Rockefeller Foundation that largely funded the New Education Fellowship between 1921 and 1946.

[38] Louis Menard, *The Metaphysical Club* (New York, 2001), part four (quote at 299); John Dewey, *Democracy and Education: An Introduction to the Philosophy of Education* (New York, 1999 [1916]).

[39] Dorothy to Leonard, 24 October 1921, LKE/DWE/10/D; Dorothy's, notes on John Dewey's lectures, [n.d.], DWE/G/S7/E/3.

holistic focus on 'life in its completeness', Dewey's pedagogy centred on the idea of the 'unity of knowledge' – meaning that the acquisition of knowledge was inseparable from the full range of real-world activities.[40] He placed a great deal of emphasis on generalised 'learning by doing', rather than on subject-specific teaching; this included learning to be a democratic citizen by engaging in group decision-making.[41]

Dorothy's pedagogical experience went well beyond theory. In New York, she was instrumental in starting the New School for Social Research in 1919, part of whose aim was to be a model for adult education, allowing ordinary citizens to learn from and exchange ideas with scholars, particularly in the sphere of the human sciences.[42] Along with John D. Rockefeller, she sponsored and helped shape The Inquiry, an organisation set up in 1921 to investigate group discussion as a mode of pedagogy and to promote this among church groups.[43] The network of scholars and reformers who surrounded her in these activities – Eduard Lindeman, who joined the New School; Walter Lippmann and Herbert Croly of *The New Republic*; academics including John Dewey who were associated with Columbia University – would provide a formative backdrop for Dartington, contributing ideas, advice and visits in person.

Dorothy's experiences in America also covered children's education. She sat on the General Education Board, a philanthropic organisation founded by Rockefeller to promote American public education, especially in the countryside.[44] She helped to establish the Lincoln School, a 'laboratory' for experimenting with education methods that was attached

---

[40] Menard, *Metaphysical Club*, 322–3.

[41] John Dewey, *The School and Society* (Chicago, 1907), 44. Many of Dewey's ideas were worked out in practice at the University Elementary School of the University of Chicago (known as the Laboratory School), which he opened in 1896.

[42] Dorothy pledged $10,000 a year to the New School for ten years. The school drew on the intellectual resources of both *The New Republic* and Columbia University, and early participants included John Dewey, Walter Lippmann, Herbert Croly and Thorstein Veblen. Peter M. Rutkoff and William B. Scott. *New School: A History of the New School for Social Research* (New York, 1986), 10–13; Jewett, *Science, Democracy and the American University*, 213–4.

[43] The Inquiry – originally called the National Conference on The Christian Way of Life – was set up by the Federal Council of Churches in Christ and coordinated by Teachers College, Columbia University (William M. Keith, *Democracy as Discussion: Civic Education and the America Forum Movement* (Lanham, MD, 2007), 123–4). Dorothy sat on several of its executive and administrative committees and contributed around $25,000 a year (Richard Pfaff Douthit, 'A Historical Study of Group Discussion Principles and Techniques Developed by "The Inquiry", 1922–1933', unpublished PhD, Louisiana State University, 1961, 155–7).

[44] James H. Madison, 'John D. Rockefeller's General Education Board and the Rural School Problem in the Midwest, 1900–1930', *History of Education Quarterly* 24 (1984), 181–99.

to Teachers College, Columbia University.[45] The Lincoln was in the vanguard of American educational reform, converting academic insight into practical experiment. Espousing Dewey's principles, it emphasised the social nature of education: its pupils were to develop 'self-control and self-direction' and the ability to co-operate through their experience at school.[46] Its approach fed into Dartington School, as did Dorothy's three children by her first marriage, all of whom had previously been attending the Lincoln. The provision for Dorothy's children through the construction of a progressive school was one of the conditions of her agreeing to move with Leonard to England.

Alongside these sources of inspiration in India and America, the Elmhirsts' pedagogical vision was inflected by eclectic other educational experiments, whose example they sometimes embraced and sometimes rejected. They were impressed by Oundle School in Northamptonshire, turned by its headmaster, F. W. Sanderson, into a leading centre for scientific and engineering education.[47] They looked to the Muños School in the Philippines, where Leonard, visiting in the early 1920s, had admired how students 'work their own little holdings, build their own cottages, keep their own accounts, run their own municipality'.[48] When the Elmhirsts went to see A. S. Neill's Summerhill school in Suffolk in 1927, they were impressed by the radical headmaster's libertarian approach but 'horrified at the mess and disorder and seeming chaos' that resulted from it.[49]

Another mixed influence was the Junior Republic in Freeville, New York, which Leonard visited when he was studying at Cornell. Philanthropist William Reuben George had set this institution up in 1895, with the aim of turning 'delinquent' adolescents into good citizens by giving them the experience of running their own community.[50] It inspired a similar English venture, the Little Commonwealth, founded by George Montagu (later Earl of Sandwich) and run by American

---

[45] Established with funds from John Rockefeller's General Education Board and sustained by further philanthropic donations, the Lincoln School (1917–1940) was intended to test and develop progressive teaching methods. Those involved included former Harvard president Charles Eliot, his protégé Abraham Flexner and Otis W. Caldwell, professor of science education at Teachers College. *The Lincoln School of Teachers College: A Descriptive Booklet* (New York, 1922); Elmer A. Winters, 'Man and his Changing Society: The Textbooks of Harold Rugg', *History of Education Quarterly* 7 (1967), 493–514.

[46] *The Lincoln School*, 7–9.   [47] Young, *Elmhirsts*, 134.

[48] Leonard Elmhirst, *Rabindranath Tagore*, 69.

[49] Joint diary of Dorothy and Leonard, 24 January 1927, DWE/G/S7/D.

[50] J. M. Hall, *Juvenile Reform in the Progressive Era – William R. George and the Junior Republic Movement* (Ithaca, 1971).

educator Homer Lane from 1913 to 1918. In the first well-documented case of alleged institutional child sex abuse in Britain, the Little Commonwealth was shut down after a scandal over Lane's sexual relationship with his female 'citizens'.[51] While the model of self-government at the Junior Republic and Little Commonwealth impressed the Elmhirsts, this scandal was often cited at Dartington and may have influenced Dorothy and Leonard's decision not to make sexual freedom an overt part of their school's agenda.[52]

3.2   Community-Minded Beginnings, 1926–1931

> Is it not possible then to give freedom to the children to try out their own experiment and to build out of the experiment something of permanent value in the very field where we need endless experiments of all kinds? But neither school nor ultimate community can afford to be in water-tight compartments and so each must grow as a vital part of the world around them, the rural or village life in that neighbourhood where they have set up.   Leonard Elmhirst (1925)[53]

In September 1926, a group of twelve met on the Elmhirsts' newly acquired estate for a five-day discussion about setting up the school.[54] The chairman of the group, the adult educator and community development specialist Eduard Lindeman, had been brought over by Dorothy from America specifically to help with planning.[55] The rest of the group was made up of those who would lead the school for the next few years: there were two formally trained teachers, Wyatt Rawson and Marjorie Wise – both had spent time in America, though they were English by birth; the others were workers from the estate, none of whom had

---

[51] Lucy Delap, '"Disgusting Details Which Are Best Forgotten": Disclosures of Child Sexual Abuse in Twentieth-Century Britain', *Journal of British Studies* 57 (2018), 79–107, at 84.

[52] Young, *Elmhirsts*, 134–5.

[53] Leonard to Eduard Lindeman, 7 January 192[4?], box 2, Eduard Lindeman Archives, Columbia University Archives.

[54] Eduard Lindeman, 'Report of meeting held to discuss plans and purposes of Dartington school', 11 September 1926, T/DHS/A/1/A. Those at the meeting including Eduard Lindeman, Marjorie Wise, Maude Ridgen, Wyatt Rawson, Roger Morel, Gustave Heuser, Christian Nielsen, Douglas Watson, Vic Elmhirst, P. W. Woods, Leonard and Dorothy.

[55] Eduard Lindeman, who was closely associated with *The New Republic*, viewed community and group work as vital to maintaining a healthy democracy. He promoted this through practical work, as a community organiser, extension worker and academic teacher, and through writing books including *The Community: An Introduction to the Study of Community Leadership and Organization* (New York, 1921) and *The Meaning of Adult Education* (New York, 1926).

taught before.[56] This reflected the Elmhirsts' intention that Dartington would be an egalitarian community of 'amateur adventurers'.[57] There was to be no division between the school and the estate, nor between teachers and pupils, who were called 'seniors' and 'juniors' and were to share equally in the process of learning.[58]

One of the group's main preoccupations was how to build a school that would be the 'foundation for democratic life'.[59] Following Dewey's ideals – that teaching social precepts apart from practice was 'teaching the child to swim by going through the motions outside the water' – they decided that each pupil must learn to be a good democratic citizen through 'life as an active member of a self-governing commonwealth'.[60] This ideal of self-governance ushered in years of school meetings that would cover everything from 'why have a meeting' to biscuit supplies and rules for swimming safely in the River Dart.[61] Student complaints that there were 'too many meetings' would go unheeded.[62] The principle of participatory democracy extended to the staffing structure; instead of a headmaster, there was to be an education committee with a rotating membership and a series of sub-committees populated by estate employees, making decisions on areas such as student health.[63] This time-consuming mode of direction produced some resentment, particularly since there was a sense that – as one teacher put it – ultimately 'the answers lay with Leonard and Dorothy' anyway.[64]

The planning sessions were also dominated by Leonard's desire to ensure the interrelation of school and the surrounding countryside.[65]

---

[56] Wyatt Rawson was an undergraduate with Leonard at Cambridge. He taught at Brown University in America before moving back to England. Marjorie Wise studied at Columbia University and was recommended to Dorothy by a lecturer at Teachers College. Leonard to Richard Elmhirst, 27 October 1923, LKE/IN/6/I; Young, *Elmhirsts*, 141.

[57] Leonard to Rabindranath Tagore, 10 November 1925, LKE/TAG/9/A.

[58] Young, *Elmhirsts*, 139.

[59] Eduard Lindeman, 'Report of meeting held to discuss plans and purposes of Dartington school', 11 September 1926, T/DHS/A/1/A; Leonard quoted in 'Third meeting to discuss school', September 1926, T/DHS/A/1/A.

[60] John Dewey, *Moral Principles in Education* (Boston, 1909), 14; Leonard, 'Outline of an educational experiment', 1926, T/DHS/A/5/E.

[61] Leonard, 'Second meeting for school', T/DHS/A/1/Al; Book of Juniors' Friday meetings, 1 June 1928–June 1931, T/DHS/A/3/B.

[62] Dorothy's son Whitney Straight, quoted in Dorothy's diary, 25 September 1926, DWE/G/S7/E/7.

[63] Leonard, 'Second meeting for school', T/DHS/A/1/A. Both the Elmhirsts were involved in these committees, which monitored everything from fuel supplies to catering, cleanliness and domestic staff. Household and health committee minutes, from September to December 1927, T/DHS/A/9.

[64] John Wales, 'The present position of the school', 1 March 1930, T/DHS/A/1/C.

[65] Eduard Lindeman, 'Report of meeting held to discuss plans and purposes of Dartington school', 11 September 1926, T/DHS/A/1/A.

He envisaged Dartington, like Siksha-Satra, as a village school for 'the children of parents with moderate means', which would form 'a dynamic centre' for the neighbourhood.[66] Extending Dewey's precept of learning democratic citizenship by practising it, children must learn 'the social and economic responsibility that life demands' by engaging with agriculture and industry.[67] Embedding the school in the rural community was, for the Elmhirsts, part of the process of reversing the general fragmentation of modern society: a way of 'bridging the gap that exists today between education and life'.[68]

When the first six pupils – several of them local – arrived to join Dorothy's own children and a boy from the estate in the autumn of 1926, their accommodation, which was eventually to be around the estate's central courtyard, was unfinished.[69] They lived for the first term with the Elmhirsts at the hall.[70] There were few formal classrooms at this point, and learning was mainly done around the estate or in the summerhouse in the gardens.[71] The Elmhirsts were certain that they wanted pupils' day-to-day existence to be an embodiment of Tagore's ideal of 'life in its completeness' – 'Garden, farm, workshops, weaving, dyeing, carpentry, pottery, exploring (geography and history), map-reading and making, worship, and festival, music, drama, dancing, colour and freedom'.[72] This unitive approach was a Deweyian tilt against 'subjects' dividing the world up arbitrarily – the 'specialization' that, Leonard wrote, 'tends to over run so much of modern life'.[73] What the Elmhirsts were less certain about was the nuts and bolts of teaching.

What emerged, beyond the first prospectus's vague promise to 'release the imagination, to give it wings, to open wide the doors of the mind', was an approach very loosely based on the Dalton Plan. Conceived by Helen Pankhurst in 1920, this was the most popular of several American educational schemes taken up in England in the 1920s; it was adopted by around 1,500 English schools, from West Green Boys' School, a state elementary school in London, to progressive boarding schools including

---

[66] Leonard, 'Prospectus', 1926, T/DHS/A/5/E.
[67] Leonard, 'The school in relation to life', T/DHS/A/1/A.
[68] Leonard, note, [n.d.], DWE/DHS/1.
[69] These were Keith and Mary Ponsford, Michael Preston, Lorna Nixon, Louis Heindinger and Oliver [surname unknown]. Dorothy, diary, 24 September 1926, DWE/G/S7/E/7.
[70] Young, *Elmhirsts*, 130.
[71] Maria de la Iglesia, *Dartington Hall School: Staff Memories of the Early Years* (Exeter, 1996), 14–5.
[72] Leonard to Dorothy, 12 December 1924, LKE/DWE/12/A.
[73] Leonard, 'Situation', September 1927, DWE/DHS/1/F.

3.1 Schoolchildren on the lawn, *c.* 1930 (© Dartington Hall Trust and the Elmgrant Trust)

Frensham Heights and Bedales.[74] Its main dictate was that children should pursue projects by themselves, assisted by their teacher, rather than being taught set lessons as part of a class.

At Dartington, the Dalton Plan was given its own idiosyncratic twist. Following the socially minded example of Siksha-Satra, students were encouraged to pursue three projects at once: one of use to the community, one 'connected with his dominant interest' but still also useful to 'the life of the group as a whole' and one 'which concerns his individual growth'.[75] Unlike in the standard Dalton Plan, pupils could also choose to engage in no learning at all. The projects they did choose to pursue were overseen by a supervisor and could take place in any of the departments of the estate.[76] Some of these projects were conducted with a

---

[74] Selleck, *English Primary Education*; Lesley Fox Lee, 'The Dalton Plan and the Loyal, Capable Intelligent Citizen,' *History of Education* 29 (2000), 129–38; William Boyd and Wyatt Rawson, *The Story of the New Education* (London, 1965), 39.

[75] Leonard, 'Outline of an educational experiment', 1926, T/DHS/A/5/E.

[76] Supervisors were instructed to 'help in relations between Junior and Community; To keep a friendly watch over Junior's welfare; To present a written report once a week to

semblance of a system – Leonard took those who wanted to learn history rambling among local ruins and then encouraged them to give talks on their findings, 'experience replacing textbooks'.[77] More often, however, the inexperienced supervisors were confounded by the task of encouraging students to plot their own educational path in the community. Dorothy, supervising Keith Ponsford, found 'great difficulty in getting him to initiate any suggestions ... his mental indefiniteness is baffling'.[78] The challenging teaching proposition that Dartington School presented – demanding not only dedication to nebulously defined progressive teaching but to the estate and to society at large – explains the rapid staff turnover, with twenty-two teachers passing through the school in its first five years.[79]

Many interwar educators, including Dewey, harked back to a traditional rural life where 'everyone had a pretty direct contact with nature and the simpler forms of industry'.[80] Dartington was unusual in ensuring that children were actually 'in touch with people who are spending their lives and earning their livelihood in a variety of ways and in perfect natural surroundings'.[81] There was regular contact between children and workers through the project system, from life-drawing in the arts department to vegetable-growing on one of the farms.[82] This symbiosis extended into the 'delightfully social' evenings shared by pupils and estate residents. In the course of one week, Dorothy wrote, there was sewing for 'boys as well as girls', dancing classes, chorus singing, boxing, a reading from a life of Buddha by Leonard and a 'thrilling' physiology demonstration by a visiting poultry expert from Cornell.[83] Sunday evening lectures – aimed at all estate personnel – included talks intended to expose pupils to lives different from their own. At one, Dartington's clerk of works described how his father had built his own cottage eighty years before; at another, a film was shown on 'the Miner and his Life'; a third saw Dorothy's friend Ruth Morgan give an eyewitness account of a meeting of the League of Nations.[84]

Recorders' Meeting; To secure a knowledge of the home situation for the Junior and arrange to keep parents informed of the Junior's development'. Minutes of recorders' meetings, 31 October 1927, T/DHS/A/4/B.

[77] Dorothy, note on the school, [1927], T/DHS/A/1/A.
[78] Dorothy, diary, 15 October 1926, DWE/G/S7/E/7.
[79] Stewart and McCann, *Educational Innovators*, vol. 2, 135.
[80] John Dewey quoted in Jay Martin, *The Education of John Dewey* (New York and Chichester, 2002), 10.
[81] Leonard, 'Situation', September 1927, DWE/DHS/1/F.
[82] Leonard, notebook, 'Problems', August 1927, LKE/G/S17/C/23.
[83] Dorothy, note on the school, [1927], T/DHS/A/1/A.
[84] The film was probably Charles Urban's *A Day in the Life of a Coal Miner* (Kineto, 1910); Leonard, 'Report on education experiment, Dartington Hall, September to December, 1926', DWE/DHS/1.

The success in drawing together the school and estate did not extend to the wider neighbourhood. School fees were set relatively low – at £100 per annum they were 'just half the boarding fee of other private schools', wrote Leonard, 'with room I hope for the children of local farmers'.[85] A few local children, such as the offspring of farmer Frank Crook and general factotum Herbert Mills, did attend Dartington. But from the beginning, the intake was skewed in favour of the children of the metropolitan elite. Aside from the issue of cost, this seems to have been to do with local suspicion about the enterprise; even a series of increasingly generous local scholarship schemes was not enough to attract many pupils.[86] Two children were taken away in the first term because of the absence of formal Christian teaching.[87] Locally and further afield, Dartington gained a reputation as a 'hot-bed of vice'.[88]

For a number of interwar progressive educators, reforming attitudes to sex was a central part of pedagogical reform, and of improving society at large.[89] 'What I hope for is that in generations to come this beginning of freedom from artificial sex taboos will ultimately fashion a life-loving world', wrote A. S. Neill.[90] Inspired by Freud, he psychoanalysed students, and his school was renowned for its sexual licence.[91] In their school's prospectus, Dora and Bertrand Russell also promoted complete frankness on the 'anatomical and physiological facts of sex, marriage, parenthood and the bodily functions', with Dora, in particular, seeing the sexually emancipated body as the foundation for a reformed world.[92]

---

[85] Leonard to Rabindranath Tagore, 10 September 1925, LKE/TAG/9/A. His assertion is borne out by the interwar data on school fees collected by W. A. C. Stewart and W. P. McCann (*Educational Innovators*, 315–9).

[86] Scholarships were, at first, offered on an informal case-by-case basis. In 1929, and again in 1944, more official schemes were set up. There was recurrent disagreement over whether scholarships should be offered on the basis of need or of academic merit (Education Committee minutes, 22 February 1929, T/DHS/A/4/C; Punch, *Progressive Retreat*).

[87] Leonard to A. S. Neill, 9 June 1927, LKE/G/24/B; Dorothy, draft statement on religion, included in letter to Leonard, 30 October 1927, DWE/DHS/1/F.

[88] R. A. Edwards, 'Dartington: A report for the Bishop of the Diocese', January 1948, DWE/G/S3/G.

[89] Carla Hustak, 'Love, Sex, and Happiness in Education: The Russells, Beacon Hill School, and Teaching "Sex-Love" in England, 1927–1943', *Journal of the History of Sexuality* 22 (2013), 446–73, at 447.

[90] A. S. Neill, *Summerhill: A Radical Approach to Child Rearing* (New York, 1960), 207, quoted in Sterling Fishman, 'The History of Childhood Sexuality', *Journal of Contemporary History* 17 (1982), 269–283, at 271.

[91] Richard Bailey, *A.S. Neill* (London, 2014); Ray Hemmings, *Fifty Years of Freedom: A Study of the Development of the Ideas of A.S. Neill* (London, 1972).

[92] Deborah Gorman, 'Dora and Bertrand Russell and Beacon Hill School', *The Journal of Bertrand Russell Studies* 25 (2005), 39–76, at 47; Stephen Brooke, 'The Body and Socialism: Dora Russell in the 1920s', *Past & Present* 189 (2005), 147–77.

Their views were echoed in the wider sex reform movement that flourished through the 1920s and 1930s, promoting access to birth control and 'a more enlightened, liberal and consciously modern approach to sexuality' as vital ways to reform society.[93]

The Elmhirsts were less strident than other utopian progressive educationists in expressing their views about sex education and its relation to social reform, but they too attempted to promote freedom and frankness in this area. Dorothy started a 'Question Club' to try to answer children's questions about sex, and some of the school's students were analysed with tools roughly fashioned from Freud.[94] Girls and boys had separate sleeping quarters in the 1920s, but all activities were coeducational, including nude bathing in the Dart. The permissiveness around sex and sexuality at Dartington seems to have discomfited some pupils: interwar students interviewed later recalled 'primitive' sex education and an all-round 'excessive preoccupation with sex', which was only increased by adults' strenuous efforts to be open and natural.[95] There is also a mention in the estate archive of older boys taking advantage of the licence allowed them to prey on younger girls.[96] The fact that this is limited to a single reference may be because it occurred infrequently, but it could also be because it was distressing for victims to mention, or was deliberately suppressed in the records.[97] The Elmhirsts were aware that sex and sexuality was a problem, impacting negatively on pupils' experiences and on the school's reputation, but they did not address this head-on and the unresolved difficulties would resurface forcefully in the 1980s, with tabloid scandals about nude swimming and underage sex.[98]

Leonard was frustrated by the elite bias of the school. He began to complain that the teaching staff did not understand his point of

---

[93] Stephen Brooke, 'Bodies, Sexuality and the "Modernization" of the British Working Classes, 1920s to 1960s', *International Labor and Working-Class History* 69 (2006), 104–122, at 109. See also Ivan Crozier, '"All the World's a Stage": Dora Russell, Norman Haire, and the 1929 London World League for Sexual Reform Congress', *Journal of the History of Sexuality* 12 (2003), 16–37.

[94] Young, *Elmhirsts*, 125, 148; Michael Young, interview with Dartington School ex-pupils, sent to Kay Starr, 11 July 1944, LKE/G/35/A.

[95] Michael Young, interview with Dartington School ex-pupils, sent to Kay Starr, 11 July 1944, LKE/G/35/A; Michael Young quoted in Roland Perry, *The Last of the Cold War Spies: The Life of Michael Straight* (Cambridge, MA, 2005), 28.

[96] Michael Young, interview with Dartington School ex-pupils, sent to Kay Starr, 11 July 1944, LKE/G/35/A.

[97] Delap discusses the way that child sex abuse is or is not recorded in 'Disgusting Details'.

[98] Notebook, Leonard to Gerald Heard, 26 December 1934, LKE/G/ 17; John R. Pfeiffer, Review of Mark Kidel's *Beyond the Classroom*, *Utopian Studies* 2 (1991), 204–7, at 204; David Gribble, *Considering Children* [online edition, davidgribble.co.uk/index.php/books2/books-english, originally published by Dorling Kindersley, 1985], 171–2.

view – that local children on scholarships represented 'all the children of England' and were a more crucial responsibility than the middle-class fee-payers.[99] Yet even as he criticised, the Elmhirsts were shifting their initial conception of Dartington School. To begin with, they had maintained that it should avoid 'providing "luxury" opportunities' so that its model could be copied by every village school (even while Dorothy was furnishing the boarding houses from the fashionable London store Heal's).[100] By 1930, they were allowing that, rather than providing an immediately transferable blueprint, Dartington might be understood as an experimental institution, rather like the Lincoln School. On this basis, it could be justified in having a larger expenditure than the village schools it sought to reform – and perhaps also in being less integrated with the surrounding community.[101] In confirmation that the school was a research centre as well as a model, when it was settled with an endowment in 1930, the sum was divided into the 'cost of ordinary school' and the additional cost of 'experiments in education'.[102]

Leonard admitted to A. S. Neill that 'we are fumbling beginners in the art of meeting children fearlessly on their own ground' – his language reflecting the utopian progressive educationist view that it was children, rather than adults, whose outlook on life was fundamentally right.[103] In spite of this, he was optimistic when it came to drawing up a report after the school's first term. Building a chicken house had 'led directly to intellectual questions, such as those of mathematics, decimals, fractions, areas and cubic contents'.[104] The 'large Staff engaged on Estate and school work' had settled down in a 'spirit of co-operation and sincerity'.[105] Dorothy agreed, writing (apparently with enthusiasm), 'though we have only fifteen pupils they present as many and as interesting problems as if we had a hundred ... how encouraging and splendid it all is'.[106] The school was chaotic; it was not fully integrated with its surroundings; but it seemed to be realising some of the democratic unity of the self-governing rural community. One early pupil, Dougie Hart,

[99] Leonard to Dorothy, 1 November 1927, LKE/DWE/12/E.
[100] Leonard, 'The school in relation to life', 1928, T/DHS/A/1/A. A. S. Neill warned the Elmhirsts that 'you will sooner or later be up against the problem ... the tables or the children? ... It may arise that for the development of his soul a boy must smash a wonderful machine' (4 June 1927, DWE/DHS/2/D). The Heal's furniture did quickly become dilapidated and was not replaced.
[101] Leonard, 'The school in relation to life', 1928, T/DHS/A/1/A.
[102] Education Committee minutes, 28 March 1930, T/DHS/A/4/C.
[103] Leonard to A. S. Neill, 9 June 1927, LKE/G/24/B.
[104] Leonard, 'Report on education experiment, Dartington Hall, September to December, 1926', DWE/DHS/1.
[105] Ibid.   [106] Dorothy to Helen Page, 16 March 1927, DWE/G/8/E.

remembered that he got only a 'little bit of education', but 'a love and respect for the community in general'.[107]

The Elmhirsts sent the prospectus and the first report to their acquaintances across the world.[108] For George Montagu, founder of the Little Commonwealth, Dartington was 'admirable'.[109] Town-planner Patrick Geddes, whose son had worked with Leonard at Sriniketan, wrote that he had discussed the prospectus with American educator Professor Charles Hanford Henderson and with an Indian teacher who had worked at Gandhi's school and the Rousseau Institute in Geneva and they were all three 'without criticism to speak of'.[110] Others, preoccupied with social welfare concerns rather than progressive pedagogy, were more equivocal. Phyllis Potter, a director of the Caldecott Community nursery, which cared for deprived children, criticised the lack of social mission, regretting that Dartington was clearly not 'for the children of the people' when 'so few people are in a position to found a school for these'.[111] Albert Mansbridge, co-founder of the WEA, warned that creating an 'ideal school' was not enough; the Elmhirsts must show 'how you are going to weave it in to the educ[ation] system as it is'.[112]

Dorothy and Leonard pondered these viewpoints, conscious that their experiment was in its early stages. Although they were often asked to contribute articles and give talks on their school, including by the New Education Fellowship's co-founder Beatrice Ensor, they refrained, insisting that 'we are much too near the beginning of things to be able to be of use to anybody else'.[113] Their sense that they were not, on their own, managing to effect the integrated education that they wanted was hinted at by their attempt, in 1929, to recruit Kenneth Lindsay – a young

[107] David Gribble (ed.), *That's All Folks: Dartington Hall School Remembered* (Crediton, 1987), 16.
[108] Leonard, 'Prospectus', 1926, T/DHS/A/5/E and 'Report on education experiment, Dartington Hall, September to December, 1926', DWE/DHS/1.
[109] George Montagu to Leonard, 19 October 1925, T/DHS/A/1/H.
[110] Patrick Geddes to Leonard, 15 January 1926, LKE/IN/6/E.
[111] Phyllis M. Potter to Leonard, 26 October 1925, LKE/G/S4/E. There was a short-lived suggestion of building a Caldecott house on the Dartington estate for 'the real co-education of middle class with "working class" children'. Margery L. Spring Rice to Leonard, 5 February 1929, LKE/G/S4/E.
[112] Albert Mansbridge to Leonard, 10 November [1925?], T/DHS/A/1/H.
[113] Beatrice Ensor to Leonard, 1 June 1926; Leonard to Dorothy Matthews, 16 January 1927, T/DHS/B/10/A. There was some early publicity – Dorothy wrote 'Dartington Hall, Totnes, Devonshire, England' for the *Junior League Magazine* in March 1928 (DWE/DHS/1). There were also non-Elmhirst-sanctioned articles published, including in the *New York Herald Tribune* (April 1926) and the *Western Morning News* (26 and 27 June 1926, February 1927).

Labour politician who had just published *Social Progress and Educational Waste*, advocating national educational reform – to take charge of education at Dartington.[114] As well as the school, the proposition was '300 to 400 working men, 30 to 40 apprentices in from the neighbourhood, rural teachers building up a new kind of secondary education which should unite technical with general and general with social education'.[115] Preoccupied with state policy, Lindsay refused the post. The rejected offer marked the end of the first phase of the Elmhirsts' efforts to fit progressive education with their wider mission of rural regeneration and the beginning of a new era in which pedagogical specialists would shape the direction of the school.

3.3   Years of Crisis, 1928–1931

To begin with, Dartington pupils were conceived as equal partners – or even leaders – in a democratic enterprise. By the late 1920s, however, the sense that the school lacked 'coherence and continuity' was enough to persuade Dorothy and Leonard to bring in educationists and psychologists for advice.[116] This was in line with a general shift on the estate towards importing specialists, and echoed the wider process in Britain in the interwar years by which, as Adrian Woolridge puts it, 'professionalism was gaining the upper hand'.[117] It also signalled a move towards the non-utopian progressive educationist mindset: rather than being able to point adults to a better way of living, children were repositioned as immature beings who needed to be managed by adults.[118] The input of professionals who did not share the Elmhirsts' preoccupation with connecting education and rural regeneration precipitated the school's transition from a group that blended with the rest of the Dartington enterprise into a more conventional educational establishment.

---

[114] Kenneth Lindsay was an admirer of Dorothy's before she met Leonard. He worked at Toynbee Hall, was the first General Secretary of the think-tank Political and Economic Planning, and later an Independent National MP and secretary to the Board of Education. His *Social Progress and Educational Waste: Being a Study of the "Free-Plan" and Scholarship System, etc.* (London, 1926) concluded that the chief barrier to a good education was poverty, and that a new system of secondary schooling was needed that was free and catered for all children based on their desires and the needs of production, rather than just preparing the upper echelons to rule.

[115] Leonard to Kenneth Lindsay, 24 April 1929, LKE/PEP/4/J.

[116] Leonard, 'The school in relation to life', [1928], T/DHS/A/1/A.

[117] Adrian Wooldridge, *Measuring the Mind: Education and Psychology in England, c. 1860–1990* (Cambridge, 1994), 43.

[118] Tisdall, *Progressive Education*, chapter 1.

Among the first experts to arrive were Professor and Mrs Frederick Gordon Bonser, educationists visiting from Teachers College, Columbia University.[119] They approved of Dartington School's philosophy, in which – like many early visitors – they saw an echo of their own ideals. It offered an 'organic unity' of 'all the best that has been discovered, accepted and advocated by the foremost students of psychology and educational theory in recent years'; the Elmhirsts understood that the 'unfolding of forces within the child' was best promoted in a rich natural and social environment and under the stewardship of good teachers.[120] The Bonsers' criticisms were reserved for the way these ideals were being applied. The school staff lacked a proper knowledge of progressive education. Better records should be kept so that the school was 'genuinely scientific'. Although, in theory, a 'more hopeful and satisfying environment could scarcely be imagined' for testing educational philosophies, the interface between the estate and school had not been thought through. Younger students needed purpose-built practical activities that were 'less technical and complex' than those that the commercial enterprises offered. Older students needed more constructive ways to connect 'occupational and community life' with their academic work.[121] The notions that childhood should be decisively separated from adulthood and divided into developmental stages were ones that started to become more common in English pedagogy from the 1930s, and which would be central to mainstream educational progressivism after the Second World War.[122]

Psychological theory was popular among interwar progressive educators: both disciplines, as Wooldridge writes, were based on the assumption 'that the mind to be educated, not the tradition to be transmitted, is the proper starting point of all instruction'.[123] While Leonard was dubious about the current state of psychology – he feared that 'analysed, laid out in front of us in pieces, recorded in files', its subjects tended to become 'pieces of human disintegration' – he thought it had potential to achieve 'positive synthesis' in education.[124] The Elmhirsts imported

[119] Professor Frederick Gordon Bonser was a strong believer in child-centred education and also developed a system of social-industrial education that he propounded in *Industrial Arts for Elementary Schools*, co-written with Lois Coffey Mossman (New York, 1925).
[120] Professor and Mrs Frederick Gordon Bonser, 'Observations and suggestions relative to the educational experiment at Dartington Hall, 1–20 June 1928', T/DHS/A/1/G.
[121] Ibid.   [122] Tisdall, *Progressive Education*, 169 and passim.
[123] Wooldridge, *Measuring the Mind*, 55. For more on the relation between psychology and progressive education, see Mathew Thomson, *Psychological Subjects: Identity, Culture and Health in Twentieth-Century Britain* (Oxford, 2006), 110–31.
[124] Leonard Elmhirst, untitled note, [n.d.], LKE/G/S8/F.

an American child psychologist, Helen Mayers, to report on their school and to see whether it would benefit from employing a psychologist permanently.[125] This was not a success. Mayers reported that she felt she had failed to connect meaningfully with the children. She also pointed out a prevailing insecurity among school staff about what they were supposed to be doing: they lacked a 'central idea' or 'unity of aim'.[126] At the same time, the Bonsers were discouraging the Elmhirsts from using any psychology at all. In an echo of the advice about community-building given by Frederic Bartlett, they declared that in a life 'filled with wholesome, interesting, educational and recreational activities' the emotional side would 'take care of itself'.[127]

Dartington's education committee was deeply puzzled over how to translate experts' advice into practical measures – especially when this advice was conflicting. Should psychology be used or avoided? Should the Bonsers' advocacy of (limited) freedom be followed, or should they obey a report written by the local doctor, warning that freedom was 'not the natural condition of the child' and was giving students 'chronic mental fatigue'?[128] They tried drafting in yet another specialist, Clarice Evans from Teachers College, to help with the process of incorporating expert recommendations, but she merely made the situation worse by using the 'turgid jargon of "child-centred" education', which few understood.[129] The quandary foreshadowed the crisis of confidence in English education in the late 1960s and early 1970s, when a deluge of fashionable theories from progressive educationists and left-wing sociologists, few tested and some mutually incompatible, resulted in widespread uncertainty about how to proceed.[130]

The disorientation was exacerbated by the departure of Marjorie Wise and Wyatt Rawson, the only two of the school staff with any training in education. In 1927, the teachers, both unmarried, had been seen kissing in the garden at Dartington while Leonard and Dorothy were in America. Such affairs were common at Dartington: as Rawson put it, the estate was 'a laboratory – but for life', and the 'private lives' were not

---

[125] Dorothy to Lindeman, 29 January 1930, box 2, Eduard Lindeman Archives; [n.a.], 'Particulars of research with reference to Miss Mayers', [n.d.], DWE/DHS/2/D.

[126] Helen Mayers, 'Memorandum to the Education Committee', 18 November 1929, DWE/DHS/2/D.

[127] Bonsers, 'Observations', T/DHS/A/1/G.

[128] Dr S. R. Williams, 'Observations, criticisms, and suggestions', May 1930, T/DHS/A/1/C.

[129] John Wales, 'Personal note on extant records', September 1973, T/DHS/A/2/F.

[130] Adrian Wooldridge, 'The English State and Educational Theory', in S. J. D. Green and R. C. Whiting (eds.), *The Boundaries of the State in Modern Britain* (Cambridge, 1996), 231–58, at 251.

excluded from the experiment.[131] But not all residents were in favour of such goings-on. The education committee decided to sack the two teachers and, somewhat bizarrely, to appoint the head gardener, P. W. Woods, in their place.[132] On their return, the Elmhirsts persuaded the committee to rescind the decision, but afterwards, frustrated by tensions within the committee and by the absence of a consistent pedagogical line, Rawson and Wise left the school.

In 1929, Rawson moved to London to work for the New Education Fellowship. He continued to receive money from the Elmhirsts, who saw this as a 'natural outgrowth of our own work'.[133] Wise embarked on a survey of Devon village schools, intended to shape Dartington's local engagement and to be of general use to educational reformers.[134] The survey attracted the interest of the Board of Education and the Local Education Authority (LEA), although it was conducted independently of them.[135] Rawson and Wise's activities spoke to Leonard's hope that Dartington could be of use to the wider educational world, but their departure, along with the Elmhirsts' growing preoccupation with other estate departments, meant the school lost momentum. The failure of the self-governing dimension of the Elmhirsts' enterprise had rarely been clearer.

At the same time, there was growing tension on the estate between the school's educational objectives and the for-profit aims of the commercial enterprises around it. Employees resisted having to help with student projects. The managing director of the newly formed company Dartington Hall Ltd demanded efficiency from every department and was hostile to anything that interfered with it. Lacking a strong champion or a certain direction, the school sank 'from the position of being the focus of the whole experiment, to that of a poor and rather disreputable relation'.[136] 'Was there anywhere a clear plan for the school?' its teachers asked. 'Who was really in charge?'[137] Observers who had seen possibilities of social salvation in the school now complained, with some justice, that all the Elmhirsts had to show for their grand ideas was 'a handful of children not larger than many a mid-Victorian family, to whom a staff of master, mistresses, matrons etc. – nearly as large – are (from a decent

[131] Wyatt Rawson to Eduard Lindeman, July 1927, DWE/G/7/C.
[132] Young, *Elmhirsts*, 151.
[133] Rawson worked as NEF founder Beatrice Ensor's assistant. He later became joint director of the English section of the NEF.
[134] Marjorie Wise, *English Village Schools* (London, 1931).
[135] Education Committee minutes, 17 May 1929, T/DHS/A/4/C.
[136] John Wales, 'The present position of the school', 1 March 1930, T/DHS/A/1/C.
[137] Ibid.

modern social or democratic standpoint quite unjustifiably) devoting their lives'.[138]

Dorothy and Leonard resorted to full re-organisation.[139] They separated the school off from the rest of their experiment. Having been housed around the central courtyard, it was now divided into a primary school and a main school (catering for pupils up to the age of eighteen) and moved into new, more distant buildings.[140] Each subject was given its own centre – library, pottery, garden, music, kitchen, laboratory – independent of the estate departments.[141] The greatest change, however, was their decision to appoint a headmaster, 'someone with a name and definite educational status that would be recognised by the outside world'.[142] The appointment of W. B. Curry, after a three-year search for a suitable head, signalled their letting go of the idea of the school as part of a joint, democratic project between children and adults to build an integrated utopia.[143] In the 1930s, ideological debates around the school would turn on a tension that was common in progressive education – between freedom and social responsibility – rather than on how to integrate education with a mission of rural reconstruction. The school's departure from the Elmhirsts' original vision gave fresh impetus to their efforts to use education as a tool of social regeneration outside its bounds.

3.4   Beyond Dartington School: Continuing and State Education

Lawrence Goldman calls the years after the First World War 'climacteric' for adult education, with widespread interest in the subject in government circles and volunteer movements.[144] For both British and American interwar progressives, adult education was one of the tools in

---

[138] William St John Pym, response to 1931 questionnaire, T/PP/P/1/E.

[139] According to Leonard's brother Richard, the Elmhirsts also considered closing down the school entirely at this point. Interview with Michael Young, December 1977, T/HIS/S20/D.

[140] These buildings were called Aller Park and Foxhole. Victor Bonham-Carter, *Dartington Hall: The History of an Experiment* (London, 1958), 50.

[141] Leonard, 'Note on scheme for the re-organisation of the educational departments, Dartington Hall,' 21 July 1928, T/DHS/A/1/A.

[142] Education committee minutes, 23 December 1929, T/DHS/A/4/C.

[143] While the Elmhirsts were finding a head, the school was directed by temporary joint heads, Vic Elmhirst and John Wales. John Wales, 'Personal note on extant records', September 1973, T/DHS/A/2/F.

[144] Lawrence Goldman, *Dons and Workers* (Oxford, 1995), 191, and 'Education as Politics: University Adult Education in England since 1870', *Oxford Review of Education* 25 (1999), 89–101.

the push towards democracy – a 'new means of liberals', as Eduard Lindeman put it in *The New Republic*.[145] To Dorothy and Leonard, it had additional significance as a way of reinvigorating cultural life in the countryside, preventing the departure of young people to towns.[146] But in Leonard's early experience of continuing education – working with the YMCA, the WEA and, briefly in 1919, with the School of Agriculture at Dublin University to prepare soldiers for demobilisation – he had found that while 'every abstruse angle' was covered by lectures, there was little effort to engage with participants or offer them instruction that was practically useful.[147] He felt this was a mode that might suit urban workers, but not rural ones. His ambition in reforming adult education was therefore to uncover an approach specifically suited to country-dwellers: 'the idea has got abroad that by lecturing we pave the road to Paradise', he complained to Henry Morris, whereas he believed rural people learned through 'Passionate perception' – which for him was something akin to Dewey's 'learning by doing', but with the suggestion of emotional, or even spiritual engagement.[148] Leonard also wanted to get beyond the WEA's top-down model to a self-directing mode of educational organisation that would make each village more 'autonomous'.[149] To him, it was not what was studied that mattered so much as how it was studied.

This section considers some of the Elmhirsts' initiatives to make their estate part of an infrastructure for democratic education, while Chapter 4 will look at methods tried at Dartington to evoke 'passionate perception' through the arts. The focus, as in the Elmhirsts' reform-thinking generally, panned gradually outward from making the estate itself a model

[145] Eduard Lindeman, 'Adult education: A new means of liberals', *The New Republic* 54 (1928), 26–9.

[146] The Elmhirsts' hope that education would prevent rural youth migrating into towns was not unusual – it was, for instance, shared by Henry Morris, and by O. E. Baker of US Department of Agriculture (O. E. Baker to Leonard, 19 April 1934, LKE/PEP/1/A).

[147] Leonard, untitled note, October 1946, T/AG ECON/1/B.

[148] Leonard to Henry Morris, 1 July 1934, T/HIS/21/A. The phrase was borrowed from John Maynard Keynes, a close associate of the Elmhirsts, who argued for the cultural responsibility of welfare capitalism 'to furnish those few, who are capable of "passionate perception", with the ingredients of a way of "good life"'. Leonard's interpretation of the phrase was more democratic, implying community growth rather than elite leadership. Maynard Keynes quoted in Alan Sinfield, *Literature, Politics, and Culture in Postwar Britain* (Berkeley; Los Angeles, 1989), 50.

[149] Education committee minutes, 1928–36, LKE/G/S17/C/24. In spite of his reservations about the WEA, Leonard continued to support it, making a large donation during a financial crisis in the organisation in 1932 and being awarded with 'a benedictory duet' from R. H. Tawney and J. J. Allon, the warden of Toynbee Hall, who wrote that 'in the obscurity Dartington Hall is a lighthouse' (J. J. Allon to Leonard, 11 January 1932 and 18 February 1932, LKE/G/22/F).

community to contributing to state-run schemes. In large part, this was because the educational initiatives at Dartington, whilst suggesting new possibilities and echoing broader efforts to shift the adult education model from a paternalistic to a social-democratic one, never coalesced into a coherent alternative scheme to the ones that were already available.[150]

The Elmhirsts' initial intention was that all Dartington's commercial departments would have an educational component organised by their workers, but soon it became clear that profit-making would be a challenge even without this distraction.[151] Education was displaced to the realm of clubs and classes. By 1933, the numerous offerings on the estate, advertised in *News of the Day*, included plumbing, dance technique, shorthand and international relations.[152] Some classes were organised in conjunction with the WEA or LEA, some were based in the nearby town of Totnes, but most were run at Dartington and by its staff. Soon this lively adult education scene began to meet with difficulties. As employee numbers grew, more and more workers lived off the estate and were reluctant to attend classes in the evenings.[153] The relatively small scale of the Dartington community meant that – as journalist H. N. Brailsford found with a group he took for modern history – classes were 'too small, and too varied in age and development, to attain the best results'.[154] Another significant problem was the absence of any overarching ideal or direction in the programme of activities.

From 1931 the Dartington School headmaster W. B. Curry was nominally in charge of adult education, but he was unenthusiastic about the role, refusing to comply with WEA 'red tape' or to let the school, which he saw as a bastion of socialist idealism, be associated too closely with the commercial departments that he thought aimed merely at the 'betterment of their employees'.[155] A plan was drawn up at the Elmhirsts' request by WEA tutor-organiser F. G. Thomas for a workers' council to control adult education, but it was blocked by Curry and the estate's managing director W. K. Slater, on the basis that the workers were not ready for self-government.[156] A suitable democratic structure for adult

[150] Lawrence Goldman, 'Education as Politics: University Adult Education in England since 1870', *Oxford Review of Education* 25 (1999), 89–101.
[151] Leonard to Rathi Tagore, 9 December 1929, LKE/IN/21/B.
[152] Supplement to *News of the Day*, 17 January 1933, T/DHS/B/18/H.
[153] Education committee minutes, 19 February 1930, T/DHS/A/4/C.
[154] H. N. Brailsford, 'For the Dartington Hall Report,' December 1928, DWE/G/1/C.
[155] Letters between W. B. Curry and J. G. Trevena, district secretary of the WEA, 1933, T/DHS/B/9/A; W. B. Curry at Sunday evening meeting, 25 February 1934, LKE/G/13/B.
[156] F. G. Thomas, scheme for workers' council, 25 May 1933, LKE/EDU/2/B.

education was never found. In the absence of any other solution, Dartington's adult classes became the responsibility of the arts department, which ran them chaotically. In the 1940s, a separate, arts-oriented adult education centre was built to serve the local community.[157] This solution, reached in conjunction with the local authority, echoed the short-lived movement led by the newly-formed Arts Council after the Second World War, which aimed to build arts centres in every town in Britain.[158]

The Elmhirsts' second scheme to turn the estate to good account in adult education was to use it for vocational training for school leavers.[159] They thought that the permanent removal of rural youth to universities would 'guarantee the unlikelihood of their returning': 'men of the soil' should be trained in situ, exposed to the 'lore that creeps into the countryman's very bones'.[160] The Education Act of 1918 prescribed the establishment of part-time continuation classes for school leavers, but, as David Parker writes, these remained 'virtual dead letters' in the interwar years because of the economic slump.[161] The few exceptions were the continuation schools supported by private enterprise: one in Rugby, which was dependent on local industry; another at Bournville, built by the Cadbury family.[162] The Elmhirsts experimented with informally setting up 'a kind of continuation school' through a 'part-time earning, part-time learning' apprenticeship scheme with boys from the local villages and the estate school.[163] Without definite rural training of their own, there was concern that 'drudgery and monotony' would settle on village girls and they would 'rebel against country life', so a parallel residential course in domestic science was set up for them, based around running a guest house and a hostel where some of the estate workers

---

[157] Leonard, 'Conclusions from the Dartington experiment', c.1954, LKE/G/S8/1.
[158] Richard Weight, '"Building a New British Culture": The Arts Centre Movement, 1943–53', in Richard Weight and Abigail Beach (eds.), *The Right to Belong: Citizenship and National Identity in Britain, 1930–1960* (London, 1998), 157–80.
[159] The school leaving age was raised to 14 in 1921 as a result of the 1918 Education Act. 'School leavers' tended to be defined as children from the age of 14 to 16.
[160] Leonard, 'Education and the farmer', 25 May 1942, T/AG ECON/3/C.
[161] David H. Parker argues that there was continuing interest in the expansion of practical and vocational education among some Local Education Authorities in spite of the economic slump – as part of an impulse to promote national efficiency. '"The Talent at its Command": The First World War and the Vocational Aspect of Education, 1914–39', *History of Education Quarterly* 35 (1995), 237–59, at 237; G. E. Sherington, 'The 1918 Education Act: Origins, Aims and Development', *British Journal of Educational Studies* 24 (1976), 66–85.
[162] H.W. Bull, 'Industrial Education at Cadbury in the 1930s', *The Vocational Aspect of Education* 94 (1984), 59–62.
[163] Leonard to Douglas Rous Edwardes-Ker, 3 February 1927, LKE/LAND/4/F; Leonard to J. R. Currie, 24 September 1929, T/AG/ECON/1/A.

lived.[164] Its supervisor, Gudrun Larsen, came from Ankerhus College, Denmark's first centre for training domestic teachers.[165]

The girls' course, in particular, was seen as a social experiment as well as an educational one, aiming at 'a democratic mingling of two groups, – the eight girls and the eight or so adult residents' of the hostel, who joined each other for meals and recreation.[166] The hostel's residents disagreed over whether this was a success. Roger Morel, head of the orchards department, thought it made the girls 'all better citizens'.[167] For Leonard's brother Richard, it failed because 'our outlooks and methods of life were so entirely different that both girls and residents could not act spontaneously, and all of us had, with rare exceptions, to force our weekly gatherings until they at last dissolved'.[168] Richard blamed the 'mentality of the girls', which was 'of the subservient village type' and 'a relic of feudal times': 'they had been brought up and educated to give lip-service' and could not adjust to a community of equals.[169] Christian Nielsen, a farmer from Denmark, put the responsibility on the other side, suspecting that the girls 'had the feeling that they were being made the object of study, experimented with, and regarded by us somewhat as curiosities'.[170] What the girls themselves thought is not on record – an example of how muted local and workers' voices are in the Dartington archive. But the apparent discomfort of all concerned reflects the difficulties that progressives across Britain were encountering in trying to live out their theories of social equality.[171]

---

[164] Ruth Morgan, note, [n.d.], DWE/DHS/1; [n.a.], 'Training course in domestic science for girls from fourteen to sixteen years of age', [n.d.], T/AE/1/A; Gudrun Larsen, 'Report on the domestic science training experiment at the Old Parsonage, Dartington, from June 1928 to December 1929', March 1930, T/AE/1/A.

[165] Ankerhus College was set up in 1902 by Magdalene Lauridsen, a pioneering feminist who also founded the innovative Soro School of Home Economics. Folmer Dam, Lauridsen's stepson, was scheduled to visit Dartington, but was ultimately replaced by Gudrun Larsen, who, on the basis of recommendations from Folmer Dam and Peter Manniche of the International High School, was appointed supervisor of girls' training. Folmer Dam to Leonard, 26 July 1926; Leonard to Gudrun Larsen, 9 December 1926, T/AE/1/A.

[166] R. C. Morel, 'The domestic science training experiment at the Old Parsonage, Dartington', March 1930, T/AG ECON/S7/A.

[167] Ibid.

[168] Richard Elmhirst, 'Domestic training experiment, the Old Parsonage, 1928–1930', 6 March 1930, T/AG ECON/S7/A.

[169] Ibid.

[170] Christian Nielsen, 'The domestic science training experiment at the Old Parsonage, Dartington', March 1930, T/AG ECON/S7/A.

[171] Alison Light, *Mrs Woolf and the Servants: The Hidden Heart of Domestic Service* (London, 2007); Seth Koven, 'The "Sticky Sediment" of Daily Life: Radical Domesticity, Revolutionary Christianity, and the Problem of Wealth in Britain from the 1880s to the 1930s', *Representations* 120 (2012), 39–82.

Neither the boys' nor the girls' continuation scheme lasted more than a couple of years. Their closure was blamed on heavy administrative costs and – as so often at Dartington – on the failure to formulate a 'definite policy'.[172] In the 1930s, the Elmhirsts looked to support government initiatives in continuing education rather than to instigate their own. When Leonard visited Rugby, for instance, he was 'delighted' by their continuation school.[173] He wrote to Lord Halifax, president of the Board of Education, pushing for the roll-out of state-supported continuation schools across the country.[174] The Elmhirsts also gave money and equipment to the new South Devon Technical College and supported the County Agricultural Organiser, Colin Ross, who pioneered a model of travelling teaching units for giving instruction to young people in agriculture.[175]

The problem of how best the Elmhirsts could contribute to the wider educational landscape was tied up with interwar debate over the question of rural social control – whether this lay with church or squire, with the local community or the central state.[176] After a 1927 visit to the village school neighbouring the Dartington estate, in a rare use of the traditional terminology of landownership, Leonard complained that it was in a 'disgraceful state' and that it was 'vital to us and especially to me as Lord of the Manor' that it be reformed.[177] The Elmhirsts organised fetes to raise money for rebuilding and tried to arrange for the village school-children to use the estate's facilities to gain practical experience in 'dairying, orcharding, crafts and domestic science'.[178] English education in this period was only loosely directed by central government – Adrian Wooldridge calls it 'a shambles rather than a system' – and in theory the Elmhirsts might have had a strong influence on the village school.[179]

---

[172] Gudrun Larsen, 'Report on the domestic science training experiment at the Old Parsonage, Dartington, from June 1928 to December 1929', March 1930, T/AG ECON/S7/A; Roger Morel, response to 1929 questionnaire, T/PP/P/1/D.
[173] Leonard to Max Nicholson, 12 March 1935, LKE/PEP/3/C.
[174] Leonard to Lord Halifax, 27 March 1935, LKE/DCC/1/B.
[175] R. N. Armfelt to Leonard, 9 June 1932, LKE/DCC/1/B; Lynne Thompson, 'Agricultural Education in the Interwar Years', in Paul Brassley, Jeremy Burchardt and Lynne Thompson (eds.), *The English Countryside Between the Wars: Regeneration or Decline?* (New York, 2006), 53–72.
[176] Jeremy Burchardt, 'State and Society in the English Countryside: The Rural Community Movement 1918–39', *Rural History* 23 (2012), 81–106; Alice Kirke, 'Education in Interwar Rural England: Community, Schooling, and Voluntarism', unpublished PhD thesis, University College London, 2016, introduction.
[177] Leonard to Edgar Fowles, 9 August 1927, LKE/DCC/6/A.
[178] Leonard to Mr Miller, 30 June 1927, LKE/DCC/6/A; Leonard to Anna Bogue, 18 July 1927, DWE/US/2/B.
[179] Wooldridge, 'The English State and Educational Theory', 232–3.

Their efforts, however, were blocked by local hostility, and in particular by a key figure on the school's governing board, the conservative Dartington vicar, J. S. Martin.[180] Leonard was appointed to the village school board in 1935, but his efforts to enact cooperative schemes with the estate were continually stymied by Martin.[181]

In response to the mooted re-organisation of the state secondary school in nearby Totnes, the Elmhirsts proposed setting up a second, state school at Dartington. Two different visions put forward for this school encapsulate another aspect of interwar tension over the locus of rural social control – between the local community and central state.[182] In 1927, Leonard had written that 'the ultimate school is the small one'.[183] Like Tagore, he saw the ideal educational unit as a self-governed 'miniature community'.[184] By 1929, however, he was proposing to the County Council Education Committee a larger, less autonomous model – 'a central rural school at Dartington collecting the 11 plus children from the ten neighbouring villages'.[185] He drew on America for inspiration, pointing in particular to Waterville central school in New York state as 'the high water mark in centralised schools in small country towns in America'.[186] Waterville was inspired by a study of education in New York, which recommended closing down smaller, grass-roots rural schools and building a more efficiently coordinated programme centred on a large high school that would be closely monitored by the government.[187]

The Elmhirsts' offer of Dartington land for a state high school was not taken up in the 1920s. The idea of a new school resurfaced in 1936, when the headmaster W. B. Curry made a push to exclude Dartington's day pupils, by that time numbering about fifty, because their parents,

[180] Leonard to Edgar Fowles, 9 August 1927, LKE/DCC/6/A; Dorothy, note, [1928?], DWE/DHS/1.
[181] For example, J. S. Martin to Leonard, 21 August 1937, LKE/DCC/6/C.
[182] Burchardt, 'State and Society in the English Countryside', 81–106.
[183] Leonard, manuscript note in the margin of a letter from T. E. Johnston, secretary of the Rural Industries Bureau, 10 June 1927, enclosing evidence that it might be economically desirable to centralise the rural school system, C/RIB/1/A.
[184] Leonard, 'Siksha-Satra'.   [185] Leonard to Pitman, 16 October 1929, LKE/DCC/8/A.
[186] Leonard sent information on Waterville Central School to Mr Draper, 14 October 1930, LKE/DCC/8/A.
[187] The study involved Cornell University and a number of state institutions. G. A. Works and others, *Rural School Survey of New York State*, vol. 1, 208–11, cited by Julian E. Butterworth in 'A State Rebuilds the Schools of its Rural Areas: The Central Rural School District of New York', *The Journal of Educational Sociology* 14 (1941), 411–21. See also Tracy L. Stegges, *School, Society, and State: A New Education to Govern Modern America, 1890–1940* (Chicago, 2012), 106–8.

estate workers and locals, tended to want 'greater orthodoxy' and more certification than was on offer.[188] In response, Jean Sutcliffe, a McMillan-trained nursery teacher working at Dartington, suggested setting up a separate, state day school on the estate – but this time one which would 'grow out of the real desires of the working class people' and 'fit the children of the workers in this rural area for the part they should play as adults in the community'.[189] Sutcliffe envisaged this school as a 'centre for the locality', with a hall, workshop, classrooms and library used by adults out-of-hours, 'a grand mixing ground for all types and conditions of people'.[190] Above all, it would not be an 'imposition from above'. It would have an endowment and would initially be overseen by Curry, but 'the community should become more and more responsible' and it would be 'run eventually largely by the workers themselves'.[191]

The Elmhirsts were keen supporters of Henry Morris's village colleges, from which Sutcliffe's plan took its inspiration, but they did not adopt her idea and the day pupils excluded by Curry went to study in Totnes instead.[192] In 1936 the Elmhirsts' offer of land for a school was finally accepted by the Board of Education, but the result was a large, conventional, state-controlled senior school that opened in 1939 where Dartington land bordered Totnes, rather than in the heart of the estate as initially hoped.[193]

The fact that, by 1931, Henry Morris, the county education secretary for Cambridgeshire, saw Dartington as approaching education 'from the intensive psychological point of view', rather than 'dealing with the schools and public services of an actual local government area' was a disappointment to the Elmhirsts.[194] Yet Dorothy and Leonard's lavish sponsorship of Morris's village colleges – a series of state institutions that combined the conventional function of a school with educational, social and cultural functions that served the entire community – suggests that they had dropped the hope of building a model for a locally useful

---

[188] W. B. Curry, untitled statement, June 1936, DWE/DHS/3/A.
[189] Jean Sutcliffe, 'Proposal for the foundation of the day school which might possibly become the nucleus of a social centre for the workers within the Dartington rural development scheme', November 1936, T/DHS/B/18/A.
[190] Ibid.   [191] Ibid.
[192] W. B. Curry, untitled statement, June 1936, DWE/DHS/3/A.
[193] Leonard was appointed to the management committee of the new school and spoke at its opening. 'New Senior School', 25 February 1939, *The Totnes Times and Devon News*, British Library Newspaper Archives.
[194] Henry Morris to Leonard, 25 November 1931, LKE/EDU/10/E.

educational hub themselves. Morris's colleges were intended as centres of community integration and life-long learning that 'a child would enter at three and leave only in extreme old age'.[195] Although they were state-controlled, Morris was keen to emphasise that they were 'not a foreign organisation thrust on the rural community' but 'a union of *local* social services'.[196]

A final education scheme, for rural teachers, was inspired by the Elmhirsts' attendance at a teachers' conference on the estate of the reforming landowner Christopher Turnor in 1925.[197] Five residential courses for teachers were held at Dartington between 1928 and 1933 in conjunction with the Board of Education and the LEA – a demonstration of one type of compromise between centralised/state and local/private control over education.[198] Leonard envisaged teachers coming, not for a discrete academic or agricultural course, but for a holistic experience that would involve the arts and crafts, enlarge their outlook and offer contact with the rural workers they were preparing their students to become.[199] The first course, taught by Professor L. M. Roehl while on sabbatical from Cornell, modelled its aims on the Federal Board of Vocational Education in America, 'enlarging the outlook and improving the teaching of men whose schools are rightly influenced by a marked rural bias'.[200] In a sign of the ongoing negotiation between the government and the private and voluntary sector in the countryside, the teachers' courses ended in the early 1930s amid acrimony over who was in charge of them – the

---

[195] Henry Morris laid out his principles in *The Village College, Being a Memorandum on the Provision of Educational and Social Facilities for the Countryside, with Special Reference to Cambridgeshire*, which appears in Harry Ree, *The Henry Morris Collection* (Cambridge, 1984). Sawston, Bottisham, Linton and Impington Village Colleges opened between 1930 and 1939. They provided the model for many post-war developments in community education, including Countesthorpe Community College. T. Jeffs, *Henry Morris: Village Colleges, Community Education and the Ideal Order* (Nottingham, 1998).

[196] Henry Morris to Jack Pritchard, 3 March 1936, LKE/G/25/D.

[197] Leonard to Christopher Turnor, 22 June 1931, LKE/LAND/2/H.

[198] The courses were jointly funded by the Board of Education, LEA and the Elmhirsts. The first two courses were for Devon teachers, then three bigger courses were held for teachers from the whole of the South West. Teachers training at the University College of the South West also spent time at Dartington, observing the school and nursery. 'Report on short course for rural teachers at Dartington Hall', 10–20 April 1928, T/AE/1/C; Extracts from five essays on Dartington Hall School, written by Exeter University College students who visited in 1934, T/DHS/B/15/A.

[199] Leonard to Mr Howard, 20 December 1927, T/AE/1/C.

[200] Board of Education, South West Division, 'Report on short course for rural teachers at Dartington Hall', 10–20 April 1928, T/AE/1/C. The Federal Board of Vocational Education, set up in 1917, provided federal funds to train those preparing to enter agriculture, industry and home economics.

county authorities or the Elmhirsts – and whether they were relevant to teachers in the state system.[201]

Through the 1930s and into the Second World War, the Elmhirsts continued to look for ways that their estate could be used to reform national education. They suggested Dartington might collaborate with the NEF to survey the country's education system, sent evidence to the Luxmoore Committee on agricultural education and hosted a visit by some of its members.[202] But this period saw the fading of their early hope that the integration of education into their estate's activities would fore-shadow the use of education to reinvigorate rural democratic communities more widely.

The dwindling of this ambition was partly because Dartington School had diverged into another form of progressivism, leaving a hole at the centre of the education project. J. J. Findlay, a professor of education who spent his retirement beginning on a social survey of Dartington, condemned the 'deep cleavage' between Dartington's rural reconstruction work and its 'highbrow' school, whose 'children and teachers could be put into charabancs and transplanted to Kent or Essex without any serious disturbance to the social outlook'.[203] Others agreed that the Elmhirsts had gone astray. Eduard Lindeman advised Dorothy to drop her sponsorship of experimental schools altogether (her philanthropic fund in America supported other progressive institutions including the Lincoln School and the Little Red House School).[204] The Elmhirsts' ideas about educational style had now been sufficiently demonstrated, he argued, and were only benefiting the middle class.[205] They should concentrate instead on how to 'spread the newer methods of education in such a manner as to make them available for all'.[206] While Dartington failed in the 1930s to demonstrate how to integrate education and rural regeneration, W.B. Curry was turning the school into a showcase for a different kind of pedagogy.

[201] Leonard to Fred Gwatkin, 22 November 1932, LKE/LF/15/F; Leonard to L. C. Schiller, 22 May 1952, T/DHS/B/18/C.
[202] W. B. Curry to Dr H. G. Stead, 29 July 1942, T/DHS/B/10/F; 'Evidence to be placed before the Luxmoore Committee by the Dartington Hall Trust', 21 October 1942, C/DHL/5/C.
[203] J. J. Findlay, *The Dartington Community: A Story of Social Achievement*, unfinished manuscript written 1937–9, LKE/G/13/B.
[204] DWE/US/4.
[205] Eduard Lindeman, memorandum on 'Experimental schools and childhood education', 24 June 1932, in 'Agenda for meeting of Committee of Commitments, 14 August 1932', DWE/US/4/A.
[206] Ibid.

3.5 W. B. Curry's 'Modern School', 1931–1945

> A modern school is one which recognizes that the social order must be radically changed if civilization is to survive at all and which also recognizes that education will have perhaps the most difficult and the most important part to play in the changes which must come about.
>
> W. B. Curry (1934)[207]

Dartington's first headmaster, William Burnlee Curry, was a flamboyant, contradictory character. A committed socialist, his extravagances nonetheless included owning two Rolls-Royces, a Bentley and a Hispano-Suiza (later used in the film *The Third Man*).[208] A passionate advocate of individual freedom, he was more inclined in his personal dealings to dictate than to cooperate. He was also a pacifist, atheist and all-round iconoclast who viewed reforming education as essential to avert 'disaster for mankind'.[209] Before he arrived in Devon, he had run Oak Lane Country Day School in Pennsylvania, founded in 1916 by a group of businessmen who wished to apply John Dewey's principles. Curry was tempted back to England by the opportunity that the Elmhirsts offered 'to develop a first-class school, run along modern lines, but much better financed than any other progressive school has been' – the kind of opportunity, he wrote, 'which only occurs about once a century'.[210]

Curry believed that an education that promoted freedom, rational, responsible behaviour, co-operation, respect and love would take the fire out of nationalism and individual competition.[211] It would produce democratic, internationally minded citizens fit to populate 'a cosmopolitan co-operative commonwealth'.[212] He wanted to use Dartington School to demonstrate this to an international progressive elite. Curry's evangelicalism was a long way from the Elmhirsts' sense of their school in the 1920s as a tentative experiment that they hoped 'would demonstrate itself and not have to be talked about'.[213] It was also a far cry from the Elmhirsts' vision of education at Dartington as a motor for local rural

---

[207] W. B. Curry, *The School and a Changing Civilisation* (London, 1934), xii.

[208] Maurice Punch, 'W.B. Curry (1900–1962): A Re-assessment', T/DHS/B/1/I. Many character sketches are given by staff and students in De la Iglesia, *Memories* and Gribble, *That's All Folks*.

[209] W. B. Curry, 'The School', in *News of the Day*, supplement to the 500th number, 13 March 1934, MC/S4/42/F1.

[210] W. B. Curry to Jerome J. Rothschild, one of Oak Lane's trustees, 16 October 1930, T/DHS/B/1/A.

[211] W. B. Curry, 'The School', in Bonham-Carter, *Dartington Hall*, 202.

[212] W. B. Curry, 'The School', in *News of the Day*, supplement to the 500th number, 13 March 1934, MC/S4/42/F1.

[213] Leonard to Sir Henry Lopes, 14 February 1928, LKE/DEV/3/D.

regeneration: they had hoped Dartington School would have 'roots in the neighbourhood', but by 1935 they were reflecting disconsolately that 'at present it tends to root and blossom in Bloomsbury'.[214] As was their usual approach when they brought in experts, however, Dorothy and Leonard gave the new headmaster their full backing, accepting that this was 'the beginning of a new era'.[215] He was 'a great educator' and 'an extraordinarily fine human being', Dorothy wrote. 'Leonard and I simply don't know how to thank our stars for him.'[216]

As a condition of his appointment, Curry had insisted on total control of the school, without interference from the Elmhirsts.[217] On his arrival in 1931, he immediately began to assert this right. He sacked all but two of the old, mostly unqualified staff and brought in American and British teachers. Some had a background in progressive education. Margaret Isherwood, a psychologist and teacher who became one of Dorothy's companions in her spiritual questing, came with him from Oak Lane. Fred Seyd was brought in from Bedales School.[218] Others, like Raymond O'Malley, were recruited directly from university.[219] Curry actively discouraged his employees from mixing with the rest of the estate, asserting that he could see no 'logical connection' between the school and the other departments.[220] A few rebelled: Seyd, for example, insisted on running gym classes for dancers and actors from the arts department.[221] For others, though, Curry's school was the only thing of value on the estate. 'I couldn't throw myself into the larger Dartington', wrote O'Malley, who found it difficult to accommodate his radical left-wing ideas with the estate's wealthy founders and profit-oriented commercial departments. 'I could never get Leonard to do anything but talk *at* me', while Dorothy was unreachably insulated by her wealth.[222]

The architect Oswald Milne had designed a new building, Foxhole, for the school when the Elmhirsts decided to house it away from the main courtyard.[223] Milne's creation resembled a traditional university

[214] Leonard to Frederic Bartlett, 21 May 1935, LKE/G/13/B.
[215] Dorothy to Anna Bogue, 10 April 1932, DWE/US/3/D.   [216] Ibid.
[217] W. B. Curry to Jerome J. Rothschild, 16 October 1930, T/DHS/B/1/A.
[218] Fred Seyd was educated at Bedales and Oxford and then worked at Bedales before joining Dartington. Fred Seyd, 'History', [n.d.], T/DHS/B/31/A.
[219] Cambridge University was a popular source, with three teachers, Raymond O'Malley, David Lack and John Hunter all moving straight from there to Dartington.
[220] Sunday evening meeting, 25 February 1934, LKE/G/13/B.
[221] Beatrice Straight to Fred Seyd, 1 October 1936, T/DHS/B/31/A.
[222] Raymond O'Malley to Michael Young, 5 January 1983, T/HIS/S20/D.
[223] Oswald Milne was a pupil of Edwin Lutyens and one of four architects who designed new buildings for the estate in the 1930s. For more on Dartington's architecture, see Chapter 5.

college – in 'rather feeble, formal neo-Georgian', according to architecture historian Nikolaus Pevsner.[224] For Curry, this traditionalism seemed a 'missed opportunity': he considered progressive education and modernist architecture to 'speak the same language', both 'discarding dogma, taking nothing for granted' and both working with the whole – whether it be the whole child or the whole building.[225] The Swiss-American modernist architect William Lescaze had designed Oak Lane, and Curry persuaded the Elmhirsts to bring him in to plan a headmaster's house and three new boarding houses at Dartington, praising Lescaze's method of 'working from function outwards rather than from façade inwards'.[226] Lescaze's designs for Dartington School were some of the earliest in Britain to be built in the international modern style. While the Devon climate would quickly take its toll on his clean-cut, white cube structures, they were enthusiastically received by the architectural press and helped inspire two visiting educators, Clive and Janet Nield, to set up the modernist progressive Koornong School in Australia.[227] Lescaze went on to be commissioned by the Elmhirsts for a series of other projects including the construction of their estate's central office.

Celia Jenkins characterises New Education as 'pedagogic bricolage' – an eclectic, evolving mixture of ideas and practices.[228] This was reflected in Curry's educational approach, which – like the Elmhirsts' – was defined by no clear, single technique or theory. Many practices stayed the same as before his arrival, albeit running with less 'nervous strain'.[229] The project method continued – one pupil at the school, Michael Young, tried poultry farming, motorcycle repair and market gardening.[230] Student activities remained broad, ranging from pottery and film-making to outdoor swimming and expeditions to Dartmoor and the sea. There

---

[224] Nikolaus Pevsner, *Devon* (Harmondsworth: Penguin, 1989 [1952]), 315.

[225] W. B. Curry, 'Modern Buildings for New Schools', *The Survey* 41 (1931), 496–8, at 497; W. B. Curry to William Lescaze, 19 December 1930, quoted in Gaia Caramellino, *Europe Meets America: William Lescaze, Architect of Modern Housing* (Newcastle, 2016), 134.

[226] W. B. Curry 'The School', 180. Lescaze had an international reputation and his work was included in the renowned 'Modern Architecture: International Exhibition' at the Museum of Modern Art, New York, in 1932.

[227] They were featured in international publications such as *Country Life* 27 (1933), 548–53, *Architectural Record* 75 (1934), 384–5, and *The Architects' Journal* 82 (1935), 477–86. Philip Goad, 'A Chrome Yellow Blackboard with Blue Chalk': New Education and the New Architecture: Modernism at Koornong School', *History of Education* 39 (2010), 731–48, at 735–6.

[228] Celia M. Jenkins, 'New Education and its Emancipatory Interests (1920–1950)', *History of Education* 29 (2000), 139–51, at 149.

[229] W. B. Curry to Margaret Isherwood, 21 March 1932, T/DHS/B/15/C.

[230] Gribble, *That's All Folks*, 12.

were also differences. Curry tried to ensure that his students were insulated from the estate – for example, by running a separate school farm rather than giving them the freedom of the estate's agricultural ventures.[231] Self-government continued, but Curry placed less reliance on the school council than the Elmhirsts had, writing privately that he did not 'believe in self-government to any extent' in schools – the council merely provided a point of view, rather than an ultimate authority.[232] Pupils remembered, anyway, that their headmaster had a 'quasi-dictatorial role' and 'could out-argue anyone ... so he always got his way, regardless of our so-called democracy'.[233]

There were other changes. The classic dilemma for progressive educators was whether to prioritise the freedom or the worldly success of their pupils, since the two aims seemed incompatible.[234] Even so radical a Dartington parent as Aldous Huxley worried that the school would turn his son Matthew into 'a man with the desirable spirit and opinions but lacking in the efficiency required to make that spirit an effective force for good'.[235] Receiving his son's poor report card, Huxley chided Curry that freedom was all very well, but 'no educational system can afford to ignore the facts of the present and probable future social order', in which getting a good job required qualifications.[236]

Curry, in fact, was inclined to agree with Huxley. While he prized liberty, he wanted his students to 'prove to the world that what people considered a crank school could win scholarships to Cambridge'.[237]

---

[231] W. B. Curry, 'The School', 173.

[232] W. B. Curry to Margaret Crallan, 28 October 1936, T/DHS/B/11/D. The councils, in which every pupil and member of staff had an equal vote, still continued to make rules about such subjects as bedtimes, rest, washing and bullying. They also settled disputes, meted out punishments and even instigated experiments with alternative forms of school government. Kidel, *Beyond the Classroom*, 31.

[233] Gribble, *That's All Folks*, 44. Dartington was not unique in this. At the similarly progressive Beacon Hill school, adults also dominated the school council. Bertrand Russell, who founded the school with his wife, recalled that 'there was a pretence of more freedom than in fact existed'. Bertrand Russell, *Autobiography, vol. 2* (London, 1969), 155.

[234] Such tensions, for example, plagued the Cambridge Malting House school, whose parents – mostly intellectuals – found it difficult to come to terms with the implications of their children being raised in total freedom. Shaul Bar-Haim, 'The Liberal Playground: Susan Isaacs, Psychoanalysis and Progressive Education in the Interwar Era', *History of the Human Sciences* 30 (2017), 94–117.

[235] Aldous Huxley to W. B. Curry, 31 December 1934, T/DHS/B/67/B. David Bradshaw gives an account of Huxley's tortured relationship with progressive education in general and Dartington School in particular in 'Huxley and Progressive Education: Daltonism and the Dartington Hall Débâcle', *Aldous Huxley Annual* 15 (2015), 1–20.

[236] Bradshaw, 'Huxley and Progressive Education', 11.

[237] Interview with Leonard, quoted by Maurice Punch in 'W. B. Curry (1900–1962): A Reassessment', T/DHS/B/1/I.

3.2 Children with ponies in the Dart, *c.* 1935 (© Fritz Henle Estate)

The 1932 school prospectus mentioned exams and university preparation for the first time.[238] Under Curry, many students were prepared for
the school certificate, and prepared – as one student remembered – 'in a
conventional way': 'teaching methods lagged considerably behind ideas
on almost every other facet of School society' and children who did not
take the certificate were 'comparatively neglected'.[239] Curry's arrival
signalled a move away from the utopian progressive idea of children at
Dartington – as pure beings who, freed from corrupt adult norms, could
reshape society for the better – and towards a non-utopian conception of

---

[238] W. B. Curry, 'Prospectus', April 1932, T/DHS/A/5/G.
[239] Michael Young, interview with Dartington School ex-pupils, sent to Kay Starr, 11 July
1944, LKE/G/35/A.

children as beings limited by their immaturity and in need of adult educators to guide them to becoming responsible citizens, capable of thriving in the world as it was.

Students who had started at the school in the pre-Curry era regretted the new exam orientation and their separation from the rest of the estate. The school had 'become less of a protest' against the existing order; they were nostalgic for the time when 'it was an experiment: being part of it gave us a sense of being part of something really significant'.[240] The Elmhirsts, too, lamented the rise of 'all those examination aims and ideals which a place like Cambridge dangles in front of the professional headmaster'.[241] The softening of Dartington School's radicalism in the 1930s in favour of a 'sound' education and achieving wider impact reflects what Celia Jenkins finds was a common trajectory among Britain's progressive schools away from the social fringe.[242] Since, in the same period, progressive values were increasingly being adopted in state education, the distinctiveness of independent progressive schools was diminished.[243]

Dartington School nonetheless continued to attract outré idealists who saw society's salvation lying with children. One such was the American proto-eugenicist William Sheldon, who, staying on the estate in 1934, hoped to turn Dartington School into a 'psychological nursery' where children would be categorised through an association of their physiology and psychology.[244] Huxley, who made friends with Sheldon, went on to popularise his categorisation system of 'endomorphs', 'ectomorphs' and 'mesomorphs' through his essays and fiction.[245] Like many progressive educators, Curry was interested in mental testing, which was widely seen as 'the most effective means to prevent the standardization of educational method' by furnishing knowledge of individual needs.[246] At Dartington he regularly used the Stanford–Binet intelligence tests that he brought with him from America. But, disliking the intervention of outsiders in the school, and perhaps put off by Sheldon's messiah-like zeal, he did not try

---

[240] Ibid.   [241] Leonard to Frederic Bartlett, 21 May 1935, LKE/G/13/B.
[242] Celia M. Jenkins, 'The Professional Middle Class and the Social Origins of Progressivism: A Case Study of the New Education Fellowship 1920–1950', unpublished PhD, Institute of Education, University of London, 1989, 169.
[243] For the pervasiveness of progressive values in the state system in the 1930s, see Selleck, *English Primary Education*, and Tisdall, 'Teachers'.
[244] William Sheldon to the Elmhirsts, 1 February 1935, DWE/G/9/E.
[245] L. G. A. Calcraft, 'Aldous Huxley and the Sheldonian Hypothesis,' *Annals of Science* 37 (1980), 657–71; Aldous Huxley, *Island* (London, 2005 [1962]).
[246] William Boyd (ed.), *Towards a New Education: Based on the Fifth World Conference of the New Education Fellowship at Elsinore, Denmark* (London and New York, 1930), 273. See also Wooldridge, *Measuring the Mind*, 207.

out the American's methodology.[247] Sheldon complained to the Elmhirsts, with a frustration frequently echoed among Dartington participants, that Curry had 'utterly incoordinate ambitions' and was 'building for his own ends' not for 'the wider plan that really underlies the thing that he has been entrusted with doing'.[248]

Eugenics lingered at the edges of Dartington School as it did around interwar progressivism more widely – seen as one possible avenue for the improvement of human society.[249] Students were subjected to idiosyncratic intelligence tests developed by biology teacher Raymond Cattell, who went on to write a controversial work of psychology as a research fellow at the Eugenics Society.[250] Another Raymond, the literary critic Raymond Mortimer, thought that since a utopian community like Dartington should be the preserve of a strong and healthy race, 'all subnormal or very odd children' should be excluded from the school because they would 'handicap the place most unfairly'.[251] For retired educator J. J. Findlay, who dedicated his final years to studying Dartington, 'the problems of human "stock"' was 'one of the greatest issues facing mankind'.[252] Under a draft chapter in his survey of the estate headed 'Will Dartington breed true to type?' he bemoaned that 'cultured populations' were in decline because they were more focused on entertainment than reproduction. It would be 'the crowning victory of the Whitney-Elmhirst control if this miasmic atmosphere' could be lifted by 'the clean pure atmosphere of good eugenic family life'.[253] Such sentiments, as well as being an indicator of the dubious types Dartington attracted, show what a diversity of ideas interwar progressivism encompassed. For Curry, however, as for the Elmhirsts, the determinist theories of eugenics were antithetical to progressive education and social progressivism generally – both of which aimed to protect the freedom of the individual.[254] Here, at least, was a point of view that Curry shared with most other members of the wider Dartington project.

---

[247] Although not widely deployed in Britain, intelligence tests had become standard references for interwar American psychologists, especially within the education system. Adrian Wooldridge attributes their popularity in America to the rapidly expanding school population, the heterogeneity of its members and the education system's decentralised structure that called for some method of easy, mass comparison (*Measuring the Mind*, 159–69).
[248] William Sheldon to Leonard, 9 May 1935, DWE/G/9/E.
[249] Chris Renwick, *British Sociology's Lost Biological Roots: A History of Futures Past* (Basingstoke, 2012), especially chapter 2; Michael Freeden, 'Eugenics and Progressive Thought: A Study in Ideological Affinity', *Historical Journal* 22 (1979), 645–71.
[250] Raymond B. Cattell, *The Fight for Our National Intelligence* (London, 1937).
[251] Raymond Mortimer to Dorothy, 30 November 1932, DWE/DHS/2/D.
[252] Findlay, *The Dartington Community*, LKE/G/13/B.   [253] Ibid.
[254] W. B. Curry, 'The School', 203.

3.5.1   W. B. Curry versus the Estate

In his first eight years as headmaster, Curry increased Dartington School from 30 to 200 pupils.[255] Rather than trying to attract locals, he turned it into what one pupil remembered as the 'village school of the Bloomsbury intellectual'.[256] As well as Huxley, parents included Bertrand Russell and Victor Gollancz, Ernst Freud, Barbara Hepworth and Ben Nicholson.[257] Many of them shared Huxley's view that orthodox education was to blame for the lamentable state of society – for 'the newspaper-reading, advertisement-believing, propaganda-swallowing, demagogue-led man – the man who makes modern democracy the farce it is'.[258] It was not only English intellectuals and artists who were catered for. By the later 1930s, the school roster included the children of progressives from sixteen different countries, ranging from refugees from totalitarian regimes in Europe to Etain Kabraji, the daughter of a meteorologist in India.[259] Unlike the Elmhirsts, Curry was comfortable catering to an elite subculture that had already espoused progressive values and wanted to prepare its children for a future of more of the same.

The ease of his task is illustrated by the trajectory of a few of his pupils: Matthew Huxley, son of Aldous, would go on to become an anthropologist; Breon O'Casey, son of playwright Sean O'Casey, joined the artists' colony at St Ives, Cornwall; Susan Williams-Ellis, daughter of architect Sir Clough – designer of the eccentric holiday resort of Portmeirion – started the entrepreneurial Portmeirion Pottery.[260] Ann, daughter of American educator Alexander Meiklejohn – founder of the University of Wisconsin Experimental College – took a doctorate in psychology and joined Berkeley's Institute for Human Development.[261] Etain Kabraji became a teacher at St Paul's School in London.[262] By contrast, the younger children of Frank Crook – among the few Devonian natives still

---

[255] Maurice Punch, 'W.B. Curry (1900–1962): A Re-assessment', T/DHS/B/1/I.

[256] Ex-pupil interviewed for Punch's *Progressive Retreat*, 35.

[257] For more examples of the widespread enthusiasm for educational reform among interwar progressives, see the writing of Bertrand Russell, Anthony Powell, Christopher Isherwood, W. H. Auden and H. G. Wells.

[258] Aldous Huxley, *Proper Studies* (London, 1927), 115.

[259] Etain Todds was sent from India in 1937 by her father, who was a great admirer of Tagore. Author interview with Etain Todds (née Kabraji), 17 May 2015.

[260] Anne Pimlott Baker, 'Ellis, Susan Caroline Williams- (1918–2007)', *Oxford Dictionary of National Biography* (Oxford University Press, Published online 6 January 2011, published in print 7 March 2013) [www.oxforddnb.com/view/article/99216].

[261] The Experimental College (1927–1932) was a self-governing community of students seeking to link Greek democratic values with modern America. Adam R. Nelson, *Education and Democracy: The Meaning of Alexander Meiklejohn, 1872–1964* (Wisconsin, 2001), 144 and 221.

[262] Author interview with Etain Todds (née Kabraji), 17 May 2015.

attending the school in the 1930s – went on to local jobs similar to those that might have been expected of people of their socio-economic background had they not gone to an experimental institution.[263]

Through the 1930s, Curry vigorously promoted the school and its philosophy outside the estate. He lectured on 'Education and Peace' and 'Education and Democracy' everywhere from Hampstead Heath Babies' Club to the WEA and the BBC, and he crossed the Atlantic several times to attract students and 'interpret Dartington for America'.[264] Usually, he refused requests by others wanting to write about the school – 'It is difficult for it not to err in emphasis, if not in fact, if we do not write it ourselves' – and instead he published his own accounts of his pedagogy, most notably *The School and a Changing Civilisation*.[265] By the mid-1930s, he was at the centre of a web of correspondents and visitors: students of education; teachers from as far afield as Sweden and America wanting advice or jobs; parents, including one of an unborn child, wanting guidance on how to bring up their children in a progressive mould.[266] He had succeeded in turning Dartington into a New Education show window and in making himself, as W. A. C. Stewart and W. P. McCann write, 'one of the best-known names in progressive education'.[267] In an indication of the importance of educational reform to progressives more widely, Dartington School also continued to draw interest from idealists from many fields. Those who took up Curry's invitation to give a talk at the school included sociologist Barbara Wootton, art historian Herbert Read, housing consultant Elizabeth Denby and utopian philosopher Karl Mannheim.[268]

While Curry's charisma and energy enriched the school's culture and increased its renown, his domineering personality narrowed down the opportunity for other educational experiments at Dartington, even when these were supported by the Elmhirsts. A case in point was a plan for a

---

[263] Michael Young interview with Mrs Crook, 23 August 1977, T/HIS/S20/D; Herbert Mills, reminiscences, 21 January 1970, LKE/G/31/E.

[264] T/DHS/B/8/A and B; BBC debate, 'The Child, the Parent and the Teacher', broadcast 20 April 1932 and 29 November 1934, T/DHS/B/18/G.

[265] W. B. Curry to Dexter Morand, 1 August 1934, T/DHS/B/18/D; W. B. Curry, *The School*.

[266] Close correspondents included Konni Zilliacus, an internationalist and Labour politician working with the League of Nations in Geneva; his brother, Laurin Zilliacus, a central figure of progressive education in Finland; and Hugh Heckstall-Smith, a Quaker, farmer, agricultural economist and schoolmaster who sent his son, Dick Heckstall-Smith, to Dartington. For many visitors, it was not just Curry's educational policy but his political attitude that impressed. The left-wing author Geoffrey Trease enjoyed the presence of the *Daily Worker* and the *Moscow Weekly News* in the library (Geoffrey Trease to Curry, 16 March 1935, enclosing 'An impression of Dartington Hall', T/DHS/B/2/C).

[267] Stewart and McCann, *Educational Innovators*, 137.   [268] T/AE/4.

new nursery. Dorothy, prompted by the birth of her last children – Ruth in 1926 and Bill in 1929 – wanted to turn the informal nursery that had started in the estate's earliest days into a more substantial and innovative enterprise.[269] Like other reformers, including Dora and Bertrand Russell, Dorothy had visited Margaret and Rachel McMillan's open-air nursery school in Deptford and been impressed by how it brought together child development theory and socialism in a practical project.[270] Dorothy hoped to combine its example with an American model in which higher education institutions such as Teachers College worked closely with schools.[271] To achieve this, she recruited Winifred Harley, an Englishwoman who had been teaching at the Merrill-Palmer School in Detroit, to establish a nursery-cum-department-of-child-development-study at Dartington in order to set higher standards 'percolating through the whole of primary education'.[272] As with the Elmhirsts' deployment of psychologists in the field of socio-spiritual questing, the hope was that this project would achieve the synthesis of academe and practical experience that England lacked, 'bringing together the results of specialists in different fields of study, planning research where it is needed, and passing on scientific knowledge not only to nursery school workers but also to parents in all classes of society'.[273]

Harley arrived in 1931, and by 1932 her nursery had seventeen children and was, she wrote, 'the only one in England definitely incorporating American ideals'.[274] Its innovations included using Merrill-Palmer tests to assess the progress of children – a psychologist at the University of London was set to re-purpose the American material for English use.[275] The experimental nursery was short-lived, however, because

[269] Nancy Astor's 'Ten year plan for children', advocating improved nursery education, is in the Dartington archive, but there is no evidence of her discussing it with the Elmhirsts (LKE/EDU/11/D). Kevin J. Brehony, 'Lady Astor's Campaign for Nursery Schools in Britain, 1930–1939: Attempting to Valorize Cultural Capital in a Male-Dominated Political Field', *History of Education Quarterly* 49 (2009), 196–210.

[270] The institution also trained teachers and nursery nurses and had, since 1919, been supported by the LEA. Dorothy donated £100 to it and remained in contact with Margaret McMillan and E. Stevenson, a teacher at the nursery. Dorothy to Margaret McMillan, 17 November 1927, DWE/DHS/2/D; Pam Jarvis and Betty Liebovich, 'British Nurseries, Head and Heart: McMillan, Owen and the Genesis of the Education/Care Dichotomy', *Women's History Review* 24 (2015), 917–37.

[271] Dorothy to E. Stevenson, 24 February 1928, DWE/DHS/2/D.

[272] The Merrill Palmer School was founded in 1920. As a 'Child Development Laboratory', it offered academic programmes in child development and family functioning and served as a training site and community resource. Winifred Harley, 'The English and American Nursery Schools Contrasted', *New Era*, November 1930, T/DHS/B/15/E.

[273] Ibid.   [274] Winifred Harley to Harvey Walker, 2 June 1932, T/DHS/B/15/G.

[275] Stewart and McCann, *Educational Innovators*, 136.

Harley and Curry were at opposite ends of the spectrum of progressive pedagogy and the Elmhirsts had yielded Curry full control of education on the estate. For Curry, freedom was at the root of education; Harley's concentration on rules, theories and science was anathema to him. A row broke out over Harley's making a 'moral issue of "clean plates at meals"', a policy, Curry wrote, which 'runs counter to the principles upon which I have been trying to build the rest of the school'.[276] He refused to direct the nursery with Harley running it and she was forced to resign.[277]

Curry also resisted efforts by the Elmhirsts and others to re-attach the school to Dartington's wider ambition to promote rural regeneration. He accepted that the education and commercial departments of the estate were both striving to create 'civilised, competent and creative products' for a better world.[278] But he viewed his own stock-in-trade – social values – as superior to the industrial and agricultural departments' material output and saw no reason why he and they should work together. He was unconcerned by his lack of integration with the surrounding community. He did not mind that he had 'no local friends other than those connected with the school' and that 'most of my outside contacts are much further afield, and are mainly in London'.[279] He humorously told friends that the locals thought that his school was 'under the influence of Moscow' and that he was 'the direct agent of the devil' – his response in sharp contrast to the Elmhirsts', who continued to be distressed by their failure to build cooperative relations with their neighbours.[280] He was equally unconcerned by his pupils' insularity. Looking back, many of them remembered an idyllic education, but one that was cut off from the real world and did not prepare them for life.[281] One recalled regarding the neighbouring town of Totnes as 'foreign territory, ordinary and boring'.[282] There was 'a lot of elitism', another remembered, and difficulty, after leaving, in 'finding out what ordinary life was about'.[283] This, for

---

[276] W. B. Curry to Winifred Harley, 10 November 1932, T/DHS/B/15/G.

[277] The nursery continued without Harley's leadership, but along more conventional lines.

[278] W. B. Curry, 'The School', in *News of the Day*, supplement to the 500th number, 13 March 1934, MC/S4/42/F1.

[279] W. B. Curry to Claude Scott, 1 March 1939, T/DHS/B/2/D.   [280] Ibid.

[281] Michael Young, interview with ex-pupils, sent to Kay Starr, 11 July 1944, LKE/G/35/A. Only Clement Freud said he had not been happy: 'no one told us how good the lessons were nor how to work at things one did not like'. Conrad Russell, the youngest son of Bertrand Russell (not in Young's interview) also did not like the school and was moved to Eton instead (Young, *Elmhirsts*, 173).

[282] Author interview with Etain Todds (née Kabraji), 17 May 2015.

[283] Gribble, *That's All Folks*, 32.

Curry, was part of the point – he was preparing elite children for an elite culture, not for 'ordinary' life.

Curry was more outspoken than the Elmhirsts in his support for sexual freedom, insisting that 'sexual ideas and play in children' were normal, amalgamating the boys' and girls' accommodation, and talking frankly to his pupils about sex at every possible opportunity.[284] This approach exacerbated the gossip that already abounded about Dartington School, with one school inspector (who had not actually visited) calling it 'nothing but a brothel'.[285] Dartington Hall Ltd's managing director W. K. Slater complained that the company's potential customers were put off by 'salacious rumour' about the school: its politics – communist; its morality – libertarian; and its religion – non-existent.[286] The sales manager, James Harrison, estimated that the school cost the company £1,000 a year in fees to 'the Editorial Section of the London Press Exchange merely as a defensive measure, to prevent, as far as we can, the Yellow Pages from champing its jaws over sensational tit-bits'.[287] It was not only a case of reduced sales; Curry received numerous complaints from estate workers and locals about vandalism and theft by pupils.[288]

Curry's enthusiasm for sexual freedom extended to his own relationships. In 1935, he began an affair with one of the school's housemothers, Marsie Foss, and then divorced his wife, provoking disapproval across the estate and beyond.[289] A neighbouring villager warned the Elmhirsts that the local vicar and 'a certain MP' were plotting to 'shut the place up'.[290] Gerald Heard, who acted as an informal representative for Dartington in London, reported that people were gossiping about Curry's behaviour in the capital. What was at stake, he said, was the whole cause of progressivism: 'not only would Dartington suffer but liberal education and indeed all liberalism'.[291] To defuse the ill-feeling,

---

[284] W. B. Curry to Dr Susan Isaacs, 1 February 1940, T/DHS/B/22/E; [n.a.], notes from meeting with Leonard, Gerald Heard and Felix Green, 3 or 4 November, LKE/G/17/E; Gribble, *That's All Folks*, passim, De La Iglesia, *Memories*, passim.
[285] Gerald Heard to the Elmhirsts, 2 November 1935, LKE/G/17/E; Marjorie Wise to Dorothy, [n.d.], quoting a conversation with Thyra Smith of Her Majesty's Inspector of Schools, T/DHS/B/15/A.
[286] W.K. Slater, 'Questions for Mr Curry's talk on Sunday 1 March 1936', 25 February 1936, T/DHS/B/18/A.
[287] James Harrison to W. K. Slater, 29 February 1936, T/DHS/B/18/A.
[288] For example, R. S. Lynch to W. B. Curry, 14 June 1937; James Harrison to W. B. Curry, 20 October 1937, T/DHS/B/24/B.
[289] Michael Young notes the furore the divorce caused on the estate (*The Elmhirsts*, 177–9), and there are many agonised reflections scattered through Dartington's archive.
[290] Sydney R. William to the Elmhirsts, 4 July 1935, T/DHS/B/1/H.
[291] Notes from meeting between Leonard, Gerald Heard and Dartington parent Felix Green, November 1935, LKE/G/17/E.

the Elmhirsts asked Curry to justify his views on 'morality, religion, politics' at a Sunday evening meeting.[292] The headmaster gave a spirited defence, arguing that what would suffer if his teaching was curtailed or if he was forced to leave Dartington was the cause of individual freedom.[293] While many on the estate continued to resent him, the Elmhirsts were won over; they were unwilling, anyway, to sack a man who had so successfully led their school. The 'emancipation of parts, or divergence of sub-ends' in the community, Leonard concluded diplomatically, was natural and should not detract from 'the psychological reality of the "common end"'.[294] The incident illustrates how Elmhirsts' tolerance and inclusiveness were at once Dartington's great strength – making it a draw for all kinds of idealists – and its great weakness, since it meant there were few clear shared concepts, beyond a vague ideal of holistic integration, to hold participants together.

3.5.2   The New Education Fellowship and Beyond

Formed at a conference in Calais in 1921, the New Education Fellowship (NEF), with its journal, *Education For the New Era*, was the closest that the often discordant progressive education movement came to having a mouthpiece in the interwar years.[295] Like many reforming organisations between the wars, its ethos was strongly international: its headquarters were in London, but, by 1937, it had branches across America, Europe, Asia and Australasia; and each of the seven conferences it held before the Second World War was in a different country.[296] Curry was closely involved with the NEF until the late 1930s, and his

---

[292] W.K. Slater, 'Questions for Mr Curry's talk on Sunday March 1st, 1936', 25 February 1936, T/DHS/B/18.

[293] Leonard, notebook, July 1936, LKE/G/S17/C/27.

[294] Leonard, untitled note, [n.d], LKE/G/S8/B.

[295] The NEF archives were damaged by an air raid in 1941 and histories of the organisation are in short supply. The most comprehensive account remains *The Story of the New Education* by William Boyd and Wyatt Rawson. More recent studies, focusing on narrower areas, include Kevin J. Brehony, 'A New Education for a New Era: The Contribution of the Conferences of the New Education Fellowship to the Disciplinary Field of Education 1921–1938', *Paedagogica Historica* 40 (2004), 733–55; Jenkins, 'New Education and its Emancipatory Interests' and 'The New Education Fellowship 1920–1950'; Christopher Clews, 'The New Education Fellowship and the Reconstruction of Education: 1945 to 1966', unpublished PhD, University of London, 2009.

[296] Jenkins, 'New Education and its Emancipatory Interests'; Clews, 'Reconstruction', 192; Brehony, 'Conferences', 734.

determination to make Dartington a space for demonstrating its ideas gave the school a new framework when he became headmaster.[297]

In the 1920s, the NEF's pedagogical philosophy aligned quite closely with that of the Elmhirsts. Inspired in part by the theosophical beliefs of its co-founder Beatrice Ensor, the organisation saw an education that was rooted in freedom and holistic fulfilment as the way to access the 'spiritual powers latent in every child' – and, by doing so, to 'create a new world where all might find true happiness'.[298] This was approximately the same as the 'utopian progressives' viewpoint, as Tisdall terms it: that children left to their own devices, preferably in a rural setting, would not only thrive individually but might lead society at large into a better pattern of living.[299] In the 1930s, the NEF moved away from this utopian approach towards one that concentrated more on preparing children for the immediate economic, social and political problems of contemporary society.[300] This reflected a wider sense among progressives of the era that – in part because of the rising threat of fascism – they needed to start grappling with 'real world' problems.[301] The NEF also largely abandoned its spiritual interests in favour of positivism and empiricism, incorporating psychology and mental testing: progressive education became more about assessing children and tailoring their education to suit them than about freeing children completely.[302] Curry bridged the earlier and later phases in the NEF: he saw liberated children as harbingers of a better society, but he was ambivalent about quite how much freedom they should be allowed, and had no interest at all in spirituality.

The English branch of the NEF spanned a wide spectrum: it encompassed marginal progressive schools, often single sex and relatively traditional; moderate progressive schools, retaining orthodox elements – a uniform, emphasis on academic success – but still at the centre of progressivism; and radical progressive schools, including A. S. Neill's Summerhill and Dora and Bertrand Russell's Beacon Hill, whose commitment was less to a particular vision of education than to the freedom

---

[297] For letters relating to W. B. Curry and the New Education Fellowship, see file T/DHS/B/10/C.
[298] Boyd and Rawson, *The Story of the New Education*, 67; Margaret Mathieson, 'English Progressive Educators and the Creative Child', *British Journal of Educational Studies* 38 (1990), 365–80, at 376; Jenkins, 'The New Education Fellowship 1920–1950'.
[299] Tisdall, *Progressive Education*, chapter 1.   [300] Stewart, *Progressives and Radicals*, 362.
[301] Martin Green, *Children of the Sun: A Narrative of 'Decadence' in England after 1918* (London, 1977), 309.
[302] Brehony, 'Conferences', 743; Jenkins, 'The New Education Fellowship 1920–1950', 280.

of the child.[303] Curry identified with the last group, and visits, students, staff and letters of advice were exchanged between Summerhill, Beacon Hill and Dartington through the 1930s.[304] In 1934, the Elmhirsts settled a substantial endowment on Dartington School and Curry was regarded with a certain degree of envy by the Russells and Neill, whose finances were precarious. Kate Russell, who moved from Beacon Hill to Dartington after her parents' divorce in 1932, remembered her 'aston-ishment at the luxury of the place: delicious food, a room to myself, wonderful and plentiful bathrooms ... All that American money made a difference.'[305]

At Dartington, Summerhill and Beacon Hill, lessons were optional and freedom was central. Their heads eschewed the fine distinctions about method that were often the focus of other members of the NEF.[306] Beacon Hill was 'not run on Dalton lines, but in a much freer way'; Dartington was not wedded to any 'organized system'; and at Summerhill children were free 'to live according to their inner nature'.[307] Neill's guiding light was Freudian psychology, and – inspired by Homer Lane of the Little Commonwealth – he often framed his school in terms of a therapeutic community.[308] He was ambivalent about even belonging to the NEF because, as he wrote to Curry, 'You and Dora R[ussell] and I talk a different language from them; we are the only ones who make child psychology the basis of our job. I can't waste my time going to town to hear a lot of bilge about Self gov[ernmen]t and Montessori etc.'[309] He took Curry to task for not 'making psychology nearly important enough. What is happening to your kids' anal-eroticism, hate, destruction, parental complexes, masturbation guilts? My dear lad, I fear me they are repressing em.'[310] Like the Elmhirsts, however, Curry placed his faith in the curative powers of freedom – including

---

[303] Maurice Punch uses this categorisation in *Progressive Retreat*, 9–10. See also Blewitt (ed.), *The Modern Schools Handbook* and L. B. Pekin, *Progressive Schools* (London, 1934).

[304] A. S. Neill to W. B. Curry, 24 January 1936, T/DHS/B/21/C; Peter Cunningham, 'Innovators, Networks and Structures: Towards a Prosography of Progressivism', *History of Education* 30 (2001), 444.

[305] Kate Tait (neé Russell), quoted in Gribble, *That's All Folks*, 30.

[306] A contrast is provided in the pages of *Education for the New Era*, when specific educational methods such as the Project Method, the Dalton Plan, the Winnetka Technique and Platoon Plan are discussed at length.

[307] Dora Russell to F. C. Needles, 7 December 1933, quoted in Gorman, 'Dora and Bertrand Russell', 70; W.B. Curry, 'Prospectus', April 1932, T/DHS/A/5/G; A.S. Neill, *Summerhill: A Radical Approach to Education* (London, 1962), 107.

[308] A. S. Neill, *That Dreadful School* (London, 1937). Neill met Homer Lane while on leave from the army during the First World War (Bailey, *Neill*, 24–5).

[309] A. S. Neill to W. B. Curry, 25 November 1932, T/DHS/B/21/C

[310] A. S. Neill to W. B. Curry, 18 February 1933, T/DHS/B/21/C.

sexual freedom – rather than in actively liberating pupils from their repressions through Freudian psychology.[311]

Curry's pedagogical commitments were more akin to those of the Russells. While Dora and Bertrand dabbled in psychology, in particular behaviourism, they chiefly regarded their educational work as part of a wider project of social reconstruction.[312] Bertrand hoped that progressive education, by encouraging cooperation and giving 'the mental habits required for forming independent opinions', would make democratic, humane and morally responsible citizens.[313] Dora focused on the potential of education to redefine social relations and patterns of authority: 'by rearing a child in a free democratic community, rather than in the restrictions and shelter of his family patterns or under a school autocracy, we will prepare him better for life in the modern world'.[314] Curry venerated Bertrand in particular – there was a Dartington School saying in the 1930s, 'There is no God but Russell and Curry is his prophet' – and he also felt that education was a means to a social end.[315] For him, it was not, as for Neill, primarily about liberating the individual child; it was about liberating the child in order to liberate the world. 'I have never been able to get excited over teaching methods', he wrote – explaining, in part, his school's failure to make much of a mark in the wider history of progressive pedagogy – in his view Dartington's 'pioneering significance' was its social organisation.[316] Neill, the Russells, and to a lesser extent Curry, have come to be identified by historians as 'figureheads of child-centred education' in the interwar years, but in reality, as Laura Tisdall

---

[311] W. B. Curry, *The School*, 28, 31; Maurice Punch, 'W. B. Curry (1900–1962): A Reassessment', T/DHS/B/1/I. Nonetheless, through the 1930s, Curry corresponded on teaching strategy with the educational psychologist and psychoanalyst Susan Isaacs, head of the newly formed department of child development of the University of London and previously a teacher at the experimental Cambridge Malting House school. Isaacs contrasted Curry's approach – 'free from doctrinairism' – favourably with that of Neill and the Russells, who applied psychological theory in a way that she considered 'far too simple to fit the facts'. Isaacs to Curry, 29 May 1934, T/DHS/B/22/B.

[312] Richard F. Kitchener, 'Bertrand Russell's Flirtation with Behaviorism', *Behavior and Philosophy* 32 (2004), 275–91.

[313] Bertrand Russell, *Principles of Social Reconstruction* (London, 1971 [1917]), 144–5; *On Education: Especially in Early Childhood* (London, 1957 [1926]); *Education and the Social Order* (London, 1932). See also Philip Stander, 'Bertrand Russell on the Aims of Education', *The Educational Forum* 38 (1974), 447–56.

[314] Dora Russell, 'Beacon Hill', in Blewitt (ed.), *The Modern Schools Handbook*, 29–42, at 41.

[315] W. B. Curry read Bertrand Russell's *Principles of Social Reconstruction* in 1919, and it fuelled his interest in education and peace, in particular in its emphasis on the necessity of the 'reverence' of those in authority towards the young. Maurice Punch, 'W. B. Curry (1900–1962): A Re-assessment', T/DHS/B/1/I; Young, *Elmhirsts*, 164.

[316] Curry, 'The School', 218.

argues, they were 'positioned outside the mainstream of progressive educational thought', in large part due to this concern with social reform over new educational theories and techniques.[317]

It was because of Curry's focus on the social end-point that the NEF's influence on him did not last. From the mid-1930s, the organisation began to be dominated by more conventional, mainstream educators; a reconsideration of its principles had been triggered, in particular, by the fact that some of them had been adopted to promote fascism in Italy.[318] Curry complained that the NEF had become detached from the bigger picture: it was turning into 'a forum for the exchange of ideas, no matter of what sort', just when the international political situation was worsening and the NEF's earlier role as 'a propagandist body aiming to spread a particular class of ideas' was most essential.[319] It had lost sight of its foundational belief that 'radical changes in education were necessary if there was to be any chance of organising a peaceful world'.[320] Wyatt Rawson, former Dartington teacher and now joint director of the English section of the NEF with Beatrice Ensor, tried to placate Curry by explaining that 'to capture and help transform education throughout the World' the organisation must engage with 'official England', but Curry could not be persuaded of this line.[321]

Instead, as he wrote, he became 'more and more desirous of linking my education work with some such notion as the Wellsian Open Conspiracy'.[322] The idea behind H. G. Wells' influential *The Open Conspiracy: Blue Prints for a World Revolution* was of a loose, decentralised network of individuals, an educated elite, dedicated to bringing about a rational and progressive vision of a world that was 'politically, socially and economically unified'.[323] Like Neill and Bertrand Russell, Curry joined 'The Open Conspiracy Society', set up in 1932 by H. G. Wells and Cyril Joad for 'the demonstration of the inter-relatedness of many progressive causes'.[324] He began putting more and more of his energies

---

[317] Tisdall, 'Teachers', 260.
[318] Jenkins, 'New Education and its Emancipatory Interests', 143; Brehony, 'Conferences', 754.
[319] W. B. Curry to Walter Laffan, 12 November 1936, T/DHS/B/10/D.
[320] W. B. Curry to Miss Soper, 9 December 1936, T/DHS/B/10/D.
[321] Wyatt Rawson to W. B. Curry, 31 October 1932, T/DHS/B/10/B.
[322] W. B. Curry to Lord Allen of Hurtwood, 29 December 1932, T/DHS/B/11/A.
[323] H. G. Wells, *The Open Conspiracy: Blue Prints for a World Revolution* (London, 1928).
[324] Also known as the Progressive League and the Federation of Progressive Societies and Individuals, its members, all called 'vice presidents', included Vera Brittain, Julian and Aldous Huxley, A. S. Neill, Bertrand Russell, Rebecca and Geoffrey West, Leonard Woolf and Barbara Wootton. Curry spoke regularly for the organisation and – in an indication of his winning articulacy – was given its presidency in 1937 on the basis that 'no lecturer who has appeared on our platform has been more appreciated'. Hugh

into this organisation at the expense of the school. The slow-burn project of education no longer seemed to him the most effective vehicle for bringing about urgently needed social and political reform. Detached from the NEF, no longer the focus of its headmaster, in the late 1930s Dartington School sank in importance in the progressive landscape, as, in the late 1920s, it had in the landscape of the estate.

On the eve of the Second World War, Curry stopped innovating at Dartington and stopped lecturing on education. Instead, he joined an assorted group of intellectuals who were convinced that the only solution to militant nationalism was replacing nation-states with a world democratic federation.[325] He devoted his attention to promoting this idea of federal union, both to the general public and to such pacifist groups as the Peace Pledge Union and the World Union of Freethinkers International Congress.[326] In 1939, he published *The Case for Federal Union*, which sold over 100,000 copies in six months.[327] The enthusiasm it aroused was such that a Conservative MP, Harry Selley, tried, unsuccessfully, to get the book suppressed by Parliament.[328]

In the 1920s, Dartington School pupils had a sense of being part of a unique, shared experiment in community-building.[329] In the early 1930s, under the full blast of Curry's attention, they had continued to have a feeling of being at the centre of something of wider importance. Although no longer making a key contribution to building a small utopia in the here-and-now, they were members of a progressive international elite being prepared as leaders for a reformed society of the future. Curry was opposed to federal union or any other political movement being promoted

Leakey to W. B. Curry, 12 October 1937, T/DHS/B/11/D; Lesley A. Hall, '"A City That We Shall Never Find"? The Search for a Community of Fellow Progressive Spirits in the UK between the Wars', *Family & Community* 18 (2015), 24–36.

[325] Federal Union, founded in 1938, had around 10,000 members in Britain by 1940, including Barbara Wootton, Lionel Curtis, Lord Lothian and Lord Beveridge. Andrea Bosco, 'Lothian, Curtis, Kimber and the Federal Union Movement (1938–4)', *Journal of Contemporary History* 23 (1988), 465–502; W. B. Curry, *The Case for Federal Union* (Harmondsworth, 1939), 20.

[326] T/DHS/B/8/A and B.

[327] Curry received a huge array of responses to his book, from Europe and America and as far afield as New Zealand. Most were enthusiastic – including from Norman Angell, Julian Huxley, the Archbishop of York, members of the NEF and a German refugee who advocated everyone learning Esperanto as a way of forwarding the plan. Some objected to Federal Union's oversimplification and lack of economic practicality. T/DHS/B/5/C and D. For the background to federal union, see Mark Minion, 'The Fabian Society and Europe During the 1940s: The Search For a "Socialist Foreign Policy"', *European History Quarterly* 30 (2000), 237–70.

[328] *Hansard Parliamentary Debates*, House of Commons debates, 20 November 1941, vol. 376 (1941), column 506W.

[329] Michael Young, interview with ex-pupils, sent to Kay Starr, 11 July 1944, LKE/G/35/A.

3.3 Evacuees outside one of the Aller Park boarding houses, 1940
(© Dartington Hall Trust and the Elmgrant Trust)

in schools, seeing it as 'anti-educational' to enlist children in causes when their minds should still be 'open and searching'.[330] Nonetheless, his early students picked up on his interest in and optimism about politics, with many joining the Communist Party or becoming pacifists.[331] In the late 1930s, however, with their school detached from the wider landscape of progressive education and with their headmaster mostly either distracted or absent, pupils were affected by 'a mood of fatalistic disillusionment'.[332] Curry returned from campaigning once to find placards saying, 'Down with Federal Union. We want our headmaster'.[333]

3.6   Into the Future

During the Second World War, many parents withdrew their children from Dartington, which was vulnerably close to the Plymouth docks.

---

[330] W. B. Curry, 'The School', 210.
[331] Michael Young, interview with ex-pupils, sent to Kay Starr, 11 July 1944, LKE/G/35/A.
[332] Ibid.   [333] Young, *Elmhirsts*, 183.

There was discussion of evacuating the remainder of the pupils to America or Canada – although in the end the difficulty of organising and paying for this proved too great an obstacle.[334] Instead, the diminished school retreated to a small part of its premises. The three junior boarding houses and upper floor of the school were taken over for military billeting and the classrooms leased to the LEA for use by schools evacuated from London, Gravesend and Plymouth.[335] Many teachers were called up or set to work on the land as conscientious objectors. In response to shortages of labour, an hour of 'useful work' was introduced into students' routine, helping with domestic or farm tasks after breakfast – Curry's school inadvertently taking on an echo of students' community service at Siksha-Satra and at last being integrated with the estate.[336]

In theory, this moment offered another chance for the school's – and Dartington's – progressive education to be shared with a wider base of people. Evacuees and the refugee children from Europe who had trickled into the estate in the 1930s rubbed shoulders with refugee artists and with burned airmen sent to Dartington so that they could walk in the protection of its shady woods.[337] Yet the Elmhirsts were distracted by the war, making a long tour of the United States to drum up support for Britain, and Curry was preoccupied with political campaigning. In place of any active effort to integrate the newcomers, there was a prevailing passive assumption that the refugees and working-class children from the inner cities would thrive simply because they were in a healthy rural environment: Dorothy saw Dartington's 'greatest contribution to the war' as 'the change we have brought about in all the hundreds of evacuee children'.[338] Journalist H. N. Brailsford enthused over children exchanging 'the squalor of their slums' for 'one of the loveliest corners of our island', calling it a 'social experiment of great promise'.[339]

In reality, although some new arrivals found Dartington 'a golden world', others were less happy there.[340] Pupils of Dartington School

---

[334] T/DHS/B/20/C.
[335] Minutes of a trustees meeting, 1 December 1940; Philip Connolly, *Evacuees at Dartington 1940–1945* ([n.p.], 1990).
[336] [n.a.], 'Report to Dartington Hall trustees, January 1941', DWE/DHS/3/A.
[337] The artists included Oskar Kokoschka, an Austrian expressionist painter, and Naum Slutzky, a designer for the Bauhaus. Author interview with Etain Todds (née Kabraiji), 17 May 2015; author interview with Mary Bride Nicholson, 23 June 2016.
[338] Dorothy to Simone Moser, 7 May 1941, DWE/S/2/B.
[339] H. N. Brailsford, 'My American talk', 1941, broadcast in America, DWE/S/2A/C.
[340] Author interview with Etain Todds (née Kabraji), 17 May 2015. One evacuee drowned while swimming in the River Dart and was buried in the Dartington churchyard. Connolly, *Evacuees.*

proper remembered being 'far too self contained and selfish' to mix with the disoriented new arrivals.[341] Dorothy's unsympathetic response to two children who showed a 'refugee mentality' and were 'unprepared to take their share in the daily obligations of the community' was that they should be sent to join the 'less favoured' children at the Totnes day school, which would 'bring them up against reality which they seem unable to face here at Dartington'.[342] The war years, with their national narrative of 'self-sacrifice, social levelling and community spirit', brought the hope that Dartington's ambitions were on their way to being writ large; dissent and uncooperativeness were not part of the programme. Jose Harris's argument that the concept of a socially levelling, solidarity-building British wartime should be taken with a pinch of salt is borne out by this kind of experience at Dartington.[343]

The Second World War, Laura King finds, resulted in an intensification of the (non-utopian progressive) conception of children as 'future citizens, vessels in which to invest' to order to ensure the collective future of Britain.[344] This idea, combined with Labour's victory in 1945, seemed to promise that a reformed, more progressive education would now be made available to all children, preparing them to be part of an enhanced, egalitarian social order.[345] The Elmhirsts and their estate's trustees saw engagement with the process of centralised reconstruction as the way forward for Dartington School – while retaining its 'experimentalism', it should be 'linked as closely as possible with the Devonshire LEA and with the public school systems'.[346] This view was echoed by a new generation of progressive educators who concentrated their energies on state education rather than on autonomous experimental schools.[347]

But W. B. Curry was still at the helm when Dartington emerged from the war – by now a demoralised man who felt that a 'world which appears to be so obstinately uninterested in its own survival is one in

---

[341] Peggy Wales in De la Iglesia, *Memories*, 22.

[342] Dorothy to Mrs Margesson, 16 November 1940, DWE/S/2/A.

[343] Jose Harris, 'War and Social History: Britain and the Home Front during the Second World War', *Contemporary European History* 1 (1992), 17–35, at 17. See also Sonya Rose, *Which People's War? National Identity and Citizenship in Britain 1939–1945* (Oxford, 2003).

[344] Laura King, 'Future Citizens: Cultural and Political Conceptions of Children in Britain, 1930–1950s', *Twentieth Century British History* 27 (2016), 389–411, at 393.

[345] Wooldridge, *Measuring the Mind*, 253; Mathew Thomson, *Lost Freedom: The Landscape of the Child and the British Post-War Settlement* (Oxford, 2013).

[346] Michael Young to the Elmhirsts, 8 May 1944, LKE/G/35/A.

[347] Jenkins, 'The New Education Fellowship 1920–1950', 121; Christopher Clews in 'Reconstruction'; Maurice Ash, *Who Are the Progressives Now?* (London, 1969), 6.

which long-term hopes for our sort of education are hard to sustain'.[348] He refused to engage with the reconstruction of national education and resisted governmental inspection of Dartington School. He argued that it was important to guard educators' independence amid the decline of liberalism and to oppose the 'modern tendency for the tentacles of the state to reach out further'.[349] In the event, the first government inspection of Dartington, carried out in 1950 under the 1944 Education Act, was not particularly critical, merely noting 'a peculiar difficulty about writing a report on this school since its life is determined by ideas about freedom'.[350] Becoming increasingly difficult to work with, Curry was forced by Dartington's trustees to resign in 1957.[351]

It was not until Dr Royston Lambert, a sociologist from Cambridge University, was appointed as Dartington School's headmaster in 1968 that the Elmhirsts' desire for the school to be of use to the wider community was finally realised – albeit on a small scale and not through supporting local regeneration. Lambert had undertaken research for the second Newsom Report, a government investigation that looked into integrating the private school and state school systems, and he hoped to make Dartington School useful to wider society.[352] His most successful scheme linked the school, through student exchanges, with Northcliffe High School in Conisbrough, a deprived coal-mining town in Yorkshire with which Leonard's family had close links.[353] This project became a touchstone for Michael Duane, head of Risinghill Comprehensive School in North London, a rare and short-lived effort to build a radically progressive state school.[354] Lambert started another programme for Dartington School leavers, assisting a village called Scopello in northwest Sicily.[355] While both these initiatives spoke to the Elmhirsts' hopes of integrating their school with wider society, they were hugely costly

---

[348] Bonham-Carter, *Dartington Hall*, 188–9.

[349] W. B. Curry, 'Memorandum concerning inspection', [1949], T/DHS/B/18/C; W. B. Curry to Leonard, 18 May 1938, T/DHS/B/18/A.

[350] Report by H. M. Inspectors on Dartington, 2 September 1950, T/DHS/B/18/C.

[351] Bonham-Carter, *Dartington Hall*, 188–9.

[352] Royston Lambert set out his plans in 'What Dartington Will Do', *New Society* 13 (1969), 159–61.

[353] Kidel, *Beyond the Classroom*, chapter 3; Pat Kitto, *Dartington in Conisbrough* (London, [2010]).

[354] Leila Berg, *Risinghill: Death of a Comprehensive School* (Harmondsworth, [1968] 1974).

[355] Running from 1969 to 1974, the scheme involved Dartington school leavers learning Italian, Sicilian and a craft, then joining ex-Dartington teacher Julian David in running a craft centre in Scopello, promoting rural industries that included knitting, pottery and horticulture. T/DHS/D/12; Kidel, *Beyond the Classroom*, chapter 3.

and not sustainable for an institution that was already running at a significant deficit.[356] In the post-war years, inflation had begun to eat into the school's endowment, starting a process of accumulating financial difficulty that would be one of the reasons for the school's closure in 1987.

The utopian progressive ideal of setting the rising generation free from the corrupt adult status quo – which had been a key inspiration in the foundation of Dartington School – did not thrive in the decades after the Second World War.[357] Instead, the non-utopian progressive movement became central to mainstream education, aiming to give children the most suitable education for each stage of their development in order to fit them to become responsible participants of the welfare state.[358] Much in Dartington's direction of thought, as well as that of other interwar progressive schools, was nonetheless writ large in the post-war reform of the state system: the focus of teaching shifted 'from instructing students about subjects, to recognising students as subjects'; intelligence testing, greater freedom in the classroom and psychoanalytical observation of students were all embraced.[359] The prediction made to the Elmhirsts by Sir Michael Sadler in 1927 that '[f]ifty years from now, the principles you are trying to establish will be recognised as inevitable in education' was not far off the mark.[360] Some of the groundwork for this development was laid in the state sector in the 1930s, but there is little evidence that Dartington and other independent progressive schools were directly significant in influencing government policy.[361]

There were connections. In 1932, the Board of Education's official advisory committee on educational reform, led by Henry Hadow, catechised ex-Dartington teacher Wyatt Rawson about pedagogical practices on the estate and later produced six reports strongly infused with

---

[356] Ivor Stolliday, 'Dartington's Money', unpublished note, 2007 [accessed by courtesy of the author).

[357] The ideal of liberating children completely did crop up again though, in the 1960s and 1970s, with the utopian 'de-schooling' movement, which focused on abolishing schools and bringing education into the community. Tisdall, *Progressive Education*, 223–5.

[358] Tisdall, *Progressive Education*, passim.

[359] Thomson, *Psychological Subjects*, 131; Harold Silver, *Education, Change, and the Policy Process* (London, 1990), 156.

[360] *News of the Day*, 15 December 1927, T/PP/EST/1/001.

[361] Laura Tisdall finds that state-school teachers in the interwar years were often rather more wholehearted in their embrace of progressive, child-centred theory than they were in the 1950s and 1960s, when they felt their position threatened by the 'permissive shift' in society as a whole. 'Teachers', 260 and passim.

New Education philosophy.[362] And when, in 1963, another review of primary education was set up, Michael Young, one of Dartington's pupils and then trustees, sat on the committee. The resultant Plowden Report widened many of the recommendations that Hadow had made – and Dartington had practised – in the 1930s, such as suggesting incorporating child psychology and experiential education into the state system.[363] Overall, however, Dartington School was not a direct progenitor of progressive values in the state system. Nor did the Elmhirsts' aspiration to tie life-long education in with rural regeneration leave a significant practical legacy. The education schemes at Dartington, sitting amid a panoply of utopian ideas and projects in the 1920s and 1930s, nonetheless foreshadowed and helped to temper the state mentality that would embrace some elements of progressive education after the war.

---

[362] Wyatt Rawson to Leonard, 23 October 1932, T/DHS/A/5/C. The six reports produced between 1923 and 1933 by Hadow's committee – whose members included Leonard's acquaintances R. H. Tawney and Albert Mansbridge – were strongly infused with New Education ideas. The most influential reports, *The Education of the Adolescent* (1926) and *The Primary School* (1931), became standard handbooks for teachers. The latter, with strong echoes of Dartington's early educational ideals, introduced the school as 'not a place of compulsory learning, but a community of old and young, engaged in learning by cooperative experiment'. It recommended cross-disciplinary, project-based restructuring of the curriculum in 'closer correlation with the natural movement of children's minds' (*Report of the Consultative Committee on the Primary School* ([n.p.], 1931), xvii).

[363] *Children and Their Primary Schools* (London, 1967), 7.

4   Creativity for All

> [T]he Dance and Mime School, the Music and Drama undertakings at Dartington are not merely spires, finials and crockets, on a super-cowshed and factory farm, but are themselves essential parts of the structure.   Gerald Heard (1934)[1]

For the Elmhirsts, the arts offered a source of unity in an age of specialisation, division and fragmentation. They were 'essential to any completeness' of life.[2] Yet there was considerable divergence in Leonard and Dorothy's understanding of the way the synthesising powers of the arts should be deployed. Leonard believed that the arts should primarily be socially useful. While working with Rabindranath Tagore he had approvingly observed a community in which the arts were integral to the everyday, aiding 'the ultimate perfection of our relationship, first within our own complex personalities, then to one another as well'.[3] Promoting creativity formed part of his overall ambition to regenerate the countryside by making life there as attractive as in the town – if not more so. Beyond their utility as a social unifier, he did not place a high value on the arts; they certainly did not need to be highly accomplished to be useful. Peter Cox, Dartington's arts administrator from 1940 to 1983, thought that if Leonard had not married Dorothy, he would have likely been content to have the arts embodied only in an education department.[4]

Dorothy, meanwhile, following the example of her father – 'a lover of the arts', as she called him, who filled his house with 'Raphaels, Titians,

---

[1] Gerald Heard, 'The Dartington Experiment', *Architectural Review* 449 (1934), 119–22, at 121.
[2] Dorothy, 'My talk in the Barn Theatre on the eve of my departure for Chekhov in America', [1939], DWE/A/15/E.
[3] Leonard, 'Dartington Hall and its department of the arts', [n.d.], LKE/G/S8/C. See also Leonard Elmhirst, 'Personal Memories of Tagore', in Kissoonsingh Hazareesingh (ed.), *A Rich Harvest: The Complete Tagore/Elmhirst Correspondence and Other Writings* (Stanley, Rose-Hill, Mauritius, c.1992).
[4] Michael Young interview with Peter Cox, 24 May 1978, T/HIS/S20/D.

Van Dykes' – became one of England's foremost collectors.[5] Her taste
was for a 'domesticated', English form of modernism: Alfred Wallis's
naïve boats in the Cornish seascape; Christopher Wood's primitivist fruit
and flowers; naturalistic landscapes and still lives by Ben and Winifred
Nicholson before they turned to abstraction in the late 1930s.[6] Such a
synthesis of experimentalism with the local and everyday echoed a wider
'romantic modernism' in England – a contrast to the abstract tendencies
of Continental modernism.[7] While the contents of Dorothy's collection
spoke to the Dartington agenda of combining traditional rural values
with progressivism, her collecting habits followed a conventional patrician mode. She bought through London galleries and, resisting encouragement to open up a public gallery, mostly displayed her acquisitions in
the family's private quarters.[8] Her collecting did not perform a direct
social reform function and overlapped little with the life of the estate.

Yet, in the 1920s, Dorothy also began to see the creative process in
spiritual terms, as a unity-seeking act that should be explored at
Dartington – part of the search for a guiding philosophy for herself and
for society at large. At this point, the professional artist began to take on a
second guise for her, not the distant receiver of patronage, but a spiritual
guide or guru. Once her close involvement with Dartington School came
to an end on the appointment of a headmaster, her main preoccupation
became nurturing professional artists and her own creativity-driven spiritual self-exploration – the latter in the company of the former, insofar
as possible.

Between 1925 and 1945 the Elmhirsts initiated diverse programmes at
Dartington in drama, dance, music, arts education, film, crafts and the

[5] Dorothy, [n.d.], Sunday evening talk, 'Background and foreground – a personal pattern', DWE/S/1/E. Dorothy's sister-in-law, Gertrude Vanderbilt Whitney, was a similarly passionate patron of the arts, as well as a sculptor in her own right, founding the Whitney Museum of American Art in New York in 1931.
[6] Rachel Esther Harrison, 'Dorothy Elmhirst and the Visual Arts at Dartington Hall 1925–1945', unpublished PhD, University of Plymouth, 2002, 76 and 80–1. Dorothy's collection also included work by Frances Hodgkins, Henri Gaudier-Brzeska, Henry Moore, Eric Gill, David Jones, Graham Sutherland, John Piper and Jacob Epstein. Many of the artists she collected were members of the Seven and Five (later, 7 & 5) Society, some of whom spent time at the artist's community in St Ives, Cornwall, fairly close to Dartington.
[7] Alexandra Harris explores the idea of modernism 'coming home' to England in *Romantic Moderns: English Writers, Artists and the Imagination from Virginia Woolf to John Piper* (London, 2010).
[8] H. S. 'Jim' Ede, a collector and a curator at the Tate, encouraged Dorothy to start a gallery. She showed some interest, but the idea never took off. Jim Ede to Dorothy, 11 October 1935, DWE/A/1. The way Dorothy displayed her collection is discussed in Harrison, 'The Visual Arts' and in Peter Cox, *The Arts at Dartington, 1940–1983: A Personal Account* (Exeter, 2005), 142–3.

visual arts to further their unitive visions.[9] This chapter focuses on theatre, dance and the crafts, as the disciplines that were most central to the debates about how the arts could play a part in social reform. The development of the arts department falls into three phases. At the beginning, the community-minded strand dominated. A series of artists arrived – dancers, musicians, potters, painters, mime artists, sculptors – invited by Dorothy, by other people on the estate, or introduced by outside supporters. Some were given grants or salaries, others cheap housing or studios and some nothing more than the opportunity to pursue their art in lively surroundings. In spite of a lack of close definition of their function and terms of engagement, these early arrivals tended to share Leonard's view that the artist should contribute to the immediate community: they organised exhibitions, gave evening classes, taught at the school and offered their designs to estate industries such as furniture-making.

In the early 1930s, the arts department underwent a process of formalisation as part of the push to make Dartington profitable and more replicable by others; this was, in part, a response to the rise of totalitarianism on the Continent, which provoked a feeling that there was an urgent need to offer an alternative social model. An arts administrator was appointed. Chris Martin's values were closer to Dorothy's than to Leonard's – in the sense that he wanted to employ more professional artists and to make the estate a centre of international renown, rather than of a holistically integrated local life. His appointment was an example of how Dorothy's views shaped Dartington, in spite of Leonard's more public leadership. Some of the early artists departed and were replaced by others with more established reputations, many of them refugees from Europe. The new arrivals also hoped their art would promote social unity, but in a more abstract sense that was often related to questions of spiritual transcendence and unity between the arts. They tended to view their ideals as best furthered by their excelling at their own practice and promoting it to a wide audience, rather than by engaging with locals. Their external focus was fuelled by their urgent desire to counteract the influence of the fascist regimes from which they had fled.

With the onset of the Second World War, many of the refugee artists were either interned as aliens or ordered by the government to leave the estate since Dartington was close to the coast and to the Plymouth docks.

[9] An overview of all the arts is given by Victor Bonham-Carter in *Dartington Hall: The Formative Years, 1925–1957* (Dulverton, Somerset, 1970) and Peter Cox, *The Arts at Dartington, 1940-1983: A Personal Account* (Exeter, 2005).

In a third phase, Leonard's notion of the arts as socially useful returned to the fore – this time, however, oriented not to the local community group, but to deploying arts in the construction of the welfare state. The culmination of this was the Elmhirsts' sponsoring of the Arts Enquiry.[10] This large-scale investigation into the state of the visual arts, music and film in England and Wales had a significant influence on government policy in the late 1940s and contributed to Dartington's developing into a hub for arts education after the war.

The Elmhirsts' wealth, connections and enthusiasm meant that their arts department drew in a remarkably rich and varied international line-up: along with British practitioners, artists came from backgrounds as diverse as the Cornish School of Music and the Chicago Little Theatre in America, the German Bauhaus, the Danish International People's College and the *Mingei* ('People's Art') movement in Japan. Many of these artists shared the Elmhirsts' interest in art's unifying potential, but they also brought in new variations on this theme. There was the aspiration to unify the arts themselves and a desire to defend the unity of process, ensuring the craftsman remained in charge of his product from beginning to end. As international politics grew stormy in the 1930s, there were pressing debates over what community art ought to be helping to unify – whether the village, the nation or global humanity. Amid all these various unitive visions, the medieval community was a common touchstone – harking back, as Leonard wrote, to a time when the arts and religion were not 'special subjects', but interwoven with each other and with the everyday, forming 'part and parcel of a way of life'.[11] A second, related inspiration was the nineteenth-century Arts and Crafts movement, which also had wide-ranging dreams about the complete life that could be brought about through the arts.[12] This movement held up the artist-craftsman as a symbol of integration in a fragmenting world, signifying unity of the spirit, heart and hand; of the processes of production; and between community members.[13]

---

[10] The Arts Enquiry, *The Visual Arts: A Report Sponsored by the Dartington Hall Trustees* (London, 1946).

[11] Leonard, 'Talk to Plymouth Playgoers' Circle', 10 March 1935, LKE/G/S8/A.

[12] The deployment of Arts and Crafts ideals by British artists and craftsmen of the early twentieth century is discussed by Tanya Harrod in *The Crafts in Britain in the Twentieth Century* (Yale, 1999) and by Michael Saler in *The Avant-Garde in Interwar England: Medieval Modernism and the London Underground* (New York and Oxford, 1999).

[13] Tom Crook, 'Craft and the Dialogics of Modernity: The Arts and Crafts Movement in Late-Victorian and Edwardian England', *The Journal of Modern Craft* 2 (2009), 17–32; Alan Crawford, 'Ideas and Objects: The Arts and Crafts Movement in Britain', *Design Issues* 13 (1997), 15–26.

4.1 Willi Soukop, possibly with his wife Simone, making a plaster statue, *c.* 1935 (© Fritz Henle Estate)

In spite of a common belief at Dartington that the arts could promote unity, the different visions of how it could do so butted against one another and could not easily be reconciled. These tensions echoed wider debates about the role of creativity in society. In the following chronological survey, each is elaborated on at the point at which it came to the fore at Dartington. The earliest arising was the tension between Dorothy and Leonard's viewpoints, which exemplified a wider debate between modernist 'formalist' art – 'eschewing any wide social or historical meanings in its quest for self-sufficiency' – and avant-garde 'functionalism' that, building on Arts and Crafts ideals, 'worked to restore the medieval integration of art and life'.[14] The second was the tension between the craftsman-controlled, unified production process and more commercially oriented notions of the relation between art and industry – with the latter gradually winning out at Dartington. The third was the question of unifying the art forms themselves, which became central to the shape of the arts department in the 1930s. Also arising mainly in the 1930s, stoked by stormy international politics, there was the issue of the type of community that art was intended to unify: whether it should

[14] Michael Saler's term for the 'functionalists' is 'medieval modernists', in consequence of their desire to restore the integration of the Middle Ages to the present day. *The Avant-Garde*, 5 and 19.

be the local 'folk', the nation, or a harmonious, global society. The difficulty in finding a coherent policy for the arts department meant that – as in other areas – the Elmhirsts gradually gravitated away from making the estate itself a replicable model for how the arts should unite society, and towards it contributing to centralised, government-led initiatives instead. This paralleled a wider dethroning of ideas of elite patronage of the arts in favour of state-sponsored interventions (although this process was always uneven and partial).[15]

The Elmhirsts' experimentation with the arts echoed other efforts to democratise culture – to insist on culture as a shared creation of the everyday imaginative life of the people and the exalted work of a cadre of professional artists. The BBC, for example, aimed to forge a 'culture for democracy'.[16] Like Dartington, some of its participants favoured elite-led 'uplift' – reflected in Director-General John Reith's paternalistic assertion that it was 'better to over-estimate the public mentality than to under-estimate it' – while others wanted to meet popular demand, founding a Listener Research department that aimed to make 'democracy function' by turning the BBC into 'the sympathetic interpreter' of public opinion.[17] More expansively, the history of the arts at Dartington speaks to discussions about the nature of a 'common culture', a conversation in which the Marxist critic Raymond Williams figures large. Born in 1921 in rural Wales, growing up during Dartington's first two decades, and coming to international prominence in the 1950s, Williams dwelt all his life on the same subject that preoccupied the Elmhirsts: the relationship between democracy and culture. He argued that culture was not just the preserve of 'a body of intellectual and imaginative work' – it was 'also and essentially a whole way of life'; and that a 'genuinely common culture' was only possible in the context of democracy, strong community feeling and 'a move towards a more actual and active conception of human beings and relationships'.[18] These were beliefs that Dorothy and Leonard also held, hoping that Dartington could show how culture was – or could become – a shared, unifying part of the everyday life of all people.

[15] Brian Foss, 'Message and Medium: Government Patronage, National Identity and National Culture in Britain, 1939–45', *Oxford Art Journal* 14 (1991), 52–7; *War Paint: Art, War, State and Identity in Britain, 1939–1945* (New Haven, CT and London, 2007), chapter 6.

[16] D. L. LeMahieu, *A Culture for Democracy: Mass Communication and the Cultivated Mind in Britain Between the Wars* (Oxford, 1988), 188–90.

[17] J. C. W. Reith, *Broadcast over Britain* (London, 1924), 34; Scott Anthony, *Public Relations and the Making of Modern Britain: Stephen Tallents and the Birth of a Progressive Media Profession* (Manchester, 2018), 137.

[18] Raymond Williams, *Culture and Society* (London: Vintage, [1958], 2017), 425, 436–7.

4.1   Community-Minded Beginnings

For Leonard, art was an integrating force both psychologically and socially – he saw the arts as 'increasing our own sensitivity in every direction'.[19] It was the socially unifying aspect that he identified as being of most use to Dartington. In the estate's first years, when Dorothy was preoccupied with the school and her own collecting, his desire to promote amateur art prevailed. A rich adult education programme sprang up. The school music teacher, Nevison Robson, ran an estate choir; Erica Inman, the school secretary, started a drama club. By 1930, thirty people belonged to this club, ten to a competing drama group and thirty-five to a singing club.[20] At the estate's Sunday evening meetings, discussion about and performance of the arts featured prominently.[21] Creative pursuits twined into the life of the estate in a typical week:

We have a Dancing class every Tuesday night which is great fun. It consists of the older boys in the school, the school staff, some of the workers on the Estate, the maids in the house, and one or two outsiders .... Then on Wednesday evenings we all sing together in a big chorus .... Here again, the Estate people join us, the farmer, the gardener, etc .... Before Christmas, we, as school staff, have a play, 'The Importance of being Earnest', for all our own people on the Estate.[22]

The socialist dancer and choreographer Margaret Barr embodies the philosophy of these years.[23] Barr ran a professional performing group and gave classes in drama and folk dancing on the Dartington estate and in nearby villages. 'She has all of us dancing,' wrote Dorothy, 'workmen, apprentices, and even the children in the village school'.[24] Barr called her technique of story-telling through movement 'dance-mime' and was clear that its main purpose was community-building: in dance-mime, she wrote, 'each idea sets its own standards – born of the community itself – not projected in from the outside'.[25] In improvisation sessions with amateurs, she encouraged students to elaborate on dramatic incidents she suggested, using 'singing, chanting, elemental sounds' and 'every plastic movement necessary to aid the idea'.[26]

[19] Leonard, 'Dartington Hall and its department of the arts', [n.d.], LKE/G/S8/C.
[20] Education committee minutes, 19 February 1930, T/DHS/A/4/C.
[21] Sunday evening meeting committee minutes, 4 October 1929, T/DHS/A/4/C.
[22] Dorothy to Frances 'Blix' Livingtone, 11 February 1927, DWE/G/7/A.
[23] Born to Anglo-American parents in India, Margaret Barr trained as a dancer in America. She was heavily influenced by the nationalist, modern American dance of Martha Graham. Larraine Nicholas, *Dancing in Utopia: Dartington Hall and its Dancers* (Alton, Hampshire, 2007).
[24] Dorothy to Anna Bogue, 7 October 1930, DWE/US/2/F.
[25] Margaret Barr, 'Dance-Mime Work', November 1933, T/AD/2/B1.
[26] Margaret Barr, 'Spring term report, 1931–1932', T/AD/2/B1.

Even with Barr's professional group, her ambition was to produce art that was connected to ordinary people's lives, contributing to 'the liberation of the workers by means of culture and self-expressiveness'.[27] Her choice of subject tended to be political and cycle-of-life dramas, like *The People*, which criticised contemporary social conditions.[28] Prior to arriving at Dartington, Barr had been at the Cornish School in Seattle, set up by Dorothy's friend Nellie Cornish to promote integrated education in the arts.[29] She brought the ideal of unifying the various art forms into her work at Dartington, where she hoped to create something more vibrant and accessible than was offered by formal theatre – 'a new Theatre-form springing from movement, sound, form, light and colour'.[30] Her performances involved stark, dramatic lighting, emotive scores and dynamic choreography, whose effect was heightened by the use of simple, draped costumes.[31] Barr's sense of the rich possibilities of drama for strengthening community was echoed beyond Dartington, with several interwar government reports presenting drama as a way of honing the cooperation and responsibility required of a good democratic citizen.[32] Barr's activities adhered more closely to Leonard's ideals than Dorothy's, but her intense political viewpoint meant that she never comfortably fitted with either of the Elmhirsts: 'she was too far out – left', one dancer remembered, whereas the Elmhirsts leaned towards the elitist, only-once-the-masses-are-educated school of democracy.[33] Dorothy and Leonard wanted Barr to promote organic social unity at Dartington, but Barr hoped to promote the international solidarity of the proletariat.

Another central figure in this period was the first head of the visual arts, the potter Jane Fox-Strangways, who was passionate about 'trying

[27] [n.a.], 'Report of year's work, Sept 1932-July 1933', T/AD/2/A.
[28] Leonard in transcripts for 'Man Alive', a programme for the BBC transmitted 29 November 1972, editor Adam Clapham, producer Richard Thomas, LKE/G/S13/L.
[29] Established in Seattle 1914 as a music school, the Cornish School expanded to encompass drama, dance and the visual arts, since Nellie Cornish believed that artists were best educated through exposure to all art forms. In 1977, the school was accredited to offer degrees and it continues to the present as the Cornish College of the Arts. Ellen Van Volkenburg Browne and Edward Nordhoff Beck (eds.), *Miss Aunt Nellie: The Autobiography of Nellie C. Cornish* (Seattle, 1964).
[30] Margaret Barr and group to the Elmhirsts, 'General principles', July 1934, T/AD/2/B.
[31] For more on Barr's approach, see Anna Neima, 'The Politics of Community Drama in Interwar England', *Twentieth Century British History* 31 (2019), 170–96.
[32] Harley Granville-Barker quoted in Adult Education Committee, *The Drama in Adult Education. A Report by the Adult Education Committee of the Board of Education, Being Paper No. 6 of the Committee* ([S.I.], HMSO, 1926).
[33] The comment is Paula Morel's, quoted in David Edward Hilton, 'Film and the Dartington Experience', unpublished PhD, University of Plymouth, 2004, 35. Larraine Nicholas discusses Barr's radical politics in *Dancing in Utopia*.

to get people to realise the artistic side of whatever they were doing'.[34] She held regular 'Design and Workmanship' exhibitions. These exhibitions, of 'any portable work done on the Estate by anyone of any age, which has been made with an eye to beauty of design', emphasised that 'craft' could extend even to the act of typing up a letter or polishing boots.[35] Like Barr, her activities were, as David Jeremiah writes, 'tinged with Bauhausian ideas on the unity of the arts' – although they lacked the high-level theorisation of the Bauhaus.[36] Fox-Strangways shared Leonard's belief that art could and should be socially and economically useful. If all were taught creative expression, she wrote, 'artists will no longer be a race apart, and the improvement of commercial design no longer a problem'.[37] The value Fox-Strangways and others in the community put on creativity arising out of daily life echoed the 'New Art' movement that emerged in Britain in the interwar period, inspired by the work of Franz Cižek in Vienna: Cižek saw children, in particular, as possessing a pure creative instinct, and uniquely positioned to make art out of their everyday experience.[38] His ideas influenced English educational reformers, including Christian Schiller and Robin Tanner, who, in the 1930s, emphasised the importance of self-expression in the educational process (for both pupils and teachers).[39] In the 1950s and 1960s, Schiller and Tanner would run teachers' courses at Dartington to encourage a flexible, creative approach to education.[40]

If, in these early years, Barr and Fox-Strangways spoke mostly to Leonard's hope that art could strengthen community, the painter and Bahá'í devotee Mark Tobey supported Dorothy's growing perception of creativity as a source of spiritual succour.[41] Besides pursuing his own art, Tobey gave estate drawing classes, taught at the school, worked with

[34] Education committee minutes, 25 October 1929, T/DHS/A/4/C.
[35] *News of the Day*, 9 October 1928, T/PP/EST/1-8.
[36] David Jeremiah, 'Beautiful Things: Dartington and the Art of the Potter and Weaver', in Tanya Harrod (ed.), *Obscure Objects of Desire: Reviewing the Crafts in the Twentieth Century* (London, 1997), 163–76, at 166.
[37] Jane Fox-Strangways, 'First art studio at Dartington Hall', 1927, T/AAP/3/A.
[38] Laura Tisdall, *A Progressive Education: How Childhood Changed in Mid-Twentieth-Century English and Welsh Schools* (Manchester, 2019), 51–2.
[39] Catherine Burke, 'About Looking: Vision, Transformation, and the Education of the Eye in Discourses of School Renewal Past and Present', *British Educational Research Journal* 36 (2010), 65–82.
[40] DWE/A/3; T/AA/3/B.
[41] Mark Tobey, dubbed 'the Sage of Seattle', came from the Cornish School like Margaret Barr, and was at Dartington from 1931 to 1938. He painted Cubist-style landscapes and still-lives and later became a pioneer in mining traditional Asian culture as a resource for Western modernist art.

Barr's dance-mime school and with a group exploring documentary film.[42] He infused all of this work with his fervent spirituality. One of his teaching methods, for example, was to emphasise the connection between body and spirit and between different art forms by pinning up huge sheets of paper in the studio and asking students 'to experience the whole being making marks with chalk to music'.[43] As well as integrating the material and spiritual worlds, Tobey sought to overcome perceived divisions between the artist and the rest of society. For Tobey, conventional education systems invoked a 'feeling of separateness resulting in specialized avenues of thought'.[44] He was determined that his teaching role was not to make 'artists in the more or less accepted views', but to make his pupils 'better equipped to know of what a real unity is composed – not uniformity – but unity of related parts'.[45]

In the absence of a shared religion or a comprehensive manifesto about what the Elmhirsts were trying to do, art in the 1920s and early 1930s formed the heart of their community. The artists drawn to the estate realised Leonard's ambition to improve society by joining together students, employees and the surrounding villagers in creative endeavour, and Dorothy's to explore spiritual possibilities. The apogee of this period was an outdoor production of Milton's *Comus* in 1929, organised by English-born theatre producer Maurice Browne and American puppeteer Ellen van Volkenburg, both founders of the progressive Chicago Little Theatre.[46] The Elmhirst family, along with other amateurs from the estate, took central roles.[47] The play was helped along by many of Dartington's dancers, musicians and designers. It drew a considerable local audience, who sat cheek-by-jowl with visitors from London and abroad on wooden boards that had been laid out on the lawn.[48]

---

[42] Hilton, 'Film and the Dartington Experience', 35. Beatrice Straight describes the success of Tobey's drawing classes in a letter to Nancy Wilson Ross, 11 October 1935, 156/2, Nancy Wilson Ross Archives.

[43] Martin Sharp, *Michael Chekhov: The Dartington Years* (DVD, Palomino Films, 2002).

[44] Mark Tobey, 'What is an artist?', 10 May 1936, MC/S4/42/F1.

[45] Mark Tobey, 'Paper for reading to first drawing class', 1931, T/AV/1A.

[46] Maurice Browne and Ellen Van Volkenburg were part of the America-wide Little Theatre Movement, established in 1912, which sought to free experimental theatre from the limitations imposed by the need to make money. Browne's play *The Unknown Warrior* was performed to great acclaim in London and at Dartington. The Elmhirsts then backed his subsequent production of R. C. Sherriff's *Journey's End*, one of the few arts endeavours which made them significant money. Donald F. Tingley, 'Ellen Van Volkenburg, Maurice Browne and the Chicago Little Theatre', *Illinois Historical Journal* 80 (1987), 130–46.

[47] *News of the Day*, 24 May 1929, T/PP/EST/1.

[48] Herbert Mills, reminiscences, 21 January 1970, LKE/G/31/E.

Leonard was confident that the play had 'lifted us out of ourselves', giving a utopian 'glimpse of what might be'.[49] Afterwards, the Elmhirsts sent round a questionnaire that summarised their shared hopes for the arts as a source of social and spiritual unity: 'All down the ages the Church has used drama to bring focus to bear on the deeper meaning of life. Do you think drama can yet be made, in any way, an expression of the deeper significance of our life here as a community?'[50] The surviving answers were cautiously optimistic. The teacher Wyatt Rawson thought that, while the estate was establishing itself, 'not much energy can wisely be diverted into such a field', but at the same time thoroughly supported 'the idea of drama (i.e. symbolic action) as an opportunity for common self-expression'.[51]

In these first, experimental years, the Elmhirsts were reluctant to publicise their efforts at using art as a means of community building, just as they were reluctant to commit to working with outside initiatives in the field of education. Dorothy put off a request for an article by Geoffrey Whitworth, founder of the British Drama League, an organisation that also aimed to use drama to strengthen community life. She explained that the process by which professional artists were helping estate workers find 'in dance and drama the imaginative explanation of their lives' was 'still in its infancy'.[52] J. G. Trevena, district secretary to the WEA, who suggested Leonard give a lecture on the arts and adult education, got even shorter shrift. 'Our whole experiment at present is dependent for its success on our keeping our mouths shut in public', Leonard responded in 1927.[53] Before the Elmhirsts' could gain the confidence to begin to publicise, there would be a swing away from early, amateur-oriented ideals, towards professional values and ambitions for recognition on the national and international stage.

4.1.1 Arts and Crafts or Art for Industry?

> In my mind I have defined your estate, its communal, industrial and educational life as a refined and sand-papered microcosm of the world .... I have tried to place the artist in relationship to this microcosm. He is a terrific difficulty ...   William McCance (1929)[54]

For Dorothy, the artist's relationship with the economy was simple: 'great artists' should be sheltered by their patrons – their role was not

---

[49] Leonard, notebook, 14 July 1929, LKE/G/S17/C/23.
[50] Leonard, 1929 questionnaire, 4 November 1929, T/ADR/2/A.
[51] Wyatt Rawson to the Elmhirsts, November 1929, T/DHS/A/5/C.
[52] Dorothy to Geoffrey Whitworth, 25 November 1931, DWE/A/11/C.
[53] Leonard to J. G. Trevena, 3 November 1927, LKE/EDU/1/A.
[54] William McCance to Leonard, 30 January 1929, LKE/G/22/E.

to contribute to the financial well-being of society but to its spiritual or aesthetic health.[55] The Scottish artist William McCance, who considered joining Dartington in 1929, articulated the opposite extreme: the artist was 'a misfit in any commonwealth which is based on utilitarian and economic values, and every commonwealth must be of this nature'.[56] Instead of being 'a dead weight on the young community', McCance thought that the artist must 'drop his artistic identity into the will of common effort' and take up 'ordinary' work 'amongst the actual workmen'.[57] Leonard, while not going quite this far, certainly preferred to think of Dartington as a blueprint for how art could be made integral to the life of every village, rather than a 'rich man's phantasy' of subsidised professionals.[58] He offered McCance a starting post at Dartington as a smithy's apprentice. But McCance did not take it – put off by the prospect of hard graft and by Leonard's warning that 'readiness of tongue might lead you into trouble with a number of practical minded people'.[59] It was a foretaste of how difficult it would be to make the arts a source of profit as well as of social integration.

Dorothy's non-economic viewpoint predominated in the case of the arts proper, but the crafts were a different matter. As a potential part of the commercial side of operations, Leonard saw them as subject to the 'economic yardstick'.[60] In the 1920s, they were carried out on a sufficiently small scale that disagreement over the formalist and functionalist views did not become a central issue; it was understood that they were there as much to expand the horizons of the school's pupils as to create rural jobs. Pottery, the school prospectus declared, would demonstrate 'an art which is directly related to the needs of our life': 'A department definitely engaged in the production of pots for use, as well as in the research that is necessary for building up an old handicraft, can play an

---

[55] Dorothy, 'The arts at Dartington', 21 February 1950, DWE/A/4/E.
[56] William McCance to Leonard, 30 January 1929, LKE/G/22/E. McCance, painter, teacher and art critic, worked in Wales for the Gregynog Press but flirted with the idea of moving to Dartington. The ambitions of Gregynog founders Gwendoline and Margaret Davies bore a notable resemblance to those of the Elmhirsts: they wanted their estate to become both an arts community and a centre for social improvement. Dorothy A. Harrop, *A History of the Gregynog Press* (Middlesex, 1980).
[57] William McCance to Leonard, 30 January 1929, LKE/G/22/E.
[58] Leonard, note on Dartington's financial structure, January 1931, LKE/G/S11A.
[59] William McCance to Leonard, 30 January 1929 and Leonard to McCance, 6 March 1929, LKE/G/22/E.
[60] Bernard Leach to Leonard, 6 December 1932, T/AAP/3/A2.

important part in the following out of our ideal of education.'[61] In the 1930s, however, tensions grew. With the appointment of a managing director to oversee the tightening of estate finances, there was a schism between those who envisaged artist-craftsmen as industrial technicians and those who saw them as the last bastion against the advance of mechanised industry and mechanised, economics-driven life in general.

Of the main three crafts on the estate, furniture-making was reasonably lucrative, while the weaving enterprise and pottery – discussed here – both continuously lost money and therefore became battlegrounds between those who saw financial success as a sine qua non and those who thought the arts should be free from economic pressure. As a side note, in spite of the strong feminist engagement with the crafts in inter-war Britain, explored by Lucy Delap and Zoë Thomas, at Dartington the crafts remained a peculiarly male province – evidence that, in spite of the sexual experimentation on the estate, gender politics remained relatively conservative.[62] This predominance of men is reflected in the language of the following.

Arguments over the position of the artist-craftsman at Dartington spoke to other efforts to adapt Arts and Crafts ideals to the conditions of the twentieth century, both in Britain and further afield.[63] Potter Bernard Leach, for instance, who joined Dartington in 1932, was a member of the Japanese White Birch Group, a coterie of artists and intellectuals who were inspired by, among others, William Morris and Rabindranath Tagore, and who were concerned with the preservation of creativity in labour.[64] The group set up Atarashiki Mura (the 'New Village') in southern Japan in 1918, an experimental community combining the arts and agriculture on a smaller scale but in a similar fashion to Dartington.[65] Leach also had close links with the crafts community at

---

[61] [n.a.], untitled note on the school 'as an extension of our statement in the prospectus', [n.d.], T/DHS/A/1/A.

[62] Lucy Delap, *The Feminist Avant-Garde: Transatlantic Encounters of the Early Twentieth Century* (Cambridge, 2007), chapter 6; Zoë Thomas, *Women Art Workers and the Arts and Crafts Movement* (Manchester, 2020). The weaver Elizabeth Peacock created a series of banners for the Dartington Great Hall between 1933 and 1938, representing each department of the estate. But her stay in the community was very brief and she was largely based at Ditchling when making these banners.

[63] Harrod, *Crafts in the Twentieth Century*, 95 and chapter 3; Saler, *The Avant-Garde*, passim.

[64] Tessa Morris-Suzuki, 'Beyond Utopia: New Villages and Living Politics in Modern Japan and Across Frontiers', *History Workshop Journal* 85 (2018), 47–71. Bernard Leach first met the Elmhirsts in 1925. He kept his own workshop in Cornwall running under a series of deputies at the same time as setting up a studio at Dartington.

[65] Anna Neima, *The Utopians: Six Attempts to Build the Perfect Society* (London, 2021), chapter 2.

Ditchling in Sussex, where the weaver Ethel Mairet, calligrapher Edward
Johnston, sculptor Eric Gill and others aimed to demonstrate a unified
craft community along Morrisian lines.[66] At Ditchling and Atarashiki
Mura, the objective was integration – of the creative process with the
economic, the spiritual with the material, the individual with the community. Gill complained that the lack of creativity permitted to factory
workmen meant that they became 'obedient tools, ants rather than
men'.[67] Leach agreed: the craft tradition alone represented the 'unifying
culture out of which fresh traditions can grow'; it was the counterbalance
to all the objectionable divisions in modern society – the rupture between
work and leisure, craftsmanship and industry, art and religion, East
and West.[68]

This strand of thinking wove through interwar British social and
economic thought – but it was not uncontested. For some reformers,
the way to heal the rifts generated by industrialisation was not to escape
to a craft utopia, but to 'spiritualize capitalism' with art.[69] As Michael
Saler finds, London Transport manager Frank Pick thought the 'transcendent spirit of art' could restore a moral dimension to capitalist
society.[70] He commissioned Edward Johnston of Ditchling to draw up
a London Transport alphabet and sought out artists and architects to
design posters and stations that would integrate good design with the
everyday.[71] The economic slump of the 1930s gave fresh impetus to such
efforts: artists, pushed into poverty, were forced to diversify into industry
and commercial activity.[72]

The government, too, came to see the lack of integration between
design and industry as a significant factor in exacerbating Britain's economic difficulties. In 1934, it set up the Council for Art and Industry to
improve design in the products of industry, making Frank Pick the first
chairman.[73] There was, however, ambiguity over how the crafts fitted
into this organisation: for some, the council was intended to incorporate
hand-makers; for others – including the refugee Bauhaus founder Walter
Gropius – it should stand for the success of a brave new world of

[66] Emmanuel Cooper, *Bernard Leach: Life & Work* (New Haven, CT and London, 2003).
[67] Eric Gill, *Art and a Changing Civilisation* (London, 1934), viii; for more on Gill's views, see Fiona MacCarthy, *Eric Gill* (London, 1989).
[68] Bernard Leach, *A Potter's Book* ([n.p.], 1940), 4 and 10.
[69] Saler, *The Avant-Garde*, vii.   [70] Ibid, 92–6.
[71] John Elliot, 'Pick, Frank (1878–1941)', rev. Michael Robbins, *Oxford Dictionary of National Biography* (Oxford University Press, first published 23 September 2004, revised 27 May 2010) [www.oxforddnb.com/view/article/35522].
[72] Andrew Stephenson, 'Strategies of Situation: British Modernism and the Slump, c.1929–1934', *Oxford Art Journal* 14 (1991), 30–51.
[73] Saler, *The Avant-Garde*, 122–5.

modernist design, opposed to the 'dilettante handicraft spirit' which should now be set aside.[74] The difficulties at Dartington of reconciling craft ideals and commerce reflected these unresolved wider debates: the estate was cited as an inspired example of 'the formation of new factories' by Roger Fry in his essay for the 1932 Gorrell Report on the promotion of good design in Britain – but the internal workings of the community did not bear out this optimistic reading.[75]

The pottery enterprise established by Bernard Leach indicates a common trajectory among the estate's craft industries. Leach saw his aim as twofold: to make goods whose utility and simplicity of design were 'of human quality for daily use'; and to ensure they were designed and produced from start to finish by one artist-craftsman in a 'completely unified human expression'.[76] In his early years, he was convinced that making by hand in a workshop was the mode of production most likely to achieve these ends; the factory had 'split the human personality' while the workshop contributed to social unity and the 'organic' unity of the production process.[77] By 1931, however, the finances of his workshop in Cornwall had reached rock bottom, and he was willing to concede that the prospects of an isolated craftsman 'working by hand in a machine age' were 'desperate', and that some amalgamation 'with science, and machinery, and organisation, and distribution and the capital' might be necessary.[78] The shift echoed that of Leach's hero William Morris towards factory production in the previous century.[79] It also reflected Leach's links with Japan, where he had lived for eleven years and where the *Mingei* or 'People's Art' movement celebrated functional work made by an anonymous team. At this juncture, the Elmhirsts, who had been buying Leach's pots since the 1920s, invited him to establish a pottery at Dartington.

Leach told them that their estate represented 'the best environment I have seen' in which to experiment with small-scale factory production

---

[74] Walter Gropius, 'The Formal and Technical Problems of Modern Architecture and Planning', *Journal of the Royal Institute of British Architects*, 41(1934), quoted by Tanya Harrod, who covers the debate between crafts and modernist design in *Crafts in the Twentieth Century*, 118–21.

[75] *Art and Industry: Report of the Committee Appointed by the Board of Trade Under the Chairmanship of Lord Gorrell on the Production and Exhibition of Articles of Good Design and Everyday Use* (London, 1932), 15.

[76] Bernard Leach to Leonard, 11 December 1931, T/AAP/3/A2; Leach, *A Potter's Book*, 4.

[77] Leach, *A Potter's Book*, 258.

[78] Bernard Leach to Leonard, 11 December 1931, T/AAP/3/A2.

[79] Fiona MacCarthy, *William Morris: A Life for Our Time* (London, 2015); Charles Harvey and Jon Press, 'John Ruskin and the Ethical Foundations of Morris & Company, 1861–96', *Journal of Business Ethics* 14 (1995), 181–94.

4.2 Bernard Leach at Shinner's Bridge Pottery, Dartington, *c.* 1935
(© Fritz Henle Estate)

while retaining 'the conception of work as responsibility and enjoyment' instead of 'industrial serfdom'.[80] There was a community to supply, the next generation to educate, and 'a sympathetic and progressive spirit'.[81] He hoped to combine hand-making, mechanical mass production and teaching at the school: 'the knowledge of a century could be gathered round the new craftsman – the factory to him instead of him to the factory'.[82] In response to Leonard's warnings about financial accountability, Leach

---

[80] Bernard Leach to Leonard, 11 December 1931, T/AAP/3/A2.   [81] Ibid.
[82] Bernard Leach quoted in Harrod, *Crafts in the Twentieth Century*, 142.

conceded the necessity of the '"economic yard-stick" as an antidote to experiment which is costly and time taking and which gets labelled "idealism"'.[83] He planned to produce a range of light, hard-wearing utilitarian tableware, rooted in tradition but serving modern needs.[84] The Elmhirsts agreed that such a pottery as Leach suggested could 'find its natural place as an art, a science and a utility as well as in the education scheme as an introduction to formal design'.[85]

Within less than a year, Leach was disenchanted. He complained that there were 'two main trends of thought in School and Estate, the one towards science, intellect, and plan, the other towards art, intuition, and warmth of human relationship', and that the former risked the 'sacrifice of essential human relationship and also of quality of product'.[86] He butted heads with the estate's managing director W. K. Slater. His workforce rebelled against his efforts to introduce a system of division of labour.[87] As with his own pottery at St Ives, Leach's small experimental pottery at Dartington lost money. Slater imposed strict monitoring on its designs and finances. In response, Leach delayed the promised move from workshop to factory production, preferring to exercise his ingenuity by making large, one-off pieces rather than turning out the easily replicable range he had promised the Elmhirsts. He spent increasing periods of time away from the estate, including making a long trip to Japan in 1934, paid for by the Elmhirsts, to research how to produce stoneware in large quantities.[88] While he was away, his son David, who worked with him, was encouraged by Leonard and Slater to undertake a period of technical training in factory production at Stoke-on-Trent. David went, much to the fury of his father who deemed the factories to be making exactly 'the wrong kind of pottery'.[89]

When Bernard Leach returned from Japan he promised again 'to step out from the studio' and into 'the small factory where quality of design and material is preserved, while science and organisation are put to the service of the artists and craftsman'.[90] Yet he also continued to insist on

---

[83] Bernard Leach to Leonard, 6 December 1932, T/AAP/3/A2.

[84] Cooper, *Bernard Leach*, 177.

[85] Leonard to Bernard Leach, 3 December 1931, LA5832, Leach Archive, Crafts Study Centre, University Centre for the Creative Arts.

[86] Bernard Leach to Leonard, 6 December 1932, T/AAP/3/A2.

[87] Harry Davis to Bernard Leach, 19 April 1935, Leach Archive.

[88] Bernard Leach to Kay Starr, 20 December 1923, 2542, Leach Archive. For details of this journey, part of which he undertook with the painter Mark Tobey, see chapters 8 and 9 of Cooper, *Bernard Leach*.

[89] Leonard to Bernard Leach, 15 January 1935, T/AAP/3/A4. David Leach trained at the North Staffordshire Technical College in Stoke-on-Trent from 1934 to 1936.

[90] Bernard Leach to W. K. Slater, 19 December 1935, T/APP/3.

having autonomy over technique and design. Slater wrote him a stern memorandum, 'Report on the centralised control of the artist craftsman', which emphasised that the artist-craftsman was a 'technician' whose value lay in 'the improvement of design' and suggested that Leach take advice on consumer taste from the newly established Dartington sales department, rather than relying on his own judgement.[91] To Leonard, Slater complained that Leach seemed to imagine himself 'in a fool's paradise', expecting the same kind of 'freedom on design and technique' that he would get if Leonard were 'patron to a studio' – and, indeed, the lavish way that the Elmhirsts financed Leach's activities and bought his work did suggest an artist–patron relationship.[92]

The gap between rhetoric and practice (in part a reflection of the divide between Dorothy's patronage and Leonard's sense of commercial imperative) was indicative of the general lack of unified thinking about the arts at Dartington. A puzzled journalist asked Leonard in 1933 to clarify whether or not the 'William Morris school of thought' had been 'abandoned in favour of styles associated with modern machine production' – and, if so, how Leach, 'one of our ablest exponents of the primitive or peasant school', fitted into this.[93] He did not get an answer from Dartington – and probably, outside of a broad, unity-seeking ambition, there was not one. In the national arts, however, people like Frank Pick and initiatives like the Design and Industries Association were demonstrating that there need be no absolute dichotomy between an Arts and Crafts philosophy and one that harnessed machinery and took account of consumer taste.[94]

Sidestepping the problem, in 1937 Leach arranged to receive £3,000 from the Elmhirsts over the course of three years to experiment with stoneware at his own pottery in St Ives and further discussion of a ceramics factory at Dartington was quietly dropped.[95] Leach nonetheless retained a base, in the form of a caravan, on the estate up until 1949 and produced the most tangible outcome from his time at Dartington, *A Potter's Book*, with Elmhirst funding between 1939 and 1940. This manual, a seminal contribution to the philosophy and practice of British twentieth-century handicraft, became popular in the 1960s, attracting

---

[91] W. K. Slater, 'Report on the centralised control of the artist craftsman', 2 December 1935, T/AAP/3/A4.

[92] W. K. Slater to Leonard, 3 December 1935, T/AAP/3/A4.

[93] Christian Barman, industrial designer and editor of *The Architectural Review*, to Leonard, 10 March 1933, LKE/G/S3/D.

[94] Saler, *The Avant-Garde*, passim.

[95] [n.a.], 'Memorandum on the re-organisation of the Leach Pottery', 21 June 1937, T/AAP/3.

disaffected members of the New Age counterculture with its promise of the possibilities of an independent, contemplative 'craft life'.[96] It placed a heavy emphasis on self-fulfilment – indicating the broader therapeutic turn taken by the crafts by this point – and did not mention Leach's earlier factory plans at all.

As well as the Arts and Crafts movement, a modernist European strand of unity-seeking design thinking fed into estate ambitions to unite craft and industry. There was a suggestion that Walter Gropius would take up a year-long contract to build up a group of designers, establish links with industry and 'secure a unified character for the Dartington products' – but in the end, his salary requirements were deemed too high and his methods too experimental.[97]

Craft economics had been analysed at Dartington and found wanting. Instead of modelling a craft community on the estate, the Elmhirsts began to outsource their support for the discipline. In conjunction with the Rural Industries Bureau, an organisation founded by the government in 1921 to preserve and develop rural industry, they sponsored a survey of craftsmen and tradesmen in Devon by Rex Gardner, previously a craftsman on their estate.[98] Following this survey, again with the Elmhirsts' support, Gardner worked towards the formation of an Agricultural Trades Guild for South Devon, and, in 1938, arranged the first Devon Agricultural Industries Conference at Dartington with the object of 'raising the status and working conditions of the crafts'.[99] More than 160 people attended – reflecting the relative success, in terms of tangible impact, of the Elmhirsts' contributions to centralised initiatives by comparison with their early, more local efforts.[100]

---

[96] Harrod, *Crafts in the Twentieth Century*, 221.
[97] Walter Gropius to W. K. Slater, 6 January 1935, T/EST/7/D; 'Minutes', 20 March 1936, C/STAV/1. The hopes of other Bauhaus figures, including Fraulein Otti Berger, head of the Bauhaus weaving department, of joining Dartington also came to nothing – in part because during the 1930s the estate was inundated with applications from refugees, in part because it did not seem sufficiently clear to these artists what their role would be in the community. Charles Ross to Leonard, 29 January 1933, LKE/USA/6/G9.
[98] Architect-craftsman Rex Gardner arrived at Dartington in 1927 and was responsible for designing buildings, then running the crafts studio. His survey of Devon, running from 1934 to 1936, resulted in a card index of a thousand businesses and was maintained until the outbreak of World War II. E. Havelock of the Development Commission to W. K. Slater, 3 May 1935, C/RIB/1/A; Rex Gardner, 'Rural trades in Devonshire, organizer's report to 28 February 1937', C/RIB/1/A.
[99] 'Preliminary draft agenda for Devon Agricultural Trades Conference', 19 June 1937, C/RIB/1/A.
[100] *News of the Day*, 25 June 1937, C/RIB/1/A.

In 1952, Leach, too, returned temporarily to Dartington, to organise the first International Conference of Craftsmen in Pottery and Textiles. This gathered practitioners to discuss the role of the craftsman in contemporary society and, like Gardner's Conference of Agricultural Industries, was indicative of Dartington's move away from isolated experimentation and towards coordination with outside institutions and initiatives. Although there was much mention at the conference of the importance of building links with industry, the fundamental tone was anti-industrial.[101] An accompanying exhibition of pottery and textiles then toured the country with government sponsorship. To outsiders, it had an archaic quality – the critic Robert Melville wrote that 'the general effect is of an ethnographical exhibit of the remains of a lost civilisation'.[102] By the end of the Second World War, the project of integrating the ideals of the artist-craftsman into modern industry had largely fallen out of favour politically and in arts circles. Efforts to stimulate post-war economic recovery emphasised quantity over quality, fulfilling consumer desire over the holistic life of the producer, and the arts themselves moved towards exploring values of 'plurality, ephemerality, and contingency'.[103] Nonetheless the workshop spirit would continue to be kept alive by a range of alternative groups through the 1950s and 1960s.[104]

4.2   The 1930s: 'A Great Interrelation Centre'[105]

The constitution of the Dartington Hall Trust in 1931 to oversee the running of the non-commercial branches of the estate was prompted in part by the fact that the various departments had grown too big and too complex for the Elmhirsts to oversee themselves. More than this, though, Dorothy and Leonard hoped the trust would offer a model that could be replicated by others and would ensure the continuity of their enterprise after their deaths.[106] This kind of trust formation was an innovative measure in the cultural sphere – in 1935, Leonard thought that the closest parallel he could find to Dartington was London Zoo.[107] In reality,

[101] Peter Cox, Michael Cardew, Marguette Wildenhaim, Patrick Heron, Robin Tanner and John Bowers, *The Report of the International Conference of Craftsmen in Pottery and Textiles at Dartington Hall, Totnes, Devon, July 17–27, 1952* (Totnes, 1954).
[102] Robert Melville, 'Exhibitions', *Architectural Review* 112 (1952), 343–4.
[103] Saler, *The Avant-Garde*, 172.   [104] Harrod, *Crafts in the Twentieth Century*, part II.
[105] The term is sculptor Willi Soukop's. Interview with Michael Young, 1 April 1979, T/HIS/S22.
[106] Leonard, 'Summary of Dartington constitution', April 1931, LKE/G/SG.
[107] Leonard to Fred Gwatkin, 8 October 1935, LKE/LF/16/D.

a number of general-purpose philanthropic trusts of vast scale preceded it in America, many of them supporting cultural enterprise. One of the biggest was the Carnegie Corporation of New York, mandated in 1911 'to promote the advancement of knowledge and understanding'.[108] What was unusual about the Dartington Hall Trust, though, was its connection to a specific community. After the Second World War, several rural cultural enterprises conceived in the interwar period, such as John Christie and Audrey Mildmay's opera festival at Glyndebourne, would follow suit, turning themselves into trusts – although this related to a desire to perpetuate the founders' intention and to avoid tax, rather than to strengthen local community.[109]

Following the establishment of the trust, arts and adult education briefly became the responsibility of Dartington School's new headmaster, W. B. Curry. He showed little interest in the job, however, and unaccounted spending, 'quarrels, jealousies and a sense of complacency' continued to plague the arts.[110] In 1934, one of Dartington's new trustees, solicitor F. A. S. Gwatkin, insisted on the constitution of a proper arts department with an administrator and a finite endowment that was separate from the rest of the estate. Chris Martin, an orderly minded young man just down from Oxford and a nephew of the local (Dartington-averse) rector J. S. Martin, was appointed as the head of the new department.

At first sight, Chris Martin was an odd choice. He had little interest in community-building art. He defined amateurism disdainfully as 'the placing of work and results in a category second in importance to personal predilections and personal comfort'.[111] He saw Dartington as 'a very loose association of people all working within one enterprise, and not a community'.[112] The estate's aim should not be internal integration, he thought, but through 'a whole hearted striving for results worthy to stand with the best either in England, America or on the Continent' to become an international centre of excellence that would elevate the way

[108] Frederick P. Keppel, *The Foundation: Its Place in American Life* (Oxford; New York, 2017 [1930]).
[109] The Glyndebourne Arts Trust was formed in 1954 to perpetuate the work of John Christie and Audrey Mildmay who had founded the opera festival in 1934 – and who consulted Leonard about trusts in the 1930s (John Christie, founder of Glyndebourne to Leonard, 15 December 1938, T/ADR/1). Another example, the Springhead Trust, was set up in 1973 in memory of Rolf Gardiner, who had bought the estate for his farming and cultural projects in 1933.
[110] Cox, *The Arts at Dartington*, 10.
[111] Chris Martin, 'Report to Dartington Trustees', 14 July 1934, T/AA/1.
[112] Chris Martin, 'Dartington Hall – a social experiment', [1936], T/AA/1/I.

people thought of culture.[113] This was a long way from Leonard's amateur-art-for-local-unity model, but it provided a solution to what he increasingly recognised was a problem: Dartington had 'two dialectically, i.e. essentially antagonistic aims: to be as good a community as possible, and to be a spring of values recognized by, and in their turn raising, the standards of the world at large'.[114] A new policy that envisaged art's unifying function on a larger canvas might go some way to reconciling the two. Rather than focusing on uniting everyone on the estate, he hoped Dartington could incubate a 'maximal culture' that would 'transcend' its bounds, being 'a cooperative product of mankind'.[115] The professional artist would inspire and unite society at large – guiding and drawing people together in a fashion akin to Matthew Arnold's 'great men of culture' – and rendering marginal the issue of unity at Dartington itself.[116]

Martin's policy was given impetus by broader European history. Hitler's rise in Germany produced many refugee artists, a number of whom found their way to Dartington. Their cultural background and political experiences bred a different aesthetic ideology to the one that had, so far, dominated on the estate: less focused on the daily life of the organic local community and more on national or international impact. The high standard of work and the attention which these artists brought Dartington meant that the Elmhirsts, with many other calls on their time, fell in with Martin's hopes for the arts department as they had with Curry's for the school. Nonetheless, the sheer number of new arrivals, each with their own agenda, made it difficult for Martin to organise them. His position was further complicated by the Elmhirsts' propensity to respond to artists' appeals for support over his head; and by the difficulty of keeping spending within the sums generated by the endowment when more, and more costly, artists kept joining the community. Nonetheless, 1934 ushered in a new, professional phase in the history of the arts department: from this point and until the war, it was focused on more abstract notions of the unity that could be achieved by the arts – relating to the spiritual and the relations between the arts themselves, rather than on how to integrate the estate and local area through making creativity part of everyone's everyday life.[117]

---

[113] Chris Martin, 'Report to Dartington Trustees', 14 July 1934, T/AA/1.
[114] Leonard, untitled note beginning 'to appreciate what Dartington has achieved', [n.d.], LKE/G/S8/B.
[115] Ibid.
[116] Matthew Arnold, 'Culture and Its Enemies', *Cornhill Magazine* 16 (1867), 36–53.
[117] Chris Martin, 'Arts administration: report to Dartington Trustees', 21 November 1941, T/AA/1/G.

4.2.1   'Arts – Place of Escape or Share in Community'?[118]

Between 1934 and 1939, there were fewer projects to use the arts to promote community feeling at Dartington – although, as discussed later, Leonard still found opportunities to pursue these outside the estate. Mark Tobey, feeling his spiritually oriented methods incompatible with those of the new arts administrator, moved to the Far East. Martin tried to dissolve Margaret Barr's professional group and make her responsible for adult education only, on the basis that her group's work was of a low standard and that the estate was not big enough to support more than one dance troupe.[119] She protested to the Elmhirsts that 'our whole line of action has been based on the knowledge we are not a professional dance school, but rather ... exploring the potentialities of the community', but, as with Curry, Dorothy and Leonard stood by their new appointment and Barr left to work with left-wing theatre groups in London.[120]

In place of the old guard, Dartington began to fill with professional, mainly European artists, many of them fleeing the Nazis. Among them were the Germans Kurt Jooss and Sigurd Leeder, with the dancers, musicians and designers of the ballet school and touring company they had run in Essen.[121] Rudolf Laban, a leader of German modern expressive dance, was attached to their group, as was the stage designer Hein Heckroth. German conductor Hans Oppenheim arrived to take charge of music; Willi Soukop came from Austria to carry on his sculpture; the Russian Michael Chekhov (nephew of playwright Anton) established a theatre school; Uday Shankar (Ravi's brother) stayed for a summer with his troupe of Indian dancers.[122] Instead of the earlier expectation that

---

[118] Leonard, untitled note, 21 February 1935, LKE/G/S9/A.

[119] Chris Martin, 'Report to Dartington Trustees', 14 July 1934, T/AA/1.

[120] Margaret Barr and group to Elmhirsts, July 1934, T/AD/2/B. She received a grant of £1,000 from Dartington to set up her group in London. Later she went on to promote the development of indigenous modern dance in Australia. Nicholas, *Dancing in Utopia*, 86–7 and 112–6.

[121] Kurt Jooss choreographed for Rudolf Laban before starting a dance school with Sigurd Leeder. He became the director of dance at the Folkwangschule in Essen-Werden, moving his school with Leeder there. He achieved fame in 1932 as the winner of Les Archives Internationales de la Danse's first choreography competition with *The Green Table*, which parodied the posturing of politicians at the Versailles Peace Conference with a masked dance of death. He then formed a touring company, the Ballets Jooss, but when he refused to dismiss its Jewish members as required to by the Nazis, he and Leeder were forced to flee the country. Ann Hutchinson Guest, 'The Jooss-Leeder School at Dartington Hall', *Dance Chronicle* 29 (2006), 161–94; Andy Adamson and Clare Lidbury, *Kurt Jooss: 60 Years of the Green Table* (Birmingham, 1994).

[122] Hans Oppenheim, formerly of the Deutsche Musik Bühne, was Jewish and left Germany in 1933. He worked as an assistant conductor to the Glyndebourne Opera Company before joining Dartington. Willi Soukop was invited to Dartington in 1934 by the Elmhirsts' secretary Kay Starr, after studying at the Viennese Academy of Fine Arts.

artists on the estate would find niches for themselves, incomers were now given formal contracts.[123] Sometimes their duties included teaching at Dartington School or giving evening classes, but more often their work was oriented around building up professional studio schools and preparing for national or international tours. The studio schools they ran, at least in theory, offered more structured courses preparing students for professional life as an artist.[124] The Dartington Hall Trust spent disproportionately huge sums ensuring that the Jooss-Leeder Dance School, the Ballets Jooss, the Theatre Drama Studio established by Michael Chekhov and Hans Oppenheim's Music Theatre Studio each had suitable premises and their director a salary to match his international status.[125] The groups, who performed at Dartington, in London and on national and international tours, put the estate 'firmly on the professional map' as Martin had hoped.[126]

Partly because of Martin's outward-looking philosophy, partly because of the situations they were coming away from, many of the new artists were of the opinion that they owed their loyalty not to the estate or local community, nor to any nation, but to their own work. Leonard complained that 'the idea of the Patron still holds and especially in the German outlook' – the 'old court tradition holds out against group thought and planning and responsibility'.[127] Kurt Jooss was a notable adherent to this 'courtly' tradition. He saw the Elmhirsts as successors to the 'princes of the church and the world', duty bound, in consequence of the fate that had put wealth in their hands, to give no-strings support to the artists whom they needed to turn their 'cultural wishes into lasting values'.[128]

Michael Chekhov had to leave Russia after refusing to comply with the Soviet government's insistence on artists adopting a social realist style.

[123] In spite of this formalisation, confusion over artists' roles remained a feature. Willi Soukop, for example, was given no salary but used space in Rex Gardner's workshop and took wood from the sawmill in return for giving evening classes. He began to work as a paid teacher at the school in 1937, but also worked at other schools in the area. Michael Young's interview with Willi Soukop, 1 April 1979, T/HIS/S22.

[124] The Jooss-Leeder Dance School claimed to offer a three-year course with examinations at the end for a teacher's certificate to teach amateurs, and, after further tuition, a diploma to teach professionals. In reality, all the schools tended to diverge significantly from their written programmes.

[125] The average annual cost to Dartington of the Jooss-Leeder Dance School and the Ballets Jooss between 1934 and 1937 was £10,000, which constituted the entire annual budget of the arts department. Dorothy had constantly to supplement the department's formal endowment. Chris Martin, note on financial position of the arts department, [1942], T/AD/1/C.

[126] Chris Martin, 'Plan for the Arts Department', 1941, T/AA/1/H.

[127] Leonard, 'Confidential memo', 29 December 1937, T/AA/1/F.

[128] Kurt Jooss to the Elmhirsts, received 8 December 1933 [translation], T/AD/1/A.

Jooss' lack of investment in the life of estate – it was merely a 'refuge', he told Dorothy, where his art might grow 'undisturbed by the worries of the day' – was such that he campaigned (unsuccessfully) to be allowed to remove all references to Dartington in Ballets Jooss publicity material.[129] Dartington smacked of 'amateurism or provincialism', he complained, and the association could damage his company's reputation in London.[130] Other artists were equally dismissive. Viennese sculptor Willi Soukop, while impressed by what he witnessed of Mark Tobey's ability to engage artistically with all comers, believed that 'Art cannot be of great interest to everyone – only to the few'.[131] He disliked giving lessons at the school – 'A boy would look in and say "I'll come later", or ask the pupils to go riding. I could not compete with a horse'. He preferred the better-regulated, more conventional Westcountry private schools like Blundell's and Bryanston, where he also gave lessons, and where there was 'an atmosphere of work'.[132]

Other arrivals responded with enthusiasm to the community-arts ethos they found at Dartington. They saw in it the unique opportunity to realise their ideal of the arts having direct social, economic and spiritual functions.[133] Hein Heckroth, wrote one of his life-drawing students, was 'prepared to break down the barriers of the artists' trade union for the delectation of the philistine', seeing the results as of value to the students 'themselves, to their jobs, and to the world at large'.[134] The conductor Frederic 'Fritz' Waldmann, an Austrian refugee who worked as a music director for the Ballets Jooss, put forward a plan for 'building up a real musical culture based on a natural unity of professional musicians and the population'.[135] The estate would be inducted into the European tradition of *Hausmusik* ('community music-making'); professional musicians would organise an estate choir and orchestra; music courses would be conducted in the 'favourite Inns of the workmen'; groups would tour Devon's villages with a music programme design to engage and educate, giving 'detailed explanation in the programme' and engaging the audience through voting and through whistling competitions.[136] While such ambitious projects as Waldmann's were not acted on, the arts department of the 1930s

[129] Kurt Jooss to Dorothy, 13 March 1941, DWE/A/9/C; Kurt Jooss to W.K. Slater, 17 September 1935, T/AD/1/A.
[130] Kurt Jooss to W.K. Slater, 17 September 1935, T/AD/1/A.
[131] Michael Young, interview with Willi Soukop, 1 April 1979, T/HIS/S22.   [132] Ibid.
[133] For the broader debates about this idea in England, see Charles Harrison, *English Art and Modernism* (London, 1981), 238.
[134] Quoted in Harrison, 'The Visual Arts', 151.
[135] Frederic 'Fritz' Waldmann, 'Plan for the organisation of the musical life at Dartington Hall Estate, of Devonshire and for the distant future', 22 July 1935, T/AM/1/A.
[136] Ibid.

continued to be seen from the outside as a place of interest for those who wanted to bring out in modern art 'the actual, good work done, and its relation to the whole social structure and to life in general', rather than focusing on famous 'personalities'.[137] It received a steady stream of visitors, many of whom, like Barbara Hepworth and John Maynard Keynes, saw culture as an essential component of a good society.[138]

There was a gulf between the theoretical community-building ideas of a few of the new arrivals and the overall direction of the arts department. Members of the estate might be told that they were welcome in the main courtyard where the arts were based, but most of the artists did not go out to the estate, or seek to connect with the wider local community.[139] Hans Oppenheim, who was supposed to take over musical direction on the estate, 'didn't really know how to go about it, nor did he have any interest in the encouragement of amateurs', a pianist on the estate remembered.[140] Leonard hoped that he would engage with the school's students and locals, and Martin that he would unite the resident artists, but the musician did neither, preferring to concentrate on building up his own professional group and insisting that 'real enjoyment from the arts can only be *earned* by hard work over a long period'.[141]

When Leonard urged them to do so, Jooss and Leeder found it equally difficult to address the needs of locals – either in working with them or performing for them. 'If Leeder could bright up the folk dancing somehow, add a few foreign ones, and a little colour ... with the village orchestra to play, we might be getting somewhere,' wrote Leonard wistfully. 'It's the gap between antiquarianism and the Jooss Ballet, full blast on tour, that somehow Leeder, Oppenheim and Kurt ought to find some way of filling.'[142] The arts department was set to become an institution with wide renown – in 1934 some of its concerts began to be broadcast by the BBC – but with little relevance to its immediate surroundings.[143]

---

[137] Barbara Hepworth quoted in Harrison, 'The Visual Arts', 151.
[138] Dorothy arranged for John Maynard Keynes to meet Kurt Jooss and watch the Ballets Jooss perform. Keynes to Dorothy, 21 January 1935, DWE/6/E.
[139] Nicholas, *Dancing in Utopia*, chapter 3.
[140] Michael Young, interview with Ronald Anderson, 8 October 1977, T/HIS/S20/D. Anderson arrived at Dartington in 1938.
[141] Hans Oppenheim, note to W.B. Curry, 12 July 1938, T/DHS/B/22/D.
[142] Leonard to Dorothy, 20 November 1937, LKE/DWE/6/B.
[143] Ronald Biggs, director of music, to Dartington trustees, 13 January 1934, T/AM/1/A. This was seen, apparently on both sides, as a preliminary to 'much more hand-in-glove' cooperation between the organisations, with the BBC suggesting broadcasting a tour of the Elmhirsts' estate. This did not materialise in the interwar years, although the concerts continued and a BBC Third Programme was made about Dartington in 1950. Chris Martin to Leonard, memorandum, 15 July 1935, T/AM/1/A; Leonard interviewed by Victor Bonham-Carter, transcript of recording of BBC Third

This external focus was, in part, enforced by the impossibility of achieving internal harmony with such an influx of artists, each with their own ambitions.

The new configuration of the arts department bemused or incensed the rest of the estate. Dartington was supposed to be egalitarian, but artists were accorded greater privileges than everyone else. There was grumbling about the 'great revelation' Dorothy expected from professional foreign artists, 'especially if their English was not too good'.[144] An element of xenophobia crept into these complaints, as into the socio-spiritual questing of the 1930s – a view that Europeans had a 'determination in pursuit of self-interest which is strange to the Englishman'.[145] The Elmhirsts, who had initially striven to be candid about estate finances as part of their overall ambition to build a democratically run community, grew uncomfortable about disclosing spending on the arts: '£100 is as much as many men expect to earn in the year,' Leonard noted confidentially. 'How can you explain in a few words the school of dance, the ballet, and the endowment of the Arts Dep[artmen]t?'[146]

The informal give-and-take between departments of the early years was replaced by wrangling over boundaries: the school's headmaster complained to Chris Martin that no payment was made when his chairs were borrowed for performances, and to Hans Oppenheim that those coming to teach music seemed to consider it 'a sort of mere by-product of what is going on in the Arts Department'.[147] Dorothy gave the artists some protection, but when English painter Cecil Collins was criticised for the pointlessness and incomprehensibility of an exhibition of his work, he tried to defend its utility in *News of the Day*. It aimed 'to feed and sustain' the 'real life deep in each person,' he explained: 'Thus my art is truly functional.'[148] Despite efforts to bridge the gap between the formalist and functionalist aims, these years signalled a definite step away from Leonard's hope that art would contribute to knitting Dartington itself into a holistic community. As a visitor commented in 1938, the estate artist had become 'independent of his public, a specialist' and had 'gone meandering off into realms of pure form, ceasing to apply his art to everyday things'.[149]

Programme on Dartington Hall, recorded 19 June 1950, transmitted 13 August 1951, LKE/G/S13/A.

[144] Michael Young, interview with Ronald Anderson, 8 October 1977, T/HIS/S20/D.

[145] Chris Martin, 'Plan for the Arts Department', 1941, T/AA/1/H.

[146] Leonard, 'Confidential memo', 29 December 1937, LKE/G/S8.

[147] W. B. Curry to Chris Martin, 24 October 1934, T/DHS/B/20/A; W. B. Curry to Hans Oppenheim, 25 September 1941, T/DHS/B/20/B.

[148] *News of the Day*, 25 June 1937, T/PP/EST/1/019.

[149] Felicity Palmer, 'Dartington' report, 1938, LKE/G/25/A.

4.2.2   Seeking Spiritual Unity: Dorothy's Quest

> Art is always a bringing together, a synthesis, and that is why we need it
> so desperately in this age of division, of specialisation, of breaking up
> more and more into less and less, this difficult mechanised age when we
> focus on the atom .... We need the great artists; but we need also to be
> artists in our own way.   Dorothy Elmhirst (1950)[150]

In the unifying idealism of the interwar years, Michael Saler finds, art was
part of 'a common quest for underlying essences that could restore
harmony, stability, and spirituality to a "modern" world that appeared
increasingly fragmentary'.[151] This could mean knitting together community; another ambition was to promote the unity of the spiritual or
psychological self. This section considers such integrative hopes
through the prism of Dorothy's experiences. The two sections that
follow pan out: the first looking at the aspiration that the unity of
mankind could be promoted by joining together the art forms themselves; the second exploring the competing national and international
visions of unity that different artists on the estate sought to support. In
the professional phase of the arts department, these abstract forms of
unity-seeking seemed to many foreign artists more compelling than
promoting the unity of the community in which they were living – an
understandable position, given that their presence at Dartington was a
necessity rather than a choice.

Over the course of the interwar years, the arts for Dorothy became less
a realm in which to exercise patronage, and more a domain where 'man
finds the unity and harmony that his soul is forever seeking'.[152] As with
Dorothy's political views – in which an elite was a necessary component
of democracy – so too, in the field of spiritualised creativity: whilst
everyone should participate in the arts, leaders were required and should
be cultivated at Dartington.[153] Her advocacy for professionalism, high
standards and protecting the artists from economic constraints echoed
the views of other patrons of the arts of the period such as John Maynard
Keynes, although the spiritual element was unusual among those of this
mindset.[154] It was a long way from Leonard's 1920s concept of amateur
art as the glue holding together a group of pioneering equals at Dartington,
but it retained a view of art as having a unifying, public-serving, even

---

[150] Dorothy, 'The arts at Dartington', 21 February 1950, DWE/A/4/E.
[151] Saler, *The Avant-Garde*, 6.
[152] Dorothy to R. A. Edwards, 2 August 1942, DWE/G/S3/G.
[153] Dorothy to Leonard, 27 August 1921, LKE/DWE/10/C.
[154] Anna Upchurch, 'John Maynard Keynes, the Bloomsbury Group and the Origins of the
Arts Council Movement', *International Journal of Cultural Policy* 10 (2004), 203–17.

missionary function. With a 'deeper life of the imagination,' wrote Dorothy, 'there might indeed be a new synthesis of faith and works even in our generation'.[155]

The Russian actor-director Michael Chekhov conformed most closely to Dorothy's ideal of artist as spiritual guide. Chekhov was influenced by the Austrian philosopher and reformer Rudolf Steiner.[156] Steiner's 'spiritual science' of anthroposophy stressed the importance of intuitive spiritual knowledge, free from dogma. He believed that the arts were an aid to spiritual development, a path away from the everyday self with which we normally identify and towards the creative 'higher ego'.[157] For Steiner, it was the mission of artists to 'penetrate the mysteries of the universe and reintegrate humanity with it to achieve universal love'.[158] An equally important inspiration for Chekhov was the Russian abstract artist Wassily Kandinsky. Like Steiner, Kandinsky sought to represent the underlying unity of mankind and envisaged the artist as a 'priest of beauty' who 'sees and points the way'.[159] Chekhov saw his artistic exploration of inner experience as the creative counterpart to Steiner's spiritual quest, and viewed his own role in Kandinsky's terms, as being a spiritual leader with a duty to guide society to a pinnacle of enlightenment.

Dorothy's daughter Beatrice met Chekhov in New York and recommended him to her mother for the estate. In spite of speaking practically no English, he was eager to join and, after studying the language for several months, he opened the Chekhov Theatre Drama Studio at Dartington in 1936.[160] Chekhov's three-year course promised to teach students to communicate 'inner realism' through physical gesture.[161] At the suggestion of her daughter, Dorothy joined his group of students

---

[155] Dorothy to Waldo Frank, 28 June 1938, DWE/G/4/C.
[156] Rudolf Steiner, anthroposophy and Rudolf Laban were subjects frequently touched on in Chekhov's acting lessons, as attested by Dorothy's class notebooks (DWE/G/S7/E/019) and by early drafts of the handbook, *To the Actor* (MC/S2), which Chekhov began writing at Dartington in 1938. This was published as *To the Actor: On the Technique of Acting* (Abingdon, 2002 [1953]).
[157] Valerie Preston-Dunlop, *Rudolf Laban: An Extraordinary Life* (London, 1998), 10.
[158] Steven G. Marks, 'Abstract Art and the Regeneration of Mankind', *New England Review* 24 (2003), 53–79, at 56.
[159] Wassily Kandinsky, trans. M. T. H. Sadler, *Concerning the Spiritual in Art* (New York, 1977 [1914]), 4 and 55.
[160] Michael Chekhov had previously acted in the Moscow Arts Theatre under the direction of Konstantin Stanislavsky. He then directed the Second Moscow Arts Theatre. Refusing to adopt the socialist realism that became the approved mode of art in Soviet Russia, he went into exile in 1928. Anthea Williams, 'DWE and the theatre', T/HIS/S22/B.
[161] Michael Chekhov, *Chekhov Theatre Studio, Dartington Hall*, 1936, DWE/A/15/A; Thomas Cornford, 'The English Theatre Studios of Michael Chekhov and Michel Saint-Denis, 1935–65', unpublished PhD, University of Warwick, 2012.

4.3 Chekhov Theatre Studio rehearsing in Dartington's gardens, *c.* 1935 (© Fritz Henle Estate)

and soon fell headlong under his influence. 'Beatrice urged me to join the group for an hour a day. I did this with grave misgivings,' she wrote, 'but soon it was two – three – four – five – six – hours a day and even more.'[162] Dressed in the long blue gown Chekhov insisted his students wear, she spent these hours doing rigorous exercises with the theatre group to strengthen the body, spirit and emotions.[163] Chekhov's ambition, in place of the contemporary naturalistic theatre that he saw as too superficial and imitative, was to reprise theatre's roots in the medieval mystery

---

[162] Dorothy, [n.d.], 'Background and foreground – a personal pattern', DWE/S/1/E.
[163] Jane Brown, *Angel Dorothy: How an American Progressive Came to Devon* (London, 2017), 170–1. This emphasis on repetition followed Kandinsky's lesson that 'the spirit, like the body, can be strengthened and developed by frequent exercise'. Kandinsky, *Concerning the Spiritual*, 36.

plays, aiming to see the world 'from some new and more spiritual point of view'.[164] 'All technique must be rescrutinized, and respiritualized,' he wrote – only then, would the capacity to present the audience with spiritual truths be re-acquired.[165]

For Chekhov, an artist was 'the servant of the highest in humanity', but he perceived the social function in abstract terms, with his studio having little to do with the day-to-day life of Dartington, or Britain, or the realm of politics generally.[166] Early proposals for his cooperating with the estate's other enterprises and providing classes for locals came to nothing.[167] After taking tea with him in 1937, Dorothy recorded his detached view of art's role in the face of totalitarianism: this was 'to take the long view – to have [a] different conception of time and space. Should be able to laugh at Hitler!'[168] The spiritual responsibility of art was not to the community in which it was practised but to the abstract cultivation of an elevated mental attitude. This view did not appeal to everyone – for example, the play-wright Sean O'Casey, who had moved to Totnes to send his children to Dartington School, and whose own works were marked by realism, social-ist politics, and the importance of words. For O'Casey, Chekhov's concept of the intuitive, spiritual 'entirely modern' play was 'an impossible experi-ment, and a waste of time'.[169]

Like other refugees at Dartington in the late 1930s, in spite of his desire to laugh at Hitler, Chekhov was acutely conscious of the growing threat from Germany. In 1938, he relocated his studio to the safety of an empty schoolhouse in Ridgefield, Connecticut. By then, Dorothy's work with him had been the main focus of her life for almost two years. In March 1939, after agonised indecision, she left England to join him. She justified the move as being necessary to equip herself as a drama teacher for Dartington and to continue her role in their current production, *The Possessed*.[170] She seems, however, to have been as much drawn by the 'creative, unifying experience' that the work was offering her.[171] Chekhov – 'the Master', as his students called him – brought to her

[164] Michael Chekhov, 'Chekhov Theatre Studio, Dartington Hall', [n.d.], DWE/A/15/A.
[165] Michael Chekhov, untitled notes introducing the Chekhov Theatre Studio, [n.d.], T/ADR/1.
[166] Michael Chekhov, 'Chekhov Theatre Studio, Dartington Hall', [n.d.], DWE/A/15/A.
[167] [n.a.], 'Proposed plans for theatre school at Dartington', 8 April 1935, T/ADR/1.
[168] Dorothy, 'Notes on tea with Mischa', 29 April [1937], DWE/A/15/B.
[169] Christopher Murray, *Sean O'Casey: Writer at Work: A Biography* (Dublin, 2004), 250.
[170] Anthea Williams, 'DWE and the theatre', T/HIS/S22/B.
[171] Dorothy to Anna Bogue, 13 August 1936, T/HIS/S22/B. She wrote to her son Michael that Chekhov 'has opened such a rich world of feeling and imagination to all of us that sometimes I want to sit down and cry, for the sheer wonder of it'. 3 October 1937, T/HIS/21/E.

'a different dimension from ordinary life ... free of the narrow limits of one's own personality'.[172] The Elmhirsts' marriage seems to have experienced an unusual moment of strain as a result of her enthusiasm – although there is no evidence that Dorothy's passion for Chekhov was anything but platonic.[173] She thanked Leonard for his patience 'during this strange new experience of concentrating all my energies on one thing, one idea. I see, with a kind of overwhelming gratitude, that perhaps only you would have been capable of supporting and helping me this way – asking nothing in return, and only eager to see new vistas of life opening for me.'[174] The incident gives a glimpse into the Elmhirsts' relationship ten years on: still romantic, still mutually supportive, still allowing both parties a great deal of leeway to pursue their own interests.

Chekhov's group in Connecticut was, Dorothy wrote to Leonard, 'the perfect pattern for monastic life, a group without restriction of age or sex, intent upon a task, and under the direction of a great leader'.[175] Chekhov's allure for Dorothy echoed the appeal that gurus such as Meher Baba, G. I. Gurdjieff and Jiddu Krishnamurti had for elites amid the social and political turbulence of the interwar years, with some men and women abandoning their earlier lives completely in order to follow these spiritual guides.[176] In Dorothy's case, the outbreak of the Second World War brought her back to Dartington and her husband – and a position that was far more engaged with mainstream society than before. Her teacher, meanwhile, moved to Hollywood, where one of his most famous students, Marilyn Monroe, would find in him some of the same inspiration that Dorothy had, writing that 'with Michael Chekhov acting became more than a profession to me. It became a sort of religion.'[177]

4.2.3   Seeking Spiritual Unity: Uniting the Arts

Alongside Dorothy's quest, a wider spiritual ambition drove the arts at Dartington: to join the different art forms themselves into a synthetic whole. A diverse range of influences fed into this. One was the Arts and Crafts movement, which idealised medieval workshop traditions where

[172] Dorothy, 'My talk in the Barn Theatre on the eve of my departure for Chekhov in America', [n.d.], DWE/A/15/E.
[173] The only suggestion that Dorothy was in love with Chekhov is the speculation of dancer Paula Morel in an interview with Michael Young, 23 August 1976, T/HIS/S22.
[174] Quoted in Young, *Elmhirsts*, 368.
[175] Dorothy to Leonard, 9 April 1939, T/HIS/S22/B.
[176] Mathew Thomson, *Psychological Subjects: Ideas, Culture and Health in Twentieth-Century Britain* (Oxford, 2006), 78.
[177] Marilyn Monroe quoted by Simon Callow in 'Foreword' to Chekhov, *To the Actor*, xxvii.

artists strove together to express the common spiritual ideals of the organically integrated community.[178] This ambition informed Bernard Leach's work at Dartington, as well as the formation of a short-lived Craftsmen's Studio, led by Rex Gardner, a former employee of the Arts and Crafts furniture maker Ernest Gimson.[179] Another influence was, again, Kandinsky, who assumed correspondence between the various branches of art – 'that painting could replicate the psychological effect of music or poetry and vice versa' – and that all, combined, could achieve a spiritual effect that would bring the viewer closer to the universal.[180] Under Kandinsky's inspiration, Rudolf Laban, who fled from Germany to Dartington in 1938, had already experimented earlier in his career with the concept that movement could unify the arts under the rubric of *Tanz, Ton, Wort* (dance, sound, word).[181] Dartington seemed to offer another possibility of realising Kandinsky's theories.

The third and perhaps most significant shaper of the ambition to unite the arts at Dartington was the Bauhaus, where Kandinsky had briefly taught.[182] Walter Gropius, in his Bauhaus manifesto of 1919, advocated unifying all the creative arts under the primacy of architecture: 'Let us strive for, conceive and create the new building of the future that will unite every discipline, architecture and sculpture and painting, and which will one day rise heavenwards from the million hands of craftsmen as a clear symbol of a new belief to come.'[183] The Arts and Crafts movement was an inspiration for the Bauhaus vision – though where William Morris extolled the romance of hand-making in rural communities, Gropius and his fellow artists embraced machine manufacture for the modern city. With the closure of the Bauhaus under pressure from the Nazis in 1933, its ideals were widely disseminated – its members

---

[178] Saler, *The Avant-Garde*, 11. Printer and puppeteer H. D. C. Pepler, part of the Arts and Crafts community at Ditchling, tried without success to interest the Elmhirsts in sponsoring a cooperative theatre where 'design, interpretation, costume, lighting, music, the dance, and pure mime' would all be 'adapted to a unified purpose'. H. D. C. Pepler to Dorothy, 2 July 1937 and 12 July 1937, DWE/A/10/G.

[179] For an account of the craft studio, see Chapter 5.

[180] Wassily Kandinsky would paint a watercolour, give it to a musician to 'play' into music, and then to a dancer to 'dance' to both watercolour and sound. Marks, 'Abstract Art and the Regeneration of Mankind', 55; Kandinsky, *Concerning the Spiritual in Art*.

[181] Preston-Dunlop, *Rudolf Laban*, 19–21.

[182] Nikolaus Pevsner traces the connection between the founding fathers of the Arts and Crafts movement and the Bauhaus in *Pioneers of the Modern Movement from William Morris to Walter Gropius* (London, 1936).

[183] Walter Gropius, *Manifesto and Programme of the Weimar State Bauhaus*, 1919 [www.bauhaus100.de/en/past/works/education/manifest-und-programm-des-staatlichen-bauhauses/].

contributing to the founding of Black Mountain College in North Carolina in 1933 and the Institute of Design in Chicago in 1937.[184]

Walter Gropius and László Moholy-Nagy both went briefly to Dartington, where they found a project that they recognised.[185] Gropius, first visiting in 1933, thought that the estate mirrored his own hopes, 'the junction of all parts and details and the bringing them into relation to the whole life was my principal aim too'.[186] The Elmhirsts commissioned him to redesign the Barn Theatre, but his presence on the estate was opposed by several of the incumbent artists, who were concerned that he would overshadow their own efforts. The project was only partly completed.[187] Instead, Dorothy and Leonard supported his collaboration with Maxwell Fry and Henry Morris, Secretary to the Cambridgeshire Education Committee, in designing a village college at Impington – the only complete example of Gropius' work in Britain. Although the Bauhaus founder's mark was not set obviously on the fabric of the estate, Bauhaus ideals fed into the hope in the 1930s 'to bring together the four schools of drama, dance, design and music theatre'.[188]

Sam Smiles writes that, because Dartington retained a strong element of the backward-looking, of the Arts and Crafts tradition, it missed 'fulfilling its potential as an artistic community, a British Bauhaus uniting all the arts and crafts with architecture and progressive education in a truly radical enterprise'.[189] This reading risks missing the Elmhirsts' overall aspiration, which was to regenerate the countryside, rather than to promote an artistic

---

[184] Albert and Anni Albers emigrated to America, where they taught at the experimental Black Mountain College. László Moholy-Nagy eventually went to the Chicago, via Dartington, opening the Institute of Design in 1944. JoAnn C. Ellert, 'The Bauhaus and Black Mountain College', *The Journal of General Education* 24 (1972), 144–152. Fred Turner describes the refugee artists from the Bauhaus coming together in America with intellectuals and artists to create a 'democratic surround' that would go on to feed, more distinctly than in Britain, into the counterculture of the 1960s. *The Democratic Surround: Multimedia and American Liberalism from World War II to the Psychedelic Sixties* (Chicago and London, 2013).

[185] In addition to Gropius and Moholy-Nagy, there was further contact between Dartington and the Bauhaus. In the Dartington archive, for example, there are two anonymous letters on how lessons were taught at the Bauhaus (22 October 1932 and 17 December 1932, DWE/G/S4/D). Dorothy's friend, the writer Nancy Wilson Ross, who studied at the Bauhaus in the early 1930s, visited Dartington several times and saw the projects as closely connected (Nancy Wilson Ross, interview with Anthea Williams, 25 April 1977, T/HIS/S22/A).

[186] Walter Gropius to W. K. Slater, 21 July 1933, T/EST/7A/D1.

[187] David Elliott, 'Gropius in England', in Charlotte Benton (ed.), *A Different World: Emigré Architects in Britain 1928–1958* ([London], 1995), 107–24.

[188] Leonard to John Christie, 9 February 1938, T/ADR/1.

[189] Sam Smiles, 'Refuge or Regeneration: Devon's Twentieth Century Identity', in Sam Smiles (ed.), *Going Modern and Being British: Art, Architecture and Design in Devon c. 1910–1960* (Exeter, 1998), 1–14, at 11.

movement per se. Yet, even though no single aesthetic school of unity-seeking theory – Bauhaus, Arts and Crafts or otherwise – was ever fully embraced at Dartington, for a brief moment in the late 1930s the ideal of integrating the arts did come close to realisation, with the formation of a Music Theatre Studio in 1937 under the direction of Hans Oppenheim and the Art Studios in 1939 under Hein Heckroth.

The Music Theatre Studio was planned as both a school and a touring group. With shades of Richard Wagner's ideal of the theatre as a *Gesamtkunstwerk*, or 'total work', synthesising all the arts, it was intended to establish a new form of 'modern operatic theatre': 'the world on the stage must as regards sound, rhythm and dynamics be perfectly blended with the world of the orchestra, to form a unified, living and harmonious cosmos'.[190] Hein Heckroth would give lessons in stage and costume design; Kurt Jooss and Sigurd Leeder in musical mime; the Chekhov Theatre Studio in acting; and there would be further classes in expressive movement and body control.[191] Similarly, the Art Studios were to offer a three-year course run by Hein Heckroth, Bernard Leach, Cecil Collins and Willi Soukop. They would provide direction in painting, sculpture, pottery and a 'working knowledge of practice and basic principles as these have existed in all art from ancient to modern masters'.[192] When the Second World War started, however, many of the European artists had to leave Dartington. The Art Studios were disbanded before they could properly begin. The Music Theatre Studio managed one production, Handel's opera *Rodelinda*, performed at Dartington and the Old Vic in London, before it closed down.[193]

Hans Oppenheim had hoped to revive a specifically English syncretic tradition of art, following in the footsteps of Henry Purcell, 'who wrote music and words in a single composition that involved dance, chorus, drama, opera and orchestra, and an intimate understanding of all five'.[194] But his aim had also been that his Music Theatre Studio would combat 'political cramps' – by which he meant totalitarianism and the rising threat of war – by joining together a 'ring of similarly-thinking minds around the world', whose 'new and genuinely creative life' would bring 'a resurrection of a new Mankind'.[195] The advance of these

---

[190] Hans Oppenheim, 'A singer's studio at Dartington', T/AM/1/D.
[191] [n.a.], Introductory pamphlet for the Music Theatre Studio, [n.d], T/AM/1/B.
[192] [n.a.], 'Dartington Art Studios', [n.d.], T/AV/2.
[193] Peter Cox, 'The Dartington Hall Arts Department and Its Music Training Centre', 1 February 1945, T/AM/1/F.
[194] Hans Oppenheim's ambitions were described by Leonard in a letter to H. Gee of the Ministry of Labour, 30 June 1937, T/AM/1/C.
[195] Hans Oppenheim, 'A singer's studio at Dartington', [n.d.], T/AM/1/D.

political cramps had put a quick end to his nationally specific but internationalist project. Oppenheim was not alone in his desire to combat international tensions. In the 1930s, the Dartington arts department was a testing ground for a range of communitarian and internationalist ideas for promoting social harmony.

4.2.4   Internationalist and Nationalist Visions

> Troupes of dancers and actors from Chelsea, Boston and the more exotic cultural capitals of Europe disported in the numerous theatres and dancing arenas, but endeavours to develop an indigenous artistic tradition satisfying the needs of the countryside petered out.   Rolf Gardiner (1941)[196]

For the Elmhirsts, the harmonious progress of civilisation lay not with the nationalist mentality – which they, like many of their generation, deemed responsible for the First World War – but with people who were simultaneously committed to their local community and sympathetically attuned to the rest of the world (Kwame Appiah's 'rooted cosmopolitanism').[197] Their pacifist internationalism was shared by a large number of people in the 1920s and by many of the artists drawn to Dartington.[198] The 1930s, however, introduced a more complex dialectic. The rise of totalitarian regimes and the arrival on the estate of refugees fleeing them meant that some began to see nationalism as not only culturally desirable but also necessary for defence. The result was passionate, unresolved debate across the estate over whether the community should be internationally or nationally minded, and whether such ideals would be most effectively promoted through local amateur art or through professional performance on a larger stage. That Dartington was able to host contending viewpoints was symptomatic of a lack of intellectual rigour and coordinated direction, but these characteristics also contributed to its creative richness, making it a conduit for many of the cultural currents of its age.

Kurt Jooss was representative of the large-stage and internationalist side of the argument. In Germany, in response to Nazi nationalism, he had developed a modernist choreographic style that was 'an

---

[196] Rolf Gardiner, 'Rural Reconstruction', in H. J. Massingham (ed.), *England and the Farmer: A Symposium* (London), 1941, 91–107, at 106–7.

[197] Leonard, Notes on Dartington, January 1931, LKE/G/S11A; Leonard, 'Time Budget 1934–5', 8 November 1934, LKE/G/S8/I; Kwame Anthony Appiah, *The Ethics of Identity* (Princeton), 2005, chapter 6.

[198] Jeanne Morefield details the variety of liberal plans for furthering internationalism in *Covenants Without Swords: Idealist Liberalism and the Spirit of Empire*, Princeton, 2005.

4.4 Ballets Jooss dancers on a break, *c.* 1935 (© Fritz Henle Estate)

internationally focused fusion of ballet and modern dance'.[199] Both he and Leonard hoped that the Ballets Jooss would further Dartington's agenda by promoting international unity, carrying its ideals 'right across national bounds' and contributing to 'the building of one commonwealth of nations recognizing one common weal'.[200] His company, performing successfully in London, Europe and America, and his dance school, drawing a cosmopolitan array of students, certainly gave Dartington international status.[201] Yet, Fritz Cohen, the Ballets' composer, saw a problem: the company would be ineffectual at propagandising in foreign countries unless it was properly integrated with the estate: 'to lead far reaching propaganda for Dartington Hall ideas .... We all have to become much more a part of Dartington Hall'. The 'spirit of the group' might identify with Dartington 'but the spirit alone is not enough: it has to work in flesh and blood ... within the much wider order of the Arts Department and the entire estate'.[202] Leonard agreed with Cohen that internationalism should begin with building a unified society on the local scale, but Jooss did not. His extrovert ambitions for his group

---

[199] Ramsay Burt, *Alien Bodies: Representation of Modernity, 'Race' and Nation* (London, 1998), 106.
[200] Leonard, Ballets Jooss programme, 1939, T/AD/1/A/G.
[201] In 1936, twelve of the students were Dutch, five Swedish, five German, two American, two Swiss, two Polish, one Danish, one Romanian, one French and one Russian. 'Jooss-Leeder School of Dance Register 1934–6', T/AD/1. Hutchinson Guest, 'The Jooss-Leeder School', 168.
[202] Fritz Cohen to the Elmhirsts, [extract], 1938, DWE/A/9/B.

tended to pull the arts department 'out of shape', as arts administrator Chris Martin complained.[203]

Other observers thought the foreign artists and internationalist agenda of the 1930s were anathema to Dartington's original ambition – which they interpreted as being to discover a good standard of English rural life. For the left-wing theatre director Rupert Doone, who tried and failed to get the Elmhirsts to adopt his theatre group, Dartington should be 'a realistic experiment which may provide the basis upon which the big landlord-estates may be liquidated ... not a "Pleasaunce of the Arts" and of international talent'.[204] It was not that Doone condemned the 'internationality of aesthetics' per se. Nor did he think that artists ought to be excluded from the estate. He only argued that, in order to align with the Elmhirsts' wider objectives, artists should be representative of the locale, rather than being admitted 'regardless of their affinity for the country or their ability to represent it'.[205] Doone's ideas about indigenous art echoed those of the interwar folk revivalists, who, as Georgina Boyes finds, saw village dances and songs as the means of regenerating '"Merrie England"'.[206]

Chris Martin was satisfied with a situation in which his department represented a collaboration between Dartington and 'the best elements in the theatre of Weimar Germany', and had even become 'something new' that was 'neither German nor English' – but some refugee professional artists agreed with Doone.[207] The object of art was 'to develop the particular traits of the natives and the land'.[208] Art's purpose was inherently nationalistic – or at least locale-specific. Oppenheim hoped to revive the English 'art of music theatre' that had been pursued by Purcell before the 'national tradition and school of music fell prey to fashion from abroad'.[209] Rudolf Laban, a leading theorist of modern expressive dance, had been practising a systematic approach to nation-

[203] Chris Martin, 'Report to Dartington Trustees, 21 November 1941', T/AA/1/G.

[204] Rupert Doone's criticisms were quoted by W. B. Curry in a letter to Chris Martin, 21 May 1936, T/DHS/B/20/A. Rupert Doone's own Group Theatre (1932–53) was a socialist experiment founded with Robert Medley and intended to create 'realistic fantasy' that would provide a commentary on modern life. It attracted the involvement of Christopher Isherwood, Stephen Spender and W. H. Auden. Michael Sidnell, *Dances of Death: The Group Theatre of London in the Thirties* (London, 1984).

[205] Rupert Doone quoted by W. B. Curry in a letter to Chris Martin, 21 May 1936, T/DHS/B/20/A.

[206] Georgina Boyes, *The Imagined Village: Culture, Ideology and the English Folk Revival* (Manchester, 1993), 65.

[207] Chris Martin, 'Report to Dartington Trustees', 18 May 1939, T/AA/1/E.

[208] Rupert Doone quoted by W. B. Curry in a letter to Chris Martin, 21 May 1936, T/DHS/B/20/A.

[209] Leonard to H. Gee of the Ministry of Labour, 30 June 1937, T/AM/1/C.

building dance in Germany and saw in Dartington an opportunity for continuing with his experiments in this sphere.

For Laban, as for the Elmhirsts, art was a source of social and spiritual unity: a means of achieving 'a right functioning of our individual as well as community life' and a 'connection and communication with the life-force'.[210] From 1912, in the Swiss experimental community of Monte Verita, he had run a summer school that offered movement, nature and spiritualism as antidotes to the mechanisation of modern society.[211] In the 1920s and 1930s, in Germany, he developed this culture of dance into a more elaborate community-building ideology. Its mainstay, the movement choir ('*Bewegung-schor*') – a choreographed 'folk' celebration – involved large numbers of amateurs. Laban's ideology, along with the broader *völkisch* movement of which it formed part, was gradually co-opted by the Nazi state, with the folk idea metamorphosing into the ideal of a master race.[212] While Laban himself was more interested in strengthening local community than in fascist nationalism, he cooperated in this process.[213] 'We want', he wrote, 'to place our means of expression and the language of our eager energy in the service of the great tasks which our nation is fulfilling.'[214] In 1936, he choreographed a large dance demonstration for the Berlin Olympic Games.[215] Soon after, he fell out of favour with the regime. Accused of being a Freemason (true) and homosexual (false) he was forced to flee the country.[216]

When Laban arrived in Devon in 1938 to recover his health and write a book, he continued to pursue his hope of nation-building through communal creativity, seemingly not minding that he was now part of a

---

[210] Rudolf Laban to Leonard, 10 March 1939, T/AD/3.
[211] This was called *Schule für Lebenskunst* ('School for the Art of Life'). Patricia Vertinsky, *Disciplining Bodies in the Gymnasium: Memory, Monument, Modernism* (London, 2004), 277.
[212] John Alexander Williams, *Turning to Nature in Germany: Hiking, Nudism, and Conservation 1900–1940* (Stanford, 2007).
[213] There is broad consensus that Rudolf Laban was either apolitical or politically naïve and did not fully comprehend the implications of the association of his cultural efforts with the Nazi regime. Martin Green, *Mountain of Truth: The Counterculture Begins, Ascona, 1900–1920* (Hanover and London, 1989); Valerie Preston-Dunlop, *Laban*; and Carole Kew, 'From Weimar Movement Choir to Nazi Community Dance: The Rise and Fall of Rudolf Laban's "Festkultur"', *Dance Research: The Journal of the Society for Dance Research* 17 (1999), 73–96.
[214] Rudolf Laban quoted in Vertinsky, *Disciplining Bodies*, 286.
[215] Preston-Dunlop, *Laban*, 189–98.
[216] Patricia Vertinsky, 'Schooling the Dance: From Dance under the Swastika to Movement Education in the British School', *Journal of Sport History* 31 (2004), 273–95.

different nation.[217] He suggested to Leonard 'a splendid idea to join the marvellous unfolding of the professional dancing at Dartington [to] an organisation of the modern community dance chorus' – showing no concern that many of the professional artists were refugees from the regime he had until recently been supporting.[218] He imagined that this could be linked to the movement promoting national fitness.[219] He presented to Leonard a scheme similar to his earlier plans for a state dance college in Nazi Germany, although now he was less trusting of the state.[220] He thought that such a movement should grow locally, 'in an organic way': 'the laws of movement cannot be forced upon anybody by a violent and spasmodic effort'.[221] Nothing came of Laban's idea, but it says much for Dartington's ideological capaciousness that it could simultaneously support his nationalistic urges and other refugees' pacifist internationalism.[222]

Nationalist art gained little traction on the estate in the 1930s because the Elmhirsts' approach was fundamentally internationalist. Nonetheless, Dartington was brushed by the interwar enthusiasm for national regeneration through folk art.[223] Rolf Gardiner, who trained in forestry on the estate and then went on to build a multifaceted rural regeneration project at Springhead in Dorset, saw folk music and dance as the 'unifying magic of a purposeful society'.[224] He returned to Dartington with a touring troupe to give a 'semi-mystical' folk performance at a Sunday evening meeting – for him, a demonstration of how authentic folk culture could counter the bankruptcy of a materialist, individualist civilisation.[225] Leonard's secretary spoke for a wider response among the audience when she recorded her puzzlement over the religious solemnity of the occasion, at which no applause was allowed. 'For the people who like that sort of thing,' she wrote, 'that's

---

[217] Born a Hungarian, Rudolf Laban obtained German nationality in 1935 and from 1938 spent the rest of his life in England – his trajectory perhaps influencing his sense that national loyalty might be easily transferred.
[218] Rudolf Laban to Leonard, 10 March 1939, T/AD/3.
[219] Rudolf Laban, 'Practical outlook', [n.d.], T/AD/3.
[220] Rudolf Laban to Leonard, 10 March 1939, T/AD/3.   [221] Ibid.
[222] After the war Laban set up an 'Art of Movement' studio in Manchester with the Elmhirsts' sponsorship, and his ideas about dance entered the curriculum of many British schools. Vertinsky, 'Schooling the Dance'.
[223] Boyes, *The Imagined Village*; Matthew Jefferies and Mike Tyldesley (eds.), *Rolf Gardiner: Folk, Nature and Culture in Interwar Britain* (Farnham, 2011).
[224] Rolf Gardiner, 'Reflections on Music and Statecraft', first published in 1934, compiled in Andrew Best (ed.), *Water Springing from the Ground: An Anthology of the Writings of Rolf Gardiner* (Oxford, 1972), 95–100, at 97.
[225] For more on Rolf Gardiner, see Patrick Wright, *The Village that Died for England: The Strange Story of Tyneham* (London, 1995), 151–63 and 176–202.

the sort of thing they like.'[226] Gardiner, 'chilled' by his reception, complained that Dartington lacked the 'fire of dedication': the arts department, full of 'good Americans who feel far more at home in New York', would never generate a 'living tradition of dance and mime' until it was 'based on fundamentally English, northern instincts of carriage and socially on the life and occasions of the estate'.[227] Dartington's participants, he wrote, thought of art as 'production or performance' put on for them, rather than 'festival solidarity'.[228] He would perhaps have looked with more approval on the 1929 community performance of *Comus*.

Outside the European context, the Elmhirsts were more willing to support cultural nationalism. They welcomed the visit of the Japanese potters Yanagi Soetsu and Hamada Shoji, whose *Mingei* movement advocated turning back to the functional beauty of everyday goods made by unknown traditional craftsmen as the basis for constructing a new national culture for Japan.[229] Dorothy and Leonard also consistently supported the work of Tagore, whose university of Visva-Bharati was a touchstone for regenerating the national arts. And, after the Indian dancer and choreographer Uday Shankar had used Dartington as a base in 1936 for successful European and American tours with his troupe, the Elmhirsts provided £20,000 for him to set up a school for arts education in the United Provinces in northern India[230] Shankar was celebrated by supporters of the Indian cultural renaissance, including Tagore, for his embrace of a pan-regional style of Indian ballet, 'developing the indigenous arts as symbolic carriers of nationhood'.[231] His short-lived school in Almora promised an 'all-India character' and intended not to take on any

---

[226] Kay Starr to Leonard Elmhirst, 22/23 September 1933, LKE/G/31/A.

[227] Rolf Gardiner to Leonard, 16 June 1933, LKE/G/15/B.

[228] Rolf Gardiner to Leonard, 28 September 1933, LKE/G/15/B.

[229] The association was through Bernard Leach, who was central to the early *Mingei* movement. Yanagi Soetsu to Leonard, 4 August 1929, T/AAP/3/A; Yuko Kikuchi, 'The Myth of Yanagi's Originality: The Formation of *Mingei* Theory in its Social and Historical Context', *Journal of Design History* 7 (1994), 247–66.

[230] The troupe was called 'Uday Shankar and his Hindu Ballet'. Initially Dorothy's daughter Beatrice Straight, one of Shankar's most enthusiastic students whilst he was at Dartington, was going to put up the money for the Uday Shankar India Culture Centre. She also briefly considered marrying him. Partly to protect her from what they saw as a passion that would be short-lived, her parents took over the funding. The centre flourished momentarily, attracting the interest of the Indian government, but within five years internal tensions and financial problems forced it to close. Correspondence between Shankar and the Elmhirsts and papers relating to the Uday Shankar India Culture Centre are in file LKE/India/19/A-D and DWE/A/8/A; Ruth K. Abrahams, 'Uday Shankar: The Early Years, 1900–1938', *Dance Chronicle* 30 (2007), 363–426, at 365.

[231] Rabindranath Tagore, 'Tagore's Tribute to Shankar', trans. Basanta Koomar Roy, *The American Dancer*, February 1937, 13; Nicholas, *Dancing in Utopia*, 93.

Western students for the first five years.[232] Promoting European nationalism, in the shadow of the First World War and then the Second, ran against the Elmhirsts' vision for Dartington as a hub of world unity; supporting cultural nationalism in non-European countries seemed to them a very different proposition. This contradiction, not uncommon in the interwar years, bore a flavour of primitivism. There was a sense that non-Western nations were ahistorical or apolitical: that they were lower down or separate in the world order and unlikely to harm the project of building an internationalist utopia even if they developed an independent identity.[233]

This primitivism – the idealisation of earlier cultures or 'timeless' non-Western cultures that are seen as 'other' and outside modernity – led the Elmhirsts and others on the estate to place a strong value on Eastern culture.[234] They viewed the art of non-Western cultural traditions, as well as their religion, as embodying superior values: opposing urban decadence, materialism and individualism with rustic honesty, spiritual enlightenment and locally rooted, collective living.[235] The Elmhirsts saw Uday Shankar's dance and music performances as unique in the way they united life and the arts.[236] Japanese art, for Bernard Leach, was a source of spiritual authenticity, while for Mark Tobey it collapsed oppositions 'between the insignificant and the overwhelming', accessing universality through details in a way Western approaches could not.[237] These views echoed a wider sense in the early twentieth century of an aesthetic and social vitality located beyond the West, a vitality that modernists from Pablo Picasso to Igor Stravinsky strove to channel, and that the Elmhirsts sought to capture in their community.[238]

---

[232] Uday Shankar to G. B. Pratt, the Premier of the United Provinces, [n.d.], LKE/India/19/A.

[233] The intersection of primitivism, nationalism and imperialism is explored in the French context by John Warne Monroe, 'Surface Tensions: Empire, Parisian Modernism, and "Authenticity" in African Sculptures, 1917–1939', *American Historical Review* 117 (2012), 445–75. Morefield discusses the contradiction between universalism and the hierarchy of colonial and colonised countries in *Covenants Without Swords*, 2, 131 and passim.

[234] Ben Etherington, *Literary Primitivism* (Stanford, CA, 2018), 10.

[235] Partha Mitter, 'Decentering Modernism: Art History and Avant-Garde Art from the Periphery', *The Art Bulletin* 90 (2008), 531–48, 543.

[236] Diana Brenscheidt, *Shiva Onstage: Uday Shankar's Company of Hindu Dancers and Musicians in Europe and the United States, 1931–38* (Berlin, 2011), 119.

[237] Christopher Reed, 'Sublimation and Eccentricity in the Art of Mark Tobey: Seattle at Midcentury', in *Bachelor Japanists: Japanese Aesthetics and Western Masculinities* (New York, 2017), 201–90, at 240.

[238] David Matless, 'Nature, the Modern and the Mystic: Tales from Early Twentieth Century Geography', *Transactions of the Institute of British Geographers* 16 (1991), 272–86, at 283; Etherington, *Literary Primitivism*, 4–5.

4.3   Looking Outwards and Looking Forwards

The high point of the professional era of the arts department was the summer of 1938. There were some sixty foreign artists working and studying at Dartington. Chekhov's Theatre Studio, the Ballets Jooss and Oppenheim's Music Theatre Studio were building the estate's international renown.[239] Dartington modelled in miniature the effect that sculptor Barbara Hepworth saw émigrés having nationally. 'Suddenly England felt alive and rich – the centre of an international movement .... We all seemed to be carried on the crest of this robust and inspiring wave of creative energy. We were not at that time prepared to admit that it was a movement in flight.'[240] When the Second World War began and many artists on the estate left, Chris Martin found himself with a skeleton of a department and a depleted endowment. Dorothy, coming back from her work with Chekhov, was more concerned to promote Anglo-American unity as part of the war effort than to stabilise the arts department.

At this point, Leonard's unifying ideal came back to the fore: not high standards, but community utility; not international success, but how 'to train other Mark [Tobey]s to start groups in the villages and schools'.[241] Experimentation with community involvement stretched back through the 1930s, when Leonard had pursued it in Devon independently of the arts department. When war broke up the professional status quo, Chris Martin shifted his position to follow Leonard's lead. His new focus was to make the estate a training centre for teachers taking arts into the surrounding countryside.[242] There would also be schools of dance, drama, music and the visual arts, each with a performing group to give students experience by touring regionally and working with amateurs. Rather than the local initiatives of the 1920s – the socialist pluralist model of social improvement through autonomous units – this iteration of the community-building ideal leaned towards national progressive collaboration with the state. The next sections look at the work that Leonard did to support community arts outside the professionalised Dartington arts department in the 1930s, following these efforts to their culmination in cooperation with the government during and after the Second World War.

---

[239] Chris Martin, 'Plan for the Arts Department', 1941, T/AA/1/H.
[240] Barbara Hepworth, *A Pictorial Autobiography* (London, 1985). See also Daniel Snowman, *The Hitler Emigrés: The Cultural Impact on Britain of Refugees from Nazism* (London, 2002).
[241] Leonard to Dorothy, 20 November 1937, LKE/DWE/6/B.
[242] Chris Martin, 'Plan for the Arts Department', 1941, T/AA/1/H.

4.3.1   Community Drama in the 1930s

Leonard had supported the Workers' Educational Association (WEA) since his youth in Yorkshire, attending lectures and donating funds. He was nonetheless chary of committing Dartington to a 'fixed mode of cooperation' with this or any other external organisation in the estate's experimental early stage.[243] In the 1930s, once he and Dorothy had become more open to collaboration, the problem became the limited structures available with which to work. The Elmhirsts were frustrated by the organisational chaos in adult education: 'the WEA, Women's Institutes, County Council, University College, local institutions such as our own, all try to attack this vast problem from different angles'.[244] In a letter to R. H. Tawney, Leonard compared it to 'the field of marketing': 'Between competitive retailers and middlemen, the public is getting neither quality nor quantity'.[245] Further complicating matters, Leonard's experiences at Sriniketan, with the Young Men's Christian Association and then at Dartington, had led him to disapprove of the WEA's general mode of approach in the countryside: rather than through lectures and discussions, he wrote, rural people actually learned through '"Passionate perception"'.[246] For him, this meant through the arts.

The vehicle Leonard found for furthering this agenda was the Devon Extension Scheme (DES). Established in 1927 as a collaboration between the WEA, Devon County Council and University College of the South West (UCSW), its central figure was F. G. Thomas, the tutor-organiser appointed to head up its operations.[247] Along with seven other tutors, Thomas worked to marshal dramatic organisations in Devon – the British Drama Society, the UCSW, various local repertory companies – into cooperating to hold classes and put on plays and festivals.[248] Leonard spoke at the first DES conference, sat on its governing committee and then, in 1935, became its chairman.[249] He supported and advised Thomas, sharing with him a sense of the importance of the arts in extra-mural extension programmes and of helping 'all the various activities of

[243] Leonard to John Murray of the University College of the South West, 25 December 1927, LKE/EDU/1/A.
[244] Leonard to John Murray, 30 April 1929, LKE/EDU/1/C.
[245] Leonard to R. H. Tawney, 27 February 1928, LKE/EDU/10/B.
[246] Leonard to Henry Morris, 1 July 1934, T/HIS/21/A.
[247] An account of the work of F. G. Thomas and his wife Irene is given by Mick Wallis in 'Drama in the Villages: Three Pioneers', in Paul Brassley, Jeremy Burchardt and Lynne Thompson (eds.), *The English Countryside Between the Wars: Regeneration or Decline?* (New York, 2006), 102–115.
[248] F. G. Thomas to Leonard, 23 March 1928, LKE/EDU/1/B.
[249] F. G. Thomas, 'Birthday Party at Hay Tor', *Western Times*, 2 December 1927, British Library Newspaper Archives.

the village which are making for the good of the community as a whole'
rather than supporting one particular educational organisation.[250] For
Thomas, community drama was a form of adult education superior to
lectures, radio or film because it was universal, crossing class and intellectual barriers, and because it was 'centripetal', bringing villages
together and demonstrating their unity.[251]

When Leonard took up the chairmanship of the DES, he hoped he would
be presiding over 'a pioneer experiment' in bringing education to 'the
isolated rural population', free from the 'petty squabblings' which he had
experienced in other areas of local activism.[252] He was disappointed, however, and was soon comparing the work to being 'back in India discussing
communal representation'.[253] Interwar adult education was a shifting
field, a messy patchwork of voluntarism and state-sponsored services.[254]
There were tensions between district and centre. The WEA, county authorities and universities jockeyed for power.[255] Thomas was caught in the
crossfire. His post was funded by the Carnegie UK Trust for its first three
years, but he remained attached to the WEA and his pioneering approach
aroused the wrath, first of the WEA district secretary, J. G. Trevena, then
of the WEA's central bureaucracy.[256] The WEA tried to tie Thomas down
to teaching orthodox, grant-earning tutorial classes and to restrict his
collaboration with other organisations working in the villages.[257]

Leonard put considerable effort into pulling the institutional strings
required to allow Thomas to go on doing 'just the kind of educational
work that is most needed'.[258] He asked the National Council of Social
Services to review the situation, accusing the WEA, UCSW Extra-Mural
Department and county authorities of deliberately failing to cooperate.[259]
He helped Thomas in his successful application for a Rockefeller

---

[250] [n.a.], 'Weekend school to be held at Pinchaford Farm', 19–20 November 1927, LKE/
EDU/1/A.
[251] F. G. Thomas, *The New Learning: An Experiment with Educational Films in the County of
Devon* (London, 1932), 115.
[252] Leonard, 'Time Budget 1934–5', 8 November 1934, LKE/G/S8/1.
[253] Leonard to E. Green, organising secretary of the WEA, 21 February 1935, LKE/EDU/
3/A.
[254] Jeremy Burchardt, 'State and Society in the English Countryside: The Rural
Community Movement 1918–39', *Rural History* 23 (2012), 81–106.
[255] Wallis, 'Drama in the Villages', 111.
[256] E. Green of the London WEA warned Leonard of the danger of Thomas's work
impinging on that of the WEA district secretary, J. G. Trevena (20 February 1935,
LKE/EDU/3/A). Trevena himself also strove throughout the 1930s to curtail
Thomas's remit.
[257] See files LKE/EDU/1–10.
[258] Leonard to J. G. Trevena, 28 March 1928, LKE/EDU/1/B.
[259] Leonard to Captain Ellis of the National Council of Social Services, 23 February 1928,
LKE/EDU/1/B.

Foundation scholarship to get experience in better-organised American extra-mural education.[260] When Thomas returned from this trip, his path had been smoothed by a chance change in Board of Education regulations so that he could be transferred to working directly for the UCSW.[261] Earlier, Leonard had supported the idea of multiple independent schemes for social reform – a form of socialist pluralism – but his experience with Thomas and the DES pushed him towards championing a planned, centralised system for adult education and the social services more generally.

Leonard also supported Mary Kelly, founder of the Village Drama Society, in his search for dynamic ways to promote community arts. Kelly began the society after the First World War in her home village and helped it to expand, but she always insisted, like Thomas, that not too much should be imposed from above – on 'the growth of this village movement from within, rather than the application of imitative drama from without'.[262] The Elmhirsts were regulars at her 'folk dramas', which used original scripts based on local history.[263] In 1935, at Leonard's instigation, Kelly was appointed the honorary director of drama for the DES, working alongside F. G. Thomas. In an indication of the untidy nature of adult education, despite this appointment, the British Drama League (into which the Village Drama Society was incorporated in 1932) still had to pay her salary.[264] Kelly's trajectory paralleled that of the Elmhirsts and other elites in the voluntary sector: beginning as 'a gentrywoman exercising class patronage', she moved to collaborating with the state and charitable agencies in the interwar years, and by the 1940s was working for a publicly funded institution.[265]

---

[260] F. G. Thomas's emphasis on community-building rather than the acquisition of intellectual knowledge in adult education reflected the attitude of many progressives in America. Joseph F. Kett, *The Pursuit of Knowledge Under Difficulties* (Stanford, 1994), 313–5.

[261] Under Article XI of the amended Regulations of 1931, universities were given funding for full-time tutors delivering pioneering work as well as tutorial classes. Mick Wallis, 'Drama in the Villages', 113–4.

[262] Mary Kelly was referred to the Elmhirsts by Geoffrey Whitworth of the British Drama League. The Elmhirsts gave her a gift of £50 and guaranteed an overdraft for her. Mary Kelly to Dorothy, 13 July 1932, DWE/A/11/C.

[263] Dorothy to Thelma Cazalet MP, 3 May 1940, DWE/A/11/C; Andrew Walker, 'The "Uncertainty of Our Climate": Mary Kelly and the Rural Theatre', in Kristin Bluemel and Michael McCluskey (eds.), *Rural Modernity in Britain: A Critical Intervention* (Edinburgh, 2018), 121–34, at 122.

[264] Mary Kelly to Leonard, 6 August 1935, T/ADR/2/B.

[265] Mick Wallis, 'Kelly, Mary Elfreda (1888–1951)', *Oxford Dictionary of National Biography* (Oxford University Press, first published 23 September 2004, revised 27 May 2010) [www.oxforddnb.com/view/article/69833?docPos=1]; Mick Wallis, 'Unlocking the Secret Soul: Mary Kelly, Pioneer of Village Theatre', *New Theatre Quarterly* 16 (2000), 347–58.

Through all, she retained a sense of being a 'natural' leader of society. It was not an uncommon path or point of view. James Hinton finds that even the Second World War, for all its democratic rhetoric, just as often reinforced the authority of traditional social leaders as it stimulated radical challenge from below.[266]

Leonard hoped that the Dartington arts department would contribute to the efforts of the DES. The gulf between the ideas of such community organisers as Kelly and Thomas and those that were dominant among Dartington's professional artists in the 1930s, however, was indicated by Michael Chekhov's reaction to seeing a performance put on by one of Thomas's drama groups: 'I imagine you must have many different aims for your work, and that you do not mean to try to make actors'.[267] Although Thomas had asked for constructive feedback, Chekhov saw village drama as so far from his own work that it scarcely registered on the same scale of analysis. In consequence of the difficulty of knitting Dartington into broader efforts for adult education, and of Leonard's unsatisfactory experience of coordinating the patchwork of private and public organisations working in Devon, in the late 1930s he turned his mind to a new fulcrum of social reform. This would be oriented around strong central or regional planning, with adult education properly coord-inated by the universities or county councils.[268] He hoped Dartington could lead the way in the development of this centralised system.

4.3.2   Supporting the National Arts: The War Years and After

With the outbreak of war, Chris Martin changed tack. He began to argue that 'the foreign musician or man of the theatre' would 'not easily find himself at home in England' and that Dartington should turn its atten-tion 'to the amateur and educational world'.[269] Just as he had wanted his professional foreign artists to be nationally renowned, in this turn to community arts he hoped to replace the extemporised local activities of the arts department's early years with long-term, large-scale collaborative projects with government and voluntary organisations. He also saw such collaboration as an opportunity to access more money. 'We ought to make every effort to depart from our position of splendid isolation and forge a link between ourselves and other individuals and organisations working in the same field,' he wrote in a 1941 plan for the arts

---

[266] James Hinton, *Women, Social Leadership, and the Second World War* (Oxford, 2002).
[267] Michael Chekhov to F. G. Thomas, 27 April 1936, LKE/EDU/4/B.
[268] F. G. Thomas, 'The basis of an extension department of the UCSW, Exeter', 1935, LKE/EDU/3/D.
[269] Chris Martin, 'Plan for the Arts Department', 1941, T/AA/1/H.

department, 'particularly those working with public money'.[270] He imagined Dartington as 'a type of centre which does not exist anywhere else in England', combining a close-textured knowledge of 'the problems and difficulties in the area' with links to national organisations.[271] This national-scale vision absolved participants of the need to make the arts part of the community at Dartington; instead, the arts – and Dartington – would do public service in helping to integrate British society as a whole, chiming in with the war-years' vogue for central planning.[272]

Busy with war work, the Elmhirsts asked Martin to take over liaison with the DES, and to collaborate with the Local Education Authority (LEA) to set up the Devon County Committee for Music and Drama.[273] This committee, which also involved the UCSW and representatives of local organisations, was to promote arts classes in villages and schools and organise festivals and courses, effectively taking over the work that F. G. Thomas had pioneered.[274] It was the start of a connection between the Dartington arts department and the state that would grow over several decades, culminating, in 1974, in the department's receiving national funding as a college of arts.[275] The work brought Martin into contact with others all over the country who were promoting the arts in rural areas, including the Rural Music Schools Association and the Carnegie UK Trust.

In the interwar years, F. M. Leventhal argues, 'public expenditure to subsidize the performing arts in Great Britain was widely perceived as objectionable'.[276] The tendency towards the nationalisation of culture under the Nazis and in Soviet Russia confirmed this prejudice against what seemed to be a manifestation of totalitarian centralisation. The propaganda requirements of the Second World War, however, along with the desire to shore up the national framework of culture during wartime, radically altered this view.[277] The result was the setting up of

---

[270] Ibid.   [271] Ibid.

[272] If politicians 'don't do some thorough planning now it will be too late when the war ends', Leonard wrote to Professor Stanley Watkins of University College (10 January 1940, LKE/EDU/7/A). Daniel Ritschel, *The Politics of Planning: The Debate on Economic Planning in Britain in the 1930s* (Oxford, 1997).

[273] The DES was paid for by the University Extra Mural Board and a grant from the Elmhirsts. It tried to negotiate funding from the Carnegie UK Trust for the salary of a director but was deemed 'too grandiose a scheme' for Carnegie to sponsor. [n.a.], Note on Devon County Committee for Music and Drama, [n.d.], DWE/A/6/B.

[274] Chris Martin, 'Report to Dartington Trustees', 7 February 1941, T/AA/1/G.

[275] Sam Richards, *Dartington College of Arts: Learning by Doing. A Biography of a College* (Totnes, 2015).

[276] F. M. Leventhal, '"The Best for the Most": CEMA and State Sponsorship of the Arts in Wartime, 1939–1945', *Twentieth Century British History* 1 (1990), 289–317, at 289.

[277] Foss, *War Paint*.

the Council for the Encouragement of Music and the Arts (CEMA) in 1940 and the launch of an ambitious project to take visual art, music and drama to audiences throughout the country.[278] Initially, although CEMA operated under the supervision of the Board of Education, it was paid for by the Pilgrim Trust, a philanthropic organisation set up in 1930 by American millionaire Edward Harkness.[279] By the end of the war, however, it had transitioned to being wholly funded by the state.

The change in the Dartington arts department's direction at this moment coincided with the change in the government's – in part because they were by this point intimately linked. Martin was in close contact with CEMA from the start, and it was even suggested that Dartington might become the organisation's headquarters.[280] Although this did not happen, other more transient proposals for cooperation did reach fruition, many of them related to music. In 1940, under a scheme co-organised by the arts department and the Devon LEA, for example, Hans Oppenheim's Dartington Hall Music Group played for eleven schools; the same year, in collaboration with CEMA, it toured local towns and villages.[281] Another group, the Dartington Hall Piano Quartet, also gave touring concerts, funded by a combination of the Pilgrim Trust and CEMA. Despite, or perhaps because of, the privations of war, Dartington's arts programme was finally integrating with the wider community in the way the Elmhirsts hoped.

These small, disparate endeavours were drawn together in 1942 by the arrival of musician Imogen Holst.[282] The idealistic daughter of composer and adult educator Gustav Holst, she first came to Dartington temporarily as one of CEMA's Music Travellers – a band of musicians charged with organising musical activities among amateurs in rural areas during

---

[278] The War Artists' Advisory Committee (established in 1939) had a similar impetus to CEMA – as well as recording the war, it was intended 'to raise public taste, foster a national culture, and lay the groundwork for post-war patronage of art by the state'. Foss, *War Paint*, 9 and 193.

[279] Edward Harkness and Dorothy both made substantial gifts for student buildings at American universities, owned mansions on the same avenue in New York and supported the arts in Britain – but do not seem to have been intimate acquaintances. Roger L. Geiger, *To Advance Knowledge: The Growth of American Research Universities 1900–1940* ([n.p], 2017), 119 and 128.

[280] Cox, *The Arts*, 12.

[281] Chris Martin, 'Report on the visit of the Dartington Hall Chamber Music Group to LEA schools in Devon', [1940], T/AM/1/E; Chris Martin, Memorandum, 14 January 1941, T/AM/1/E.

[282] Imogen Holst was a member of the English Folk Dance and Song Society from 1923, part of the English folk revival. After leaving Dartington in 1951, she went to Aldeburgh, Suffolk, remaining there for the rest of her life and running the Aldeburgh Festival, a celebration of English classical music founded by Benjamin Britten and Peter Pears.

the war.[283] Martin was impressed by her skill in combining amateurs into a vibrant music community within a few weeks, and invited her to remain and start a training course at Dartington, primarily for rural music teachers and county music organisers.[284]

Holst's thorough-going socialism made her initially sceptical of the wealth of Dartington, but she was reconciled by how egalitarian she found its day-to-day functioning, and over the next eight years she established the foundations of a music school.[285] It would become one of the chief components of the estate's post-war arts department.[286] Holst also represented Dartington at Devon County Music Committee meetings, spreading its influence more widely, and contributed to turning the estate into 'an arts centre for the locality' by launching a full programme of music, from gramophone recitals to composition lessons and an amateur choir and orchestra.[287] A pupil at Dartington School remembered playing the cello on open strings next to Leonard, who had started learning at the same time as herself: 'Everyone, but everyone was involved in playing music.'[288] In 1961, the arts department was transformed into the Dartington College of Arts on the foundations that Holst had laid. This part-publicly, part-Dartington-Hall funded institution offered courses that prepared students for a career of teaching in the arts – the first to do so for state-school students.[289]

Art and theatre took a back seat to music during the war but similarly moved towards local and national community participation. In 1940, Dartington hosted two public exhibitions in conjunction with the London Gallery, 'the first major showing of surrealist work in a British

---

[283] Gustav Holst was for a time director of music at Morley College, a philanthropic adult education institute set up in South London in 1889 to improve working class access to 'good' culture. The Music Travellers were the invention of musician and broadcaster Sir Walford Davies. They were originally intended just for Wales but were subsequently applied to the whole of the country. They were first funded by the Pilgrim Trust and then taken over by CEMA during the war.

[284] Cox, *The Arts*, chapter 4.

[285] Imogen Holst, interview with Michael Young, 21 March 1977, T/HIS/S22/A.

[286] The music school began with students aged sixteen to eighteen. The forty-three students who had graduated from the course by 1949 went on to become rural music school directors, music teachers, administrators or professional performers. In 1951 a drama course was launched to parallel the music course, but it quickly folded and from then on drama was mainly continued through association with external institutions including Bath Academy. T/AM/1/G.

[287] Holst's activities are detailed in Peter Cox and Jack Dobbs (eds.), *Imogen Holst at Dartington* (Dartington, 1988).

[288] Author interview with Etain Todds (née Kabraji), 17 May 2015.

[289] Richards, *Dartington College of Arts*, 15.

provincial gallery'.[290] In 1949, a successful 'Teacher and the Arts' course was run for the LEA, bringing together ninety teachers and cementing a long-term relationship with the LEA.[291] Dartington's arts department formed close links with other bodies, new and old. It supported the Devon Guild of Craftsmen, founded in 1955. It ran a 'Made in Devon' exhibition in 1950 at the behest of the County Federation of Women's Institutes and Townswomen's Guilds, which wanted to help its member organisations prepare for the Festival of Britain. Walter Gropius' Barn Theatre became the home of a new community theatre group, the Playgoers Society, and was also used by a patchwork of amateur and university drama groups, and as an annual meeting place for county drama organisers.[292] The move back to community-oriented, collaborative arts initiatives undertaken by Chris Martin at the onset of the Second World War defined the shape of Dartington's activities for decades to come, yielding more tangible and far-reaching results than the inward-looking iteration of the same philosophy in the 1920s had managed to achieve.

4.3.3   The Arts Enquiry

The Arts Enquiry was the apotheosis of the community-utility approach to the arts at Dartington. It was a survey launched by the Dartington Hall Trust in 1941 with the cooperation of a number of public and private organisations to make a comprehensive investigation into the state of the visual arts, music and film in England.[293] Over the course of eight years, it brought together arts professionals, artists, philanthropists and public thinkers in specialist committees to look at the social value of the arts, their place in education and their economic structure. It was funded by the Dartington Hall Trust, published by the Elmhirst-sponsored think-tank Political and Economic Planning (PEP), and represented significant

---

[290] With the outbreak of war, Roland Penrose and E. L. T. Mesens of the London Gallery decided to locate their collections at Dartington, allowing them to be used in public exhibitions. Six exhibitions were planned, but only two took place, 'Panorama', a survey of modern art, and 'Before Cubism, Negro Art, Cubism and Chirico', both in 1940. David Jeremiah, 'Dartington' – A Modern Adventure', in Smiles (ed.), *Going Modern and Being British: Art, Architecture and Design in Devon c. 1910–1960* (Exeter, 1998), 43–78, at 68.

[291] Cox, *The Arts*, 81–2.

[292] Joan Chissell, 'Dartington', *The Musical Times* 91 (1950), 337–41, at 40.

[293] The members of the investigation into visual arts included F. A. S. Gwatkin (Dartington Hall trustee), G. D. H. Cole (Nuffield College), M. C. Glasgow (CEMA), M. A. Hamilton (Reconstruction Secretariat), B. I. Evans (British Council), A. D. K. Owen (PEP), J. Wilkie (assessor to the Carnegie Trust) and Julian Huxley. To begin with, Chris Martin was the director and Peter Cox the secretary.

private sector involvement in arts policy research for policy formation.[294] Its influence on the Labour Party's arts policy after the war was substantial.[295]

The enquiry stemmed in part from Leonard's burgeoning interest in national planning. This interest reflected a wider vogue for planning, which moved from being 'the foremost radical panacea of the day' in the 1930s to become, during the war, a government preoccupation that would define the shape of the post-war British state.[296] Chris Martin was more specifically inspired to organise the enquiry by his friendship with G. D. H. Cole. The Labour intellectual was the director of the Nuffield College Social Reconstruction Survey, a government-backed investigation into education, social services, the location of industry and the distribution of population.[297] Martin feared that, in post-war reconstruction, 'industry and professions, education and the social services will all put forward plans for their own betterment and claims for some measure of state support', but that the arts would have no unified lobbying platform.[298] He proposed an investigation of the arts as supplementary to, though unaffiliated with, the Nuffield Survey.

The government did not back the Arts Enquiry directly, but it sent a representative from the Reconstruction Secretariat to sit on its committee and requested reports of its findings. As well as undertaking the survey for the purposes of contributing to national planning, both Leonard and Martin saw the enquiry as a way of gathering information that would provide fresh direction for Dartington itself.[299] In that sense, the motivation behind the project had two strands. One was assisting the government. The other, part of a wider culture of surveying that Dartington had supported since its instigation, was about being a

---

[294] The Elmhirsts spent £19,000 over the course of the six-year Arts Enquiry. Upchurch, *The Origins of the Arts Council Movement*, 95–8.

[295] There was a personal connection between Dartington and post-war Labour arts policy in the form of Michael Young. The former Dartington school pupil and protégé of the Elmhirsts drafted the 1945 Labour manifesto for the general election, *Let Us Face the Future*, which emphasised the need 'to assure our people full access to the great heritage of culture in this nation' (London, 1945), 9. When Labour was elected, its commitment to building art into the democratic state was confirmed by its turning CEMA into a permanent body, the forerunner of the Arts Council of Great Britain.

[296] Ritschel, *The Politics of Planning*, 4. See Chapter 5 for further discussion of planning.

[297] The Nuffield College Social Reconstruction Survey, begun in 1941 and based in Oxford, was an attempt to foster cooperation between academics, politicians and business leaders in planning reconstruction. It prepared reports at the request of government departments.

[298] 'The Arts Enquiry', [n.d.], T/AAE/1/B.   [299] Ibid.

community project whose example and investigations would help other like-minded people and operations to help themselves.[300]

There were four projected areas of investigation: the visual arts, theatre, music and factual film.[301] The first report became the most substantial. With Chris Martin as the committee chairman, *The Visual Arts* was intended to be 'an objective and fact-finding survey of the present situation', a yardstick against which to measure the merit of a 'multitude of schemes in the air' for the future of the arts.[302] Soon after work began, Martin fell ill and the direction of the Arts Enquiry was taken over by his assistant, Peter Cox. Martin's position as chairman was given to public intellectual, biologist and social reformer Julian Huxley. Long associated with the Elmhirsts through friendship and through his work with PEP, Huxley had very different ambitions for the survey to Martin.

Huxley had been inspired by the state sponsorship of artists he had seen in the 1930s in New Deal America under the Federal Arts Project. Rather than just collating facts, he wanted the enquiry to advocate a similar model of reconstruction; state funding should replace private patronage and art should be used to give 'society a consciousness'.[303] Huxley succeeded in widening the scope of the Arts Enquiry to making recommendations, but in doing so he alienated some members of the committee. CEMA's representative, Mary Glasgow, objected that the expectations of her own organisation and of the government – that the enquiry would be concerned with objective fact-finding – were being betrayed.[304] The enquiry was claiming to have official support, whilst being 'a purely private venture' sponsored by Dartington.[305]

---

[300] The surveys conducted by Dartington – for example J. R. Currie and W. H. Long's *An Agricultural Survey in South Devon* (1929) – were connected to a wider movement for regional survey in Britain between 1918 and 1939 that was inspired, in particular, by Patrick Geddes. Geddes saw regional surveying as a means of utopia-building: both making the most of an individual place and encouraging participative citizenship, giving people the sense of being 'at once a local, national and world citizen'. David Matless, 'Regional Surveys and Local Knowledges: The Geographical Imagination in Britain 1918–1939', *Transactions of the Institute of British Geographers* 17 (1993), 464–80.

[301] *The Visual Arts* was published in 1946. *Factual Film*, published in 1947, and *Music*, in 1949, had less impact. A projected fourth on theatre was never completed.

[302] [n.a.], 'The Arts Enquiry' [n.d.], T/AAE/1/B.

[303] Julian Huxley quoted in Harrison, 'The Visual Arts', 214. Huxley's views on the international social function of art – put forward in his capacity as secretary-general of the UNESCO preparatory commission – can be found in *UNESCO, Its Purpose and Its Philosophy* ([London], 1946).

[304] Mary Glasgow would be the fulcrum of the organisation for over a decade, becoming secretary-general, first of CEMA then of the Arts Council. 'Discussion between Miss Glasgow and Peter Cox', 29 March [1943], T/AAE/1/B.

[305] [n.a.], 'Minutes of 30 May 1944 Arts Enquiry', T/AAE/1/B.

The consequence of this disagreement was that the central visual arts committee was disbanded, but not before the bulk of research was complete and the writing-up begun.[306]

The specialists who reported to the visual arts committee, based at CEMA's offices in London, echoed many of the diverse, sometimes incompatible, ambitions that the Dartington arts department had tried to cultivate since its inception. The architecture historian and German refugee Nikolaus Pevsner, for example, argued that the arts and crafts should be taught together, and with an eye to the needs of industry; that there should be a planned building up of 'a school-cum-workshop-cum-sales organisation'; and that the populace should be encouraged to engage with art through 'an enlightened policy of exhibitions and museum display, concerned with objects of everyday use'.[307]

A frequently recurring point of discussion – echoing a long-running debate at Dartington – was whether to support popularly accessible standards and amateur creativity or to raise the level of mass taste through professional example. Did democratising art mean 'the democratic acceptance of different taste cultures' or the paternalistic 'co-opting of "the people" into the interests and expectations of the elite'?[308] Kenneth Clark, director of the National Gallery, and economist John Maynard Keynes were two exponents on the visual arts committee of the high-standards school, effectively seeing popular taste as bad taste.[309] Conversely, Philip Hendy, Slade professor of art history at Oxford and director of the Leeds City Art Gallery, warned Huxley that, since 'the whole of the organisation for consuming and producing art' was at present 'essentially oligarchic' – including the committee members themselves – it was crucial that the Arts Enquiry fought against the danger of replicating rather than reforming that model.[310] He contrasted the cultural paternalism of England unfavourably to the more democratic, consumer-oriented approach in America, where market research was used to determine public desire.

Ultimately, although the will of the people was referenced reverently, the Arts Enquiry tended towards a dismissal of popular standards in

[306] It was decided that, since the Arts Enquiry had devolved from 'a little body of non-experts' into 'many panels of specialist opinion', the central committee should not have to sign off on the final report before publication. [n.a.], 'Minutes of the Arts Enquiry Group meeting, 2 May 1944', T/AAE/1/B.
[307] Nikolaus Pevsner, 'Memorandum of the position of the designer for British industries after the war', [n.d.], T/AAE/2/A.
[308] Foss, 'Message and Medium', 56.
[309] Leventhal, '"The Best for the Most"', 289. Their views influenced both CEMA and the Arts Enquiry.
[310] Philip Hendy to Julian Huxley, 31 December 1942, T/AAE/2/A.

favour of fostering artistic excellence and raising public taste through a system of state patronage. 'The majority of people do not know how to look at works of art,' ran the report. 'They need help and guidance.'[311] It was an elitist approach that reflected Dorothy's overall philosophy more than Leonard's – although such paternalist proponents of high culture as Clark and Keynes had neither the modernist nor the spiritually unitive aims that had been put forward by their analogues at Dartington in the years between the wars.

The 'raise or spread' debate – whether to put money towards improving exemplary professional performance or towards broadening the amateur arts – would recur within the Arts Council, CEMA's successor organisation, for many years to come.[312] It was evident at the 1951 Festival of Britain, which, in spite of its populist rhetoric, was, as F. M. Leventhal writes, 'an unleashing of talented professionals egged on by the great and the good'.[313] Among the great and good was Leonard Elmhirst, invited to serve as a member of the Festival of Britain organising council.[314] It was a sign of how far he and Dorothy had moved from the anti-establishment experimenters they considered themselves when they began Dartington – it was also indicative of a broader rapprochement between elite reformers and the state.[315]

Dartington's hope that elite and popular culture could be reconciled would be taken up by the New Left from the 1950s, with Raymond Williams, in particular, arguing that this division was not necessary; that culture could be a collective collaboration, uniting all members of society in a common social project and transcending such conceptual divisions as 'elite' and 'popular'.[316]

The Arts Enquiry's recommendations significantly influenced postwar policy.[317] The chief suggestion, setting up the Arts Council and the Council for Industrial Design, substituted 'a permanent and organic relationship of the State to the fine arts for the haphazard policies of the

---

[311] The Arts Enquiry, *The Visual Arts: A Report Sponsored by the Dartington Hall Trustees* (London, 1946), 27.

[312] Nicholas, *Dancing in Utopia*, 131.

[313] F. M. Leventhal, '"A Tonic to the Nation": The Festival of Britain, 1951', *Albion: A Quarterly Journal Concerned with British Studies* 27 (1995), 445–453, at 448.

[314] The Festival of Britain element Leonard was particularly involved with was the 'Country Pavilion' for the exhibition for rural crafts. LKE/FES.

[315] Richard Weight, 'State, Intelligentsia and the Promotion of National Culture in Britain, 1939–45', *Historical Research* 69 (1996), 83–101.

[316] Williams, *Culture and Society*, 417–8, 436–7.

[317] Rachel Harrison and Anna Upchurch both argue that the influence of the Arts Enquiry on government policy has been underestimated. Harrison, 'The Visual Arts'; Anna Upchurch, '"Missing" From Policy History: The Dartington Hall Arts Enquiry, 1941–1947', *International Journal of Cultural Policy* 19 (2012), 610–22.

past'.[318] State patronage of the arts was, by the 1950s, widely accepted, and only a few isolated figures like Herbert Read still held that it risked fascist-style state control.[319] Other suggestions from the enquiry that were taken up by the government included improving professional arts schools; elevating the position of the arts in the school curriculum; and increasing the public's access to art by such measures as incorporating concert halls, theatres and art galleries in new town plans.[320] The central argument, that 'the visual arts are integral to a civilisation', was a case of Dartington's ideals writ large.[321] After much experimentation, the Dartington arts department had managed to combine some of Leonard's ideas about community engagement with Dorothy's hopes for high standards and spiritual renewal (albeit with the spiritual being interpreted in a more affective than religious sense). The resulting vision and practical prototype of arts administration were convincing enough to influence policymakers and contribute substantially to national reconstruction.

[318] Extract from *The Times*, 9 May 1946, 'Artists and Patrons', T/AAE/1/C. The recommendation to set up a permanent arts organisation had, in fact, already been carried out by the time the report was published, but the process of the enquiry had had a strong impact on thinking about it.
[319] Foss, 'Message and Medium', 56.   [320] The Arts Enquiry, *The Visual Arts*, passim.
[321] Ibid, 42.

5   Regenerating Rural Life

> [W]hat could stay the annual exodus of 50,000 farm labourers and smallholders to the towns and the general breakdown of rural life, and what future was there in the countryside except as a playground for the wealthy or as a vast national park for urban and suburban communities?   Leonard Elmhirst (1939)[1]

For the Elmhirsts, regenerating a community meant modelling a deepened democracy, with democracy construed in John Dewey's sense, as meaning participation in all aspects of social life that maximise self-realisation – the economy, education, culture and governance.[2] They hoped that the influence of their experiment in democratic community-building would be international, but they saw a small patch of country-side as the vital test bed for their efforts – as the essential social unit. It was an idea they held in common with many other reformers of the interwar years, both in Europe and America.[3] 'The social pattern of the countryside was the root pattern,' Daniel Rodgers writes of the trans-atlantic interest in rural reform: 'To mold it into more "sociable" forms, to infuse it with more intensive "collective social action", was to take hold of a nation's core historical template.'[4]

In spite of the widespread idealisation of the small-scale, local and traditional, the early twentieth century was an age of rapidly expanding domestic and international communications and transport.[5] Ideas and people moved faster than ever before, both between town and country

---

[1] Leonard quoted in 'Dartington Hall', *The Lady*, 28 December 1939, 802, clipping in DWE/G/S4/D.

[2] John Dewey, *Democracy and Education: An Introduction to the Philosophy of Education* (New York, 1999 [1916]); Robert B. Westbrook, *John Dewey and American Democracy* (Ithaca, 1991).

[3] Jeremy Burchardt sees the reconstructed ideal of the village in interwar Britain as strongly influenced both by American ruralist thinkers and by English idealists such as T. H. Green. 'Rethinking the Rural Idyll,' *Cultural and Social History* 8 (2011), 73–94.

[4] Daniel T. Rodgers, *Atlantic Crossings: Social Politics in a Progressive Age* (Cambridge, 1998), 326.

[5] Stephen Kern, *The Culture of Time and Space, 1880–1918* ([n.p.], 1983), 109–130.

and between nations – this was the very context that fuelled ruralist dreaming.[6] Dartington was a product of the accelerating globalisation: it drew on American dollars and on an international network of idealists, artists and reformers to forge a model of 'local' community that was meant to be replicable around the world. The Elmhirsts' philosophy of rural regeneration – attempting to combine, as Leonard wrote, the 'microscopic' support for community life with the 'macro-scopic or telescopic mode of approach' which was international in its outlook – prefigured and helped shape a phenomenon central to the later twentieth century.[7] The sociologist Roland Robertson calls this 'glocalisation': a process by which local community is reconfigured, and even strengthened, by global forces – the possibility of alternative, cosmopolitan identities increasing interest in local attachment and belonging.[8]

The trajectory of rural regeneration at Dartington paralleled that of education and the arts. It began as a cluster of internationally influenced, but localised projects that aimed to 'set an ideal for all groups to work to' – be it a poultry factory farm or a democratic discussion group – and ended by making contributions to national reconstruction – whether through agricultural surveys or the employment of departmental personnel by the state.[9] The Elmhirsts encountered the same tensions in this sphere as in other areas of their estate: how to reconcile democratic ideals with their lack of faith in people's ability to govern themselves; whether to prioritise economic or socio-spiritual well-being; the conflict between promoting good taste and making affordable products; the difficulty of cultivating a 'traditional' rural community in the context of urbanisation and globalisation. In spite of these challenges, a number of Dartington's innovations in the spheres of industry, agriculture and social governance caught the imagination of reformers nationally and internationally.

Many utopian endeavours of this period critiqued the dominant capitalist system by refusing to engage with it, adopting subsistence-based,

[6] Some of these tensions are touched on by Jess Gilbert in *Planning Democracy: Agrarian Intellectuals and the Intended New Deal* (New Haven, 2015) and by Raymond Williams in *The Country and the City* (London, 2017 [1973]) – although Williams focuses principally on the British context.
[7] Leonard, untitled note, October 1946, T/AG ECON/1/B.
[8] Roland Robertson, 'Glocalization: Time-Space and Homogeneity-Heterogeneity', in Mike Featherstone, Scott Lash and Roland Robertson (eds.), *Global Modernities* (London, 1995), 25–44. See also Mike Savage's research on the effects of globalisation on local identity in Manchester, including (with Gaynor Bagnall and Brian Longhurst), *Globalisation and Belonging* (London, 2005), ix.
[9] Leonard to Dorothy, 19 May 1923, LKE/DWE/11/C.

cooperative economic models.[10] The Elmhirsts, however, were determined to influence society as a whole, and for them that meant speaking the language of that society: the language of capitalism. Their efforts to humanise the way that capitalism functioned – by demonstrating how profit-making could be combined with communality and holistic fulfilment – connected Dartington to a wider endeavour to make capitalism moral.[11] In particular, it mirrored the efforts of the moral economists R. H. Tawney, Karl Polanyi and E. P. Thompson to reform capitalist individualism by promoting social integration as an alternative. This trio of intellectuals all argued, in different fashions, that laissez-faire capitalism had caused an atomisation that left the poor demoralised beyond relief, and that it was not the state, but humane, low-key, informal solidarities (Thompson's 'moral economy') that could re-integrate a more human economics back into wider society.[12] Dartington – its ambitions, as Gerald Heard put it, 'more latent than explicit, more practical than theoretical' – adds to intellectual history narratives by showing how such speculative ideas about reforming the connection between the economy and society were translated into real-world action[13] 'Had it merely been in the realm of theory,' wrote a visitor to the Elmhirsts' estate in 1929, 'I might have been able to grasp it at least as an intellectual ideal, but its bigness as a reality defeats one's practical conception'.[14]

This chapter begins by positioning rural regeneration at Dartington amid the many and varied interwar reform projects with which it cross-pollinated. The next section turns to the fields of agricultural and industrial revival – the economic side of rural regeneration. Here, early hopes to create a 'self sufficing and self supporting' community were quickly replaced by outward-looking or profit-making ambitions: be it to create a collection of exemplary rural businesses, a blueprint for how big landowners could revive their fortunes, or a research centre leading the field in agricultural and industrial experimentation.[15] The final section of the chapter looks at the Elmhirsts' ambition to promote democratic

---

[10] See, for example, Dennis Hardy, *Utopian England: Community Experiments 1900–1945* (London, 2000); Anna Neima, *The Utopians: Six Attempts to Build the Perfect Society* (London, 2021).

[11] Stefan Berger and Alexandra Przyrembel (eds.), *Moralizing Capitalism: Agents, Discourses and Practices of Capitalism and Anti-Capitalism in the Modern Age* (Cham, 2019).

[12] Tim Rogan, *The Moral Economists: R.H. Tawney, Karl Polanyi, E.P. Thompson and the Critique of Capitalism* (Oxford and London, 2017).

[13] Gerald Heard, 'The Implications of Dartington Hall to a Visitor', *News of the Day*, supplement to the 500th number, 13 March 1934, MC/S4/42/F1.

[14] William McCance to Leonard, 30 January 1929, LKE/G/22/E.

[15] Leonard to Dorothy, 12 December 1924, T/HIS/S20/A.

communal participation. In this area, too, their plan to build a self-governing and holistically integrated collective yielded to one that was more externally focused. The vision that they had reached by the late 1930s – of Dartington as an outpost of centralised social planning – dovetailed effectively into the expansion of state control during the Second World War and into plans for national reconstruction. State participation did not, however, mean the total eclipse of the localised, social democratic ideal: this re-emerged in the decades after the war in the Elmhirsts' contributions to the field of community development in Britain and in India.

5.1   The Countryside in Context

It was in the English countryside that Dartington evolved, but the primary influence on the estate's rural regeneration work came from India. From the late nineteenth century, as Subir Sinha finds, American missionaries and academics, British colonial officials and Indian nationalists had been diagnosing agrarian poverty and social fragmentation as India's most pressing problems, and looking to the 'traditional' village as 'both a model of the good life and a road map for getting there'.[16] The result was a series of village experiments that brought together ideas, people and funds from across the globe – including Rabindranath Tagore's Institute for Rural Reconstruction, Sriniketan, in Bengal, which Leonard helped set up in the early 1920s.[17]

Sriniketan aimed to join social and economic regeneration together with creative self-expression and spiritual growth.[18] It attracted an international cast of participants and was inspired by approaches to reform from around the world, including the Irish cooperative movement,

---

[16] Subir Sinha, 'Lineages of the Developmental State: Transnationality and Village India, 1900–1965', *Comparative Studies in Society and History* 50 (2008), 57–90, at 70. Leonard tended to see the 'village problem' in England and in India as similar; others, such as the Punjab bureaucrat Francis Brayne, saw English villages as already possessing the principles that should be applied to India. Francis Brayne, *The Indian and the English Village* (London, 1933).

[17] Other village reform projects included the Gurgaon Rural Uplift Experiments of Francis Brayne and the Marthandam Rural Development centre started by the American missionary Spencer Hatch. Sinha, 'Lineages of the Developmental State'; Sunil S. Amrith, 'Internationalising Health in the Twentieth Century', in Glenda Sluga and Patricia Clavin (eds.), *Internationalisms, a Twentieth-Century History* (Cambridge, 2017), 245–64, at 252.

[18] For accounts of Sriniketan, see Leonard K. Elmhirst, *Poet and Plowman* (Calcutta, 1975) and *Rabindranath Tagore: Pioneer in Education. Essays and Exchanges between Rabindranath Tagore and L.K. Elmhirst* (London, 1961); and Neima, *The Utopians*, chapter 1.

British progressive education and American rural survey techniques.[19] This and other village experiments of the era – including Dartington Hall and novelist and reformer Mushanokōji Saneatsu's Atarashiki Mura ('New Village') in Japan, which was also inspired by Tagore – all shared a paradox.[20] They championed locally driven generation, but they were nodes in the newly burgeoning international regime of rural reform, incorporating foreign ideas, expertise, funds and the top-down operating principle.[21] They were early examples of the glocal impulse. Arthur Geddes (son of Patrick), who worked with Leonard at Sriniketan, emphasised the problem of its 'crab-like organisation' – with 'Regional and International Ideals' in planning and sociology and practical work in the locality so little aligned that the project 'walks to one side or [the] other'.[22] The task of redefining what it meant to reform a local community in a modern, globalised age would prove an equal challenge for the Elmhirsts.

Once Leonard had left Sriniketan, he and Dorothy continued to support the institute, visiting several times, hosting Tagore at Dartington in 1930 and financing Sriniketan until the Indian government took over control after independence. Dartington was founded, as Leonard wrote to Tagore, on 'an ideal we owed entirely to one source, yourself':[23] like Sriniketan, it began as a small experiment outside the mainstream; combined a rhetoric of bottom-up, democratic reform by locals with international ideas and participants; and aimed to be of international service, a 'great outpouring', that 'encircled the world'.[24] The Elmhirsts did not directly acknowledge that different social problems might affect India and England, the latter one of the foremost urban industrial nations. Tagore foresaw that failing to recognise this could lead to difficulties. He cautioned Leonard against 'translating' Sriniketan directly into English, a language that was 'too rich and mature', with 'condensed, ready-made phrases that are sure to obtrude and clog the

---

[19] Uma Das Gupta, 'Tagore's Ideas of Social Action and the Sriniketan Experiment of Rural Reconstruction, 1922–41', *University of Toronto Quarterly* 77 (2008), 992–1004.

[20] For the story of Atarashiki Mura, see Morris-Suzuki, 'Beyond Utopia' and Neima, *The Utopians*, chapter 3.

[21] The global reconfiguration of philanthropy from the late-nineteenth to early-twentieth centuries, which 'transformed the scale and intensity of interregional connections in the shaping of health and welfare in Asia', was epitomised by the expanding work of the Rockefeller Foundation. Established in 1913, the foundation had an unprecedented global reach by the 1920s. In international health alone, it funded study tours, scholarships, consultancies and large-scale research-driven public health campaigns in Europe, South America, South Asia and China. Amrith, 'Internationalising Health', 247.

[22] Arthur Geddes to Leonard, 24 April 1923, LKE/IN/6/D.

[23] Leonard to Rabindranath Tagore, 22 June 1934, LKE/TAG/9/A.   [24] Ibid.

spontaneity of creative outflow'.[25] His warning went unheeded, however. Leonard was determined to convince the 'bullet headed Britishers' that the Sriniketan ideals were indeed 'workable in other than a purely rural country'.[26]

During Leonard's two-year course in agricultural economics at Cornell University, he absorbed two further lessons that would shape the approach to rural regeneration at Dartington.[27] The first was that, rather than treating farming as 'a Science, or a Hobby, or a tradition', the English must run it as a 'National Business', employing efficient modern industrial methods and scientific experts.[28] Leonard's second lesson was Cornell's usefulness to the surrounding countryside. The university had a thriving agricultural extension scheme. Instead of the earlier style of top-down extension teaching methods – lectures and correspondence courses – this revolved around demonstration work run as a collaboration between academics and 'farmer-students'.[29] It was part of a nation-wide interwar agricultural extension movement in the United States that was notably more successful than equivalent projects to educate English farmers.[30] A central aim of American agricultural extension was to promote scientific methods and greater profit-making. But for many reformers, including Liberty Hyde Bailey, leader of agricultural extension at Cornell, the movement was also meant to reform the quality of rural life in an affective or spiritual sense, revitalising community spirit in the face of social atomisation in the countryside.[31] Leonard was attracted by both economic and socio-spiritual elements. At Dartington, and in wider debates about rural regeneration, the challenge of promoting economic modernisation at the same time as nurturing 'traditional' community spirit would be ongoing.[32]

[25] Rabindranath Tagore to Leonard, 11 October 1925, LKE/TAG/9/A.

[26] Leonard to Dorothy, 19 May 1923, LKE/DWE/11/C.

[27] Gould P. Colman, *Education and Agriculture: A History of the New York State College of Agriculture at Cornell University* (Ithaca, 1963).

[28] Leonard to Seebohm Rowntree, 29 December 1921, [extract], LKE/IN/24/A.

[29] Joseph F. Kett, *The Pursuit of Knowledge Under Difficulties* (Stanford, 1994), 301–6 and 316–19.

[30] Colin J. Holmes, 'Science and the Farmer: The Development of the Agricultural Advisory Service in England and Wales, 1900–1939', *The Agricultural History Review* 36 (1988), 77–86; Lynne Thompson, 'Agricultural Education in the Interwar Years', in Paul Brassley, Jeremy Burchardt and Lynne Thompson (eds.), *The English Countryside between the Wars: Regeneration or Decline?* (New York, 2006), 53–72.

[31] Liberty H. Bailey, *The Country Life Movement in the United States* (New York, 1911).

[32] Philip Conford, 'Finance Versus Farming: Rural Reconstruction and Economic Reform 1894–1955', *Rural History* 13 (2002), 225–41; Leo Marx, *The Machine in the Garden: Technology and the Pastoral Ideal in America* (Oxford, 1999 [1964]).

Over the course of the 1930s, as the Elmhirsts' estate in Devon struggled to achieve either economic efficiency or social cohesion, America provided them with another source of inspiration – this time for how grassroots democratic endeavour need not be autonomous but could be combined with centralised leadership. Through his time at Cornell and his marriage to Dorothy, Leonard built friendships with many American agriculturalists – not only Cornell professors, but political figures including Henry Wallace, Secretary of Agriculture, who became Vice President in 1941, and M. L. Wilson, Undersecretary of Agriculture and later director of federal extension, who played a key role in formulating a short-lived but distinctive phase in the agrarian New Deal.[33] This phase, which Jess Gilbert terms the 'Intended New Deal', ran from 1938 to 1942.[34] It favoured a distinctive mode of rural 'democratic planning' that was state-driven and deployed expert knowledge, but also involved close collaboration with local citizens. The outcome was a national network of local organisations, combining farmers, adult educators, social scientists and administrators to plan and coordinate land use – the kind of decentralised democratic planning to which the Elmhirsts hoped Dartington could contribute. Frequent trips by American agriculturalists and by the Elmhirsts themselves to and fro across the Atlantic meant that Dartington developed with close reference to the United States.[35]

The estate also evolved in dialogue with reformers closer to home. The British countryside after the First World War was deemed by most observers to be in decline.[36] The challenge arising from cheap overseas production since the 1870s, momentarily alleviated by the First World War, was renewed afterwards. Agricultural depression was given fresh impetus by the post-war withdrawal of guaranteed cereal prices and the collapse of world primary commodity prices.[37] Rural culture as a whole was seen as being in danger of collapse, ground down by factors including the withdrawal of the aristocracy from the land, international

---

[33] See files LKE/USA/7/F and LKE/USA/7/I and Jess Gilbert, 'Rural Sociology and Democratic Planning in the Third New Deal', *Agricultural History* 82 (2008), 421–38, at 423. Henry Wallace was also an editor of *The New Republic* from 1946 to 1947.

[34] Gilbert, *Planning Democracy*.

[35] Agricultural economist W. I. Myers toured the estate with Leonard prior to purchase; Gustave Heuser, Professor of Poultry at Cornell, helped set up a Dartington poultry unit; C. E. Ladd, Director of Cornell Agricultural Extension, helped establish the estate's agricultural economics research department.

[36] Alun Howkins, 'Death and Rebirth? English Rural Society, 1920–1940', in Brassley et al. (eds.), *The English Countryside*, 1–25, at 24.

[37] Edith Whetham, *The Agrarian History of England and Wales*, vol. 8 (Cambridge, 1978).

competition, the economic and cultural allure of the town and the impact of mechanisation on village crafts.[38] Concern about the state of rural society was compounded by a long-standing tendency to define England as a whole in terms of the countryside (although, as Peter Mandler points out, this tendency was a limited, contested phenomenon, rather than the universal rule that has sometimes been portrayed).[39]

The countryside attracted reformers from across the political spectrum and from both progressives and nostalgics.[40] Dartington, never defining its own manifesto, drew the interest of many different types. The Elmhirsts' interest in social democracy aligned them with the various left-leaning rural settlements flourishing in interwar England, their pedigree stretching back to William Morris through the middle-class anarchist and socialist communities of the 1880s and 1890s.[41] One example was the Sanctuary community in Sussex where Vera Pragnell, inspired by the socialist principles of Edward Carpenter, gave plots of land to anyone willing to cultivate them.[42] Leonard's belief in science and economic efficiency, however, meant that he mostly spurned collaboration with these small-scale, uncommercial endeavours. He thought that those who idealised the 'self-sufficient, insulated, isolated community' risked building a 'rural slum'.[43] He rebuffed ruralists like Montague Fordham, founder of the Rural Reconstruction Association, who sought to involve him in a small-holding resettlement plan that would 'absorb about 2,000,000 persons

---

[38] Peter Mandler, *The Fall and Rise of the Stately Home* (New Haven, CT and London, 1997), chapter 6; Brassley et al. (eds.), *The English Countryside*. The lament over rural decline became a characteristic interwar literary genre – see, for example, A. G. Street's *Farmer's Glory* (Oxford, 1959 [1932]).

[39] Paul Brassley, Jeremy Burchardt and Lynne Thompson, 'Introduction', in Brassley et al. (eds.), *The English Countryside*, 1–9; David Matless, *Landscape and Englishness* (London, 1998); Peter Mandler, 'Against Englishness: English Culture and the Limits to Rural Nostalgia, 1850–1940', *Transactions of the Historical Society* 7 (1997), 155–75.

[40] The wide appeal of ruralism in interwar Britain is suggested by a joint letter published by the leaders of the three main political parties before the 1929 election, affirming that, in spite of their differences, they agreed 'in advocating the preservation of our countryside in its rich personality and character'. Quoted in Griffiths, *Labour and the Countryside: The Politics of Rural Britain, 1918–1939* (Oxford, 2007), 81–2.

[41] Matthew Thomas, *Anarchist Ideas and Counter-Cultures in Britain, 1880–1914* (Aldershot, 2005).

[42] Like Dartington, the Sanctuary, which ran from 1923 to the early 1930s, had a vague, inclusive agenda, and attracted a wide range of participants, including artists, spiritualists and anarchists. Vera Pragnell, *The Story of the Sanctuary* (Steyning, 1928). For other examples, see Susanna Wade Martins, 'Smallholdings in Norfolk, 1890–1950: A Social and Farming Experiment', *The Agricultural History Review* 54 (2006), 304–30.

[43] Leonard in transcript of recording of BBC Third Programme, recorded 19 June 1950, transmitted 13 August 1951, LKE/G/S13/A.

into work'.[44] He was equally dismissive of government smallholding schemes: Lloyd George put forward rural resettlement as part of a wider platform for social reform after the First World War, and in the 1930s the idea surfaced again to combat mass unemployment.[45] Such schemes resonated with the Elmhirsts' belief that a rural existence was the most holistically fulfilling one, but they did not meet Leonard's objective of economic efficiency.

Leonard instead strove to associate Dartington with the growing impulse to subject the countryside to a vigorous process of economic modernisation.[46] Increasingly, in the 1930s, this led to dialogue with the state, both with officials in the Ministry of Agriculture and Fisheries and the Development Commission, and with the government-funded Rothamsted Experimental Station – where modern industrial methods, along with intervention in the countryside generally, were being embraced.[47]

Leonard also cultivated a loose network of wealthy landowners, agents and tenants who shared his reforming aspirations. Among the many visitors who toured Dartington were Francis Acland, Christopher Turnor, Rolf Gardiner, Philip Oyler and John Drummond.[48] Leonard did not overlap with these men in all their beliefs: Turnor, for instance, admired Hitler's 'plan to use the land as a means of regenerating the nation', using scientific experts to nurture 'new self-supporting

---

[44] Montague Fordham to Leonard, 16 September 1933, LKE/LAND/7/C. The Rural Reconstruction Association, founded in 1926, was a guild-socialism-influenced and pro-protection rural reform group that wanted to revive agriculture, redress its balance with industry and increase protectionism.

[45] Andrew Fenton Cooper, *British Agricultural Policy 1912–1936: A Study in Conservative Politics* (Manchester, 1989), 45 and 70.

[46] Cooper, looking at Conservative Party policy, suggests that the interwar years were the first time that agricultural policy was subordinated to economic progress, rather than tied to considerations of social stability (*British Agricultural Policy*, 2). For Leonard, in spite of his focus on economic efficiency, the ultimate objective continued to be reforming rural society in a more general sense.

[47] Sir John Russell, director of Rothamsted Experimental Station, visited Dartington and encouraged Leonard to write 'a detailed account which would serve as guidance to other landowners', 28 February 1938, LKE/LAND/4/E. Griffiths, *Labour and the Countryside*, 13–4.

[48] Francis Acland was MP for North Cornwall from 1932 to 1939 and an enthusiastic supporter of rural regeneration generally. Christopher Turnor was a reformer who admired scientific models of land management and applied their techniques on his estate at Stoke Rochford. Philip Oyler, a founding member of the Soil Association, visited Dartington at the recommendation of Lord Sandwich (Oyler to Leonard, 10 January 1934, LKE/G/24/G). John Drummond, 15th Baron Strange, who was in the army with Leonard in the First World War, upset his friend by calling Dartington 'a place to play Trianon' (John Drummond, draft chapters for unpublished book, LKE/DEV/3/C).

hereditary peasant farms'.[49] Gardiner, too, favoured a quasi-feudal system with a 'modern peasantry' rather than a social democracy, and he also railed against the Elmhirsts' privileging 'scientific calculative' over 'inductive lore'.[50] Dartington was able to accommodate association with many dissonant agendas, up to a point – partly because its founders were themselves torn between positions. Wanting to reverse the 'breakdown of cooperative village life in competition for profits' and to defend a spiritual notion of the wholesomeness of the traditional country community, they still believed that efficient modern business methods must be applied to all aspects of rural life.[51] Theoretically, in favour of localised social democracy, they nonetheless often behaved like traditional landowners themselves, and leaned heavily on the outside guidance of an international community of experts.

5.2   Scientific Agriculture

The agricultural businesses started at Dartington – including forestry, poultry, orchards, a mixed farm and a dairy farm – were intended to reflect those traditionally found in rural England, but also to prove the capacity of science to reform farming.[52] They were framed in terms of a two-stage process: planning and fine-tuning would be followed by the demonstration of profitability and the production of results useful to the outside world. Alongside these enterprises, the Elmhirsts set up a research department, whose function was to help the agricultural enterprises through their two stages and to develop and publicise new techniques. 'The best insurance against insularity is our expenditure on Research,' wrote Leonard in 1931. 'This is our means of touch with the outside world .... The more Research the more the advance guard of society and the more international in spirit we are likely to be.'[53]

Most of Dartington's agricultural enterprises did not reach stage two. The Elmhirsts – Leonard in particular – were poor at choosing managers and often changed their approach before results were produced. The effect of the Depression, as Leonard wrote, was to put the estate 'in the

[49] Christopher Turnor, *Land Settlement in Germany* (London, 1935), 16–8.
[50] Rolf Gardiner to Leonard, 16 June 1933, LKE/G/15/B; Rolf Gardiner, *England Herself: Ventures in Rural Restoration* (London, 1943).
[51] Leonard to Arthur Geddes, 24 February 1923, LKE/IN/6/D. See also Leonard to Seebohm Rowntree, 29 December 1921 [extract], LKE/IN/24/A.
[52] Leonard, 'Dartington Hall as a research centre', 9 January 1927, C/DHL/1/B. See also Michael Young, *The Elmhirsts of Dartington: The Creation of a Utopian Community* (London, 1982), 291.
[53] Leonard, 'Notes on Dartington', January 1931, LKE/G/S11A.

somewhat unfortunate position of trying to build up a sound economic basis to the experiment at a moment when nothing in the world has such a basis'.[54] The greatest problem, though, was the near-impossibility of combining disparate small-scale experimental work with large-scale, economically successful farming.

The heart of Dartington's agricultural experiment was a comparison between two farms. One was run by a local, Frank Crook, as a traditional mixed Devon farm; the other was managed under the newest theories of dairying by Christian Nielsen, a farmer with extensive agricultural training whom Leonard had met in Denmark, a country that led the field in modernising peasant production.[55] Nielsen's farm received much attention. The modernist architect Maxwell Fry, for example, thought its 'nearly factory-like' organisation instructive for farmers, manufacturers and architects alike, particularly its pioneering architecture 'based on organisation and economy' – but it continually lost money. The traditional farm made money – not the result Leonard wanted.[56] In addition, the two farmers did not get on, putting little effort into the project of comparison so that the overall experiment was largely worthless.[57] In 1932, Leonard visited the Soviet Union. In doing so, he followed the path of many interwar progressives, but one of the lessons he brought back was unusual.[58] Impressed by Russian demonstrations of artificial insemination techniques, he established a cattle-breeding centre 'to educate the farmers in the neighbourhood'.[59] From this centre there developed the nationwide use of artificial insemination – one achievement in dairying, at least, that met the Elmhirsts' hope of influencing wider rural regeneration.

---

[54] Leonard, 'Dartington Hall', [n.d.], LKE/G/S8/A.
[55] Frank Crook ran a traditional mixed dairy and livestock farm. Christian Nielsen tore out hedges to create large, prairie-style fields for mechanised farming, designed new farm buildings and cultivated a selectively bred herd of South Devon cattle. Young, *Elmhirsts*, 273; Ingrid Henriksen, 'The Contribution of Agriculture to Economic Growth in Denmark, 1870–1939', in Pedro Lains and Vincente Pinilla (eds.), *Agriculture and Development in Europe Since 1870* (London, 2009), 117–47.
[56] Edwin Maxwell Fry to Leonard, 22 November 1932, LKE/PEP/1/B. The buildings featured in architectural and farming journals and several of them were reproduced at the Agricultural Research Council's farm at Stafford.
[57] Young, *Elmhirsts*, 277.
[58] Paul Hollander, *Political Pilgrims: Travels of Western Intellectuals to the Soviet Union, China and Cuba 1928–1978* (New York, 1981).
[59] [n.a.], 'The basis of fixing rent for the Dartington Hall Artificial Insemination Centre', 1944, T/AG ECON/1/B. Leonard worked with Dr John Hammond, who was experimenting with artificial insemination at the School of Agriculture in Cambridge. Further trials were made at Dartington in 1933 and 1943, before the breeding centre was set up.

5.1 Christian Nielsen and others making hay in the summer of 1928
(© Dartington Hall Trust and the Elmgrant Trust)

Many of the agricultural schemes on the estate encountered difficulties. Leonard's brother Richard set up a model poultry factory farm with
the help of Gustave Heuser, a Cornell professor.[60] It flourished briefly,
selling 200,000 eggs a year at its peak.[61] One visitor, Avice Trench, who
was working on setting up jobs for unemployed miners in the Rhondda in
Wales, thought it exemplary.[62] But the flock, kept in close confinement,
was repeatedly swept by disease. In the 1930s, the project moved from
commercial production to smaller-scale experimentation; then, with the
quality of the birds still deteriorating, it was closed down at the end of the
Second World War.[63] Like Nielsen's dairy farm, the Dartington poultry
factory foreshadowed the large-scale, intensive style of farming that
would be widely embraced after the war, but it failed to prove its economic case.[64]

[60] The government, wanting to commercialise British poultry production, tried
unsuccessfully to enlist Gustave Heuser to head up the British National Poultry
Institute. Leonard to Mr Irons, 15 July 1927, LKE/USA/3/K.
[61] Young, *Elmhirsts*, 274.   [62] Avice Trench to Leonard, 14 May 1929, LKE/G/32/A.
[63] Victor Bonham-Carter gives an overview of Dartington's agriculture and industry in
Dartington Hall: History of an Experiment (London, 1958), chapter 3.
[64] Andrew Godley and Bridget Williams, 'Democratizing Luxury and the Contentious
"Invention of the Technological Chicken" in Britain', *The Business History Review* 83
(2009), 267–90.

Other ventures struggled in a similar fashion, including experiments with pigs, sheep, apples and soft fruit. Even the better-managed schemes – the 2,000 acres of forestry, for example, which were Leonard's particular passion – still did not turn a profit.[65] Dartington's serial failures were echoed by parallel projects of the period. At Leckford, John Spedan Lewis's estate in Hampshire, agricultural experiments were run on the same enlightened business principles that Lewis applied to his department stores.[66] Bladen, the Dorset estate of businessman Sir Ernest Debenham, operated on the novel basis of having separate specialist enterprises for supplying feed and other inputs and marketing produce.[67] Like Dartington, both estates lost large sums of money. Agricultural experimentation at the slow-paced rhythm required of anything involving the natural world did not harmonise with the large-scale, scientifically efficient profit-making that these estate owners wanted their farms to demonstrate.

The Elmhirsts hoped the Dartington research department could imitate the close relationship found in America between agricultural research institutions and surrounding farmers, providing an 'informal local extension agency which could try out improved methods of agricultural production, and if they worked out promote their prompt adoption'.[68] More broadly, Leonard wanted Dartington's research department to show 'the kind of channels along which scientific discovery should flow easily towards the increase of human welfare'.[69] As with the estate's use of psychologists, it would be an example of how experts could make themselves socially useful, contributing to – but not directing – democratic progress.

Unfortunately, the agricultural economist the Elmhirsts chose to coordinate the Dartington research department, J. R. Currie, was ill-suited to the job. He composed numerous memoranda on the tasks he could potentially perform – studies on farm management, on cost accounting, on markets and consumers, including consumer cooperatives – but he

---

[65] Wilfrid Hiley, *A Forestry Venture … Foreword and Chapter 'The Venture in Perspective' by L.K. Elmhirst* (London, 1964).

[66] Roy Brigden, 'Leckford: A Case-Study of Interwar Development', in Burchardt et al. (eds.), *The English Countryside*, 200–11.

[67] Brian Short, *Battle of the Fields: Rural Community and Authority in Britain During the Second World War* (Woodbridge, 2014), 24.

[68] W. I. Myers described Leonard's early aims to Jock Currie, 4 December 1962, quoted in Anthea Williams, 'First draft of C7', March 1979, T/HIS/21/A. Leonard was influenced particularly by C. E. Ladd's work at Cornell and that of Professor H. C. M. Case at the University of Illinois. Leonard, 'Notes for J. R. Currie', 11 November 1931, T/AG ECON/1/A.

[69] Leonard to Rathi Tagore, 28 June 1937, LKE/IN/21/D.

failed to carry out most of them or to win the confidence of the workers and surrounding farmers.[70] Relations with local farmers were not helped by Dartington's paying a higher labouring wage than the average.[71] 'I noticed that the Danish manager of one of the farms at Dartington Hall ... had made a clean sweep of his banks,' wrote author J. A. Scott Watson, recording a tour of Devon in *The Listener*. 'But I could see nobody following his example.'[72] Dorothy, in a rare moment of irritation with Leonard in 1931, asked him 'whether there was any sign that what we were doing here was likely to have any effect on the local farmer – if not, when, if never, why were we doing it?'[73]

A second problem was the difficulty of combining the research department's twin roles, promoting profit and conducting experiments. The agricultural research centres that did produce useful results in this period – such as Long Ashton and Rothamsted Experimental Stations – focused purely on the latter.[74] In addition, whilst, like Dartington, these centres were originally begun by the privately wealthy (in 1843 and 1893, respectively), in the interwar years they were taken over by the government. If the Elmhirsts had not started Dartington with the aspiration of building an independent, community-serving enterprise, the history of their agricultural activities might have looked very different.

The research department was not without impact, but only once it shifted away from serving the estate and local community. In 1929 Currie was joined by a scientist, J. B. E. Patterson, whose more productive work included analysing products from the estate ranging from milk to dye, conducting fertiliser trials and stocking the estate's scientific library.[75] By the late 1930s Leonard was sending off Patterson's findings to Sir Thomas Middleton, an advocate of scientific farming and secretary of the Development Commission, set up by the government in

---

[70] For examples of J. R. Currie's memoranda, see 'Functions of the research department', [n.d.] and 'Outline of the work being carried out by the Economics Research Department', 1929–30, T/AG ECON/1/A.

[71] Frank Crook's wife remembered that the local farmers were 'very bitter' against the Elmhirsts because they paid workers thirty-two shillings a week compared with the usual fifteen (Interview with Michael Young, 23 August 1977, T/HIS/S20/D).

[72] J. A. Scott Watson, 'Rural Britain Today and Tomorrow – vii: Tradition and Experiment in the West', *The Listener*, 22 November 1933, 797.

[73] Dorothy's manuscript comment on Leonard's 'Notes for J. R. Currie', 11 November 1931, T/AG ECON/1/A.

[74] Paul Brassley, 'Agricultural Research in Britain, 1850–1914: Failure, Success and Development', *Annals of Science* 52 (1995), 465–80.

[75] The estate science laboratory was founded in 1927. W. K. Slater was director from 1928–9, then was succeeded by J. B. E. Patterson until its closure in 1946. Young, *Elmhirsts*, 276.

1909 to promote agricultural research.[76] Patterson's most remarkable achievement was opening the first soil-fertility analysis service for farmers, which was parlayed in 1939 into a soil survey for England and Wales, undertaken for the Ministry of Agriculture. Dr L. L. Lee, who had set up an experimental soil testing station for farmers in New Jersey, crossed the Atlantic to help Patterson begin the Dartington survey.[77] In an indication of how avant garde the estate was in this area, when Patterson left Dartington in 1946, it was to join the newly established National Agricultural Advisory Service, which sought to help British farmers in the way the Elmhirsts' research department had been trying to model for twenty years.

Leonard was acutely conscious, a decade after Dartington had started, that he had still not proved the capacity of science to reform English farming. He often repeated the 'wish that we had been going a little longer' so that 'we can back our faith with actual figures'.[78] Yet, in his focus on the (undoubted) failure of most projects to meet their financial benchmarks, he was not able to appreciate the constructive impact of Dartington's agriculture on the wider world, especially from the late 1930s. This included not only pioneering artificial insemination, soil survey and poultry factory-farming but also devising a scheme for state support of private forestry owners, which fed into the Forestry Acts of 1947 and 1951.[79]

As early as 1930, outsiders were impressed by the Elmhirsts' agricultural department, seeing it as a useful model. Diplomat James Grover McDonald wrote to Lord Lothian that if Dartington were a template, 'Britain would reduce her unemployed by tens of thousands, and at the same time reduce her yearly imports of butter, eggs and other dairy products by millions of pounds sterling'.[80] Observers including M. L. Wilson of the New Deal, business magnate J. D. Rockefeller, and Sir Anderson Montague-Barlow, chair of a royal commission on the location

---

[76] Leonard to Sir Thomas Middleton, 16 November 1938, LKE/LAND/2/B; Paul Brassley, David Harvey, Matt Lobley and Michael Winter, 'Accounting for Agriculture: The Origins of the Farm Management Survey', *Agricultural History Review* 61 (2013), 135–53, at 139.

[77] *News of the Day*, 25 Oct 1929, T/PP/EST/1–8; Leonard in transcripts for 'Man Alive', a programme for the BBC transmitted 29 November 1972, editor Adam Clapham, producer Richard Thomas, LKE/G/S13/L.

[78] Leonard to Max Nicholson, 14 December 1935, LKE/PEP/3/C.

[79] Leonard's scheme, the culmination of a sustained interwar campaign to make the Forestry Commission give more help to private owners, was submitted to the government in 1944. Young, *Elmhirsts*, 297.

[80] James Grover McDonald, chairman of the Foreign Policy Association, to Lord Lothian, 15 October 1930, LKE/USA/4/I.

5.2 Richard Elmhirst and Gus Heuser in the poultry department, 1926–7 (© Dartington Hall Trust and the Elmgrant Trust)

of industry in Britain, celebrated the Elmhirsts' work.[81] Nonetheless, in the absence of statistical proof of success, Dorothy and Leonard made little effort to publicise their ventures.

---

[81] Leonard to J. R. Currie, 19 September 1933, T/AG ECON/S1/A; Sir Anderson Montague-Barlow to Dorothy, 6 January 1938, noting J. D. Rockefeller's enthusiasm, DWE/G/S3/C.

There were growing tensions in the 1930s between those who saw Dartington as a scientific experiment whose aim was to produce findings and those for whom it was a business whose success would be indicated only by profit.[82] The Elmhirsts themselves supported both viewpoints – inasmuch as both research and model production units could contribute to the economic revival of the countryside. At the same time, however, beginning to feel that estate-based research and agricultural enterprise were not proving satisfactory ways of assisting rural reform, their focus turned outward.

Leonard tried building local producer cooperatives, including a central store on the estate and an egg packing and distribution centre for the local area.[83] These efforts were inspired by the self-governing ideals of guild socialism and by the work of the Irish cooperative pioneer Sir Horace Plunkett.[84] Thinking 'more and more that the future lies in the hands of the Consumers' Cooperatives', Leonard also put out feelers about setting up such a cooperative in the nearby town of Totnes.[85] His efforts drew the interest of members of the Co-operative Union, who saw in Dartington rich possibilities for uniting distribution, production and 'the social, artistic and educational requirements which are the necessities of co-operative life'.[86] After a few failures, however, Leonard's enthusiasm for rural cooperation waned. 'Wash out any great hopes of co-op by or with farmer. 90% still are prepared to cut others' throats for sixpence', he scrawled after one meeting (although, in the British farming community as a whole, enthusiasm for working collectively was in fact on the rise).[87] Interest in cooperation re-emerged at Dartington in the late 1930s, but it revolved around the idea of an agricultural marketing collective selling goods through London-based Marks and Spencer,

---

[82] John Maxton to Leonard, 9 February 1937, LKE/DCC/6/C; Fred Gwatkin, 'Dartington Hall Ltd – proposed reconstruction', 26 May 1937, C/DHL/1/B.

[83] Leonard to Mr Greenwood, 11 February 1929, LKE/LAND/5/C.

[84] The guild socialist G. D. H. Cole was part of the coterie of socialist pluralists who influenced early ideas about Dartington (Marc Stears, 'Guild Socialism', in Mark Bevir (ed.), *Modern Pluralism: Anglo-American Debates Since 1880* (Cambridge, 2012), 40–59). Leonard had spent time in Dublin with Sir Horace Plunkett (Theodore Roosevelt's favourite agricultural reformer abroad), who saw the forging of unity in the countryside through local cooperation as a necessary pre-condition to achieving Irish political independence.

[85] Leonard to J.R. Currie, 10 December 1927, T/AG ECON/S1/A.

[86] George Walworth of the Cooperative Union to Leonard, 13 November 1929, LKE/LAND/5/C.

[87] Leonard, 'Rural ownership', 4 December 1934, LKE/LAND/8/B; Griffiths, *Labour and the Countryside*, passim.

rather than catering to locals.[88] In 1945, the South Devon Fruit and Vegetable Growers Association was finally set up, but by this time Leonard had begun to think that farmers' individualism, their lack of capital and the uneconomic size of English farms could be better combated by reforming agriculture through 'some element of central direction and control'.[89]

A more productive initiative with local farmers was a survey of the farms around Dartington, conducted jointly with Seale-Hayne Agricultural College and published in 1929.[90] This was inspired by Leonard's experience of the American survey method – popular at Cornell but yet to be widely taken up in Britain – and involved farmers in mapping land use and analysing the efficiency of different agricultural methods.[91] The democratic, grass-roots ethos of agricultural initiatives in America was reflected in the Dartington survey: it was to be a self-help initiative for farmers, part of a desire to create around Dartington 'a miniature version of the agricultural extension service which radiated information from Cornell to farmers in New York State'.[92] At the same time, echoing the way in which the New Deal surveys were supposed to feed back into state planning, it was hoped that the Dartington survey would influence public policy. American agriculturalist W. I. Myers suggested to Leonard that it would be a way to dissuade the British government from spending more 'millions of pounds' creating uneconomically sized smallholdings.[93]

Such data collection techniques were soon adopted by the British government as a way of deciding on agricultural interventions. The Farm Management Survey, set up by the Ministry of Agriculture in 1936, became a permanent part of its portfolio during and after the Second World War – fed by a growing perception that data was needed

---

[88] Leonard, 'Proposed marketing centre for fruit and vegetables', March 1939, C/DHL/8/F; [n.a.], 'Notes on conference with representatives of Messrs. Marks and Spencer, County Agricultural Department, Dartington Hall and others', 1 November 1938, T/AG ECON/S7/E.

[89] [n.a], 'First annual general meeting of the South Devon Fruit and Vegetable Growers Association', 23 February 1945, C/DHL/8/F; [n.a.], 'The blue book', [n.d.], T/PP/P/1/A.

[90] J. R. Currie and W. H. Long, *An Agricultural Survey in South Devon* (Newton Abbot and Totnes, 1929); J. R. Currie, 'A Review of Fifty Years' Farm Management Research', *Journal of Agricultural Economics* 11 (1956), 350–60, at 357.

[91] The Cornell Agricultural Experiment Station surveyed farms in New York State in 1911 and developed the idea of 'efficiency factors' such as output per labour unit. Edith H. Whetham, *Agricultural Economists in Britain 1900–1940* ([Oxford], 1981), 25–9.

[92] Young, *Elmhirsts*, 275.   [93] W. I. Myers to Leonard, 5 April 1928, LKE/USA/4/K.

by a modern state.[94] W. I. Myers wrote to Leonard that he was 'especially pleased that the Farm Management survey of Devonshire has resulted so quickly in the obtaining of a government grant for similar projects in other regions. I am firmly convinced of the value of this study to the individual farmer and to the nation as a whole'.[95] The Elmhirsts' move from on-the-ground experimentation in agriculture to work outside the estate led to far more definite achievement. The survey of South Devon marked a moment of harmonious compromise between bottom-up reform – working with and for local farmers – and top-down reform, deploying scientists and contributing to state policy.

The Farm Management Survey was the first point at which provincial agricultural economists were brought together by the state to work on a national basis, but Leonard had been involved in building bridges between agricultural economists since 1929, when the International Association of Agricultural Economists (IAAE) had its first meeting at Dartington. Like other organisations, such as the League of Nations, the International Federation of University Women and the New Education Fellowship, the IAAE was fuelled by the high enthusiasm for all things international that characterised the interwar years.[96] Those who attended the first conference saw the IAAE as 'the beginning of a new era in the development of agricultural economics, in which the world economy as well as farm economy and national economy will receive more attention'.[97]

At the same time as having an international outlook, the young discipline of agricultural economics provided a forum for a whole gamut of issues relating to rural regeneration, from rural social services to decentralising industry to speculations about better configurations of land ownership.[98] The IAAE therefore gave Leonard an outlet for his

---

[94] Paul Brassley et al., 'Accounting for Agriculture', 152. Rather than being carried out by the civil service, the farm management survey has always been the responsibility of an independent, university-based research staff working under government contract.

[95] W. I. Myers to Leonard, 19 February 1930, LKE/USA/4/K.

[96] Daniel Gorman, *The Emergence of International Society in the 1920s* (Cambridge, 2011).

[97] Comments in *News of the Day* after the first agricultural economics conference, 5 Sept 1929, T/PP/EST/1–8. At the 1929 conference, there were fifty attendees from eleven different countries. The next, larger, conference was at Cornell in 1930 and there were three others between the wars, the last held in Canada. The regular conference turned formally into the International Association of Agricultural Economists in 1964. By 1980 it had over 1,600 members worldwide. Brassley et al., 'Accounting for Agriculture', 153. See also J. R. Raeburn and J. O. Jones, *The History of the International Association of Agricultural Economists: Towards Rural Welfare Worldwide* (Aldershot, 1990).

[98] Correspondence between Leonard and A. W. Ashby, who held the first chair in agricultural economics in Britain (1929–46), LKE/LAND/1/B; Whetham, *Agricultural Economists in Britain*, 72–3.

combined desires to plan for integrated rural regeneration and to promote peaceable international fellowship.[99] As president of the conference, his duty was to visit agricultural economists and farming districts
worldwide: in 1932 he made his trip to Russia, on the basis of which he
wrote a book critical of the effects of collectivization; in 1937 he toured
seventeen countries in six weeks.[100] Agricultural economics – 'object-
ively and dispassionately studying inter-relations and measuring changes
in the economic structure' – became for Leonard, like Dartington itself, a
universal blueprint: something he hoped 'statesmen, bankers, industrial-
ists, housewives, town and country planners' would adopt, as it offered a
way 'to distinguish between scientific diagnosis on the one hand and on
the other the many short-term remedies offered by various governments
and national systems for the ills of society today'.[101] Like the agricultural
extension scheme at Cornell, it was not merely about promoting profit-
making, but about cultivating a holistic way of rural life.

Leonard's optimism was vindicated by the increasing popularity of
agricultural economics both during and after the Second World War,
although this went hand-in-hand with its narrowing into a more empirical discipline, and one less infused with affective or spiritual aspirations.
He campaigned in vain for 'a more rounded approach', remembered Ken
Hunt, Director of the Agricultural Economics Institute. 'He wanted man
to be the centre of the whole field, but this view attracted progressively
less sympathy than it did once'.[102] At the 1955 IAAE conference,
Leonard emphasised that 'technical change by itself, leading to higher
productivity, is not enough .... All change should be geared to an
integrated process of development concerned as much with social and
cultural as with technical and economic values'.[103] His views

[99] Leonard, 'The role of agricultural economists in the promotion of world order', paper
for an Agricultural Economics Society meeting, 30 June to 3 July 1939, LKE/LAND/9/
A. Finance for the IAAE came from membership fees and grants from such American
foundations as Kellogg, Ferguson, Ford and William C. Whitney as well as from the
Elmhirsts' Elmgrant fund, the British Council and individual governments.
[100] Leonard K. Elmhirst, *Trip to Russia* (New York, 1934); Leonard, 'The role of
agricultural economists in the promotion of world order', paper for Agricultural
Economics Society meeting, 30 June to 3 July 1939, LKE/LAND/9/A. He remained
president of the IAAE until 1958.
[101] Leonard, 'The role of agricultural economists in the promotion of world order', paper
for Agricultural Economics Society meeting, 30 June to 3 July 1939, LKE/LAND/9/A.
[102] Ken Hunt interview with Michael Young, 10 December 1977, T/HIS/S22. Leonard
played a large part in the growth of the IAAE after the war. In 1964, in testament to this,
a book was published in his honour, to which economists from twenty-four nations
contributed (R. N. Dixey (ed.), *International Explorations of Agricultural Economics*
(Ames, 1964)).
[103] Anthea Williams, 'LKE and agricultural economics', 15 August 1978, T/HIS/S22/B.

foreshadowed the idea of socially appropriate or intermediate technology – as opposed to unlimited technology that 'ravishes nature' and 'mutilates man' – which would be introduced in the 1970s by economist E.F. Schumacher in his book *Small Is Beautiful: A Study of Economics as If People Matter.*[104] Leonard's statement also reflected his ongoing search for the balance never quite found at Dartington – between the large-scale and the local, and between the imperatives of commercial efficiency and the holistic regeneration of rural society.

5.3   Reforming Rural Industry

Reflecting the early interest in self-sufficiency and integration, the industrial enterprises at Dartington were initially intended to process its agricultural output. They included a textiles department, a sawmill, a cider factory and a craft studio – but by the 1930s they had quietly become international in their inputs, calling for Scandinavian wood for furniture-making, French apples for cider and New Zealand wool for weaving.[105] These enterprises were intended to offer a way of 'mopping up' those put out of a job by modern, labour-saving farming that would be an alternative to the unemployed migrating into towns.[106] The Elmhirsts also saw strong industry as a necessary component of a Deweyan, social-democratic rural community: Dewey looked back idealistically to a traditional country life where 'everyone had a pretty direct contact with nature and the simpler forms of industry'.[107]

Within this framework, two competing visions of industry's place in the countryside co-existed uneasily, one of which prioritised the creation of an organically integrated community of makers, the other of which concentrated on the recurring issue of commercial viability – and, increasingly, on the consumer rather than producer as the key actor in a newly emerging form of social democracy.[108] A prominent champion of the first vision was the craftsman Rex Gardner. Trained in the Arts and Crafts tradition, his dream was that Dartington would be one of many cooperative communities of independent artist-craftsmen. Each maker

[104] E. F. Schumacher, *Small Is Beautiful. A Study of Economics as If People Mattered* (London, 1973), 293; Pauline Madge, 'Design, Ecology, Technology: A Historiographical Review', *Journal of Design History* 6 (1993), 149–66.
[105] Leonard, 'Dartington Hall as a research centre', 9 January 1927, C/DHL/1/B; Young, *Elmhirsts*, 291.
[106] Leonard to Joe Lash, 18 October 1968, LKE/USA/4/A.
[107] John Dewey quoted in Jay Martin, *The Education of John Dewey* (New York, 2002), 10.
[108] The two viewpoints were termed by Leonard the 'romantic' and 'the socio-economic'. 'Rural industries', 27 March 1939, LKE/LAND/8/A.

would achieve self-realisation in controlling the complete production process, from design to manual labour.[109] The second view, which Leonard upheld along with many of the managers the Elmhirsts brought in in the 1930s, was that rural industries must learn 'through their own inherent efficiency' to match their urban and international competitors.[110] If not, they should be closed down. This process might require dividing production into several stages, of which a worker would only experience one; it might require paying more attention to turning out what consumers wanted, rather than creatively fulfilling producers. Leonard cited Henry Ford's decentralising of car production into a series of 'village industries' in rural America as an admirable example.[111] If Dartington's industrial departments were not set on a profitable footing, he worried they would never be of wider use.[112]

The tension between these two viewpoints echoed wider debates in Britain about the social place of modern industry. In particular, the group of artists, patrons and reformers that Michael Saler terms 'medieval modernists' sought 'to spiritualize capitalism, infuse mass commodities with soul, and reshape an increasingly fragmented and secular culture into an organically integrated community' – although this group was mainly urban, seeking to infuse the city with rural spirituality, rather than, like the Elmhirsts, to modernise the countryside itself.[113] At Dartington, the tensions between the two viewpoints manifested in a series of skirmishes over methods of production and organisation. As in the country at large, the socio-spiritual viewpoint slowly yielded to the economic.

In spite of the triumph of commercial priorities, the estate's industrial departments still failed, with a few exceptions, to turn a profit until the

---

[109] Rex Gardner to Leonard, 17 June 1930, C/DHL/9/A. Rex Gardner arrived at Dartington in 1927 and was responsible for designing buildings and then running a crafts studio. He had trained with the architect-craftsman Ernest Gimson and worked at the Hampshire House workshops, part of the Hampshire House Club, a long-running social and educational enterprise set up by printer Hilary Pepler with his neighbours in Hammersmith. H. D. C. Pepler, 'Hampshire House Workshops', *Blackfriars* 31 (1950), 70–4; Bonham-Carter, *Dartington Hall*, 30–1.

[110] Leonard, 'Rural industries', 27 July 1939, C/RIB/1/A.

[111] Leonard 'Rural industries', 27 March 1939, LKE/LAND/8/A; Leonard, 'Agricultural economics, a means to what end?', 25 May 1934, LKE/LAND/8/C. Between 1920 and 1944 Henry Ford opened nineteen 'village industries', small plants for producing car parts that were located within sixty miles of the Ford Motor Company headquarters in Michigan. They were part of a number of projects in interwar America promoting decentralised industry as a way to reverse urban industrialisation, with its associated low quality of life.

[112] Leonard, 'Note on Dartington's financial structure', January 1931, LKE/G/S11A.

[113] Michael T. Saler, *The Avant-Garde in Interwar England: Medieval Modernism and the London Underground* (New York and Oxford, 1999), viii.

Second World War altered the rural economic landscape. Partly because of this failure, partly because of the incompatibility of commercial and social ideals, and partly because of the migration of their sense of the right arena for action, the Elmhirsts, by the mid-1930s, had begun to concentrate less on improving local modes of production and more on consumers as an up-and-coming political constituency that might prove a new agent of social reform. In spite of the problems of modelling industry at Dartington, the experiment interested such diverse figures as the New Deal economist Rexford Tugwell, sent by Eleanor Roosevelt to 'see whether the same general pattern might be applicable in West Virginia', and Alfred Striemer, a German government economist hoping to apply the Elmhirsts' model to his own scheme to help the unemployed.[114]

The textiles department was a typical example of the difficulties of reconciling ideals of integrated craft with successful commerce. An upper-class Anglo-Irish weaver, Heremon 'Toby' Fitzpatrick, was brought in by Dorothy to amalgamate independent village workers and centralised machine production.[115] He built a small water-powered textile factory modelled on those he had seen in Wales on a research visit paid for by the Elmhirsts, and he intended to outsource part of the labour process to cottage hand-weavers.[116] The plan for cottage weaving never materialised, however, since he failed to attract local outworkers. The factory proved a liability, with low textile quality and little market for its output – although this did not stop Leonard trying to lure M. K. Gandhi to stop by on a visit to England to see a model of 'a service centre for the supply of yarns, looms and orders for material to people living around in the neighbourhood'.[117] At all times the Elmhirsts hoped their work was contributing to a global discourse on local regeneration. The mill was later mechanised, but still served to highlight the recurring problem of Dartington's industry diagnosed by David Jeremiah: 'too big for the craft-based production with which they had started, and not large enough for the industrial-scale output that they were to move

---

[114] Leonard to Joe Lash, describing Rexford Tugwell's visit, 18 October 1969, LKE/USA/4/A; Alfred Striemer to Leonard, 29 August 1937, LKE/LAND/1/I.

[115] Dorothy to Leonard, 22 July 1925; Toby Fitzpatrick, untitled note, 14 May 1929, TEX/C/1/A.

[116] *News of the Day*, 13 December 1927, T/PP/EST/1/001. Wales was held to be 'the last stronghold of water power hand loom weaving'. Fitzpatrick's visit was in line with a number of somewhat quixotic research projects that the Elmhirsts funded, including Bernard Leach and Mark Tobey's tour of Asia.

[117] Leonard to Gandhi, 24 September 1931; Gandhi to Leonard, 30 September 1931, LKE/IN/6/B.

towards'.[118] It was only turned into a sound business proposition when a new manager, Hiram Winterbotham, outsourced much of the operation to a larger, better-equipped mill in Hampshire, thus undermining the ambition for industry to drive local regeneration.[119]

The history of the crafts department at Dartington shows the ways in which the tensions between the ideal of an organic community of craftsmen and that of commercial efficiency led the Elmhirsts to shift their focus from the village community to the individual consumer. In 1930, Rex Gardner set up a crafts studio that he envisaged as a 'centre to gather together all the small efforts of individuals to a common focus for teaching, for exhibitions, and for sales'.[120] It did not matter, in his model, that Dartington's craftsmen were producing expensive goods: they were in charge of their own process, which was both satisfying for them and set an example 'which promotes good taste even among both the workers and consumers whose pocket compels them to resort to mass-produced goods'.[121] Following the ideals of William Morris, labourers were happy at their work and in their community and were leading consumer taste in an enlightened direction.

As Dartington's industries became more centralised and commercially driven, Gardner's production methods and crafts studio came under scrutiny: it was no use workers being fulfilled by an integrated production process and having autonomy over design if the estate could not pay its way. This view reflected that of Saler's medieval modernists: Morris' model of luxury craftsmanship was inadequate because it would never reach enough people – enlightened mass production was the path of the future.[122] In 1933, a Dartington Arts and Crafts Advisory Committee of 'experts' was set up to meet in London and coordinate marketing and design.[123] Its members included J. R. I. Brooke, director of the Rural Industries Bureau, Muriel Rose, founder of the Little Gallery, and the publisher and typographer Noel Carrington. The estate craftsmen revolted. It was impossible, they insisted, to 'follow up every prospect of making revenue' and at the same time maintain 'a high standard in

[118] The second mill was designed by O. P. Milne and built by Staverton Builders Ltd, the spin-off company from the Dartington building department, on a river whose volume was so uncertain that the power it produced had to be supplemented by electricity, and in a space that was cramped between water and a steep hill, not allowing any future expansion. Jeremiah, 'Dartington', 129; Bonham-Carter, *Dartington Hall*, 99–102.
[119] Young, *Elmhirsts*, 292–3.   [120] Rex Gardner to Leonard, 17 June 1930, C/DHL/9/A.
[121] J. J. Findlay, *The Dartington Community: A Story of Social Achievement*, unfinished manuscript written 1937–9, LKE/G/13/B.
[122] Saler, *The Avant-Garde*, 13.
[123] 'Minutes of a meeting of the Brooke Committee', [n.d.], C/DHL/9/B.

design and workmanship'.[124] This echoed warnings by makers including potter Bernard Leach of the risk of the 'sacrifice of essential human relationship and also of quality of product' to economic efficiency.[125]

When the committee's leader, J. R. I. Brooke, died suddenly, its recommendations were temporarily shelved – but in 1935, Rex Gardner, criticised by the estate's managing director for his non-commercial methods and for 'the expression of political opinions during work hours', was transferred to working to help the Rural Industries Bureau survey and support Devon's craftsmen.[126] The Elmhirsts sponsored his role, paying half his salary while the other half was covered by the Development Commission.[127] This allowed them to continue to promote the notion of the independent, politically engaged artist-craftsman, but at a safe distance and in collaboration with the state.

Meanwhile, a revived Design Committee put in place a formal design procedure at Dartington to cater better to consumer demand.[128] The committee ruled that it was outside the province of a commercial organisation for an artist to 'produce unsaleable work in attempting to achieve an ideal'; instead, Dartington's workers must make what people wanted to buy.[129] Dartington was to follow the consumer, rather than to lead them – though, in order not to lose sight of what was 'basically good', the committee appointed German refugee Hein Heckroth, an 'artist in whose emotional response they had confidence', to oversee design.[130] Leonard recognised that 'from the point of view of making life within the community as "full" as possible' it was 'wiser to minister to the less developed needs of its members than to those of selected customers in New York', but the committee nonetheless envisaged wealthy, urban customers, including those from overseas.[131] This was grappling with the process of glocalisation – how to build a strong local community in an age of globalisation.

[124] Bernard Leach, Adrian Kent and Roger Morel, 'Memorandum', 16 November 1933, C/DHL/9/B.

[125] Bernard Leach to Leonard, 6 December 1932, T/AAP/3/A2.

[126] W. K. Slater to Rex Gardner, 24 April 1934, C/DHL/9/A.

[127] [n.a.], 'The relation of the Dartington trust to rural industries', 13 May 1935, C/RIB/1/A. The Rural Industries Bureau was founded in 1921 by the Ministry of Agriculture as a result of an enquiry conducted on behalf of the Development Commission. It was intended to encourage and assist in the development of rural industries. In consequence of Gardner's work with the organisation, in 1938 the first Devon Agricultural Industries Conference was held at Dartington with Leonard as chairman. 'Preliminary draft agenda for Devon Agricultural Trades Conference', 19 June 1937 and *News of the Day*, 25 June 1937, C/RIB/1/A.

[128] 'Memorandum on the position of design in the commercial departments at Dartington', 24 November 1936, C/DHL/9/C.

[129] Ibid.   [130] Ibid.   [131] Leonard, untitled note, LKE/G/S8/B, [n.d.].

The separation of designer, producer and customer represented a fragmentation of Gardner's Arts-and-Crafts ideals. One of the Design Committee's products did, however, point towards a new sort of synthesis, drawing together several departments on the estate to create a distinctive modernist piece of furniture. Heckroth, with the architect Robert Hening, designed the 'Lamda' easy chair. The fabric came from the estate textile mill, the prototype was improved in the carpentry shop attached to the sawmill, and the chair was marketed through a catalogue that was given flair by Heckroth's design and photography.[132] A number of these chairs were sold, but then the war put an end to production.

At the same time as the Design Committee was established, the conclusion was reached that it was 'not desirable to have a craft shop which depends for its success upon handworks, associated with a large industrial unit such as Dartington'.[133] The crafts studio was re-opened as a bigger retail shop with a tearoom and car park. Selling products from outside as well as inside the estate, the shop pointed towards the tourist boom after the war and became Dartington's most successful industry.[134] The divergence from the early model of an integrated community of craftsmen echoed William Morris' failure, in the previous century, to reconcile utopian ideas of production with commercial imperatives in his own business – although, as Michael Saler and Vicky Long find, others in the interwar generation found ways to rectify the disjunct between them.[135] New sorts of synthesis were evident, for example, in the work of the Design and Industries Association, formed in 1915, which combined a dedication to industrial production with an emphasis on the importance of the role of the artist in the production process – elevating public taste and therefore performing a unifying spiritual and social function.

The changing focus in the crafts was part of a wider shift at Dartington towards concentrating on efficiency, sales and consumer desires rather

[132] Bonham-Carter, *Dartington Hall*, 93; David Jeremiah, 'Dartington' – A Modern Adventure', in Smiles (ed.), *Going Modern and Being British: Art, Architecture and Design in Devon c. 1910–1960* (Exeter, 1998), 43–78, at 64.
[133] [n.a.], 'The relation of the Dartington trust to rural industries', 13 May 1935, C/RIB/1/A.
[134] Around 3,500 customers were served in tearoom in 1935, 5,000 in 1936 (P. M. Paynting to W. K. Slater, 14 January 1937, C/DHL/9/D). For the rise of rural tourism, see David Jeremiah, 'Motoring and the British Countryside', *Rural History* 21 (2010), 233–50; and David Matless, *Landscape and Englishness* (London, 1998), 95–101.
[135] Vicky Long, 'Industrial Homes, Domestic Factories: The Convergence of Public and Private Space in Interwar Britain', *Journal of British Studies* 50 (2011), 434–64, at 435; Saler, *The Avant-Garde*, 61–75.

than on creating an organically integrated community of makers.[136] From a newly built central office designed by William Lescaze, the company's managing director W. K. Slater (appointed in 1929) demanded facts, figures and healthy returns from all departments. For Slater, Dartington's activities were congregated 'mainly for administrative and practical purposes, and not as part of a prototype for the structure of society'.[137] Employees were fired when enterprises did not meet their targets, usually when the Elmhirsts were away.[138] Price Waterhouse & Co was appointed 'to set on foot a system of costings'.[139] Standardisation was the order of the day: correspondence must be in the house style and pass through the central office; advertising was only to be done by the sales department; instead of an organically evolving cooperation between departments, function charts delineated everyone's role.[140] The embodiment of bureaucratism, Slater warned personnel that although 'originally all letters were written in an extremely personal and friendly style' that was 'eminently suited to the early days', they must now 'adopt an entirely conventional form'.[141]

One visitor in the 1930s lamented that the production processes were 'monotonous and mechanical and very much like work in a factory', a departure from the early small units, 'where workers understand the whole process'.[142] 'Does it pay?' wrote the organicist Rolf Gardiner of Dartington. 'This, after the first years of idealist extravagance, became the sole criterion.'[143] Other supporters and employees who had conceived of the estate as a unique refuge where 'monetary return was important, and only important, in so far as it might make the "social" experiment possible' were also disappointed.[144] John Wales, who had been at Dartington from the beginning, vainly advocated for a proper analysis of the high turnover of casual labour and the professionalisation of management '(a) in relation to the idea of a community; (b) in relation to rural reorganization as opposed to urban proletarianisation in a rural

---

[136] J. R. Currie, 'Report upon marketing policy', 2 March 1931, C/DHL/8/A; J. R. Currie, 'The function and scope of economic research at Dartington Hall', [n.d.], T/AG/ECON/1/A.

[137] W. K. Slater, 'Notes on conclusions arrived at, Management committee', 27 July 1931, T/PP/P/1/A.

[138] Young, *Elmhirsts*, 276.   [139] *News of the Day*, 1 January 1930, T/PP/EST/1–8.

[140] W. K. Slater, 'To all departments', 29 November 1934, C/DHL/1/B; W. K. Slater, 'Memorandum of the proposed scheme of centralisation', 1932, C/DHL/1/A; W. K. Slater, 'to all departments', 10 August 1934, C/DHL/1/B.

[141] W. K. Slater to J.R. Currie, 14 October 1931, T/AG ECON/S7/B.

[142] Felicity Palmer, 'Dartington report', 1938, LKE/G/25/A.

[143] Rolf Gardiner, 'Rural reconstruction', in H. J. Massingham (ed.), *England and the Farmer* (London, 1941), 91–107, at 106.

[144] John Wales to W. B. Curry, 4 March 1936, C/DHL/1/B.

area'. Instead of building a community outside the 'cash nexus', he complained, increasingly the estate's 'techniques and motives are those of the commercial world'.[145] For the Elmhirsts, however, holistic reform had to include an attempt to integrate Dartington into society as a whole, and therefore into the consumer-capitalist system. By turning out high-quality goods at Dartington, they would make the producer socially useful – and therefore satisfied; and they would also improve consumers' taste, elevating the public socially and spiritually, as well as materially.[146] The artist would be made part of the good community in a revised, enlarged version of William Morris' communal vision.

Ironically, it was at this fractious period that the 'Dartington ideal' of a harmoniously unified local community became something to be marketed: even if participants could not live the dream, they could sell it. In 1934, a sales department was established.[147] The new manager, James Harrison, told the Elmhirsts that he found his role 'far more satisfying than the array of noughts parading to the right' that had been the aim at his previous post at Lever Brothers, and that he hoped to see 'a continued merge into one multinucleated unicellular community'.[148] The advertising copy aimed to emphasise 'the sociological angle' rather than the commercial, on the basis that those 'who know and admire the Dartington ideal are the people who will demand Dartington goods'.[149]

Harrison's tactics – appointing an advertising agent and renting an office and salesroom in London – did little to advance the estate's internal integration.[150] There was fierce criticism at Dartington, both of inaccuracies in the marketing material and of the sheer idea that the enterprise's aims should be described 'in marketing terms' at all.[151] It was objected that the estate was falsely represented in publicity materials as 'already a paying concern'; that there was no 'educational ladder' for

---

[145] Ibid.

[146] This view was akin to that of many of Michael Saler's 'medieval modernists'. *The Avant-Garde*, 73.

[147] W. K. Slater to James Harrison, 11 May 1934, C/DHL/8/C.

[148] James Harrison to Leonard, 18 July 1935, C/DHL/8/C. Lever Brothers were well-known for their care for employee welfare, building the model village of Port Sunlight in 1888 to house workers, but this was paternalistic, top-down care, with little of Dartington's democratic rhetoric.

[149] London Press Exchange, 'Editorial publicity for Dartington Hall, April-September 1935', C/DHL/7/B.

[150] The advertising agent was the London Press Exchange. In 1936, a friend of Leonard's from Cambridge, A. R. Pelly, was appointed as the estate's London representative, with a staff of seven. From this point, all estate sales except timber and farm products had to be made through the sales department. Young, *Elmhirsts*, 301.

[151] Anonymous responses to 1931 questionnaire, LKE/G/13/B; Arthur Bridges to Leonard, 9 April 1935, LKE/LAND/4/A.

employees to rise to the top of their profession as advertising claimed; and that the trust structure was not, as purported, an idealistic measure – it had been set up to avoid tax.[152] For those of a commercial bent, however, it was evident that the consumer, whether a figure to be manipulated or catered to, was increasingly a force to be reckoned with: 'the consumer's need, preference and demand should ideally be fed back to and guide the whole procedure from the production end'.[153] The marketing of Dartington as a utopia prefigured shifts in other similar enterprises. The village-cum-holiday-resort of Portmeirion, initially intended to show what good community planning could achieve in the countryside, became a springboard for its founder's daughter – Susan Williams-Ellis, educated at Dartington School – to launch Portmeirion Pottery after the Second World War, one of the first retail companies to exploit the notion of the lifestyle consumer.[154] Dartington showed, wrote one observer in 1934, that enlightened management could make an estate 'as good an investment as the manufacture of soap, motor cars or any other commercial enterprise'.[155]

The shift away from improving conditions of production to concentrating on what the consumer wanted reflected the early stages of the consumer-driven democracy that would flourish after the Second World War. The Elmhirsts were early supporters of this – in part because their effort to re-model production had not worked, and in part because they were in close contact with developments in the United States, which was several decades in advance of Britain in this field.[156] Through the Elmhirst Foundation, Dorothy gave $10,000 to the American Consumers' Club – set up in 1927 to support consumer activism.[157] The Elmhirsts later helped found the British think-tank, Political and Economic Planning, which, seeking a basis of citizenship not already tied to an existing organisation or interest associated with what it saw as an out-of-date political

---

[152] John Wales to W.B. Curry, 4 March 1936, C/DHL/1/B; LKE/G/13/B.
[153] [n.a.], 'Memorandum on the marketing of fresh vegetables, fruit and flowers, in Great Britain, and especially in Devon and Cornwall', [n.d.], T/AG ECON/S7/E.
[154] Susan Williams-Ellis began running the Portmeirion gift shop in 1953 and transformed this into Portmeirion Pottery. Will Farmer and Rob Higgins, *Portmeirion Pottery* (Oxford, 2012).
[155] Nigel de Grey, *Dartington Hall* (Totnes, 1934), 125/7b, Nancy Wilson Ross Archives.
[156] Christopher Beauchamp calls the New Deal 'a testing-ground for consumer politics'. *'Getting Your Money's Worth*: American Models for the Remaking of the Consumer Interest in Britain, 1930s-1960s', in Mark Bevir and Frank Trentmann (eds.), *Critiques of Capital in Modern Britain and America: Transatlantic Exchanges* (Basingstoke, 2002), 127–50, at 129.
[157] The Consumers' Club, set up by Frederick Schlink and Stuart Chase, was incorporated as Consumers' Research in 1929. Charles F. McGovern, *Sold American: Consumption and Citizenship, 1890–1945* (Chapel Hill, 2006), 182–4.

and economic system, increasingly put the consumer – as opposed to capital or labour – at the heart of its initiatives.[158]

Both organisations believed, as Matthew Hilton puts it, in 'the ability of information, expertise and rational individualism to modify the market, society and the economy to the needs of the people'.[159] Their philosophy foreshadowed that of the consumer organisations set up in England in the 1950s. Michael Young, ex-Dartington pupil and long-time trustee, who started the Consumers' Association in 1956 – again funded by the Elmhirsts – saw the consumer as 'the centre of a political movement which would enable the concerns of ordinary people to filter through into political expression'.[160] In place of Rex Gardner's happy craftsmen, working in a socially and spiritually fulfilling rural community and producing objects to raise the taste of society as a whole, socio-spiritual as well as economic regeneration might be led by the demands of the masses, promising far wider and more rapid reform.

5.4   Social Participation and Social Welfare

For both the Elmhirsts, the ultimate aim of rural regeneration was not to encourage healthy industry and agriculture in the countryside – though that was a sine qua non. Rather, it was the Dewey-inspired project of deepening collective fulfilment and democracy. By increasing people's participation in all aspects of social life, they aimed to reverse the self-seeking and the loss of moral meaning that they felt threatened society with fragmentation. Leonard explained to Labour politician Ellen Wilkinson that behind all his and Dorothy's work, past and future, abroad and at Dartington, lay 'a conviction that the villages of England, as also of India' had 'yet to come into their own'.[161] He told her that their aim was to help uncover in the people involved in their community – and by extension in ordinary villagers across the world – 'a deep faith in themselves, wherewith to set their own house in order, by their own

---

[158] In the late 1930s, PEP investigated the possibility of publishing independent tests of manufactured goods to empower consumers in making choices. The project failed due to concerns about British libel law. In 1934, they published *What Consumers Need* as a starting point for discussion about market reforms to strengthen the influence of shoppers. Matthew Hilton, 'Michael Young and the Consumer Movement', *Contemporary British History* 19 (2005), 311–9, at 312.

[159] Hilton, 'Michael Young', 311.

[160] Ibid, 317. See also Michael Young, *The Chipped White Cups of Dover: A Discussion of the Possibility of a New Progressive Party* (London, 1960), 11, 18–9; Lawrence Black, '*Which?* Craft in Post-war Britain: The Consumers' Association and the Politics of Affluence', *Albion: A Quarterly Journal Concerned with British Studies* 36 (2004), 52–82.

[161] Leonard to Ellen Wilkinson, 19 April 1927, LKE/G/33/I.

effort'. Dartington, Leonard wrote to Wilkinson in another letter, was 'trying to pull off the nearest thing to a communal estate that I believe is at all comparable to what is being attempted in theory, at any rate, in Russia'.[162]

The Elmhirsts' theoretical enthusiasm for grassroots democracy was accompanied by an ambivalence about it in practice that ultimately did as much to shape their estate. Dorothy had been raised in New York high society; Leonard as a traditional English squire. They were for the people, but not quite willing to be of them – a problem that plagued many early-twentieth-century intellectuals and reformers.[163] Like the national progressives of *The New Republic*, the uneasy compromise that the Elmhirsts found was to combine their ultimate faith in democratic participation with the view that the elite could – and indeed should – steer the masses in the right direction until they were ready to govern themselves.[164] Leonard described the progress of history as 'the hauling up of a load of stones from the bottom of a cliff, – a few strong men, paternalistic, enlightened, tugging and hauling by main force and the vast population on the basket sitting tight ... plastic and immobile'.[165]

This section looks first at the social structure of Dartington as it moved from the ideal of a group-run community to the reality of top-down rule. It then follows the Elmhirsts' efforts to work out how best they could contribute to social democratic reform if they could not model it themselves. They tried to make their estate a centre for the region, achieving much in the surrounding villages but encountering problems with disapproving locals. They became involved with parish and county government, seeking ways in which official instruments could be coordinated with the efforts of private activists such as themselves. When neither regional hubs nor private–public collaboration worked out satisfactorily, their sense of the proper mode of reform shifted still further away from the local. They embraced central planning, sponsoring the think-tank Political and Economic Planning and contributing to state-led schemes for post-war reconstruction.

As with the areas of agriculture and industry, Dorothy and Leonard struggled throughout this evolution in their ideas and activities to

---

[162] Leonard to Ellen Wilkinson, 28 April 1930, LKE/G/33/I.

[163] For some equivalent biographies, see Susan Pedersen and Peter Mandler (eds.), *After the Victorians: Private Conscience and Public Duty in Modern Britain: Essays in Memory of John Clive* (London and New York, 1994).

[164] Marc Stears, *Progressives, Pluralists, and the Problems of the State: Ideologies of Reform in the United States and Britain, 1909–1926* (Oxford, 2006).

[165] Leonard to Dorothy, 4 October 1921, LKE/DWE/10/D.

reconcile their faith in the importance of the local, the grassroots and a vaguely defined idea of community spirit with their belief in the efficiency of the large-scale, scientific and centralised and their reliance on international expertise. And, as in other areas, their most influential contributions were made as surveyors of the field of action and as advice-givers on larger projects, rather than as builders of a community. Yet, even as their interest in the theory of central planning was hurried into practical fruition by the Second World War, they did not lose interest in promoting localised democracy: the final section of the chapter looks at their support of post-war community development in Britain and India.

5.4.1   Self-governing Community or Benevolent Business?

> Unity of intention or purpose, community of feeling, has never been fully achieved here, and in consequence we have had to fall back upon a form of autocracy. There was no general agreement upon the purpose of education, the object of life or the nature of the good.   Wyatt Rawson (1927)[166]

In the very early years, when Dartington revolved around a small school, there was a strong sense that the estate was, or soon would be, 'a group working together' – a model for social democracy.[167] Ambitions were shaped by the emphasis placed on democracy, loving friendship and ethical day-to-day behaviour that Leonard had experienced at Sriniketan.[168] A second strong influence was Eduard Lindeman, the American expert in the theory and practice of adult education who presided over the first meetings held to plan Dartington.[169] Lindeman was opposed both to centralised 'collectivist nationalism' and to having an 'intelligence bureau' of elites interpreting democracy for the masses – ideas that were popular among a transatlantic constituency of progressives, including Walter Lippmann in America and the Fabians in England.[170] He insisted social progress would come from 'community groups being drawn together from within' – and he hoped that Dartington would be such a group.[171]

---

[166] Wyatt Rawson to Eduard Lindeman, July 1927, DWE/G/7/C.
[167] [n.a.], transcription of Sunday evening meeting, 23 September 1928, LKE/G/31/A.
[168] Leonard to Rathi Tagore, 13 March 1929, LKE/IN/21/B.
[169] 'Report of meeting held to discuss plans and purposes of Dartington school', 11 September 1926, T/DHS/A/1/A.
[170] Stears, *Progressives*, 79.
[171] Eduard Lindeman, 'The place of the local community in organized society', [n.d.], DWE/G/7/C.

Early on, the Elmhirsts, Leonard in particular, shared this ambition.[172] Yet, as soon as theoretical discussions were replaced by practical activities, it became clear that informal, organically emerging democratic direction was not going to work. The 'experiment in democracy during the autumn of 1926' was 'wholly unsuccessful', wrote one participant, responding anonymously to an estate questionnaire; there was no way that the Elmhirsts, their international experts and the workers who formed the bulk of the community were going to achieve 'subconscious homogeneity' or 'common will'.[173] 'In 1927', the respondent continued, 'we started with an autocracy.'[174] This judgement indicates a dissatisfaction that is mostly hidden in the Dartington archives by an official emphasis on communal harmony – and it is valid. Although the Elmhirsts insisted that they meant only to 'treat [Dartington] as ours until the different elements are firstly able to make a "go" of their own show, and then show ability to combine with the other elements to make a "go" of the whole thing', they gave little sign of really wanting control taken out of their hands.[175]

The ideal of collective rule was abandoned in favour of a hierarchical structure of control – topped, informally at first, by the Elmhirsts and a rotating cast of advisors, and then by a board of directors and trustees. Dartington Hall Ltd was formed in 1929, its directors controlling the commercial operations. Two years later, the Dartington Hall Trust was set up, intended to foster the non-commercial ideals behind Dartington.[176] Leonard was chairman of both company and trust, and he and Dorothy were trustees, but day-to-day guidance of the estate was increasingly devolved to an echelon of managers. Several of those involved with the estate since the beginning lamented the move from an 'attempt at living in a group' – where the emphasis was on friendship, brotherhood and love – to something 'more conventional, national and orthodox' in which 'you are free to do anything save fall below your costings keep'.[177]

Even though top-down governance had been brought in, the expectation lingered on among participants that social control, at least, would gradually be shared out through a system of committees, yielding 'a democratic result'.[178] The Elmhirsts experimented with a series of

---

[172] [n.a.], 'Report of meeting held to discuss plans and purposes of Dartington school', 11 September 1926, T/DHS/A/1/A.
[173] Anonymous response to 1929 questionnaire, T/PP/P/1/D.   [174] Ibid.
[175] Leonard to Dorothy, 29 March 1926, LKE/DWE/12/D.
[176] Victor Bonham-Carter, *Land and Environment: The Survival of the English Countryside* (Rutherford, NJ, 1971), 141.
[177] Gerald Heard to Margaret Isherwood, 17 December 1933, DWE/G/6A.
[178] Anonymous response to 1929 questionnaire, T/PP/P/1/D.

measures that fed this expectation. These ranged from works councils, through a short-lived 'Public Relations Committee', to an estate committee formed during the Second World War 'to effect interchange of ideas between the Trustees and those living or working on the Estate'.[179] At Leonard's request, the WEA tutor-organiser F. G. Thomas drew up a scheme 'for the democratic organization of the adult and social life of the workers on the estate' through a workers' council 'with statutory authority from its inception to devise, finance and organise'.[180] But the plan was blocked by the managing director W. K. Slater and the headmaster W. B. Curry – the former because self-government seemed antithetical to making a profit, the latter not wanting his freedom of action as an educator limited.[181]

The Elmhirsts, torn between 'dictation by trustees or democracy', irritated many of the estate's participants with their vacillation.[182] Slater found his position as managing director undermined by personal appeals to Dorothy and Leonard, and vainly begged them either to put in place 'the democratic methods of control through a rigidly observed committee structure' or to accept that Dartington was 'an autocracy founded on financial control'.[183] In spite of the Elmhirsts' unwillingness to choose either path explicitly, their estate drifted more and more towards the latter position, driven by financial imperatives and by their own instinctive paternalism. When a permanent joint council of trustees and managers was formed in 1945, the managers were appointed by the trustees rather than elected by the workers, and the council's role was weak and advisory.[184] Newly appointed trustee Robert Appleby – managing director of Decker and Black, advisor to the Federation of British Industry and one of the few Conservatives to sit on the Dartington board – wrote that '[t]he ideals of Dartington could only be achieved by efficiency. You would not get efficiency by molly-coddling the workers'.[185]

Regardless of who was in control, as Dartington expanded, the Elmhirsts were determined 'to make "good-will" keep pace with "structure"' and tried various means to promote collective identity.[186] In the

[179] T/PP/P/1/B and C.
[180] F. G. Thomas, scheme for workers' council, 25 May 1933, LKE/EDU/2/B.
[181] W. K. Slater to Leonard, 28 June 1933, T/AE/2/D.
[182] Leonard, jottings, 21 February 1935, LKE/G/S9/A.
[183] W. K. Slater to Leonard, 22 September 1939, C/DHL/5/B.
[184] Meeting between trustees and heads of department, 19 November 1945, C/DHL/1/E.
[185] Ibid.
[186] Leonard quoted in *Tomorrow*, the Dartington School magazine, July 1933, T/DHS/B/23/E.

absence of truly democratic government, social participation seemed to them the crucial component of democratic rural regeneration. Measures tried included a short-lived experiment with a library extension service, an equally short-lived attempt to run an estate transport service, and a successful daily news sheet, *News of the Day*, whose presence in the archives offers a source of vivid insight into the community's everyday life.[187] One employee likened *News of the Day* to the newly established BBC, both drawing together 'an audience with many points of view' (also like the BBC, the paper claimed to be democratically inclusive but was dominated by the elite).[188] Estate meetings were held every Sunday to discuss progress and direction – an echo of the New Deal's promotion of civic discussion groups to foster democratic citizenship.[189]

Yet, although estate meetings were meant to show 'in visible form the Dartington folk as a living group', some felt they excluded the '"coats off" workers' who often lived at a distance, had family responsibilities in the evenings and found the abstract nature of discussions inaccessible.[190] Socially, the community's tone was mostly set by the minority of educated, confident 'black coated workers'.[191] Newcomers, particularly local 'maids and workmen', as opposed to metropolitan middle-class idealists, complained that they did not understand what Dartington was all about. One asked for 'a sort of estate year-book, with maps and history'.[192] The absence of such a guide was an indication of the Elmhirsts' unwillingness – and their inability – to summarise what their project was about.

Dorothy and Leonard saw improving the architecture of their estate as another means of fostering community spirit: by encouraging workers to live there, and as a counter-measure to the tendency for rural people to move into towns, where living standards were higher. Their ideas about improving the built landscape paralleled the interwar rural preservation movement which, as David Matless finds, combined an interest in preservation and reconstruction with self-conscious progressivism.[193]

---

[187] *News of the Day* was first published in December 1927. Other measures are described in *Tomorrow*, July 1933, T/DHS/B/23/E.

[188] G. H. Thurley, response to 1931 questionnaire, T/PP/P/1/E.

[189] Gilbert, *Planning Democracy*, 142.

[190] Findlay, *The Dartington Community*, LKE/G/13/B; the complaint came from J. W. B. Butterworth, a worker in the plant nursery, in a letter to Leonard, 22 February 1937, LKE/DEV/1/D.

[191] J. W. B. Butterworth to Leonard, 22 February 1937, LKE/DEV/1/D.

[192] Anonymous response to 1931 questionnaire, LKE/G/13/B.

[193] David Matless, *Landscape and Englishness*, 25 and 'Definitions of England, 1928–89: Preservation, Modernism and the Nature of the Nation', *Built Environment* 16 (1990), 179–91.

Dorothy wrote that she and Leonard felt they were 'bound by a great tradition', which called on them not only to 'preserve tenderly' but to make their own additions with the same 'bigness of conception'.[194] Preservation, in Leonard's case, took the form of trying faithfully to restore the estate's medieval buildings, right down to the correct door studs and hinges.[195] One of his great pleasures, arts director Peter Cox remembered, was taking people on a tour of the buildings, 'comparing one mason's pointing with another's, clearing out a blocked drain while talking about [the estate's original owner] John Holand'.[196] Dorothy, meanwhile, focused on cultivating the garden in a way that would express 'its simple nobility of line and long human association'.[197] The garden managed more harmoniously and more consistently than the rest of the estate to be a place of integration between aesthetic styles – combining 'the classic with the romantic, the formal with the informal', as Dorothy put it, relating all the old and new elements of the estate 'in organic harmony'.[198] Overall, the Elmhirsts' interest in expensive restoration projects highlighted their position as successors to a series of lords and ladies of the manor, rather than their egalitarian hopes for Dartington's future.

Dorothy and Leonard's progressivism, conversely, was embodied in an ambitious programme of building modern, democratic houses and estate buildings. They employed no main architect or planner – partly because, as Leonard wrote, it was not easy to find one 'who had specialised in the needs of children, or of cows, or chickens, or of wage earners or of factory buildings'.[199] Partly, too, it was because the Elmhirsts wanted to incorporate as many socially or spiritually minded aesthetic schools as possible on their estate. The result was that international modernist creations like William Lescaze's Bauhaus-inspired white-cube house for the school's headmaster sat alongside Arts-and-Crafts buildings by Oswald Milne and Rex Gardner; the medieval Hall, carefully restored by William Weir, stood near clusters of small, low-cost houses with concrete block

---

[194] Dorothy, undated note, quoted in Harrison, 'The Visual Arts', 236.
[195] Young, *Elmhirsts*, 113.
[196] Peter Cox, *The Arts at Dartington, 1940–1983: A Personal Account* (Exeter, 2005), 139.
[197] Dorothy quoted in *Dartington Hall Gardens: Historical Report*, Katherine Ross and Gardens Advisory Committee (2016), 43.
[198] Quoted in Reginald Snell, *From the Bare Stem: Making Dorothy Elmhirst's Garden at Dartington Hall* (Devon, 1989), 73–4.
[199] Leonard to Nikolaus Pevsner, 1952, quoted in Nikolaus Pevsner, *Devon* (Harmondsworth, 1989 [1952]), 314.

walls and asbestos roofs designed by Louis de Soissons, the planner of Welwyn Garden City.[200]

An American visitor who toured the estate in 1935 wrote that 'if I had had to turn right back and take the steamer after leaving Dartington I should have seen the best of England – its past, present and future'.[201] Others were less inspired by the jumble of modernist and backward-looking buildings. Visitor John Drummond thought that, the estate had achieved 'no new interpretation or message in architecture, design, or country planning'.[202] John Piper, who painted Dartington Hall in 1943, called it 'an interesting survival, very much dated', with the 'over-restored Hall' and the 'beautifully hideous rolling red-earthed fields that surround it on all sides, punctured by the concrete walls and flat roofs of the houses all around that were designed by the now-forgotten famous architects of the early thirties'.[203] Nor did the Elmhirsts' buildings satisfy those who had to live in them. Workers complained that their houses – intended to provide a model for cheap building for other landowners – also looked cheap and felt cheap to live in, falling apart rapidly in the damp Devon climate.[204] Perhaps because of the number of architects involved, new houses tended to be scattered awkwardly, out of walking distance from Dartington's centre, contributing little to community spirit.[205] In spite of such shortcomings, as David Jeremiah writes, the Elmhirsts' energetic programme of restoration and building turned the once-failing fabric of their estate into 'a paradigm of the tensions between reconstruction and modernisation'.[206]

Initially, there was a feeling that the Elmhirsts' measures to promote social welfare – which included not only cheap houses to rent but 'water and electricity laid on, insurance, pensions, the nursery school' – were not the gifts of a generous employer or paternalistic landlord, but an essential part of a democratically conceived community jointly striving to

[200] David Jeremiah gives accounts of interwar architecture on the estate in 'Dartington' – A Modern Adventure', in Smiles (ed.), *Going Modern and Being British*, 43–78 and in 'Dartington Hall – A Landscape of an Experiment in Rural Reconstruction', in Paul Brassley, Jeremy Burchardt and Lynne Thompson (eds.), *The English Countryside Between the Wars: Regeneration or Decline?* (New York, 2006), 116–31. See also, Bonham-Carter, *Dartington Hall*, 116.
[201] Elsie Weil to Dorothy, 8 July 1935 DWE/G/S1/F.
[202] John Drummond, draft chapters for unpublished book, LKE/DEV/3/C.
[203] Frances Spalding, *John Piper, Myfanwy Piper: Lives in Art* (Oxford, 2009), 228.
[204] Young, *Elmhirsts*, 265.
[205] Louis de Soissons' housing estates at Huxhams Cross and Broom Park, for example, were inconveniently distant from the estate's commercial departments and isolated from the social centre formed by Dartington Hall and its immediate grounds.
[206] Jeremiah, 'Dartington Hall', 122.

raise the standard of rural life.[207] Along with the effort to make spiritual
fulfilment, education and the arts part of everyone's everyday life, they
were seen as a genuine alternative to alienated labour. With time, however, as one visitor complained, the quality of these benefits moved away
from the 'socialistic and communistic' and towards 'commercialised
feudalism'.[208] Welfare measures seemed less designed to improve social
participation and well-being for their own sake than to increase commercial efficiency or to function as a sop to make up for the 'mechanised and
stereotyped jobs' that had arisen in place of integrated work – easing the
transition to industrial capitalism.[209] The Laban Lawrence Industrial
Rhythm, for example, which was developed by choreographer Rudolf
Laban and pioneered in various Dartington departments, was meant not
just to diminish physical strain, but also to speed up production.[210]
Efficiency and worker welfare were similarly entwined in such businesses
as Rowntree where, jointly emphasised, they provided a convenient way
of fulfilling the company's Quaker ideals of service to employees and to
consumers at the same time.[211]

The interwar years marked a blossoming of interest in 'man-manage-
ment' in Britain.[212] Dartington's managers looked to the successes of
such new management techniques as 'propaganda' in the Bata Shoe
Factory in Essex, where even 'the office boy is encouraged to demand
information on such important points as profit or loss'.[213] They
complained that, by contrast, Dartington was 'barren of concrete

[207] Felicity Palmer, report on Dartington, 1938, LKE/G/25/A.
[208] William St John Pym, response to 1931 questionnaire, T/PP/P/1/E; Vicky Long writes
about the interwar narrowing of nineteenth-century utopian ideas of integrated work
into a concentration on industrial welfare, seeing it in part as a response to trade
unionism ('Industrial Homes').
[209] Meeting between trustees and heads of department, 19 November 1945, C/DHL/1/E.
[210] This system was developed by Rudolph Laban in cooperation with Frederick
C. Lawrence, a Manchester engineer. It was first used at Tyresoles Ltd in
Manchester then, in the 1950s, attracted other adherents, including Mars
Confectionary. Evelyn Doerr, *Rudolf Laban: The Dancer of the Crystal* (Lanham, MD
and Plymouth, 2008), 196–7; F.C. Lawrence to W.K. Slater, 22 May 1942, T/AD/3;
'Report upon Miss Newlove's visit to Dartington Hall Ltd. 10–21 May', 4 June 1942,
T/AD/3.
[211] Robert Fitzgerald, *Rowntree and the Marketing Revolution, 1862–1969* (Cambridge,
1995), 218.
[212] Daniel Ussishkin, 'The "Will to Work": Industrial Management and the Question of
Conduct in Inter-War Britain', in Laura Beers and Geraint Thomas (eds.), *Brave New
World: Imperial and Democratic Nation-Building in Britain Between the Wars* (London,
2011), 91–109.
[213] Hiram Hague Winterbotham, 'Memorandum', 1936, C/DHL/1/B; Joanna Smith
'"Work Collectively and Live Individually": The Bata Housing Estate at East
Tilbury', *Twentieth Century Architecture* 9 (2008), 52–68.

information' and not maximising its workers' commitment.[214]
A disenchanted employee wrote in 1936 that Dartington had become
'less rather than more' than George Cadbury's Bournville and Sir
William Lever's Port Sunlight; at least these paternalistic industrial villages were clear what they stood for, while Dartington, beginning with
higher ideals of democratic government and participation, was now
'distinguishable from other industrial undertakings merely by its ineffi-
ciency'.[215] Part of the difference between the efforts to promote democratic community spirit at Dartington compared with these other
humane, if sometimes paternalistic, projects lay in its location – in deep
Devon, rather than on the fringes of London (Bata), Liverpool (Port
Sunlight) or Birmingham (Bournville). As one observer warned the
Elmhirsts, the farms and hamlets that formed Dartington had never
had a 'community life' independent from the owner of the Hall; they
were used to being part of 'the old patriarchal regime' – and did not
necessarily hunger to be freed of it.[216]

While the overall tenor of the estate shifted from group endeavour to
enlightened business, much of the time the Elmhirsts' lives resembled
those of traditional wealthy landowners. They lived in lavish private
quarters among expensive artworks and a large staff, travelled a great
deal abroad, hosted a stream of upper-class visitors and held traditional
squirearchical events like fetes and Christmas parties for the estate children.[217] They seemed, to some employees at least, cocooned in the
'unreality generated by money'.[218] Whilst theoretically in favour of social
democracy, they never engaged with the class problem head on – assuming, rather, a fundamental harmony of interests between classes and a
future in which the masses would be raised to the level of the elite.[219]
This tension between ideology and practice was evident in the lives of
elite reformers across England in the interwar years, detailed by Alison
Light, for example, in the relations between the Bloomsbury group and
their servants.[220]

---

[214] Hiram Hague Winterbotham, 'Memorandum', 1936, C/DHL/1/B.
[215] John Wales to W. B. Curry, 4 March 1936, C/DHL/1/B; Hiram Hague Winterbotham, 'Memorandum', 1936, C/DHL/1/B.
[216] John Benson to Leonard, 1930 and 1932, T/HIS/5/A.
[217] Paula Morel, interview with Michael Young, 23 August 1976, T/HIS/S22; Michael Straight to Michael Young, 11 September 1980, T/HIS/S22/D.
[218] Raymond O'Malley to Michael Young, 5 January 1983, T/HIS/S20/D.
[219] The Elmhirst-sponsored think-tank Political and Economic Planning similarly predicted 'the shaping of a world without a proletariat' in a universal process of 'grading up'. [n.a.], 'Post-war reconstruction group', 28 August 1940, LKE/USA/11/C.
[220] Alison Light, Mrs Woolf and the Servants: The Hidden Heart of Domestic Service (London, 2007).

Some visitors, like political economist George Catlin, saw Dorothy and Leonard's top-down methods of furthering democracy as exemplary: 'the dissolving of class division' was 'a task to be performed from above, in a useful unostentatious community open to those who like its ways, not from below by force and envious proletarian legislation'.[221] The craftsman Rex Gardner agreed that 'democracy will only be possible when the weapons have been forged by autocracy. That is my interest in D[artington]'.[222] Nonetheless, Leonard was uncomfortably aware that 'Big capital' could easily '"loosen" the very idea and principle of democracy'.[223] He compared Dartington enviously with the Brynmawr Experiment – a scheme to revive the fortunes of a Welsh mining town that had a self-governing model.[224] He half-wished that Dartington was run on the same lines, but never quite brought himself to admit openly that it was not. To escape the conundrum of wanting collective government but not believing people able to effect it, the Elmhirsts turned from building a micro-democracy at Dartington to considering how the estate could serve local society as a 'mother village' instead, as 'in Saxon times a parish sometimes took on the creation of a new sub-parish under its wing'.[225]

5.4.2   Dartington as a 'Mother Village'

In India, Leonard had worried that the single village was 'too small a unit to withstand [the] attack of city and world markets'; to thrive, a community must have a 'coordinating centre' such as Sriniketan, uniting the surrounding villages and hamlets.[226] By the late 1920s, Leonard had begun to think that Dartington, too, should play such a role. The conception of the region – rather than the village or the nation as a whole – as

---

[221] George E. G. Catlin to Leonard, 7 September 1925, LKE/G/4/E.

[222] Rex Gardner, response to 1929 questionnaire, T/PP/P/1/D.

[223] Leonard to R. A. Edwards, 1 January 1947, LKE/DEV/1/K.

[224] Leonard, untitled note, LKE/G/S8/B, [n.d.]. The Brynmawr Experiment to revive the fortunes of a Welsh mining town involved a survey of the district made by its inhabitants. Afterwards, a Community Study Council was set up, drawn from all sections of the community, to put in place a series of recommendations that included establishing new industries, a children's group, adult education and a library. Echoing Dartington, it aimed at 'a new relationship – a coordinating of varied interests, as parts of a whole rather than as opposing and self contained units'. 'The Brynmawr Experiment, 1928–1933', pamphlet, [n.d.], LKE/G/S4/B; letters between Leonard and Peter Scott, one of the originators of the experiment, are in file LKE/G/S4/B.

[225] Leonard interviewed by Victor Bonham-Carter, transcript of recording of BBC Third Programme on Dartington Hall, recorded 19 June 1950, transmitted 13 August 1951, LKE/G/S13/A.

[226] Leonard to Arthur Geddes, 24 February 1923, LKE/IN/6/D.

the effective unit of rural regeneration echoed the decentralised, elite-led regionalist ideals of such ruralists as Rolf Gardiner. Yet, while the Elmhirsts might seem to fulfil Gardiner's vision of rural regeneration stemming from regional centres run by 'a new *elite* rooted in the soil', part of a re-invigorated, paternalistic landowning class, their own view was still the Deweyan one that social reform could only be brought about by ordinary people.[227] In this sense, their ideas were more aligned with those of Henry Morris, Education Secretary for Cambridgeshire, who wrote that 'the English village as a social unit is a relic of the middle ages' and that people should be 'more realistic and less romantic' and admit that it was a 'rural region' – a group of villages centred around one large village – that was the unit for furthering social progress, including encouraging a degree of self-government.[228] As elsewhere, the Elmhirsts' efforts to promote their citizen-led regionalist vision panned gradually outward, from Dartington village, to other nearby villages, to the South-West as a whole.

In 1940, the newly appointed vicar for Dartington village, R. A. Edwards, reported being 'assailed with stories of the Estate's misdeeds, of anything from a Nudist Colony to the Black Mass'.[229] While he may have exaggerated opprobrium to emphasise his own achievements as a go-between for the estate and village, the Elmhirsts had certainly met with local hostility. The Women's Institute, the parish council, the cricket club, the village hall and church were all resistant to their plans from the moment they arrived in Devon.[230] Such was the peril of setting up a radical experiment in the heart of a county that was a bastion of traditional values. After a brief effort to engage with the church, Leonard, and to a lesser extent Dorothy, were content to return the cold shoulder – seeing it as an outdated institution. But they wanted the village hall, standing just beyond the boundary of their land, to be a joint centre of estate-village life. They shared with other ruralists the belief that, as Jeremy Burchardt writes, the village hall had particular 'community-forming properties', as a place of civic discussion, self-education and democratic participation.[231]

---

[227] Rolf Gardiner, *England Herself*, 171.

[228] Henry Morris, 'The rural region', paper given at the summer conference of the Institute of Public Administration, 15 July 1938, Bristol, LKE/LAND/6/B.

[229] R. A. Edwards, 'Dartington: A report for the Bishop of the Diocese', January 1948, DWE/G/S3/G.

[230] Francis Acland to Leonard, 10 October 1936, LKE/DEV/1/B; R.A. Edwards, 'Dartington: A report for the Bishop of the Diocese', January 1948, DWE/G/S3/G.

[231] Jeremy Burchardt, 'Reconstructing the Rural Community: Village Halls and the National Council of Social Service, 1919–39', *Rural History* 10 (1999), 193–216.

The Elmhirsts found the local hall controlled by a band of wealthy local Conservatives – 'not a village hall in the true and democratic sense at all' judged Leonard.[232] After making an ill-received suggestion that the villagers borrow capital and buy these men out, the Elmhirsts mooted the idea of Dartington's founding a new, truly democratic village institute by itself.[233] Tellingly, the construction of this centre was delayed until after the Second World War by local concerns that it would be a top-down affair superimposed by the Elmhirsts, rather than 'part of the normal community managed simply by the people who belong to it'.[234] When it was finally built in the late 1940s, the local vicar complained that its ambition 'to serve as a central Institute for a wide rural area' was part of an undesirable new 'Town and Country Planning idea' that would further contribute to the 'degrading of village life'.[235] For some, Devon's traditionalism should be guarded, rather than being reformed along modern social democratic lines.

The Elmhirsts worked with several other nearby villages through the interwar years: encouraging Rattery, for instance, to expand into new types of farming and to build itself a village hall; and suggesting schemes at Dittisham for better transport and sewage facilities, a school and a playing field.[236] More ambitious but less fruitful was the speculative development of a 'community of housing with [a] utopian agenda' – a new ideal community blending rural England and Continental modernism that was to be built from scratch in the nearby parish of Churston Ferrers. Only 10 of the 500 flat-roofed, white houses the Elmhirsts planned were completed before the Second World War.[237] Proceedings were slow because Dorothy and Leonard employed a construction team that spanned the Atlantic, including pioneering American urban planner Henry Wright – part of an internationalisation of planning practices still in its early stages.[238] As much of a problem as speed was the lack of

---

[232] Leonard to R. A. Edwards, 1 January 1947, LKE/DEV/1/K.
[233] Ibid; Leonard to R. N. Armfelt of the Devon County Education Committee, 20 May 1940, T/AE/5/A.
[234] R. A. Edwards to Leonard, 16 November 1946, LKE/DEV/1/K.
[235] R. A. Edwards to Leonard, 16 May 1947, T/AE/5/A.
[236] A. A. L. Caesar, 'Visit to Dartington Hall, March 17–19', 24 March 1944, LKE/LAND/2/G.
[237] The houses cost over £1,000 each when the average price for the area was little over £500. W. K. Slater to Henry Wright, 5 December 1935; W. K. Slater to William Lescaze, 27 February and 15 March 1934.
[238] Other architects and planners involved in the project included, in America, William Lescaze and Beatrix Farrand, and, in England, Oswald Milne and Dartington's building department. Churston minutes, 3 May 1933–17 January 1935, quoted in Gaia Caramellino, *Europe Meets America: William Lescaze, Architect of Modern Housing* (Newcastle, 2016), 145; Stephen V. Ward, 'A Pioneer "Global Intelligence Corps"?

5.3 Houses designed by William Lescaze, Churston estate, 1930s
(© Dartington Hall Trust and the Elmgrant Trust)

buyers. People were put off by the expense and novelty of the modernist designs, and by the suspicion that they would be required to live a 'communal life' there.[239] Many who wanted to live in Devon did so precisely because they admired its traditional values. The pitfalls of superimposing a utopian community design drawn upon another continent and without reference to local preference were made expensively apparent. When Wright died in 1936, the Elmhirsts searched America in vain for another planner to make the project 'the experiment it ought to be'; after the war, they resigned themselves to design along more orthodox lines and finally found buyers.[240]

In the late 1930s, Leonard, as chairman of the Joint Committee for Tutorial Classes – an alliance between the University College of the South West, the Local Education Authority and the Workers

The Internationalization of Planning Practice, 1890–1939', *The Town Planning Review* 76 (2005), 119–41.

[239] Fred Gwatkin to Lescaze, 30 August 1933, C/CDC/9/H. See also David Jeremiah, *Architecture and Design for the Family in Britain, 1900–1970* (New York, 2000), 86–7.

[240] Leonard to Mr Ross, 6 October 1936, LKE/USA/6/G. A more conservative architect, Louis de Soissons, took over from Lescaze, instating a more conventional style and making Churston a reasonable financial success. Caramellino, *Europe Meets America*, 160–1.

Educational Association, supported a 'listening project' in the villages of the South-West run by tutor-organiser F. G. Thomas.[241] Groups were formed in forty-three villages to fill in questionnaires after listening to a series of regional BBC broadcasts by prominent local figures on the subject of 'the changing village'.[242] The survey, which involved 'no statisticians or skilled investigators, but an affiliation of village people', was part of a movement for regional survey in the interwar period that took much of its inspiration from Patrick Geddes, the Scottish planner and social evolutionist whom Leonard had met in India.[243] As David Matless writes, for Geddes, people's participation in surveying 'would generate good local, national, and world citizenship' and promote healthy participation in a devolved regional politics.[244] The aim of F. G. Thomas's survey, as set out by Francis Acland, MP for Cornwall, in the introduction to the pamphlet of findings, was 'making citizenship not simply a matter of being governed but a thing to be lived'.[245] It was back to John Dewey again: social reformation meant deepening active participation in democracy; teaching social precepts apart from practice was 'teaching the child to swim by going through the motions outside the water'.[246]

F. G. Thomas was inspired by his success to suggest a comprehensive agricultural, economic and social survey of Devon and Somerset by its inhabitants, financed by the BBC, supported by Dartington, and providing information both for broadcasters and for use by 'economists, sociologists and by legislative bodies'.[247] He had seen American extra-mural work at first hand on the back of the Rockefeller Foundation scholarship that the Elmhirsts assisted him in securing, and he pushed Leonard to help because of his own 'unique knowledge of this type of work both here and in America'.[248] Leonard also admired American social survey, and he corresponded with central figures in the agricultural New Deal who were embracing practical surveys by citizen-researchers as part of their

---

[241] J. G. Trevena to Leonard, 10 January 1935, LKE/EDU/3/A; Leonard to John Murray, 28 March 1935, LKE/EDU/3/A.

[242] F. G. Thomas, 'First annual report of the Rural Extension Scheme', 1936, LKE/EDU/4/B.

[243] 'Development of Devon rural life', clipping from unknown newspaper, 18 September 1935, LKE/EDU/3/F.

[244] David Matless, 'Regional Surveys and Local Knowledges: The Geographical Imagination in Britain, 1918–39', *Transactions of the Institute of British Geographers* 17 (1992), 464–80, at 472–3.

[245] F. G. Thomas, 'The Changing Village', pamphlet with foreword by Sir Francis Acland, LKE/EDU/3/F.

[246] John Dewey, *Moral Principles in Education* (Boston, c.1909), 14.

[247] F. G. Thomas to Leonard, 3 February 1936, LKE/EDU/4/A.

[248] F. G. Thomas to Leonard, 19 August 1936, LKE/EDU/4/C.

programme of reform.[249] The 'two-handed commitment to democracy' that Jess Gilbert distinguishes in these New Deal surveys – a belief in the state as a means of progressive reform combined with the view that federal authority should decentralise to local citizens – represented the ideal of collaborative bottom-up/top-down reform at which the Elmhirsts themselves were now arriving.[250]

Thomas's idea for a comprehensive survey also reflected the popularity of civic survey in Britain, with numerous such endeavours taking place in the 1920s and 1930s, not least the social research project Mass Observation, which recruited a team of untrained observers and diarists to create an 'anthropology of ourselves'.[251] Thomas saw his work as a preliminary to regional planning – the means to establish 'the nucleus of the necessary machinery' to 'initiate the first practical planned re-organisation of selected parts of a given area'.[252] The scientifically minded research department at Dartington, however, argued that a survey 'by local groups of school-children or adults who have not been specially trained' would be of no use to planners.[253] The Elmhirsts themselves, while increasingly inclined to see planning as better than organic community development, also tended to see professional social scientists and the government as necessary participants in this process. Thomas's plan did not go forward.

The Elmhirsts' focus in their experiments with Dartington as a regional coordinating centre progressed from the local village hall, to the nearby villages, and finally to the South West as a whole. Their activities were hampered by their difficulties in communicating their ideals to locals. They also encountered problems in fitting themselves, as elite philanthropists, into the democratic self-improvement that they idealised. It was mostly the schemes that they sponsored from a distance – F. G. Thomas's village survey or the birth control clinic that Dorothy helped set up in the nearby town of Totnes – that had the most direct social impact and were the least complicated as to the politics of control.[254]

---

[249] See files LKE/USA/7.
[250] Jess Gilbert, 'Rural Sociology and Democratic Planning', 423.
[251] Denis Lineman, 'Regional Survey and the Economic Geographies of Britain 1930–1939', *Transactions of the Institute of British Geographers* 28 (2003), 96–122; Gilbert, *Planning Democracy*, 245.
[252] F. G. Thomas to Leonard, 19 August 1936, LKE/EDU/4/C.
[253] Research department, note on F. G. Thomas survey, 17 February 1936, LKE/EDU/4/B; W. E. Hiley to Leonard, Memorandum, 2 March 1936, LKE/EDU/4/B.
[254] A birth control clinic was first held on the estate in 1934, with much discretion, so as not to antagonise locals. Under the aegis of Dartington, rooms were subsequently acquired for a regular clinic in Totnes. Dorothy's private secretary to Mrs Graham Murray, 9 October 1935, DWE/G/S3/C.

The realisation that they were better at advising and supporting than demonstrating on the ground, and that this was a way to accommodate themselves as elites into the social-democratic project, contributed to reshaping the Elmhirsts' hopes for Dartington. They began to consider community, or even regional, experiments as too insignificant to bring about reform; what was needed was a way to harness their estate's work to national efforts at rural regeneration.

5.4.3   Experimenting with a Public–Private Rural Regime

The First World War, which, Jeremy Burchardt writes, 'energised voluntarism and stimulated the development of state sponsored social services', also raised questions about the relationship between government and the voluntary sector in the countryside which resonated through the interwar years.[255] In the 1930s, when the Elmhirsts were looking for a way to re-purpose Dartington as something other than an independent experiment, Leonard became involved in local government. At the same time, he was briefly involved with the rural community council movement (RCC). The RCC, set up in 1920, aimed to meld villager self-help, state social services and philanthropic organisations into a democratic pattern that would supersede a rural society led by the landed elite.[256] After a very short consideration of the value of 'trying to combine charity, voluntary-ism and efficiency', however, Leonard decided that social reform would be better run by the government and social scientists along centrally planned lines, saving 'a lot of toil and trouble'.[257]

In 1931, Leonard was elected to Dartington's parish council, with education as his chief focus.[258] In 1937 he was elected as county councillor for the Harberton Electoral Division.[259] His experience of local politics did not give him a strong faith in it – he felt that most of the time it was achieving little. Although David Cannadine argues that, by the 1930s, the county councils were 'a professional hierarchy

---

[255] Jeremy Burchardt, 'State and Society in the English Countryside: The Rural Community Movement 1918–39', *Rural History* 23 (2012), 81–106, at 81. See also Margaret Brasnett, *Voluntary Social Action: A History of the National Council of Social Service 1919–1969* (London, 1969).

[256] Burchardt, 'Rethinking the Rural Idyll' and 'State and Society'.

[257] Leonard to R. N. Armfelt, secretary to the Local Education Authority, 5 February 1938, LKE/FIT/1/B.

[258] Leonard to Bryan Miller, clerk to the county council, 29 April 1931, LKE/DCC/1/A.

[259] Leonard to Francis Acland, 23 February 1937, LKE/DCC/1/D.

and structured bureaucracy', Leonard, at least, was frustrated by the paternalism, conservatism and amateurism of his colleagues – an experience echoed by Winifred Holtby's depiction of the workings of local government in *South Riding*.[260] He was upset not only by the absence of cooperation within the councils but also with other government bodies, and most particularly with independent institutions such as Seale-Hayne Agricultural College and Dartington.[261] He turned towards the notion that the rural regime needed to be reformed more fundamentally.

One route that Leonard considered was the formation of a rural community council in Devon.[262] After a brief moment of enthusiasm, however, he decided that it risked being dogged by the same 'old Norse belief in the enterprising amateur' as existing social service provision.[263] Instead, he recommended the RCC idea be evolved into a regional survey – rather like that suggested by F. G. Thomas, but led by the local university and the National Institute of Economic and Social Research instead of by ordinary citizens. It would give 'a comprehensive picture of where the social structure falls short' and would be the basis for a holistic regime of 'psycho-physical hygiene which regards the human being as one comprehensive organism and not as a series of specialist functions'.[264] For Leonard, this could lead to 'all round improvement from the bottom upwards' – involving government, universities and the church, but starting with 'John Citizen – and all his voluntary Clubs, Societies, Associations and Unions, which for a democracy represent the very life blood of any freedom'.[265] Leonard cited as a parallel a social survey of Bristol that had just been completed by Herbert Tout.[266] This notion of a complete reform of the social system informed by social science was one that would be realised in Britain, albeit in a heavily top-down form, after the Second World War.

---

[260] David Cannadine, *The Decline and Fall of the British Aristocracy* (London, 1996 [1990]), 167; Winifred Holtby, *South Riding* (London, 1936).

[261] A. J. Withycombe, clerk to the county council, to Leonard, 8 March 1938, LKE/DCC/1/E; Leonard to Bryan Miller, 29 April 1931, LKE/DCC/1/A; Leonard to Sir Henry Lopes, chairman of county council, 27 February 1937, LKE/DCC/1/E.

[262] R. N. Armfelt passed the suggestion from the National Council of Social Services on to Leonard, asking for his advice, 22 October 1938, LKE/DCC/1/E and 10 March 1939, LKE/DCC/1/F.

[263] Leonard to R. N. Armfelt, 14 March 1939, LKE/DCC/1/F.   [264] Ibid.   [265] Ibid.

[266] Herbert Tout, *The Standard of Living in Bristol: A Preliminary Report of the Work of the University of Bristol Social Survey* (Bristol, 1938).

5.4.4   Political and Economic Planning

> The gathering of all available and relevant facts and the digestion
> and interpretation of these in the light of social and economic
> trends within the framework of a policy which politicians can
> grasp and parliaments approve is the process we here describe as
> Planning.   Leonard Elmhirst (1940)[267]

Carol Aronovici, an authority on city planning based in New York, visited
Dartington in 1931 and warned the Elmhirsts that their managers were not
'inspired by the "force idea" as the French sociologist calls it, which is the
mainspring of your undertaking'; that staff were not 'conscious of working
for a specific social purpose'; and that the surrounding community was 'to
a considerable extent sceptical, ignorant and unsympathetic about your
project and aims'.[268] The same year, the Elmhirsts circulated a questionnaire on their estate, asking whether Dartington could have a bearing on
the way the country was governed. The general view of respondents was
that it was 'too far off from the mainstream political parties to have an
impact'.[269] The estate's 'bold, clean, fundamental principle of community
living' and 'the very unification of its planning with its proposed balancing
of industries (Farm, School, Factory, etc.)' meant that Dartington would
only be 'of great use to an organization state, one that owns, controls, and
regulates the necessities of existence'.[270] Dorothy and Leonard – their
early faith in social reform stemming from 'innumerable small experiments' anyway shaken by their practical experiences – felt they had to find
another way to promote democratic social progress.[271]

Meanwhile, centralised planning was proliferating across the world –
be it the economic reforms of Russia's Five Year Plan, the New Deal or
Hitler's Four Year Plan for wartime self-sufficiency. At home, the
perception was that the British government was failing to offer a
'constructive outlook' as an alternative to these: Leonard complained it
was concerned 'with retrenchment, and hardly if ever with planned
development'.[272] The Elmhirsts took the view, like many other reformers
in the 1930s, that Britain needed to adopt the panacea of planning.[273]

---

[267] Leonard, 'The place of research and planning in the process of government', 10 August
1940, LKE/PEP/S/F.
[268] Carol Aronovici, 'Tentative suggestions for Dartington Hall', 17 July 1931,
T/PP/P/1/A.
[269] Anonymous response to 1931 questionnaire, LKE/G/13/B.   [270] Ibid.
[271] Leonard to Eduard Lindeman, 7 January 192[4?], box 2, Eduard Lindeman Archives,
DWE/G/7/C.
[272] Leonard, untitled note, 13 May 1933, LKE/LAND/8/A.
[273] Leonard, 'Agricultural economics, a means to what end?', 25 May 1934,
LKE/LAND/8/C.

The particular trigger for Dorothy and Leonard's whole-hearted promotion of 'the planned research and the research-based plan' was the appointment of a National government in 1931.[274] They saw this as 'a step back': the politicians 'have, for lack of figures and facts about national income, trade, and earning power had to appeal to national sentiment and quietly haul down the flag of progressive social reform'.[275] In the absence of state leadership in the field of collective social planning, they saw it as their duty to step into the breach.

In moving from the ideal of an organically emerging local community to that of a centrally planned society, Leonard was also continuing a quest that he had been pursuing since his time at Cornell to work out how social scientists could be incorporated into the project of social regeneration. He saw social science – interpreted widely to include such fields as agricultural economics, spiritualised psychology, planning and administration – as an alluring new catch-all discipline. 'Hitherto,' he wrote, 'the social service meekly followed in the wake of problems already created by industry and individuals, but now society itself is, for the first time in history perhaps, in a position to give a lead.'[276] Government policy was dominated by 'old conservers'; university research was 'dead'; what was needed was a new kind of graduate school where 'social experience might be collected, collated, digested and utilised and the findings extended back in to the world again'.[277] Perhaps because Leonard's enthusiasm for the deployment of social science in guiding society was unusual in this period in Britain, the limited support he found for this idea came mainly from America, where the vision of the role of social science was already more socially purposive.[278] Ultimately, however,

---

[274] Leonard to Rabindranath Tagore, 15 December 1931, LKE/TAG/9/A. In early 1931, the minority Labour government seemed unable to cope with the unfolding economic crisis, while the Conservatives were riven by internal discontent and the Liberal Party was marginal and divided. From August to October, a cross-party National government was formed under Ramsay MacDonald, which also included figures with no party affiliation.

[275] Leonard to Dorothy, 26 August 1931, LKE/DWE/12/E.

[276] Leonard, 'Social trends in rural areas: administrative problems', [n.d.], LKE/LAND/9/A.

[277] Leonard to Gerald Heard, copied in a notebook, 26 December 1934, LKE/G/17.

[278] A key aspect of the New Deal was the idea of a more 'purposive' social science, which could ease, without controlling, democratic transformation (Gilbert, *Planning Democracy*, 179). For more on the development of the social sciences in America and England, see Chapter 1. Leonard's idea of a public administration college received some support from Mansfield Forbes, Cambridge academic and leader of the modernist Twentieth Century Group, and more from American psychologist William Sheldon and from Carl Ladd, Director of Agricultural Extension at Cornell (Mansfield Forbes to Leonard, 30 October 1930, LKE/G/14/A; Leonard to Gerald Heard, copied in a notebook, December 1934, LKE/G/17; Carl Ladd to Leonard, 13 March 1937, LKE/USA/4/B).

Leonard did find an English vehicle to combine his interests in social science and in centralised social reform – not a graduate college but the capitalist think-tank Political and Economic Planning (PEP).

PEP was conceived in 1931 by the editorial team of the *Week-End Review* – a product of the prevailing frustration at seeming political inertia in the face of global economic depression and domestic instability.[279] The group hoped to create a comprehensive and detailed plan for regenerating Britain, combining private enterprise and state planning to create 'the sort of society we want as an alternative to Hitler's New Order on the one hand and to our old selves on the other'.[280] Its activities were underpinned by three assumptions: that experts – social scientists in particular – could understand problems and identify solutions in a way that transcended politics; that government intervention and the greater concentration of power within industry would be beneficial; and that policy-making and social progress more generally could be advanced by circulating research and reports among the interested public.[281]

The group attracted leading figures in business, government and academia, including Basil Blackett, a director of the Bank of England; the biologist Julian Huxley, later the first director of the United Nations Educational, Scientific and Cultural Organization; Max Nicholson, ornithologist and environmentalist; Gerald Barry, editor of the *Week-End Review* and later director-general of the Festival of Britain; and the clothing retailer Lawrence Neal.[282] Along with Israel Sieff, the managing director of Marks and Spencer, Leonard and Dorothy provided it with long-term sponsorship and support.[283] Sieff shared the Elmhirsts' unusual ambition to moralise, or even spiritualise capitalism: hoping to

---

[279] PEP first met in March 1931 under the chairmanship of Sir Basil Blackett. It published reports, broadsheets, and a journal, *Planning*, and was active until 1978, when it merged with the Centre for Studies in Social Policy to form the Policy Studies Institute. John Pinder (ed.), *Fifty Years of Political and Economic Planning: Looking Forward 1931–1981* (London, 1981); Daniel Ritschel, *The Politics of Planning: The Debate on Economic Planning in Britain in the 1930s* (Oxford, 1997), 145–183; Sieff, *Memoirs* (London, 1970), chapter 9.

[280] Max Nicholson to Dorothy, 5 July 1941, DWE/G/8/B. Their initial programme, entitled 'A National Plan for Great Britain', was drafted by Max Nicholson and published in February 1931 as a supplement to the *Week-End Review*.

[281] James Vernon, *Modern Britain, 1750 to the Present* (Cambridge and New York, 2017), 367.

[282] R. C. Whiting, 'Political and Economic Planning (*act.* 1931–1978)', *Oxford Dictionary of National Biography* (Oxford University Press, first published 23 September 2004, revised 27 May 2010) [www.oxforddnb.com/view/theme/95962].

[283] Leonard was chairman and vice-president at various times up to his death in 1974. Israel Sieff gave direction in the early years and chaired the industries groups.

weave into PEP's work 'the relationship between the eternal values of the spirit and our material gains'.[284] There was mutual approval between PEP and Dartington; both were concerned with the 'altogetherness of everything', as Basil Blackett remarked, and PEP was seen as 'an organization which might take up Dartington ideas and make them much more generally applicable'.[285]

PEP was part of a dedication to state planning in Britain in the 1930s that spanned the political spectrum: Oswald Mosley launched the New Party in 1931 on a national planning platform; planning was embraced by the Next Five Years Group led by J. A. Hobson, H. G. Wells, Siegfried Sassoon and Seebohm Rowntree; and the commitment of the leftist Federation of Progressive Societies and Individuals was signalled by the title of their monthly journal, *Plan*.[286] The common element between these groups was the belief that decisions formerly made by individuals in the market should now be administered by some form of collective. They all – including Mosley – identified themselves as 'progressive', in opposition to traditional parliamentary politics, which failed to 'get things done'.[287] As was his wont, Leonard advocated cooperating with these other organisations where possible – so helping to advance 'the general movement towards rationalisation and centralisation'.[288]

Leonard's public commitment to the idea of collaborative planning was such that Dartington and PEP were conflated with the Next Five Years Group, the Fabians, the Federation of Progressive Societies and Individuals, Zionism and the Soviet state in the minds of some anti-planners. Captain Arthur Rogers, a leading member of the far-right Liberty Restoration League, spoke against Dartington in Parliament and included it in a pamphlet warning of a planning 'conspiracy' that could only be averted by 'private enterprise and full private

[284] Israel Sieff to Leonard, 12 February 1940, LKE/PEP/3/F.
[285] Basil Blackett's comment was quoted by Max Nicholson in an interview with Michael Young, 6 April 1978, T/HIS/S22.
[286] For the broad interest in planning, as well as Ritschel's *The Politics of Planning*, see Arthur Marwick, 'Middle Opinion in the 1930s: Planning, Progress and Political Agreement', *English Historical Review* 79 (1964), 285–98; Matthew Worley, 'What Was the New Party? Sir Oswald Mosley and Associated Responses to the "Crisis", 1931–1932', *History* 92 (2007), 39–63; Juliet Gardiner, '"Searching for the Gleam": Finding Solutions to the Political and Social Problems of 1930s Britain', *History Workshop Journal* 72 (2011), 103–17; Richard Overy, *The Morbid Age: Britain between the Wars* (London, 2009), 76–84.
[287] Emily Robinson, *The Language of Progressive Politics in Modern Britain* (London, 2017), 125–6.
[288] Leonard to Max Nicholson, 20 February 1934, LKE/PEP/3/B; Leonard, 'Rural industries', 27 July 1939, C/RIB/1/A.

ownership'.[289] The Elmhirsts brought a slander case against Rogers for spreading rumours about them. These rumours were even more bizarre than of the Elmhirsts being part of a planning 'conspiracy': at a London dinner party, Rogers – along with Alexandrina Domvile, wife of pro-Nazi Admiral Sir Barry Domvile – accused Dorothy and Leonard of dabbling in black magic. The charge apparently arose from the fact that a journalist who had heard that a man named Croly was staying at Dartington took this to be occultist Aleister Crowley, when in fact it was Herbert Croly of *The New Republic*.[290] The case was eventually settled out of court.

Leonard was (unusually) proud of the English as a peculiarly planning-minded nation – in particular of Sir Thomas More 'for the most adventurous planning of all, Utopia' – but his interest in planning was international.[291] He corresponded with and gave support to economist Lewis Lorwin, founder of the National Economic and Social Planning Association in Washington in 1931.[292] Similar to PEP in its organisation and aspirations, the association drew participants from government and business, published a magazine, *Plan Age*, and became the nucleus of a national movement to promote 'collective forethought and conscious social guidance'.[293] Leonard and Lorwin, unlike many planners in Britain and America (even within PEP), shared a belief that planning should be more than a national measure.[294] Lorwin proposed a 'world planning institute'.[295] Leonard saw 'no place for nationalistic barriers' in planning.[296] Their ultimate aim was a 'programme for world peace' based

---

[289] [n.a.], 'Report of a speech by Captain Arthur Rogers, OBE, Honorary Secretary, Liberty Restoration League, at a private meeting of Members of both Houses of Parliament', June 1938, LKE/LF/18/C; Arthur Rogers, *The Real Crisis* (London: Liberty Restoration League, [1938]). Richard Griffiths gives the background of this movement in *Patriotism Perverted: Captain Ramsay, the Right Club, and British Anti-Semitism, 1938–40* (London, 2015 [1998]).

[290] Valentine Holmes, legal opinion, 28 November 1936, LKE/LF/18/C; Leonard in transcripts for 'Man Alive', a programme for the BBC transmitted 29 November 1972, editor Adam Clapham, producer Richard Thomas, LKE/G/S13/L.

[291] Leonard to Miss Iredale, 27 June 1941, LKE/G/19/A.

[292] See file LKE/USA/S2/A. Claude Misukiewicz, 'Lewis L. Lorwin and the Promise of Planning: Class, Collectivism, and Empire in US Economic Planning Debates, 1931–1941', unpublished PhD, Georgia State University, 2015, 71–8.

[293] Lewis Lorwin, 'The Twentieth Century – The Plan Age', *Plan Age* 1 (1934), 1–3.

[294] Israel Sieff describes the clashes within PEP between a global view which advocated international planning and a protectionist one that wanted to restrict it to national and imperial interests in *Memoirs*, 168.

[295] Lewis Lorwin, 'A proposal for a world planning institute', 1935, LKE/USA/S2/A; Anna Bogue, 'Brief report re attendance of Mr Lewis Lorwin, Chairman of National Economic and Social Planning Association at meeting of Mrs Elmhirst's Committee on February 19, 1935', 8 April 1935, LKE/USA/S2/A.

[296] Leonard to Rabindranath Tagore, 15 December 1931, LKE/TAG/9/A.

on the 'continuous examination of social and economic affairs in all countries'.[297] Leonard envisaged linking such private organisations as the Rockefeller Foundation, PEP and Dartington with state instruments such as Roosevelt's 'Planning Board', all collating and publishing research, 'a continuous searchlight thrown on all dark corners of the world'.[298]

Their vision of a global planning utopia involved a redefining rather than a rejection of the local: the local now meant 'countless nuclei' responsible to their own communities 'for research, for digesting and regurgitation', and at the same time fuelling the universal 'grandeur ridden march of mind towards its goal of higher and ever higher consciousness'.[299] Instead of being an insular experiment, Dartington was reconceived as one such glocal nucleus, and between 1933 and 1963, PEP held many weekend gatherings on the Elmhirsts' estate. '[F]rom the beginning I have believed in and tried to act on the spirit of Dartington,' wrote one of PEP's founders, MP Kenneth Lindsay. 'As an example of rational planning based on a spiritual ideal I have used Dartington hundreds of times'.[300] This was the same Labour politician whom the Elmhirsts had tried in vain to recruit to coordinate education on their estate in the 1920s.[301] Lindsay's approval of what Dartington had become by the 1930s represented a wider view among observers that it was in its later, outward-facing iteration that the enterprise had achieved its apotheosis. Although PEP's ideas, as Paul Addison writes, had limited impact in the 1930s, the passion for planning of which it formed a significant part 'helped to prepare high-level opinion for the changes of the 1940s'.[302] During the war, many of PEP's senior figures would be recruited to help with the war effort or with post-war planning.[303]

5.4.5   Dartington as a Land Trust

Political and Economic Planning's central scheme was an economic model of industrial self-government, but in the 1930s, it was the think-tank's idea of re-organising the nation's land that had greatest influence on the Elmhirsts' evolving plans for their estate. Dartington, they hoped,

---

[297] Leonard, 'A group suggestion from D[artington] H[all] for a constructive peace policy', [October 1938], LKE/G/S5/H.
[298] Ibid; Leonard to Franklin D. Roosevelt, 4 April 1937, LKE/USA/5/E.
[299] Leonard to Gerald Heard, 26 December 1934, LKE/G/17.
[300] Kenneth Lindsay to the Elmhirsts, 21 April 1931, LKE/PEP/4/J.
[301] Leonard to Kenneth Lindsay, 24 April 1929, LKE/PEP/4/J.
[302] Paul Addison, *The Road to 1945: British Politics and the Second World War* (London, 1977), 39.
[303] Andrew Denham and Mark Garnett, *British Think-Tanks and the Climate of Opinion* (London, 1998), 31.

would be not only a research nucleus but also a test bed for a new model of land management.[304] Following PEP's faith in business-led economic rationalisation, the scheme was put forward that private landowners should cooperate in the formation of land trusts – units grouped into joint stock companies.[305] In return for participating landowners agreeing to principles of good trusteeship, the companies would support them with professional management, research, development, marketing and loans. Dartington, run by a company and a trust, foreshadowed this model and offered the opportunity for further refining it.

The Elmhirsts' interwar efforts to negotiate the transition from traditional forms of elite landownership to something more suitable for a social democracy had parallels elsewhere. Rural land nationalisation was a central feature of Labour's agricultural programme in the 1920s and 1930s.[306] Labour supporter and big landowner Charles Trevelyan, who regarded himself as merely a 'trustee of a property which under wiser and humaner laws would belong to the community', opened his estate in Northumberland to visitors free of charge and allowed it to be used as a centre for adult education.[307] Closer by, the Acland family – Liberal Westcountry allies of Leonard in his push for rural modernisation – were also deliberating over how to leave their large estate.[308] Ultimately, both the Trevelyan and Acland properties would be given to the National Trust in the 1940s.[309]

When Leonard aired the idea of the land trust at Dartington, some approved.[310] For others, however, including the socialist headmaster W. B. Curry, it was a 'save the landlord' measure that did not go far enough; what was needed was the full nationalisation of land under the government.[311] Leonard himself thought that '[o]wnership doesn't matter two hoots, management is everything'.[312] Whether run by a public land trust or a series of trusts under reformed private management, the key was that land must be treated as a 'national asset' with 'the least possible red tape and the most possible room for initiative and enterprise'.[313] This was, for him, a way back to the England of the

---

[304] Daniel Ritschel, 'A Corporatist Economy in Britain? Capitalist Planning for Industrial Self-Government in the 1930s', *The English Historical Review* 106 (1991), 41–65.

[305] Leonard, 'Observations on the proposals for a land trust', 12 December 1934, LKE/LAND/8/B.

[306] Griffiths, *Labour and the Countryside*, 230–6.   [307] Ibid, 297–8.

[308] Mandler, *Stately Homes*, 322.   [309] Ibid, 335.

[310] [n.a.], Minutes of meeting on rural ownership, 4 December 1934, LKE/LAND/8/B.

[311] Ibid.

[312] Leonard to George Wansborough, 26 June 1936, LKE/G/S1/K LKE; [n.a.], Minutes of meeting on rural ownership, 4 December 1934, LKE/LAND/8/B.

[313] Leonard, 'The land charter', [1938?], LKE/LAND/8/A.

Middle Ages and of William the Conqueror, which he idealised as a time when landowners were more than 'mere rent collectors', but had social responsibilities and duties of 'direct service to the state'.[314] The land trust more closely resembled the top-down, corporation-run rural regeneration schemes that formed a part of the main New Deal, such as the Tennessee Valley Authority (or, indeed, the National Trust in England), than the collaborative top-down/bottom-up planning favoured by the short-lived 'Intended New Deal' phase promoted by men like M. L. Wilson. Leonard's enthusiasm for it was a sign of how far he had come from his socialist pluralist beginnings.

For the Elmhirsts, the idea of a land trust, as with Dartington itself, was not just about agricultural management – it was another vehicle for achieving 'life in its completeness'. It would ensure the 'proper use, development and enjoyment of the resources and amenities of the land' for current and future generations, and could act as a referee between farming, industry, housing and amenity.[315] Each trust would have 'an Institute of Research and Planning' at its heart, based in a university and folding in a state planning board with voluntary organisations such as the National Trust.[316] Over-large towns would be 'green ribboned'; overly small and uneconomic settlements and farms would be dispensed with.[317] For the first time in the evolution of the Elmhirsts' ideas about social regeneration, this scheme confronted – if only glancingly – the fact that England was not all countryside. Planning must be as much about the town as the country: a 'system of balance, as between the purely rural and the purely urban and industrial, that will give man the maximum field of opportunity for growth, for initiative in adventure as well as the increase of his consciousness'.[318] It would provide the blueprint for a nationwide 'community, civic and industrial plan'.[319]

The land trust did not get far, and it did little practically to influence the shape of Dartington. By the late 1930s, PEP's remit had retreated from holistic society planning to independent research, in spite of Israel Sieff's urging that the organisation should not be distracted by the ease of composing 'an excellent report on some of the narrow isolated problems' and should continue to try to discover 'the needs of the community in terms of body, mind and spirit' and how 'man's material and psychic

[314] Leonard, 'Some problems facing the future of land ownership', 1 March 1935, and 'Rural industries', 27 July 1939, LKE/LAND/8/A.
[315] Leonard, 'The land charter', [1938], LKE/LAND/8/A.   [316] Ibid.
[317] Leonard to Max Nicholson, 3 March 1937, LKE/PEP/3/D.
[318] Leonard to Frederic Bartlett, 2 January 1934, LKE/G/S8/D.
[319] Leonard, 'Town and country planning', [1939], LKE/LAND/8/A.

wants are harmonised'.[320] Regardless of its lack of real-world impact, the land trust was a stepping stone in the Elmhirsts' transition from thinking of their estate as one of a series of independent, socialist-pluralist experiments to conceiving of it as an outpost of government. During the war, Leonard complained to Lawrence Neal, PEP member and deputy secretary of the Ministry of Town and Country Planning, that despite the evermore voluble talk about planning, 'we seem to hesitate to use it on a chunk of this island'.[321] He put forward Dartington as a 'nucleus' for such a state-led experiment. It was, Leonard emphasised, a socially minded company whose trustees controlled investment, laid down the principles on which the estate operated, and decided between conflicting claims on the land.[322] Others on the estate agreed. For arts director Chris Martin, Dartington could be used to demonstrate 'a new nucleation'.[323]

5.4.6   State Planning and Community Development

> We have been steadily moving towards the sort of society you have pioneered for years, but it's coming immensely faster now, and there is going to be a desperate race to make sure that the social discoveries you are making are fully recognised in our plans of reconstruction.   Max Nicholson to Dorothy Elmhirst (1941)[324]

The 1940s marked a split in the Elmhirsts' ideas and activities. On the one hand, there was the completion of the move from a vision of perfecting society via local, democratic units – of which Dartington was to be one – to social improvement through state direction, to which Dartington and the Elmhirsts would contribute. On the other, there was a renewed sense of the importance of community democracy, which was partly a reaction to the strengthened central state in Britain after the war, and partly a response to the perceived need of newly decolonised countries – India in particular – to build up the unity of their independent populations from the ground up.

The Elmhirsts' new idea of Dartington as an outpost of central planning coincided with the expansion of state control during the Second World War so that their estate's newly imagined role was quickly actualised in its contributions to the war effort and plans for national reconstruction. The estate's arts director, Chris Martin, worked for the

---

[320] Ritschel, *Planning*, 145–83; Israel Sieff to Leonard, 12 February 1940, LKE/PEP/S/F.
[321] Leonard to Lawrence Neal, 18 May 1945, LKE/PEP/2/A.
[322] Leonard, 'Some problems facing the future of land ownership', 1 March 1935, and 'Rural industries', 27 July 1939, LKE/LAND/8/A.
[323] Chris Martin, 'Dartington Hall – a social experiment', [1936], T/AA/1/I.
[324] Max Nicholson to Dorothy, 5 July 1941, DWE/G/8/B.

Nuffield College Social Reconstruction Survey and conducted the nationwide Arts Enquiry.[325] Dartington's research department provided evidence for the Scott Committee on land use in rural areas and considered the status of post-war agriculture in collaboration with the Standing Committee, the Association for Planning and Regional Reconstruction and the Economics Intelligence Division of the Ministry of Agriculture and Fisheries.[326] In 1944, a group from the Ministry of Town and Country Planning visited Dartington, was given a sketch of 'our experiments, failures and successes, in the planning of our enterprise as a piece of rural reconstruction', and in much secrecy discussed the future development of Devon.[327]

Dartington trustee Michael Young, in the thick of policy-making in London, urged the Elmhirsts to produce a history of their work, which, in its ideas on social planning, 'represents something of a long term experiment whose results can test the feasibility of some of the relevant ideas which are now being raised in rather hazy form'.[328] This idea came to nothing until Young wrote the history himself many years later.[329] But the estate's wartime contributions reflect Richard Weight's findings of how the war re-integrated much of the left-leaning intelligentsia – disillusioned with politics in the 1920s and 1930s – back into the national structure.[330]

The Elmhirsts themselves were frequently away from Dartington in the national service during the war, working particularly to further Anglo-American relations. Leonard joined a Board of Trade mission to America and he and Dorothy toured the United States at the request of its Department of Agriculture to impress on farmers Britain's need for more food.[331] Later, while Dorothy served as a volunteer speaker for the British Ministry of Information, Leonard was part of a government mission to advise on mobilising food production in the Middle East; afterwards he assisted the governor of famine-stricken Bengal.[332] When Leonard was offered a baronetcy for this work in 1946 by Clement

---

[325] [n.a.], Memorandum for the Ministry of Information, 23 February 1942, C/DHL/5/C.
[326] Ibid.
[327] [n.a.], 'Note in preparation for the visit of members of Ministry of Town and Country Planning from 16 to 19 March, 11 March 1944', LKE/LAND/2/G.
[328] Michael Young, 'History of Dartington', 1941, DWE/S/2A/A.
[329] Young, *Elmhirsts*.
[330] Richard Weight, 'State, Intelligentsia and the Promotion of National Culture in Britain, 1939–45', *Historical Research* 69 (1996), 83–101.
[331] For these activities, see file LKE/USA/12.
[332] DWE/L; LKE/DWE/18/A; Anthea Williams, 'Elmhirst, Leonard Knight (1893–1974)', rev. *Oxford Dictionary of National Biography* (Oxford University Press, first published 23 September 2004, revised 27 May 2010) [www.oxforddnb.com/view/article/31072].

Attlee, it marked the culmination of the Elmhirsts' move from independent experimentation to state collaboration. But Leonard refused national enshrinement. He wrote that, as his work had 'lain in the main among country people' in India, the United States and Devon, 'acceptance would neither be easy for me to explain nor easy for my friends to comprehend'.[333]

Nonetheless, Leonard continued to fit himself to the new opportunities offered within the post-war framework of an expanded state. He had reservations about the conservationist direction the state was taking: the post-war planning consensus that brought central planning into reality also enshrined the principle of preserving the countryside as national heritage and a source of urban amenity, rather than of making it a vibrant economic unit in its own right.[334] Yet Leonard chaired the Footpaths and Access Special Committee, part of the National Parks Committee established to carry through the Scott Report's recommendation for the creation of national parks; then, from 1949 to 1965, he worked as a development commissioner. Dartington's ideals also influenced state policy more widely through those who had visited the project in the interwar wars. W. E. Pride, introduced in the 1920s by Violet Astor when he was a young Home Office official, went on to propagate 'the novel idea of an agricultural-industries estate' within government for the next thirty years – helping to lay the 'groundwork at Brynmawr and Rhondda workshops and Board of Trade sponsored Teams Valley and the Treforest Trading Estates' and to draft the 1945 Distribution of Industry Act to redevelop depressed areas, whose principles fed into aid work of the United Nations.[335]

In spite of their support for state planning, the Elmhirsts never renounced their faith in grassroots communitarianism: as Leonard described it, 'diagnosis, research and experiment and as a result the working out, with all the residents concerned, of a comprehensive yet simple programme in which each feels a part and a responsibility'.[336]

---

[333] Young, *Elmhirsts*, 344.

[334] Helen E. Meller, *Towns, Plans, and Society in Modern Britain* (Cambridge, 1997), chapter 5. Lord Justice Scott, chair of the 1941–1942 Committee on Land Utilization in Rural Areas, wrote that farms should be regarded as the 'nation's landscape gardens'. Many of the committee's recommendations concerned the aesthetics rather than the economic or social viability of the countryside. Chris Bailey, 'Progress and Preservation: The Role of Rural Industries in the Making of the Modern Image of the Countryside', *Journal of Design History* 9 (1996), 35–53, at 37.

[335] W. E. Pride to Leonard, 28 October 1968, LKE/G/25/A.

[336] Leonard, 'Confidential memorandum for discussion by Dartington Hall Trustees Advisory Committee', February 1950, LKE/G/S8/1.

Leonard and Dorothy shared the post-war difficulties of Dartington alumnus Michael Young who, having helped to write the 1945 Labour election manifesto, struggled to reconcile Labour's focus on efficiency, nationalisation and 'bigness' with his enthusiasm for localised community democracy.[337] Dorothy and Leonard's Elmgrant Trust gave funding for Young's Institute of Community Studies, formed in 1954 to promote the latter.[338] PEP's headquarters provided the Institute's first meeting place.

Alongside community development in England, the Elmhirsts supported community development abroad. In the 1920s, Leonard had seen India as the cradle of spiritually infused social experiment: 'Madmen still survive in the East and keep their faith,' he wrote to Eduard Lindeman, 'for, life being simple, it is easier to make ideals and practice, principles and daily life meet.'[339] When the fervid years of British utopian planning in 1930s and 1940s were over, the East, with its seemingly freer rein for idealistic experimentation, called him again. Others involved in interwar agrarian or community reform followed a similar trajectory. When the community-oriented 'Intended' phase of the New Deal was over in America, some of the agriculturalists and social scientists who had been involved, including the Elmhirsts' friend M. L. Wilson, went on to apply their ideals in quasi-missionary careers in community development overseas.[340] German agricultural economist Otto Schiller, who had run experiments in peasant cooperation under the Nazis, could be found in the 1950s and 1960s working as a development economist for the United States in India and Pakistan, still promoting peasant cooperation – but by this point as a way to counter the menace of communism rather than to strengthen fascism.[341] As Nicole Sackley, Subhir Sinha and Daniel Immerwahr all find, the Cold War idealisation of the self-governing

---

[337] The tension is summarised in Michael Young, *Small Man: Big World* (London, 1949). For the wider interest in communitarian democracy after the war, see Alexandre Campsie, 'Mass-Observation, Left Intellectuals and the Politics of Everyday Life', *The English Historical Review* 131 (2016), 92–121.

[338] Funding also came from the Nuffield Foundation, the United Nation Education, Scientific and Cultural Organization and the Ford Foundation. Lise Butler, 'Michael Young, the Institute of Community Studies, and the Politics of Kinship', *Twentieth Century British History* 26 (2015), 203–24. Asa Briggs compares the communitarian thrust of the Institute of Community Studies to that of Dartington Hall, *Michael Young: Social Entrepreneur* (London, 2001), 110–54.

[339] Leonard to Eduard Lindeman, 7 January 192[4?], box 2, Eduard Lindeman Archives.

[340] Jess Gilbert, *Planning Democracy*, 260; Daniel Immerwahr, *Thinking Small: The United States and the Lure of Community Development* (Cambridge, MA and London, 2015), 55.

[341] Adam Tooze, 'A Small Village in the Age of Extremes: The Häusern Experiment', unpublished paper, 2014, 1–29, at 16–20.

village as the unit of social progress stemmed in large part from interwar development regimes.[342]

Leonard was a consultant during the planning and early stages of the Damodar Valley Corporation (DVC), which was set up by the Indian government after independence to plan a river basin both economically and socially.[343] Akin both to the Tennessee Valley Authority and to PEP's scheme for land trusts, the DVC was established as an autonomous institution, 'clothed with the power of government but possessed of the flexibility and initiative of a private enterprise'.[344] Leonard saw the DVC's success as lying chiefly with 'the villager in his village': if, with the help of international experts, the Damodar villagers could learn 'how to fight together to master their problems', he wrote, they could set an example 'for India and parts of Asia, Africa and Europe as well'.[345]

After helping with planning, Leonard continued to be involved with the DVC through the 1950s, hoping to make the Damodar Valley a glocal stronghold like Dartington: a place that drew on the best international advice, combined it with local input, and produced a model of strong community life relevant to others around the world. He advocated in correspondence and journal articles for the 'all-round attack on the village problem' trialled at Sriniketan to be scaled up for the Damodar Valley, and he hosted DVC director Sudhen Mozumdar at Dartington, so that he could see an integrated rural community at work.[346] Leonard discussed with Charles Madge, one of the founders of Mass Observation, the idea of setting up a Damodar Valley research unit to combine 'the methods of the social anthropologist' with social work in order to improve holistic village welfare.[347] He tried to pull

[342] Nicole Sackley, 'The Village as Cold War Site: Experts, Development, and the History of Rural Reconstruction', *Journal of Global History* 6 (2011), 481–504; Sinha, 'Lineages of the Developmental State', Immerwahr, *Thinking Small*.

[343] Daniel Klingensmith, *One Valley and a Thousand: Dams, Nationalism, and Development* (Oxford, 2007), 169–200.

[344] F. D. Roosevelt's description of the Tennessee Valley Authority, quoted by Ram Chandra Prasad in 'The Organisation Pattern of the River Valley Projects in India: A Study of the Board vis-à-vis the Public Corporation', *The Indian Journal of Political Science* 22 (1961), 214–25, at 215.

[345] Leonard, untitled note, [n.d.], LKE/IN/32/A.

[346] Leonard to Sri Jyoti Prasad Bhattachajee, 28 Nov 1949; and to Arthur Ashby, 22 Nov 1949, LKE/IN/31/A. Sudhen Mozumdar's visit is discussed in Leonard to Thomas, 4 October 1950, LKE/IN/31/A.

[347] Charles Madge to Leonard, 11 March 1953; Charles Madge, 'Application to the United Nations for assistance in the setting up of a Family Research Unit for the Damodar Valley and adjoining areas of West Bengal and Bihar', 25 February 1952, both in file LKE/IN/5/H; Leonard to P. S. Rau, chairman of DVC, [n.d.], LKE/IN/31/F.

together public and private funding to support this research unit – from the Indian government, the United Nations, the DVC and a wealthy American philanthropic couple, the Normans – and to ensure that the scheme would involve international experts working 'in intimate association with Indian rural life'.[348] Ultimately, funding for the scheme fell through and Madge went to Thailand instead to conduct a United Nations village survey.[349]

Others who had been involved with Dartington also turned their sights on India. Jaqueline Tyrwhitt, who worked in Dartington's central office in the 1930s and then taught at the School of Planning and Research for Regional Development in London, went to New Delhi in 1954 as the United Nations advisor for an exhibition on low-cost housing.[350] In this exhibition, she portrayed the self-governing village, offering low-cost housing and holistic fulfilment for its residents, as the 'ideal' social unit for the rural Indian, who 'has not learned to live as a townsman'.[351] The concept of the village as the 'prototypical space' for Indian development was echoed in various government papers and trade advertisements, and in governmental and non-governmental initiatives, shaping the country's struggle to re-conceive itself after independence.[352] As with the Elmhirsts' vision of the English countryside, the Indian village was (usually) not presented as a locus of immutable tradition in this discourse, but as a place for progressive social reimagining.

For Leonard, Tyrwhitt and other such social reformers, India's 'otherness' went on offering the possibility of the purest realisation of a self-governing rural utopia long after experience had tarnished their hopes of the West. Tyrwhitt's and Leonard's activities were just small elements of a burgeoning international field of community development that flourished from the 1950s to 1980s, supported, like the Indian villages experiments of the late nineteenth and early twentieth centuries, by philanthropic funds such as the Rockefeller and Ford Foundations, as

[348] Leonard to Mr and Mrs Howard Norman, 13 June 1952, LKE/IN/5/H.
[349] Charles Madge to LKE, 8 September 1953, LKE/IN/5/H; Charles Madge, *Village Communities in North-East Thailand* (New York, 1959).
[350] Ellen Shoshkes, 'Jaqueline Tyrwhitt: A Founding Mother of Modern Urban Design', *Planning Perspectives* 21 (2006), 179–197; Ellen Shoshkes, 'Tyrwhitt, (Mary) Jaqueline (1905–1983)', *Oxford Dictionary of National Biography* (Oxford University Press, first published 23 September 2004, revised 27 May 2010) [www.oxforddnb.com/view/article/106752].
[351] Farham Karim, *Of Greater Dignity Than Riches: Austerity and Housing Design in India* (Pittsburgh, 2019), 121.
[352] Ibid, 128–9.

well as by the United Nations.[353] Although the movement was fuelled by
the competing efforts of Cold War participants to expand their spheres of
influence, it nonetheless advocated a global pattern of democratic,
'co-operative, decentralized communities in harmony with nature'.[354]
This was exactly the vision of glocalisation that the Elmhirsts had long
been modelling at Dartington – the globe-trotting Anglo-American
couple, with yearnings for the East, had achieved a precociously reflexive
consciousness of the meaning of local in a globalised age.

[353] In the 1950s and 1960s, Leonard had some dealings with the Ford Foundation's
representative in India, Douglas Ensminger, in relation to Sriniketan and to rural
education (LKE/USA/S1/F). Kathleen D. McCarthy, 'From Government to Grass-
Roots Reform: The Ford Foundation's Population Programmes in South Asia,
1959–1981', *Voluntas: International Journal of Voluntary and Non-Profit Organisations* 6
(1995), 292–316; Leonard A. Gordon, 'Wealth Equals Wisdom? The Rockefeller and
Ford Foundations in India', *The Annals of the American Academy of Political and Social
Science* 554 (1997), 104–16.
[354] Ellen Shoshkes, 'Jaqueline Tyrwhitt 184.

Conclusion
The Afterlife of a Utopia

> Dartington was represented, embodied in it because of all [the Elmhirsts'] contacts, some of the great strands of utopian thought of this century – a utopian view about education, about the countryside, about the arts – very high hopes, and these high hopes came – they didn't just spring from them originally – I mean, they came out of a whole climate of thought.   Michael Young (1978)[1]

The German sociologist Karl Mannheim, who lectured at Dartington in 1941, argued that utopias are always in dialectical tension with the existing order; for all their 'incongruity' with the status quo, they remain deeply embedded within a 'historically specific social life'.[2] The fortunes of Dartington from its foundation in 1925 to the present day exemplify the messy vitality of the exchange with the real world promised in Mannheim's formulation. The estate offered countercultural alternatives. Yet its founders were determined from the outset that it would develop in symbiosis with the wider world and would 'fit into the framework of an evolutionary democratic society, such as exists in England today' rather than 'preparing for some hypothetical community' of the future.[3] Dartington's communion with the outside world was increased by the international cast of collaborators and advisors that the Elmhirsts engaged with in pursuing their capacious ideal of promoting a holistically unified life. This chapter looks at how, in the ninety-odd years since its foundation, Dartington has offered a reconfigured vision of the outside world, while being both sustained and constrained by this larger environment.

---

[1] Michael Young, a pupil then a trustee of Dartington Hall, in an interview with Peter Cox, 9 June 1978, T/HIS/S20/D, Dartington Hall Archives (unless specified otherwise, all the following archival references are to this collection).

[2] Karl Mannheim, *Ideology and Utopia, an Introduction to the Sociology of Knowledge*, trans. Louis Wirth and Edward Shils (London, 1936 [first published, untranslated, 1929]), 210; Krishan Kumar, 'Ideology and Sociology: Reflections on Karl Mannheim's "Ideology and Utopia"', *Journal of Political Ideologies* 11 (2006), 169–81. Mannheim's Sunday evening talk at Dartington was called 'The diagnosis of our time', 6 May 1941, T/AE/4/B.

[3] Leonard, 'The blue book', [n.d.], T/PP/P/1/A.

In the first decade of their enterprise, the Elmhirsts pursued a concept of social reform that was based on the idea of autonomous communities working to improve themselves. This meant that Dartington was then at its most detached from the limitations imposed by the local and wider social context. 'I am afraid we see very little of the neighbours,' wrote Dorothy, 'but for the time being we are concentrating on building up a community life among ourselves.'[4] This detachment enabled the Elmhirsts to come closest in this decade to achieving their goal of modelling 'life in its completeness', where educational, spiritual and practical aims intermingled organically. While having little mainstream impact in the immediate term, the estate attracted the interest of diverse idealists seeking social salvation in holistic 'schemes outside all the orthodox tracks'.[5] Initially exhilarating though this phase was, the inner contradictions of the Elmhirsts' utopia rapidly began to manifest themselves: the democratic rhetoric ran up against a hierarchical – even autocratic – reality; the idea of a spiritualised village community tugged in one direction and the desire for large-scale, profitable, scientific efficiency in another; the desire to involve everyone in everything proved difficult to reconcile with aspirations to make a mark in the outside world informed by experts. These conflicts and inconsistencies, together with a changing political environment, moved Dartington rapidly on to a second and more consistently outward-facing phase.

By the mid-1930s, the Elmhirsts, along with many other idealists, were less preoccupied with opposing the mainstream liberal individualist mindset than they had been in the years immediately after the First World War. They were instead concerned with opposing the dystopias they saw being consolidated in Russia, Germany and Italy. They had started to think that 'good hearted idealists' such as themselves must work out in a more 'realistic manner' how to have national impact rather than focusing on improving their own small communities.[6] Engaging more fully with the world they were trying to change and accepting some loss of autonomy might be the necessary price of achieving heightened influence. Their shift to a concept of social reform which was more centralised involved both push and pull: their frustration at their own inability to integrate the various elements of Dartington into a well-functioning whole coincided with a growing national appetite for integrated social planning. The result was a rapprochement between Dartington and the establishment.

---

[4] Dorothy to Frances Livingstone, 11 February 1927, DWE/G/7/A.
[5] Leonard to Dorothy, 19 May 1923, LKE/DWE/11/C.
[6] Leonard to Ben Nicholson, 15 March 1938, LKE/PEP/3/E.

In the mid- to late-1930s, government officials and commercial organisations were more willing than in the 1920s to engage with Dartington as a place that had established some tangible credentials for putting reforming ideas into practice. Individual experiments on the estate might have failed to perform as the Elmhirsts had hoped – whether that meant yielding a profit or a new socio-spiritual system, or providing a replicable model for access to the arts or cheap housing – but the enterprise as a whole impressed onlookers as an unusual place where theories were being applied to lived experience.[7] The Elmhirsts and their supporters now re-envisioned Dartington's place in the 'evolutionary democratic society' as being to influence and improve the shape of the central state rather than to oppose it. They experimented more and more with using their community as a test bed for initiatives with wider social impact. By 1935, Leonard could already write with satisfaction that 'Dartington staff now penetrate out into the world in all kinds of ways and are members of public bodies and research and other enterprises, in a way that secures the enterprise from ever becoming an isolated, insulated, self-worshipping sect'.[8] In line with Mannheim's theory about the evolution of utopias, Dartington's demonstration of 'life in its completeness' had expanded the sense of social possibilities in the wider landscape of reform thinking. At the same time, Dartington had been modified by the historical specificity of its context, away from pluralist communitarianism and towards an ideal of influencing and illustrating social reform led by the state.

The culmination of this shift towards working at a national level came during the Second World War. The British government began to play a more active and creative role in education, the arts and social improvement. This in turn gave Dartington a much more substantial platform to further its ideas on the national stage – ranging in breadth from soil surveys to encouraging scientific farming, from the Arts Enquiry promoting creativity for all to the general concept of holistic social planning. The Elmhirsts' rapprochement with the state during the war was echoed by that of other British idealists who, like Dorothy and Leonard, had been disillusioned with and aloof from mainstream politics in the 1920s and now lent their minds to promoting a national culture.[9]

---

[7] For example, [n.a.], 'The New Rural England', *The Architect and Building News*, 30 June, 14 July, 21 July 1933.
[8] Leonard, manuscript note on an article sent by Mrs Blitzstein, 25 April 1935, LKE/G/S8/A.
[9] Richard Weight, 'State, Intelligentsia and the Promotion of National Culture in Britain, 1939–45', *Historical Research* 69 (1996), 83–101. Cecil Day Lewis and Graham Greene, for example, undertook to produce propaganda for the Ministry of Information (Brian Foss, 'Message and Medium: Government Patronage, National Identity and National Culture in Britain, 1939–45', *Oxford Art Journal* 14 (1991), 52–7).

The Elmhirsts were unusual, in this group, in how much practical experience of social reform they had accumulated in the interwar years. Michael Young wrote to them that while 'the woolly minded' were putting forward unfounded plans for post-war reconstruction, Dartington was 'a laboratory specimen; it is itself just one of those controlled experiments which [the think-tank Political and Economic Planning] would wish the Government to sponsor'.[10] Dorothy, characteristically attributing this achievement to her husband, rejoiced in his 'almost uncanny foresight' in anticipating the trend for many-sided social planning.[11] She wrote to Leonard that the Second World War offered them the chance to 'recreate Dartington' more definitively along these state-supporting lines – 'our Second Phase'.[12] Since, at the same time, the war had made the state itself so much more receptive to their ideas, it seemed momentarily that Dartington had managed to 'break the bond of the existing order' and to turn its utopian vision into the new status quo.[13] The sense that Dartington had, successfully and without sacrificing its ideals, joined the national establishment was reinforced at a local level by Leonard's post-war roles: while he had refused a baronetcy in 1946, the next year he was serving on six Devon County Council committees, was a member of the Council of the University College of the South West and vice-chairman of the governors of three local schools.[14]

After the war, the social democracy that had once been an ideal at Dartington became a wider reality, albeit not in a utopian form. The Elmhirsts were faced with the problem of how (or whether) their estate – or any model of independent, upper-class philanthropy – could be justified in this new landscape. Should they simply allow Dartington to be absorbed into the apparatus of the state? They had never conceived of their property along traditional, aristocratic lines, 'as anything to be handed on to heirs'.[15] As Leonard wrote to Dorothy in 1926, 'there's enough of that already, and it often only hampers and confines'.[16] Even if they were interested in the traditional hereditary option, none of their offspring showed themselves suited to carrying forward a holistic utopia – each absorbing some elements of their parents' wide-ranging passions, but none their overarching interest in reforming society.

---

[10] Michael Young to the Elmhirsts, 27 October 1942, LKE/G/35/A.
[11] Dorothy to Leonard, 12 November 1940, LKE/DWE/13D.
[12] Dorothy to Leonard, 14 August 1944, LKE/DWE/14/A; Michael Young, *The Elmhirsts of Dartington: The Creation of a Utopian Community* (London, 1982), 314.
[13] Mannheim, *Ideology and Utopia*, 178.   [14] Young, *Elmhirsts*, 341.
[15] Leonard to Dorothy, 29 March 1926, LKE/DWE/12/D.   [16] Ibid.

The ideological ferment of the interwar years had divided Dorothy's children. Michael was recruited as a Soviet spy by Anthony Blunt while studying at Cambridge.[17] Whitney, a successful businessman, showed 'marked fascist tendencies', while their sister, Beatrice, determining on an apolitical acting career, remarked that her brothers were both 'criminals in their own lines' – 'I think we are a funny family.'[18] None of these three, later on, showed an appetite for taking over Dartington. Of Dorothy and Leonard's children, William Elmhirst absorbed his mother's interest in esoteric spirituality and bitterly resented not being permitted by Dartington's trustees to base his spiritual charity, Solar Quest, on the estate. Ruth settled close to Dartington, to a life of spinning, weaving and raising a family. She was the only child to become a Dartington trustee and her husband, Maurice Ash, was for some time chair of Dartington Hall Trust.

An alternative to familial inheritance was the route taken with Wallington Hall in Northumberland by the Trevelyan family (who had no heirs) and with Killerton in Devon by the Acland family (who did), both of whom gave their estates in the 1940s to the National Trust – an institution which was burgeoning into what Peter Mandler calls the 'country-house museum-keeper to Socialist Britain'.[19] Dorothy and Leonard, while claiming to be 'entirely in sympathy' with the National Trust's aims, still retained some of their ideal of community independence, as well as some ambivalence about whether they were willing to commit to full-blown rule by the masses. Rejecting both family inheritance and nationalisation, they settled instead on consolidating the trust-and-company formation that they had put in place in the early 1930s.[20] In theory, the trustees could be anyone – at last the Elmhirsts were enacting their early ambitions to give their estate to the people. In practice, the way that the trustees were appointed, by each other, almost

---

[17] Roland Perry, *The Last of the Cold War Spies: The Life of Michael Straight* (Cambridge, MA, 2005).

[18] Beatrice Straight to Nancy Wilson Ross, 1 January 1937, 156/2, Nancy Wilson Ross Archives.

[19] Peter Mandler, *The Fall and Rise of the Stately Home* (New Haven, CT and London, 1997), 329 and 523; Mary Hilson and Joseph Melling, 'Public Gifts and Political Identities: Sir Richard Acland, Common Wealth, and the Moral Politics of Land Ownership in the 1940s', *Twentieth Century British History* 11 (2000), 156–82.

[20] Left-leaning idealists including Sidney and Beatrice Webb tended to support the views of such legal philosophers as F. W. Maitland and Neville Figgis that the trust, in providing a legal basis for a group of people, could free them from certain types of state regulation – and could also promote a group's cohesion and independence in a more metaphysical sense. David Runciman, *Pluralism and the Personality of the State* (Cambridge, 1997), chapters 3, 5 and 6; Mark Bevir, 'Introduction', in Mark Bevir (ed.), *Modern Pluralism: Anglo-American Debates Since 1880* (Cambridge, 2012), 1–20, at 4.

inevitably (at least in the short term), meant that a certain type of person, socially as well as ideologically, remained at the helm. It was inheritance by elective affinity rather than by blood. Similar solutions were adopted later on by two other elite, idealistic enterprises founded in the interwar years, Rolf Gardiner's Springhead and John Christie's Glyndebourne, although these did not share Dartington's original aspirations to communitarian democracy.[21]

While Dartington's trust-and-company organisation had roots in the Elmhirsts' early ideal of the estate as a self-governing, self-supporting and egalitarian community, in reality it enshrined the control of a narrow minority. This extension of the control of the incumbent elite under a new kind of social-democratic rhetoric echoed a wider tendency in the welfare state. Mike Savage explores the 'sidestep' after the Second World War from a defence of the elite 'in terms of culture, morality, or aesthetics' to one in which their managerial or technocratic contribution to the welfare state was paramount.[22]

After the war, Dorothy and Leonard, their energy declining in their later years, were never again so intensively involved in running the estate. They initiated no new commercial endeavours themselves and spent more time on external pursuits, whether travelling to visit their far-flung children or supporting the International Association of Agricultural Economists and community development in newly independent India. They expressed the occasional flicker of disappointment that their Devon experiment had lost some of its radical edge. 'Dartington is very peaceful these days', Dorothy wrote to Margaret Isherwood in 1951. 'I sometimes wonder whether we do not need more prodding and questioning.'[23] Nonetheless, they showed no sign of regretting the use they had made of their lives. As Leonard had written to Dorothy, a few years into their experiment:

In cold blood the risks that we have taken up to date – with money, with goods, with lands, most of all with people – they appal and frighten me, perhaps because in so much of it we have been alone – and yet, though I do not deny the dangers, nor the tragedies that are the outcome of our social gambling – in this world today, in the peculiar position we are in – are we to throw up our hands and say, no, the possibility of making mistakes is so great, of damaging a human life so serious, that we should quietly retire from the scene?[24]

---

[21] The Springhead Trust was set up in 1973, two years after Rolf Gardiner's death; Glyndebourne was structured as a company and trust in 1954, eight years before John Christie died.

[22] Mike Savage, *Identities and Social Change in Britain Since 1940: The Politics of Method* (Oxford, 2010), 78 and 216.

[23] Dorothy to Margaret Isherwood, 8 September 1951, quoted in Young, *Elmhirsts*, 316.

[24] Leonard to Dorothy, 26 August 1931, LKE/DWE/12/E.

C.1 Dorothy and Leonard at Dartington's Foundation Day
celebrations, 1967 (© Dartington Hall Trust, the Elmgrant Trust
and Michael Dower)

On the whole, the Elmhirsts were content to sit back and see their
ideals pursued under the stewardship of their estate's trustees and directors. Many of the early trustees – the Elmhirsts' protégé Michael
Young and their son-in-law Maurice Ash in particular – were cast in a
similar missionary mould to the practical idealists who had formed the
backbone of interwar Dartington. Young, whom Asa Briggs calls 'the
Last Victorian' for his dedication to social service, combined working for
the Labour Party and advising Prime Minister Harold Wilson on the
creation of the Open University with helping establish the Consumers'
Association and the associated *Which?* magazine, as well as the Institute

of Community Studies.[25] Maurice Ash was a farmer, writer, environmentalist and public administrator who was introduced to Dartington through his friendship with Young. He became chairman of the Town and Country Planning Association and of the Dartington Hall Trust.

When planning Dartington in the 1920s, Leonard had written to Eduard Lindeman that ideals had 'their own cyclic appearance and market demand': though they were currently in 'a slump on the market', the wise would 'invest in the oil of idealism before the demand suddenly arises'.[26] Mainstream demand for the oil of idealism ramped up in the 1930s and 1940s with the appetite for holistic social planning: this gave Dartington a moment of heightened impact. During the booming counterculture of the 1960s and early 1970s, demand for alternative ideals again rose, and again Dartington had an upsurge of intense activity, attracting international interest.[27]

This activity contained all the elements of the Elmhirsts' founding vision of 'life in its completeness' – promoting creativity, spirituality and social and economic reform. In 1961, the arts department was transformed into Dartington College of Arts, a semi-independent entity within the national higher education system involving both Dartington trustees and representatives of the Devon County Education Committee and of the Universities of Bristol and Exeter. Under the guidance of Peter Cox – who had assisted with Dartington's Arts Enquiry in the 1940s – the college functioned as a local arts centre, a training ground for teachers in the arts, and a home for short and long courses, including a music summer school set up by Sir William Glock, Controller of Music for the BBC.[28] The college drew students and artists from across the world.[29] Like interwar Dartington, it

---

[25] Asa Briggs, *Michael Young: Social Entrepreneur* (London, 2001), 329.

[26] Leonard to Eduard Lindeman, 7 January 192[4?], box 2, Eduard Lindeman Archives.

[27] Jeremi Suri, 'The Rise and Fall of the International Counterculture, 1960–1975', *American Historical Review* 114 (2009), 45–68. Although there is no indication that he has Dartington in mind, Anthony Powell makes the connection between participants of the interwar and later counterculture in his series of novels *A Dance to the Music of Time*. *Hearing Secret Harmonies* (1975), set in the 1960s, sees figures who have passed through the bohemian 1920s, and through a more 'establishment' phase during the Second World War, embroiled in alternative culture in the form of a rural pagan cult (London, 1991 [series originally published between 1951 and 1975]).

[28] For a detailed history of the College of Arts, see Peter Cox, *The Arts at Dartington, 1940–1983: A Personal Account* (Exeter, 2005); Young, *Elmhirsts*, 251. From 1961, teachers had their musical and dramatic training at Dartington and teacher training at St Luke's College, Exeter and Rolle College, Exmouth. The music summer school was first run at Bryanston – a progressive school founded, like Dartington School, in the 1920s. It moved to Dartington in 1953.

[29] Stephen Banfield, *Music in the West Country: Social and Cultural History Across an English Region* (Suffolk, 2018), 332; Claire MacDonald, 'Desire Paths: John Cage's Transatlantic Crossing', *PAJ: A Journal of Performance and Art* 34 (2012), 35–46.

was a pioneer in many areas, from avant-garde dance to introducing Eastern musical traditions to Britain.[30] Many of its students and teachers engaged with movements that challenged or offered an alternative to the status quo, from vegetarianism, yoga and Eastern spirituality to radical feminism, anti-nuclear peace activism and environmentalism.[31]

Beyond the College of Arts, Dartington continued to support diverse experimentation and outreach work. Beaford Arts Centre and Dartington Glassworks were set up to great acclaim in North Devon in the 1960s to bring the Dartington model of arts and jobs into a poorer region of the county. In 1969, when Royston Lambert moved from King's College, Cambridge, to become Dartington School's headmaster, he brought with him a small group of researchers who founded the Dartington Social Research Unit. This went on to have a significant influence shaping local and national policy across social care, health and education.[32] Various projects were also begun on the estate to promote alternative or intermediate technology – the idea being to treat Dartington as a test bed for the use of methane digesters, hydroponics, recycled building materials and other innovations contributing to sustainability, and then to apply these technologies across Asia and Africa.[33]

In terms of community engagement, the 1960s saw a significant departure from Dartington's interwar decades; the aspiration to synthesise all the estate's various strands of activity at a community level ranged from muted to non-existent. Dartington's trustees, particularly those who had not been involved in the enterprise's holistic interwar roots and who were less intimate with the Elmhirsts themselves, saw their prime duty as being to make the estate financially viable. In the absence of a clear and compelling articulation of Dartington's purpose, they oriented Dartington's infrastructure more and more towards offering wholesome escapist sojourns and lifestyle retail products for the well-off. But at this stage Dorothy and Leonard remained a presence, albeit in the background, and Dartington retained an idealistic, evangelising

---

[30] Cox, *The Arts at Dartington.*

[31] Noel Longhurst, 'Twinned with Narnia? The Postcapitalist Possibilities of a Countercultural Place', unpublished PhD, University of Liverpool, 2010, 168, 173. Dartington became home to a Cranks vegetarian restaurant – one of a small chain that was started in London in 1961 and was a pioneer in the British whole food movement. Julia Twigg, 'The Vegetarian Movement in England 1847–1981', unpublished PhD, London School of Economics, 1981.

[32] In 2017, the charity was renamed the 'Dartington Service Design Lab'. No longer part of the Dartington Hall Trust, it continues to advise local authorities around the country on children's services.

[33] [n.a.], 'Design for Intermediate Technology', *Dartington College Looks at the Future* – a supplement to *Dartington Hall News*, 26 May 1973, 8.

tinge of mission, which touched even its engagement with tourism. The Dartington Amenity and Research Trust (DART), set up in 1967, did much work for the government as a consultancy unit in the area of rural recreation.[34] This harked back to Michael Young's hope in the 1940s that Dartington would be 'a model' for how the post-war tourist boom should be managed.[35] In an indication of how the interwar elite – and Dartington itself – had become an entrenched part of the managerial and technocratic arm of post-war social democracy, DART was run by Michael Dower, a scion of the Trevelyan family who had given up their own estates to the National Trust. Dower would go on to become Director General of the Countryside Commission (now Natural England).

In the 1920s, when Dartington was opposed to the mainstream and consciously separate from it, it had the Elmhirsts' vision and money to fuel it. From the 1930s to the 1960s, it was sustained by a mutually beneficial exchange of ideas and personnel with centralised reform projects and with wider countercultural currents. From the mid-1970s, however, both its driving idealism and its symbiosis with the wider culture came to a standstill. At the same time, through a combination of inflation, poor management and loss-making ventures, the estate's funds began to dwindle rapidly so that there was more constraint on participants' activities than in earlier years.[36] Dorothy died in 1968. Then Leonard married Susanna Isaacs, a Kleinian child psychiatrist who had gone to Dartington School. He moved to Los Angeles in 1973, dying a year later. 'We could not determine what Dartington would be without you; at the moment it seems unthinkable,' a visitor in the 1930s had written to the Elmhirsts.[37] On their deaths, it became immediately evident how crucial Dorothy and Leonard's vision had been, in the absence of any clear manifesto, to defining the parameters of the estate's activities.

Dartington's trustees were left with only a loosely worded governing document to steer by. It became increasingly clear that the meaning of this document was not self-evident in the absence of its visionary creators. As time went on, trustees were less linked to the Elmhirsts and were less in their practical-idealist mould, driven by what Leonard termed 'a sense of universal social responsibility which must find channel

---

[34] Its activities are recorded in file T/DART/RES.
[35] Michael Young to the Elmhirsts, 8 May 1944, LKE/G/35/A.
[36] Ivor Stolliday, 'Dartington's Money', unpublished note, 2007 [accessed by courtesy of the author]. Stolliday estimates that, by 1971, the trust was running at an annual deficit of around £200,000 (over £2,000,000 in today's value) and had an overdraft of nearly £400,000 (equivalent to £4,500,000).
[37] Eva Blitzstein to the Elmhirsts, 15 April 1934, DWE/A/4/I.

and expression' – the legacy of the Victorian Christian ethos of self-sacrificing service.[38] They were joined or replaced by trustees of a succeeding generation who had not known the devastation of two world wars, or what it was to strive to build up a holistic social democracy, and were less motivated by ideas of social mission.[39] As Emily Robinson and others find, by the 1970s – for a complex of reasons that included increasing affluence, rising social mobility and the belief in the equality of opportunity cultivated by the welfare state – people in Britain were increasingly focused on defining and claiming their individual rights, identities and perspectives, sometimes at the expense of identifying with wider forms of collective or community.[40]

The national climate of the last quarter of the twentieth century was not conducive to Dartington's brand of reform. Demand for the oil of idealism had sunk low, as Leonard might have put it. The economic turmoil of the 1970s – from which Dartington's finances did not escape – was succeeded by a new climate of political conservatism that was less receptive to the concept of the estate as a research station for centralised reform. Maurice Ash tried to revive a vision of Dartington as an independent community exploring a way of living that offered an alternative to the status quo and was oriented around 'the wholeness of things'.[41] But he lacked money, a coherent vision, support in wider society and the prevailing tradition of independent elite philanthropy that had sustained the Elmhirsts' confident evangelism. Since the estate was now running at a large deficit, those trustees who prioritised solvency and espoused organisational efficiency mostly won the day – although that did not mean that solvency was achieved.

Jobs were cut and departmental funding curtailed.[42] Dartington's endowment policy – which was to supply a certain sum of money to each department for general use – was replaced by a system in which grants

[38] Leonard to Dorothy, 1 February 1945, LKE/DWE/14/B.
[39] Leonard to Dorothy, 1 February 1945, LKE/DWE/14/B. Later trustees included Sir Nicholas Kenyon – who had run Radio 3 and was also a trustee of the Arts Council and director of the Barbican Centre; Sir David Green, director of Voluntary Service Overseas and the British Council and chairman of The Prince's School for Traditional Arts; and James Cornford, director of the New Labour think-tank, the Institute for Public Policy Research. For the wider picture, see James Hinton, *Women, Social Leadership, and the Second World War* (Oxford, 2002), 238–9; Callum Brown, *The Death of Christian Britain* (London and New York, 2001), chapter 8.
[40] Emily Robinson, Camilla Schofield, Florence Sutcliffe-Braithwaite and Natalie Thomlinson, 'Telling Stories about Post-war Britain: Popular Individualism and the "Crisis" of the 1970s', *Twentieth Century British History* 28 (2017), 268–304.
[41] Maurice Ash, *The New Renaissance*, 86; Walter King, 'The Lost Worlds of Dartington Hall', *Totnes Review* 2 (2007), 50–9, at 53; Peter Cox, *The Arts at Dartington*, 351.
[42] Longhurst, 'Twinned with Narnia?', 171–2.

had to be applied for specific purposes.[43] Staverton Construction, Dartington Plants, Dartington Glass and Dartington Tweeds were all spun off into independent companies – and then subsequently dissolved or merged with other businesses.[44] The Great Hall began to host weddings and corporate functions more often than artistic and reforming ones. Everything, complained trustee Michael Young, became 'bigger, more departmentalised, more specialised, less amateur and with less of the enthusiasm of the amateur'.[45] In 1977 a cluster of shops, exhibition spaces and food outlets was opened, called the Cider Press Centre. Unlike the original Dartington crafts studio, little of the centre's merchandise was linked to the estate and its enterprises – although it was still marketed under the banner of Dartington's founding ideals. As David Jeremiah writes, the centre 'took crafts retailing into a new age, a model of the good healthy life'.[46]

Maurice Ash resigned as chairman of the Dartington Trust in 1983, blaming his departure on Dartington's loss of a spiritual core.[47] His complaint echoed Rolf Gardiner's fifty years before – that there was 'a vacuum, a hollowness' where the 'flame of whole (holy) belief' should burn at the heart of the Elmhirsts' enterprise.[48] His job was taken over by a Bristol-based property developer, John Pontin, who instigated a more rapid and wholesale departure from the estate's original lines. Pontin began selling off trust assets to reduce its growing deficit.[49] This strategy, which was continued by his successors, resulted in the sale of much of Dartington's woodlands, of further acres for housing development and of much of Dorothy's modernist art collection.[50] The educational side of the trust also atrophied. In 1987, Dartington School closed – succumbing to tabloid scandal.[51] In 1989 Dartington College of Arts, facing bankruptcy, was turned into a department of Plymouth University; in 2008, the Dartington College of Arts was amalgamated with University

---

[43] King, 'The Lost Worlds of Dartington Hall', 55; Banfield, *Music in the West Country*, 335.
[44] King, 'The Lost Worlds of Dartington Hall', 55.   [45] Young, *Elmhirsts*, 342.
[46] Jeremiah, 'Dartington Hall', 131.   [47] Longhurst, 'Twinned with Narnia?', 174.
[48] Rolf Gardiner to Leonard, 16 June 1933, LKE/G/15/B.
[49] Cox, *The Arts at Dartington*, 369; King, 'The Lost Worlds of Dartington Hall', 50–9. John Pontin was chair of the Dartington Hall Trust from 1984 to 1997 and donated considerable quantities of his own funds to support it (Stolliday, 'Dartington's Money').
[50] King, 'The Lost Worlds of Dartington Hall', 50–9. Michael Young resigned his trusteeship in 1991 in protest over the management of the trust.
[51] In 1983 the headmaster made public underage sexual activity, drug use and petty criminality in the school. Soon afterwards, he was forced to resign, when photographs of him and his wife – originally taken for a sex magazine, *New QT*, in the 1970s – were republished in *The Sun*. David Gribble's *That's All Folks: Dartington Hall School Remembered* was produced as a memorial volume for the school (Crediton, 1987).

College Falmouth and relocated to Cornwall.[52] With its closure ended the vitality of a permanent student presence on the estate.

In the first two decades of the twentieth century, the trust has continued to function at a very significant loss. It sought to reduce its debt by selling off further assets: in 2011, twelve paintings given by Rabindranath Tagore to the Elmhirsts; in 2020, a number of residential properties on the estate, and two sites for large-scale housing developments.[53] The trust also sought alternative ways of raising funds. In 2018 it issued twenty million pounds of 'social impact' bonds in order 'to finance property-backed commercial activities to boost the trust's income'.[54] 'You can't rely on a few extremely wealthy philanthropists these days,' wrote the estate's then chief executive, Rhodri Samuel. 'The future of philanthropy is moving from individuals to a more collective response.'[55] While the Elmhirsts would likely have approved of the idea of group action, and of combining high ideals with commercial innovation, the share launch had a low uptake among investors, with legal fees amounting to more than the £50,000 it managed to raise.[56]

Noel Longhurst, writing on the formation of 'alternative milieus', usefully suggests studying utopias and intentional communities as local, pluralistic networks rather than as bounded entities.[57] Such a network took root around Dartington and the region bears its mark to this day. Even as the estate itself struggled to define its late-twentieth-century identity, radical idealists, many of them former students of the Dartington School or College of Arts, settled nearby and began enterprises of their own.[58] By the late 1980s, the surrounding countryside,

---

[52] Sam Richards, *Dartington College of Arts: Learning by Doing. A Biography of a College* (Totnes, 2015); Cox, *The Arts at Dartington*, 369.

[53] Maev Kennedy, 'Row as Dartington Hall Auctions Off Its Treasures', 13 November 2011, *The Guardian* [www.theguardian.com/artanddesign/2011/nov/13/dartington-hall-art-sale]; Alan Boldon, 'Latest Developments at Dartington', 24 January 2020 [www.dartington.org/latest-developments-at-dartington-hall/]; [n.a.], 'Land Sale Secures Future of Dartington Hall Estate', 3 April 2020 [www.dartington.org/land-sale-secures-our-future/].

[54] Matthew Vincent, 'The Rich Column: Modern Means to Finance an Old Country Estate', 30 November 2018, *Financial Times* [www.ft.com/content/eefd5280-cc7f-11e8-8d0b-a6539b949662].

[55] Ibid.

[56] Rob Hopkins, 'The Heart of the Matter', 22 February 2020, *The Independent* [www.independent.co.uk/independentpremium/long-reads/saving-dartington-hall-trust-country-estate-community-a9331091.html].

[57] Noel Longhurst, 'The Emergence of an Alternative Milieu: Conceptualising the Nature of Alternative Places', *Environment and Planning* 45 (2013), 2100–19.

[58] Longhurst, 'Twinned with Narnia?', 293; Philip Conford, '"Somewhere Quite Different": The Seventies Generation of Organic Activists and their Context', *Rural History* 19 (2010), 217–34.

which had once cold-shouldered the progressive Elmhirsts, had become sufficiently progressive in its own right to merit mention in a satirical guide to New Age living: '*The* area of Britain to live in is Devon. There are more natural healers, holistic health practitioners, alternative therapists and other inner-directed souls to the square mile in Devon than in any other part of the country.'[59]

In a late flowering of Dorothy and Leonard's interwar wishes, their enterprise had finally made its mark on the local community – to the extent that as Dartington shed fragments of its own radicalism, that community picked them up and took them forward. When Dartington School closed, Park School on the estate and Sand School in nearby Ashburton were founded to perpetuate its principles. Since 1985, a Steiner school has also stood on the edge of the estate. When Maurice Ash resigned as chair of the Dartington Hall Trust, it was to turn his own local estate, Sharpham, into a model 'for how life might be reordered within a disintegrating society'.[60] Ash's solutions, which included biodynamic agriculture, artisanal food production and combining Wittgenstein's philosophy with Buddhism, bore a strong flavour of prewar Dartington's holistic eclecticism.[61] Ash shared the Elmhirsts' earlier hope for Dartington: that, like the pre-Reformation monasteries, his estate would form a rural centre for spirituality, learning and innovation, a civilising task that he felt the majority of English country houses had failed to fulfil.[62]

The neighbouring town of Totnes, a bastion of conservatism in the early twentieth century, became a renowned centre of counterculture.[63] It combined artisanal production, social entrepreneurship, ecological experimentation and a lively artistic performance calendar with a general aura of alternative living and bohemianism.[64] In a sense, this micro-scale communitarian-minded social context trumped both the wider climate of individualistic materialism and the top-down, economically oriented leadership by the Dartington trustees. The holistic, democratic idealism of interwar Dartington was kept alive in a diffuse fashion that the Elmhirsts might have appreciated.

---

[59] Martin Stott, *Spilling the Beans* (London, 1986), 10.
[60] Maurice Ash, quoted in Christopher Titmuss, *Freedom of the Spirit* (London, 1991), 84.
[61] Maurice Ash's philosophy is laid out in *The New Renaissance*.
[62] Richard Boston, 'Maurice Ash', 13 February 2003, *The Guardian* [www.theguardian .com/news/2003/feb/13/guardianobituaries.booksobituaries].
[63] In the last fifty years, Totnes has spawned numerous articles of the 'Is This the Most Eccentric Town in Britain?' type (Boudicca Fox-Leonard, *The Telegraph*, 6 January 2018 [www.telegraph.co.uk/travel/destinations/europe/united-kingdom/articles/totnes-what-to-see-and-do/]).
[64] Banfield, *Music in the West Country*, 336.

Since the 1990s, the appetite for exploring practical utopian alternatives to capitalist individualism has been on the rise again.[65] New initiatives at Dartington, embedded in a flourishing local alternative culture, have gone some way to renew the estate's reputation as a nexus of broad-thinking idealism. Some of these, as in the Elmhirsts' day, have been short-lived – including the 'Abundant Life' project, a plan to turn former Dartington School buildings into a cooperative community for older people.[66] Others have had great success in influencing the local community and the wider world. The most notable of these is Schumacher College. Founded in 1991 as a teaching centre in the 'spiritual ecology' movement, the college was founded by social and environmental activist Satish Kumar and inspired by economist E. F. Schumacher, best known for his advocacy for intermediate technology and small-scale economics.[67] Offering courses on subjects ranging from sustainability to spiritual holism, this 'point of renewal' for Dartington Hall has drawn internationally recognised figures including James Lovelock, originator of the Gaia hypothesis, and environmentalist and writer Roger Deakin.[68]

Like interwar Dartington, Schumacher College places a strong emphasis on everyday behaviour – on the 'lived politics' of idealism: all students and staff are involved in domestic chores; the college strives to be carbon neutral and is vegetarian; food is grown on the grounds or sourced locally.[69] As with earlier iterations of the Elmhirsts' holistic ambitions, the turn to ecological sustainability draws on traditions of both state-centred progressivism and social pluralism. Schumacher College is embedded in state higher education, offering postgraduate

---

[65] Davina Cooper, *Everyday Utopias: The Conceptual Life of Promising Spaces* (Durham, 2014); Martin Parker, George Cheney, Valérie Fournier and Chris Land (eds.), *The Routledge Companion to Alternative Organization* (London and New York, 2014); Ruth Levitas, *Utopia and Method: The Imaginary Reconstitution of Society* (Basingstoke, 2013).

[66] Jonathan M. Lee, 'A Year Made in Dartington', 2011 [www.jonathanmlee.net/2016/05/01/a-year-made-in-dartington-dartington-hall-trust/].

[67] Dominic Corrywright, 'Network Spirituality: The Schumacher–Resurgence–Kumar Nexus', *Journal of Contemporary Religion* 19 (2004), 311–27. A former Jain Monk, Satish Kumar (born 1936) is editor emeritus of *Resurgence* and *The Ecologist*. E. F. Schumacher's 'intermediate technology' signifies that which is human-scale, decentralised, ecologically sustainable and appropriate for its purpose, an idea best captured in his book *Small Is Beautiful: A Study of Economics As If People Mattered* (London, 1973).

[68] Sir David Green, then chairman of the Dartington Hall Trust, in 'Foreword' to Anne Phillips, *Holistic Education: Learning from Schumacher College* (Totnes, 2008), 7. James Lovelock's Gaia hypothesis posits that the biosphere acts like a living organism that self-regulates to keep conditions right for sustaining life. James Lovelock, *Gaia: The Practical Science of Planetary Medicine* ([n.p.], 1991).

[69] [n.a.], 'About the College', [n.d.] [www.schumachercollege.org.uk/about].

programmes run in association with the Universities of Plymouth and
Wales. It has an international following but strives to remain small and
locally relevant, opening its doors to the community every Wednesday
and cultivating links with nearby values-driven organisations such as
the Sharpham estate and employee-owned vegetable box business
Riverford Organic Farmers.[70] Schumacher College also works with the
Transition Town movement, a decentralised, international charity
founded in 2005 and based in the nearby town of Totnes, which aims
to increase community resilience as a way to address climate change and
economic crisis.[71] The Elmhirsts' legacy is an estate that continues to
engage with the challenge of what it means to regenerate and strengthen
local community both in the national context and in an international
context of globalisation.

That Dartington has lasted for nearly a century – albeit latterly more as
a place of liberal, creative relaxation than as a forcing ground for social
change – has much to do with the characteristics that made it so influential in the first place: its founders' wealth, its strong connections with
other idealist projects and its inclusive, ever-evolving ideology. One
interwar visitor commented that the framework through which the
Elmhirsts had achieved the 'corporate embodiment' of their ideas was
'so elastic and adaptable that there is nothing to threaten their growth'.[72]
Later on, Maurice Ash saw the estate as 'a place too busy creating itself to
have lapsed into the conventional trap of commemorating itself'.[73] In the
1930s, even as they emphasised the necessity of seeking unity, Dorothy
and Leonard increasingly accepted that their lack of a definitive manifesto meant that Dartington would always be fragmented, with no one,
themselves included, having a whole view: 'there is a vertical Dartington
which reaches from the earth far away into the sky .... There is the
horizontal Dartington, which stretches over certain fields of enterprise, ...
and each person has the quadrilateral shot of which he or she is

[70] Corrywright, 'Network Spirituality'; Julia Ponsonby, 'From Farm to Feast', 2009 [www
.resurgence.org/magazine/article2824-from-farm-to-feast.html].
[71] Launched in 2006, with Totnes as the first hub, by 2014 there were 1,120 Transition
Town initiatives in 42 countries. Derk Loorbach, Flor Avelina, Alex Haxeltine, Julia
M. Wittmay, Tim O'Riordan, Paul Weaver and René Kemp, 'The Economic Crisis as a
Game Changer? Exploring the Role of Social Construction in Sustainability
Transitions', *Ecology and Society* 21 (2016) [dx.doi.org/10.5751/ES-08761-210415].
See also Rob Hopkins, 'New Report: "So What Does Transition Town Totnes
Actually Do"?', *Transition Culture* (2010) [transitionculture.org/2010/11/23/new-
report-so-what-does-transition-town-totnes-actually-do/].
[72] Godfrey I. H. Lloyd to Leonard, [n.d.], LKE/G/22/A.
[73] Maurice Ash, *The New Renaissance: Essays in Search of Wholeness* (Bideford, 1987), 150.

capable .... Out of this jigsaw Dartington builds and grows.'[74] Their enterprise was a way to negotiate 'how to be' in modern society that was not supposed to achieve its consummation in the immediate, just like the Christian faith that it in many ways replaced. And in its model of a spiritually satisfying mode of life that also contributed to the social good, it provided an answer for many.

[74] Leonard to Fred Gwatkin, 2 October 1934, LKE/LF/16/A.

Bibliography

Archives

British Library Newspaper Archives
Dartington Hall Archives, Devon Record Office
Eduard Lindeman Archives, Columbia University
Leach Archive, Crafts Study Centre, University for the Creative Arts
Nancy Wilson Ross Archives, Harry Ransom Center, University of Texas

Newspapers

Exeter and Plymouth Gazette
Nottingham Journal
The Listener
The Totnes Times and Devon News
Western Daily Press
Western Morning News
Western Times

Interviews

Author interview with Etain Todds (née Kabraji), 17 May 2015
Author interview with Mary Bride Nicholson, 23 June 2016

Printed Primary Sources

Adams, Henry, *The Education of Henry Adams*, Boston and New York, 1918.
Arnold, Matthew, 'Culture and Its Enemies', *Cornhill Magazine* 16 (1867), 36–53.
Art and Industry: Report of the Committee Appointed by the Board of Trade under the Chairmanship of Lord Gorrell on the Production and Exhibition of Articles of Good Design and Everyday Use, London, 1932.
The Arts Enquiry, *The Visual Arts: A Report Sponsored by the Dartington Hall Trustees*, London, 1946.
Badley, J. H., *Bedales: A Pioneer School*, London, 1923.

Bailey, Liberty H., *The Country Life Movement in the United States*, New York, 1911.

Beach Thomas, Sir William, 'Dartington Hall – A Great Rural Experiment', *The Listener* 29 (1933), 809–13.

Begtrup, Holger, Hans Lund and Peter Manniche, *The Folk High Schools of Denmark and the Development of a Farming Community*, London (printed in Copenhagen), 1929.

Betjeman, John, *Devon: Shell Guide*, London [1936].

Blewitt, Trevor (ed.), *The Modern Schools Handbook*, London, 1934.

Bonser, Frederick Gordon and Lois Coffey Mossman, *Industrial Arts for Elementary Schools*, New York, 1925.

Boyd, William (ed.), *Towards a New Education: Based on the Fifth World Conference of the New Education Fellowship at Elsinore, Denmark*, London and New York, 1930.

Brayne, Francis, *The English and the Indian Village*, London, 1933.

Browne, E. Martin, *The Production of Religious Plays*, London, 1932.

'T.S. Eliot in the Theatre: The Director's Memories', *The Sewanee Review* 74 (1966), 136–52.

Butterworth, Julian E., 'A State Rebuilds the Schools of Its Rural Areas: The Central Rural School District of New York', *The Journal of Educational Sociology* 14 (1941), 411–21.

Cattell, Raymond B., *The Fight for Our National Intelligence*, London, 1937.

Chekhov, Michael, *To the Actor: On the Technique of Acting*, London, 2002 [1953].

Children and Their Primary Schools, London, 1967.

Chissell, Joan, 'Dartington', *The Musical Times* 91 (1950), 337–41.

Croly, Herbert, *Willard Straight*, New York, 1925.

The Promise of American Life, Cambridge, MA, 1965 [1909].

Currie, J. R., 'A Review of Fifty Years' Farm Management Research', *Journal of Agricultural Economics* 11 (1956), 350–60.

Currie, J. R. and W. H. Long, *An Agricultural Survey in South Devon*, Newton Abbot and Totnes, 1929.

Curry, W. B., 'Modern Buildings for New Schools', *The Survey* 41 (1931), 496–8.

The School and a Changing Civilisation, London, 1934.

Education in a Changing World, New York, 1935.

The Case for Federal Union, Harmondsworth, 1939.

Dewey, John, *The School and Society*, Chicago, 1907.

Moral Principles in Education, Boston, c. 1909.

Democracy and Education: An Introduction to the Philosophy of Education, New York, 1999 [1916].

Drake-Brockman, E. D., *Staverton on the Dart: From Records of Church and Parish*, Exeter, 1946.

Elmhirst, Dorothy, *The Arts at Dartington*, St Ives, 1950.

The Gardens at Dartington Hall, Dartington, 1961.

Elmhirst, Dorothy and Leonard Elmhirst, *Outline of an Educational Experiment*, Totnes, 1926.

Prospectus, Totnes, 1926.

Elmhirst, Leonard, 'Siksha-Satra', *Visva-Bharati Bulletin* 9 (1928), 23–39.
    Trip to Russia, New York, 1934.
    Faith and Works at Dartington, reprinted from The Countryman, Totnes, 1937,
        8–11.
    *Rabindranath Tagore: Pioneer in Education. Essays and Exchanges between
        Rabindranath Tagore and L.K. Elmhirst*, London, 1961.
    Poet and Plowman, Calcutta, 1975.
    The Straight and Its Origin, Ithaca, NY, 1975.
Findlay, J. J., *The School and the Child*, London, 1906.
    Educational Essays, London, 1910.
Gardiner, Rolf, 'Rural Reconstruction', in H. J. Massingham (ed.), *England and
        the Farmer*, London, 1941, 91–107.
    England Herself: Ventures in Rural Restoration, London, 1943.
Gill, Eric, *Art and a Changing Civilisation*, London, 1934.
Gropius, Walter, *Manifesto and Programme of the Weimar State Bauhaus*, 1919,
        www.bauhaus100.de/en/past/works/education/manifest-und-programm-
        des-staatlichen-bauhauses/.
    The New Architecture and the Bauhaus, London, 1935.
Hamsun, Knut, *Growth of the Soil*, trans. W. Worster, London, 1935 [1917].
Hansard Parliamentary Debates, House of Commons debates, 20 November 1941,
        vol. 376, column 506W.
Heard, Gerald, *The Ascent of Humanity*, London, 1929.
    The Social Substance of Religion, London, 1931.
    The Emergence of Man, London, 1931.
    'The Dartington Experiment', *Architectural Review* 449 (1934), 119–22.
    The Source of Civilization, London, 1935.
    'Men and Books', *Time and Tide*, 26 (1935), 1545–6.
    The Third Morality, London, 1937.
    Pain, Sex and Time: A New Hypothesis of Evolution, London, 1939.
    'Is Mysticism Escapism?' in Christopher Isherwood (ed.), *Vedanta for the
        Western World*, Hollywood, 1945, 30–2.
Hepworth, Barbara, *A Pictorial Autobiography*, London, 1985.
Higginbottom, Sam, *The Gospel and the Plow, or the Old Gospel and Modern
        Farming in Ancient India*, London, 1921.
Hiley, Wilfrid Edward, *A Forestry Venture … Foreword and Chapter 'The Venture in
        Perspective' by L.K. Elmhirst*, London, 1964.
Holtby, Winifred, *South Riding*, London, 1936.
Hussey, Christopher, 'High Cross Hill, Dartington, Devon', *Country Life* 11
        (1933), 144–9.
Huxley, Aldous, 'Education', *Proper Studies*, London, 1927.
    Eyeless in Gaza, London, 2004 [1936].
    *Ends and Means: An Enquiry into the Nature of Ideals and Into the Methods
        Employed For Their Realization*, London, 1937.
    Adonis and the Alphabet, and Other Essays, London, 1956.
    Island, London, 2005 [1962].
Huxley, Julian, *UNESCO, its Purpose and its Philosophy*, London, 1946.

Isherwood, Margaret, *The Root of the Matter: A Study in the Connections Between Religion, Psychology and Education*, London, 1954.

Joad, Cyril, *Counter Attack From the East: The Philosophy of Radhakrishnan*, London, 1933.

Kandinsky, Wassily, *Concerning the Spiritual in Art*, trans. M. T. H. Sadler, New York, 1977 [1914].

Keppel, Frederick P., *The Foundation: Its Place in American Life*, Oxford and New York, 2017 [1930].

Knox, Ronald, *Broadcast Minds*, London, 1932.

Labour Party, *Let Us Face the Future*, London, 1945.

Landau, Rom, *God Is My Adventure: A Book on Modern Mystics, Masters and Teachers*, London, 1935.

Leach, Bernard, *A Potter's Book*, [n.p.], 1940.

The Lincoln School of Teachers College: A Descriptive Booklet, New York City, 1922.

Lindeman, Eduard C., *The Community: An Introduction to the Study of Community Leadership and Organization*, New York, 1921.

Social Discovery: An Approach to the Study of Functional Groups, New York, 1924.

The Meaning of Adult Education, New York, 1926.

'Adult Education: A New Means of Liberals', *The New Republic* 54 (1928), 26–9.

Lindsay, Kenneth, *Social Progress and Educational Waste: Being a Study of the 'Free-Plan' and Scholarship System, etc.*, London, 1926.

Lorwin, Lewis, 'The Twentieth Century – The Plan Age', *Plan Age* 1 (1934), 1–3.

Madge, Charles, *Village Communities in North-East Thailand*, New York, 1959.

Mannheim, Karl, *Ideology and Utopia, an Introduction to the Sociology of Knowledge*, trans. Louis Wirth and Edward Shils, London, 1936 [first published, untranslated, 1929].

Manniche, Peter, *Denmark, a Social Laboratory: Independent Farmers, Co-operative Societies, Folk High Schools, Social Legislation*, Copenhagen and London, 1939.

Massingham, H. J., *Country*, London, 1934.

McDougall, William, *Introduction to Social Psychology*, London, 1908.

The Group Mind, London, 1920.

Melville, Robert, 'Exhibitions', *Architectural Review* 112 (1952), 343–4.

Mitchison, Naomi, *You May Well Ask: A Memoir, 1920–1940*, London, 1979.

Moore, G. E., *Principia Ethica*, Cambridge, 1993 [1903].

Neill, A. S., *That Dreadful School*, London, 1937.

Summerhill: A Radical Approach to Education, London, 1962.

'The New Rural England', *Architect and Building News*, 30 June, 14 July, 21 July 1933.

Pekin, L. B., *Progressive Schools*, London, 1934.

Pepler, H. D. C., 'Hampshire House Workshops', *Blackfriars* 31 (1950), 70–4.

Pevsner, Nikolaus, *Pioneers of the Modern Movement from William Morris to Walter Gropius*, London, 1936.

An Enquiry into Industrial Arts in England, Cambridge, 1937.

Devon, Harmondsworth, 1989 [1952].

Powell, Anthony, *A Dance to the Music of Time*, London, 1991 [series of novels, originally published between 1951 and'75].

Pragnell, Vera, *The Story of the Sanctuary*, Steyning, 1928.

Pritchard, Jack, *View from a Long Chair: The Memoirs of Jack Pritchard*, London; Boston; Melbourne; and Henley, 1984.

Read, Herbert, *Art and Industry*, London, 1934.

Art and Society, London, 1937.

Reith, J. C. W., *Broadcast over Britain*, London, 1924.

Report of the Consultative Committee on the Primary School, [n.p.], 1931.

Reynolds, Stephen, *A Poor Man's House*, London, 1911.

Rivers, W. H. R., *Instinct and Unconscious*, Cambridge, 1920.

Rogers, Arthur, *The Real Crisis*, London, 1938.

Rolt, L. T. C., *High Horse Riderless*, Bideford, 1988 [1947].

Russell, Bertrand, *Principles of Social Reconstruction*, London, 1971 [1917].

On Education: Especially in Early Childhood, London, 1957 [1926].

Education and the Social Order, London, 1932.

Autobiography, vol. 2, London, 1969.

Scott Watson, J. A., 'Rural Britain Today and Tomorrow – vii: Tradition and Experiment in the West', *The Listener*, 22 (1933), 797.

Sheldon, William, *Psychology and the Promethean Will: A Constructive Study of the Acute Common Problem of Education, Medicine and Religion*, New York and London, 1936.

Atlas of Men, New York, 1954.

Sieff, Israel, *Memoirs*, London, 1970.

Street, A. G., *Farmer's Glory*, Oxford, 1959 [1932].

Tagore, Rabindranath, *Nationalism*, London, 1976 [1916].

The Religion of Man, New York, 1931.

'Tagore's Tribute to Shankar', trans. Basanta Koomar Roy, *The American Dancer*, 1937, 13.

Temple, William, *Christianity and Social Order*, [n.p.], 1942.

Thomas, F. G., *The New Learning: An Experiment with Educational Films in the County of Devon*, London, 1932.

The Changing Village, an Essay on Rural Reconstruction, London, 1939.

Tout, Herbert, *The Standard of Living in Bristol: A Preliminary Report of the Work of the University of Bristol Social Survey*, Bristol, 1938.

Turnor, Christopher, *Land Settlement in Germany*, London, 1935.

Waley, Arthur, *The Way and its Power: A Study of the Tao Tê Ching and its Place in Chinese Thought*, London, 1934.

Wallas, Graham, *The Great Society: A Psychological Analysis*, London, 1914.

Watts, Alan, *In My Own Way: An Autobiography*, London, 1973.

Webb, Beatrice, *My Apprenticeship*, vol. 1, London, 1926.

Wells, H. G., *The Open Conspiracy: Blue Prints for a World Revolution*, London, 1928.

Williamson, Henry, *Tarka the Otter*, London, 1945 [1927].

Wise, Marjorie, *English Village Schools*, London, 1931.

Woolf, Virginia, 'Mr Bennett and Mrs Brown' in *Collected Essays*, vol. 1, London, 1966, 319–37.

Secondary Sources

[n.a.], 'About the College', [n.d.], www.schumachercollege.org.uk/about.

[n.a.], 'Design For Intermediate Technology', *Dartington College Looks At the Future* – a supplement to *Dartington Hall News*, 26 May 1973, 8.

[n.a.], 'Land Sale Secures Future of Dartington Hall Estate', 3 April 2020, www.dartington.org/land-sale-secures-our-future/.

Abrahams, Ruth K., 'Uday Shankar: The Early Years, 1900–1938', *Dance Chronicle* 30 (2007), 363–426.

Adamson, Andy and Clare Lidbury, *Kurt Jooss: 60 Years of the Green Table*, Birmingham, 1994.

Addison, Paul, *The Road to 1945: British Politics and the Second World War*, London, 1977.

Adult Education Committee, *The Drama in Adult Education. A Report by the Adult Education Committee of the Board of Education, being Paper No. 6 of the Committee*, [n.p.], 1926.

Alam, Fakrul and Radha Chakravarty (eds.), *The Essential Tagore*, Cambridge, MA and London, 2011.

Amrith, Sunil S., 'Internationalising Health in the Twentieth Century', in Glenda Sluga and Patricia Clavin, *Internationalisms: a Twentieth-Century History*, Cambridge, 2017, 245–64.

Anderson, Walter Truett, *The Upstart Spring: Esalen and the American Awakening*, Reading, MA, 1983.

Annan, Noel, 'The Intellectual Aristocracy', in J. H. Plumb (ed.), *Studies in Social History: A Tribute to G.M. Trevelyan*, London, 1955, 241–87.

Our Age: The Generation That Made Post-War Britain, London, 1990.

Anthony, Scott, *Public Relations and the Making of Modern Britain: Stephen Tallents and the Birth of a Progressive Media Profession*, Manchester, 2018.

Appiah, Kwame Anthony, 'Cosmopolitan Patriots', *Critical Inquiry* 23 (1997), 617–39, at 633.

The Ethics of Identity, Princeton, 2005.

Aravamudan, Srinivas, *Guru English: South Asian Religion in a Cosmopolitan Language*, Princeton, 2006.

Armytage, Walter H. Green, *Heavens Below: Utopian Experiments in England 1560–1960*, London, 1961.

Arnold-Forster, Tom, 'Democracy and Expertise in the Lippmann-Terman Controversy', *Modern Intellectual History* 1 (2017), 1–32.

Ash, Maurice, *Who Are the Progressives Now?*, London, 1969.

New Renaissance: Essays in Search of Wholeness, Bideford, 1987.

Bailey, Chris, 'Progress and Preservation: The Role of Rural Industries in the Making of the Modern Image of the Countryside', *Journal of Design History* 9 (1996), 35–53.

Bailey, Richard, *A.S. Neill*, London, 2014.

Baker, Anne Pimlott, 'Ellis, Susan Caroline Williams- (1918–2007)', *Oxford Dictionary of National Biography*, Oxford University Press, www.oxforddnb.com/view/article/99216.

Banfield, Stephen, *Music in the West Country: Social and Cultural History Across an English Region*, Suffolk, 2018.

Barbeau, Aimee E., 'Christian Empire and National Crusade: The Rhetoric of Anglican Clergy in the First World War', *Anglican and Episcopal History* 85 (2016), 24–62.

Bar-Haim, Shaul, 'The Liberal Playground: Susan Isaacs, Psychoanalysis and Progressive Education in the Interwar Era', *History of the Human Sciences* 30 (2017), 94–117.

Bartie, Angela, Linda Fleming, Mark Freeman, Tom Hulme, Alexandra Hutton and Paul Readman, 'Historical Pageants and the Medieval Past in Twentieth-Century England', *The English Historical Review* 133 (2018), 866–902.

Beauchamp, Christopher, 'Getting *Your Money's Worth*: American Models for the Remaking of the Consumer Interest in Britain, 1930s–1960s', in Mark Bevir and Frank Trentmann (eds.), *Critiques of Capital in Modern Britain and America: Transatlantic Exchanges*, Basingstoke, 2002, 127–50.

Beers, Laura, *Red Ellen: The Life of Ellen Wilkinson, Socialist, Feminist, Internationalist*, Cambridge, MA, 2017.

Bell, Quentin, *Virginia Woolf, a Biography*, London, 1972.

Berg, Leila, *Risinghill: Death of a Comprehensive School*, Harmond worth, 1974 [1968].

Berger, Stefan and Alexandra Przyrembel (eds.), *Moralizing Capitalism: Agents, Discourses and Practices of Capitalism and Anti-Capitalism in the Modern Age*, Cham, 2019.

Best, Andrew (ed.), *Water Springing from the Ground: An Anthology of the Writings of Rolf Gardiner*, Oxford, 1972.

Bevir, Mark, 'Introduction', in Mark Bevir (ed.), *Modern Pluralism: Anglo-American Debates Since 1880*, Cambridge, 2012, 1–20.

Bew, John, *Citizen Clem: A Biography of Attlee*, London, 2016.

Blaazer, David, *The Popular Front and the Progressive Tradition*, Cambridge, 2009.

Black, Lawrence, 'Social Democracy as a Way of Life: Fellowship and the Socialist Union, 1951–9', *Twentieth Century British History* 10 (1999), 499–539.

'*Which?* Craft in Post-War Britain: The Consumers' Association and the Politics of Affluence', *Albion: A Quarterly Journal Concerned with British Studies* 36 (2004), 52–82.

Bland, Lucy, *Modern Women on Trial: Sexual Transgression in the Age of the Flapper*, Manchester, 2016.

Bland, Lucy and Laura Doan (eds.), *Sexology in Culture: Labelling Bodies and Desires*, Chicago, 1998.

Boldon, Alan, 'Latest Developments at Dartington', 24 January 2020, www.dartington.org/latest-developments-at-dartington-hall/.

Bonham-Carter, Victor, *Dartington Hall: The History of an Experiment*, London, 1958.

Dartington Hall: The Formative Years, 1925–1957, Dulverton, Somerset, 1970.

Land and Environment: The Survival of the English Countryside, Rutherford, NJ, 1971.

Bosco, Andrew, 'Lothian, Curtis, Kimber and the Federal Union Movement (1938–4)', *Journal of Contemporary History* 23 (1988), 465–502.

Boston, Richard, 'Maurice Ash', 13 February 2003, *The Guardian*, www .theguardian.com/news/2003/feb/13/guardianobituaries.booksobituaries.

Boyd, William and Wyatt Rawson, *The Story of the New Education*, London, 1965.

Boyes, Georgina, *The Imagined Village: Culture, Ideology and the English Folk Revival*, Manchester, 1993.

Bradshaw, David, 'Huxley and Progressive Education: Daltonism and the Dartington Hall Débâcle', *Aldous Huxley Annual* 15 (2015), 1–20.

Brasnett, Margaret, *Voluntary Social Action: A History of the National Council of Social Service 1919–1969*, London, 1969.

Brassley, Paul, 'Agricultural Research in Britain, 1850–1914: Failure, Success and Development', *Annals of Science* 52 (1995), 465–80.

Brassley, Paul with Jeremy Burchardt and Lynne Thompson (eds.), *The English Countryside Between the Wars: Regeneration or Decline?*, New York, 2006.

Brassley, Paul with David Harvey, Matt Lobley and Michael Winter, 'Accounting For Agriculture: The Origins of the Farm Management Survey', *Agricultural History Review* 61 (2013), 135–53.

Brehony, Kevin J., 'A New Education for a New Era: The Contribution of the Conferences of the New Education Fellowship to the Disciplinary Field of Education 1921–1938', *Paedagogica Historica* 40 (2004), 733–55.

'Lady Astor's Campaign for Nursery Schools in Britain, 1930–1939: Attempting to Valorize Cultural Capital in a Male-Dominated Political Field', *History of Education Quarterly* 49 (2009), 196–210.

Brenscheidt, Diana, *Shiva Onstage: Uday Shankar's Company of Hindu Dancers and Musicians in Europe and the United States, 1931–38*, Berlin, 2011.

Brigden, Roy, 'Leckford: A Case-Study of Interwar Development', in Paul Brassley, Jeremy Burchardt and Lynne Thompson (eds.), *The English Countryside Between the Wars: Regeneration or Decline?*, New York, 2006, 200–11.

Briggs, Asa, *Michael Young: Social Entrepreneur*, London, 2001.

Broadbent, D. E., 'Bartlett, Sir Frederic Charles (1886–1969)', *Oxford Dictionary of National Biography*, Oxford University Press, www.oxforddnb.com/view/article/30628.

Brooke, Stephen, 'The Body and Socialism: Dora Russell in the 1920s', *Past & Present* 189 (2005), 147–77.

'Bodies, Sexuality and the "Modernization" of the British Working Classes, 1920s to 1960s', *International Labor and Working-Class History* 69 (2006), 104–22.

Brooks, Ron, 'Professor J. J. Findlay, the King Alfred School Society, Hampstead and Letchworth Garden City Education, 1897–1913', *History of Education* 21 (1992), 161–78.

Brown, Callum G., *The Death of Christian Britain*, London; New York, 2001.

Brown, Jane, *Angel Dorothy: How an American Progressive Came to Devon*, London, 2017.

Bull, H. W., 'Industrial Education at Cadbury in the 1930s', *The Vocational Aspect of Education* 94 (1984), 59–62.

Bull, Philip, 'Plunkett, Sir Horace Curzon (1854–1932)', *Oxford Dictionary of National Biography*, Oxford University Press, www.oxforddnb.com/view/article/35549.

Burchardt, Jeremy, 'Reconstructing the Rural Community: Village Halls and the National Council of Social Service, 1919–39', *Rural History* 10 (1999), 193–216.

Paradise Lost: Rural Idyll and Social Change in England Since 1800, London and York, 2002.

'Rethinking the Rural Idyll', *Cultural and Social History* 8 (2011), 73–94.

'State and Society in the English Countryside: The Rural Community Movement 1918–39', *Rural History* 23 (2012), 81–106.

Burke, Catherine, 'About Looking: Vision, Transformation, and the Education of the Eye in Discourses of School Renewal Past and Present', *British Educational Research Journal* 36 (2010), 65–82.

Burt, Ramsay, *Alien Bodies: Representation of Modernity, 'Race' and Nation*, London, 1998.

Butler, Lise, 'Michael Young, the Institute of Community Studies, and the Politics of Kinship', *Twentieth Century British History* 26 (2015), 203–24.

Michael Young, Social Science, and the British Left, 1945–1970, Oxford, 2020.

Byrne, Georgina, *Modern Spiritualism and the Church of England, 1850–1939*, Woodbridge, UK, 2010.

Calcraft, L. G. A., 'Aldous Huxley and the Sheldonian Hypothesis', *Annals of Science* 37 (1980), 657–71.

Campbell, Colin, *The Easternisation of the West*, London and New York, 1999.

Campbell, Louise, 'Patrons of the Modern House', *Journal of the Twentieth Century Society* 2 (1996), 41–50.

Campsie, Alexandre, 'Mass-Observation, Left Intellectuals and the Politics of Everyday Life', *The English Historical Review* 131 (2016), 92–121.

Cannadine, David, *The Decline and Fall of the British Aristocracy*, London, 1996 [1990].

Caramellino, Gaia, *Europe Meets America: William Lescaze, Architect of Modern Housing*, Newcastle, 2016.

Carey, John, *The Intellectuals and the Masses: Pride and Prejudice Among the Literary Intelligentsia, 1880–1938*, London, 1992.

Carroll, Anthony J., 'Disenchantment, Rationality and the Modernity of Max Weber', *Forum Philosophicum* 16 (2011), 117–37.

Carter, Laura, 'The Quennells and the "History of Everyday Life" in England, c.1918–69', *History Workshop Journal* 81 (2016), 106–34.

Ceadel, Martin, *Pacifism in Britain 1914–1945: The Defining of a Faith*, Oxford, 1980.

Semi-Detached Idealists: The British Peace Movement and International Relations, 1854–1945, Oxford and New York, 2000.

Claeys, Gregory, 'Owen, Robert (1771–1858)', *Oxford Dictionary of National Biography*, Oxford University Press, 2004, www.oxforddnb.com/view/article/21027.

Clarke, Arthur C., 'Of Sand and Stars', in Arthur C. Clarke, *Spring: A Choice of Futures*, New York, 1984, 151–7.

Clarke, J. J., *Oriental Enlightenment: The Encounter Between Asian and Western Thought*, London, 1997.

Clews, Christopher, 'The New Education Fellowship and the Reconstruction of Education: 1945 to 1966', unpublished PhD, University of London, 2009.

Clout, Hugh and Iain Stevenson, 'Jules Sion, Alan Grant Ogilvie and the Collège des Ecossais in Montpellier: A Network of Geographers', *Scottish Geographical Journal* 120 (2004), 181–98.

Collini, Stefan, 'Sociology and Idealism in Britain, 1880–1920', *Archives Européennes de Sociologie* 19 (1978), 3–50.

    Public Moralists: Political Thought and Intellectual Life in Britain 1850–1930, Oxford, 1991.

    Absent Minds: Intellectuals in Britain, Oxford, 2006.

    Common Reading: Critics, Historians, Publics, Oxford, 2008.

Colman, Gould P., *Education and Agriculture: A History of the New York State College of Agriculture at Cornell University*, Ithaca, NY, 1963.

Colpus, Eve, 'Women, Service and Self-Actualization in Inter-War Britain', *Past and Present* 238 (2018), 197–232.

    Female Philanthropy in the Interwar World: Between Self and Other, London, 2019.

Conford, Philip, 'The Natural Order: Organic Husbandry, Society and Religion in Britain, 1924–1953', unpublished PhD, University of Reading, 2000.

    'Finance Versus Farming: Rural Reconstruction and Economic Reform 1894–1955', *Rural History* 13 (2002), 225–41.

    '"Somewhere Quite Different": The Seventies Generation of Organic Activists and Their Context', *Rural History* 19 (2010), 217–34.

Connolly, Philip, *Evacuees at Dartington 1940–1945*, [n.p.], 1990.

Cooper, Andrew Fenton, *British Agricultural Policy 1912–1936: A Study in Conservative Politics*, Manchester, 1989.

Cooper, Davina, *Everyday Utopias: The Conceptual Life of Promising Spaces*, Durham, 2014.

Cooper, Emmanuel, *Bernard Leach: Life & Work*, New Haven, CT and London, 2003.

Cooper, Jonathan, 'Friends of Dorothy', unpublished talk given at Dartington's first queer arts festival, 'A Dartington Outing', held in 2017 [access by courtesy of the author].

Cornford, Thomas, 'The English Theatre Studios of Michael Chekhov and Michel Saint-Denis, 1935–65', unpublished PhD, University of Warwick, 2012.

Corrywright, Dominic, 'Network Spirituality: The Schumacher-Resurgence-Kumar Nexus', *Journal of Contemporary Religion* 19 (2004), 311–27.

Cox, Peter, 'Creating a National Exception', *Oxford Review of Education*, 3 (1977), 135–45.

    The Arts at Dartington, 1940–1983: A Personal Account, Exeter, 2005.

Cox, Peter, Michael Cardew, Marguette Wildenhaim, Patrick Heron, Robin Tanner and John Bowers, *The Report of the International Conference of Craftsmen in Pottery and Textiles at Dartington Hall, Totnes, Devon, July 17–27, 1952*, Totnes, 1954.

Cox, Peter and Jack Dobbs (eds.), *Imogen Holst at Dartington*, Dartington, 1988.

Craig, F. W. S., *British Parliamentary Election Results, 1918–1949*, Chichester, 1983 [1969].

Crawford, Alan, 'Ideas and Objects: The Arts and Crafts Movement in Britain', *Design Issues* 13 (1997), 15–26.

Crook, Tom, 'Craft and the Dialogics of Modernity: The Arts and Crafts Movement in Late-Victorian and Edwardian England', *The Journal of Modern Craft* 2 (2009), 17–32.

Cross, Stephen J., and William R. Albury, 'Walter B. Cannon, L. J. Henderson and the Organic Analogy', *Osiris* 3 (1987), 165–92.

Crossley, Robert, 'Olaf Stapledon and the Idea of Science Fiction', *Modern Fiction Studies* 32 (1986), 21–42

Crozier, Ivan, '"All the World's a Stage": Dora Russell, Norman Haire, and the 1929 London World League for Sexual Reform Congress', *Journal of the History of Sexuality* 12 (2003), 16–37.

Cunningham, Peter, 'Innovators, Networks and Structures: Towards a Prosopography of Progressivism', *History of Education* 30 (2001), 433–51.

De la Iglesia, Maria, *Dartington Hall School: Staff Memories of the Early Years*, Exeter, 1996.

Dearlove, Pamela, 'Fen Drayton, Cambridgeshire: An Estate of the Land Settlement Association', in Joan Thirsk (ed.) *The English Rural Landscape*, Oxford, 2000, 323–35.

Delap, Lucy, *The Feminist Avant-Garde: Transatlantic Encounters of the Early Twentieth Century*, Cambridge, 2007.

  '"Disgusting Details Which Are Best Forgotten": Disclosures of Child Sexual Abuse in Twentieth-Century Britain', *Journal of British Studies* 57 (2018), 79–107.

Delap, Lucy and Sue Morgan (eds.), *Men, Masculinities and Religious Change in Twentieth-Century Britain*, Basingstoke, Hampshire, 2013.

Den Otter, Sandra, '"Thinking in Communities": Late Nineteenth-Century Liberals, Idealists and the Retrieval of Community', *Parliamentary History* 16 (1997), 67–84.

Denham, Andrew and Mark Garnett, *British Think-Tanks and the Climate of Opinion*, London, 1998.

Dixey, Roger N. (ed.), *International Explorations of Agricultural Economics. A Tribute to the Inspiration of Leonard Knight Elmhirst*, Iowa, 1964.

Dixon, Joy, *Divine Feminine: Theosophy and Feminism in England*, Baltimore, MD and London, 2001.

Dixon, Thomas, *The Invention of Altruism: Making Moral Meanings in Victorian Britain*, Oxford, 2008.

Doan, Laura, 'Topsy-turvydom: Gender Inversion, Sapphism, and the Great War', *GLQ: A Journal of Lesbian and Gay Studies* 12 (2006) 517–42.

  Disturbing Practices: History, Sexuality, and Women's Experiences of Modern War, Chicago, 2013.

Doerr, Evelyn, *Rudolf Laban: The Dancer of the Crystal*, Lanham, MD and Plymouth, UK, 2008.

Donnachie, Ian L., *Robert Owen: Owen of New Lanark and New Harmony*, East Linton, 2000.

Douthit, Richard Pfaff, 'A Historical Study of Group Discussion Principles and Techniques Developed by "The Inquiry", 1922–1933', unpublished PhD, Louisiana State University, 1961.

Dutta, Krishna and Andrew Robinson, *Rabindranath Tagore: The Myriad-Minded Man*, London, 1995.

Dutta, Krishna and Andrew Robinson (eds.), *Selected Letters of Rabindranath Tagore*, Cambridge, 1997.

Ellert, JoAnn C., 'The Bauhaus and Black Mountain College', *The Journal of General Education* 24 (1972), 144–52.

Elliott, David, 'Gropius in England' in Charlotte Benton (ed.), *A Different World: Emigré Architects in Britain 1928–1958*, London, 1995, 107–24.

Elliot, John, 'Pick, Frank (1878–1941)', rev. Michael Robbins, *Oxford Dictionary of National Biography*, Oxford University Press, www.oxforddnb.com/view/article/35522.

Eros, Paul, '"One of the Most Penetrating Minds in England": Gerald Heard and the British Intelligentsia of the Interwar Period', unpublished PhD, University of Oxford, 2011.

Etherington, Ben, *Literary Primitivism*, Stanford, CA, 2018.

Falby, Alison, 'The Modern Confessional: Anglo-American Religious Groups and the Emergence of Lay Psychotherapy', *Journal of the History of the Behavioural Sciences* 38 (2003) 251–67.

    Between the Pigeonholes: Gerald Heard, 1889–1971, Newcastle, 2008.

    'Maude Royden's Sacramental Theology of Sex and Love', *Anglican and Episcopal History* 76 (2010), 124–43.

Farmer, Will and Rob Higgins, *Portmeirion Pottery*, Oxford, 2012.

Field, John, 'An Anti-Urban Education? Work Camps and Ideals of the Land in Interwar Britain', *Rural History* 23 (2012), 213–28.

Fishman, Sterling, 'The History of Childhood Sexuality', *Journal of Contemporary History* 17 (1982), 269–83.

Fitzgerald, Robert, *Rowntree and the Marketing Revolution, 1862–1969*, Cambridge, 1995.

Foster, Roger, 'The Therapeutic Spirit of Neoliberalism', *Political Theory* 44 (2016), 82–105.

Foss, Brian, 'Message and Medium: Government Patronage, National Identity and National Culture in Britain, 1939–45', *Oxford Art Journal* 14 (1991), 52–7.

    War Paint: Art, War, State and Identity in Britain, 1939–1945, New Haven and London, 2007.

Fox-Leonard, Boudicca, 'Is This the Most Eccentric Town in Britain?', *The Telegraph*, 6 January 2018, www.telegraph.co.uk/travel/destinations/europe/united-kingdom/articles/totnes-what-to-see-and-do/.

Francis, Martin, 'The Domestication of the Male? Recent Research on Nineteenth- and Twentieth-Century British Masculinity', *Historical Journal* 45 (2002), 637–52.

Franklin, J. Jeffrey, *Spirit Matters: Occult Beliefs, Alternative Religions, and the Crisis of Faith in Victorian Britain*, Ithaca, NY and London, 2018.

Freeden, Michael, 'Eugenics and Progressive Thought: A Study in Ideological Affinity', *Historical Journal* 22 (1979), 645–71.

Liberalism Divided: A Study in British Political Thought, 1914–1939, Oxford, 1986.

Liberal Languages: Ideological Imaginations and Twentieth-Century Progressive Thought, Princeton, 2005.

Freshwater, Helen, 'The Allure of the Archive: Performance and Censorship', *Moveable Type* 3 (2007), 5–24.

Fuchs, Eckhardt, 'Educational Sciences, Morality and Politics: International Educational Congresses in the Early Twentieth Century', *Paedagogica Historica* 40 (2004), 757–84.

Gandhi, Leela, 'Other(s) Worlds: Mysticism and Radicalism at the *Fin de Siècle*', *Critical Horizons* 2 (2001), 227–53.

Affective Communities: Anticolonial Thought, Fin-de-Siècle Radicalism, and the Politics of Friendship, Durham and London, 2006.

Gardiner, Juliet, '"Searching for the Gleam": Finding Solutions to the Political and Social Problems of 1930s Britain', *History Workshop Journal* 72 (2011), 103–17.

Geiger, Roger L., *To Advance Knowledge: The Growth of American Research Universities 1900–1940*, [n.p]: Routledge, 2017.

Gilbert, Jess, 'Rural Sociology and Democratic Planning in the Third New Deal', *Agricultural History* 82 (2008), 421–38.

Planning Democracy: Agrarian Intellectuals and the Intended New Deal, New Haven, 2015.

Gildart, Keith, 'Séance Sitters, Ghost Hunters, Spiritualists, and Theosophists: Esoteric Belief and Practice in the Parliamentary Labour Party, c.1929–51', *Twentieth Century British History* 29 (2018), 357–87.

Godley, Andrew and Bridget Williams, 'Democratizing Luxury and the Contentious "Invention of the Technological Chicken" in Britain', *The Business History Review* 83 (2009), 267–90.

Goldman, Lawrence, 'Education as Politics: University Adult Education in England Since 1870', *Oxford Review of Education* 25 (1999), 89–101.

Dons and Workers, Oxford, 1995.

Gordon, Leonard A., 'Wealth Equals Wisdom? The Rockefeller and Ford Foundations in India', *The Annals of the American Academy of Political and Social Science* 554 (1997), 104–16.

Gorman, Daniel, 'Ecumenical Internationalism: Willoughby Dickinson, the League of Nations and the World Alliance for Promoting International Friendship through the Churches', *Journal of Contemporary History* 45 (2010), 51–73.

The Emergence of International Society in the 1920s, Cambridge, 2011.

Gorman, Deborah, 'Dora and Bertrand Russell and Beacon Hill School', *The Journal of Bertrand Russell Studies* 25 (2005), 39–76.

Gould, Karolyn, 'The Modest Benefactor', *Cornell Alumni News* 3 (1975), 19–21.

Green, Martin, *Children of the Sun: A Narrative of 'Decadence' in England After 1918*, London, 1977.
   Mountain of Truth: The Counterculture Begins, Ascona, 1900–1920, Hanover; London, 1989.
Gribble, David (ed.), *That's All Folks: Dartington Hall School Remembered*, Crediton, 1987.
Griffiths, Clare V. J., *Labour and the Countryside: The Politics of Rural Britain, 1918–1939*, Oxford, 2007.
Griffiths, Richard, *Patriotism Perverted: Captain Ramsay, the Right Club, and British Anti-Semitism, 1938–40*, London, 2015 [1998].
Grimley, Matthew *Citizenship, Community, and the Church of England: Liberal Anglican Theories of the State Between the Wars*, Oxford, 2004.
Grzegorz, Kosc, Clara Juncker, Sharon Moneith and Britte Waldschmidt-Nelson (eds.), *The Transatlantic Sixties: Europe and the United States in the Counterculture Decade*, Bielefeld: [transcript], 2013.
Gupta, Uma Das, 'In Pursuit of a Different Freedom: Tagore's World University at Santiniketan', *India International Centre Quarterly* 29 (2002), 25–38.
   'Tagore's Ideas of Social Action and the Sriniketan Experiment of Rural Reconstruction, 1922–41', *University of Toronto Quarterly* 77 (2008), 992–1004.
Hall, J. M., *Juvenile Reform in the Progressive Era – William R. George and the Junior Republic Movement*, Ithaca, NY, 1971.
Hall, Lesley A., '"A City That We Shall Never Find"? The Search for a Community of Fellow Progressive Spirits in the UK Between the Wars', *Family & Community* 18 (2015), 24–36.
Hankins, Gabriel *Interwar Modernism and the Liberal World Order: Offices, Institutions, and Aesthetics after 1919*, Cambridge, 2019.
Hardy, Dennis, *Utopian England: Community Experiments, 1900–1945*, London, 2000.
Harrington, Anne, *Reenchanted Science: Holism in German Culture from Wilhelm II to Hitler*, Princeton and Chichester, 1996.
Harris, Alexandra, *Romantic Moderns: English Writers, Artists and the Imagination from Virginia Woolf to John Piper*, London, 2010.
Harris, Jose, 'Political Thought and the Welfare State 1870–1940: An Intellectual Framework for British Social Policy', *Past and Present* 135 (1992), 116–41.
   'War and Social History: Britain and the Home Front During the Second World War', *Contemporary European History* 1 (1992), 17–35.
   Private Lives, Public Spirit: A Social History of Britain, 1870–1914, London, 1993.
Harris, Ruth, 'Rolland, Gandhi and Madeleine Slade: Spiritual Politics, France and the Wider World', *French History* 27 (2013), 579–99.
Harrison, Charles, *English Art and Modernism 1900–1939*, New Haven, CT and London, 1994.
Harrison, Rachel Esther, 'Dorothy Elmhirst and the Visual Arts at Dartington Hall 1925–1945', unpublished PhD, University of Plymouth, 2002.
Harrod, Tanya, *The Crafts in Britain in the Twentieth Century*, Yale, 1999.
Harrop, Dorothy A., *A History of the Gregynog Press*, Middlesex, 1980.

Harvey, Charles and Jon Press, 'John Ruskin and the Ethical Foundations of Morris & Company, 1861–96', *Journal of Business Ethics* 14 (1995), 181–94.

Hazareesingh, Kissoonsingh (ed.), *A Rich Harvest: The Complete Tagore/Elmhirst Correspondence and Other Writings*, Stanley, Rose-Hill, Mauritius, c.1992.

Hazelgrove, Jenny, *Spiritualism and British Society Between the Wars*, Manchester, 2000.

Heelas, Paul, *The New Age Movement: The Celebration of the Self and the Sacralization of Modernity*, Oxford, 1996.

Hemmings, Ray, *Fifty Years of Freedom: A Study of the Development of the Ideas of A.S. Neill*, London, 1972.

Henriksen, Ingrid, 'The Contribution of Agriculture to Economic Growth in Denmark, 1870–1939', in Pedro Lains and Vincente Pinilla (eds.), *Agriculture and Development in Europe Since 1870*, London, 2009, 117–47.

Hilson, Mary and Joseph Melling, 'Public Gifts and Political Identities: Sir Richard Acland, Common Wealth, and the Moral Politics of Land Ownership in the 1940s', *Twentieth Century British History* 11 (2000), 156–82.

Hilton, David Edward, 'Film and the Dartington Experience', unpublished PhD, University of Plymouth, 2004.

Hilton, Matthew, 'Michael Young and the Consumer Movement', *Contemporary British History* 19 (2005), 311–19.

Himmelfarb, Gertrude, 'The Age of Philanthropy', *The Wilson Quarterly* 21 (1997), 48–55.

Hinton, James, *Women, Social Leadership, and the Second World War*, Oxford, 2002.

Hogan, Anne and Andrew Bradstock (eds.), *Women of Faith in Victorian Culture: Reassessing the Angel in the House*, Basingstoke, 1998.

Hollander, Paul, *Political Pilgrims: Travels of Western Intellectuals to the Soviet Union, China and Cuba 1928–1978*, New York, 1981.

Holmes, Colin J., 'Science and the Farmer: The Development of the Agricultural Advisory Service in England and Wales, 1900–1939', *The Agricultural History Review* 36 (1988), 77–86.

Holmes, Edmond, *The Tragedy of Education*, London, 1913.

Honeck, Mischa, 'The Power of Innocence: Anglo-American Scouting and the Boyification of Empire', *Geschichte und Gesellschaft* 42 (2016), 441–66.

Hopkins, Rob, 'New Report: "So What Does Transition Town Totnes Actually Do"?', *Transition Culture* [transitionculture.org/2010/11/23/new-report-so-what-does-transition-town-totnes-actually-do/].

'The Heart of the Matter', 22 February 2020, *The Independent*, www .independent.co.uk/independentpremium/long-reads/saving-dartington-hall-trust-country-estate-community-a9331091.html.

Houlbrook, Matt, 'Thinking Queer: The Social and the Sexual in Interwar Britain', in Brian Lewis (ed.) *British Queer History: New Approaches and Perspectives*, Manchester, 2013, 134–64.

Howkins, Alun, *The Death of Rural England: A Social History of the Countryside Since 1900*, London, 2003.

Hubble, Nick, *Mass-Observation and Everyday Life: Culture, History, Theory*, Basingstoke, 2006.

Hutchinson Guest, Ann, 'The Jooss-Leeder School at Dartington Hall', *Dance Chronicle* 29 (2006), 161–94.

Hynes, Samuel, *The Auden Generation: Literature and Politics in England in the 1930s*, London, 1976.

Iglesias, Christine, 'Modernist Unselfing: Religious Experience and British Literature 1900–1945', unpublished PhD thesis, Columbia University, 2018.

Immerwahr, Daniel, *Thinking Small: The United States and the Lure of Community Development*, Harvard University Press: Cambridge, MA and London, 2015.

Jackson Lears, T. J., *No Place of Grace: Antimodernism and the Transformation of American Culture, 1880–1920*, Chicago and London, 1981.

Jackson, Mark, *The Age of Stress: Science and the Search for Stability*, Oxford: Oxford University Press, 2013.

Jarvis, Pam and Betty Liebovich, 'British Nurseries, Head and Heart: McMillan, Owen and the Genesis of the Education/Care Dichotomy', *Women's History Review* 24 (2015), 917–37.

Jefferies, Matthew and Mike Tyldesley (eds.), *Rolf Gardiner: Folk, Nature and Culture in Interwar Britain*, Farnham, 2011.

Jeffs, T., *Henry Morris: Village Colleges, Community Education and the Ideal Order*, Nottingham, 1998.

Jenkins, Celia M., 'The Professional Middle Class and the Social Origins of Progressivism: A Case Study of the New Education Fellowship 1920–1950', unpublished PhD, Institute of Education, University of London, 1989.

'New Education and Its Emancipatory Interests (1920–1950)', *History of Education* 29 (2000), 139–51.

Jenkins, Philip, *The Great and Holy War: How World War I Became a Religious Crusade*, Oxford, 2014.

Jeremiah, David, 'Beautiful Things: Dartington and the Art of the Potter and Weaver', in Tanya Harrod (ed.), *Obscure Objects of Desire: Reviewing the Crafts in the Twentieth Century*, London, 1997, 163–76.

'Dartington – A Modern Adventure', in Smiles (ed.), *Going Modern and Being British: Art, Architecture and Design in Devon c. 1910–1960*, Exeter, 1998, 43–78.

Architecture and Design for the Family in Britain, 1900–1970, New York, 2000.

'Dartington Hall – A Landscape of an Experiment in Rural Reconstruction', in Paul Brassley, Jeremy Burchardt and Lynne Thompson (eds.), *The English Countryside Between the Wars: Regeneration or Decline?*, New York, 2006, 116–31.

'Motoring and the British Countryside', *Rural History* 21 (2010), 233–50.

Jewett, Andrew, *Science, Democracy, and the American University: From the Civil War to the Cold War*, Cambridge, 2012.

Karim, Farham, *Of Greater Dignity Than Riches: Austerity and Housing Design in India*, Pittsburgh, 2019.

Keith, William M., *Democracy as Discussion: Civic Education and the America Forum Movement*, Lanham, MD, 2007.

Kennedy, Maev, 'Row as Dartington Hall Auctions Off Its Treasures', 13 November 2011, *The Guardian*, www.theguardian.com/artanddesign/2011/nov/13/dartington-hall-art-sale.

Kennerley, Alston, *The Making of the University of Plymouth*, Plymouth, 2000.

Kent, John, *William Temple: Church, State, and Society in Britain, 1880–1950*, Cambridge, 1992.

Kent, Susan Kingsley, *Making Peace: The Reconstruction of Gender in Interwar Britain*, Princeton, 1993.

Kern, Stephen, *The Culture of Time and Space, 1880–1918*, [n.p.], 1983.

Kett, Joseph F., *The Pursuit of Knowledge Under Difficulties*, Stanford, 1994.

Kew, Carole, 'From Weimar Movement Choir to Nazi Community Dance: The Rise and Fall of Rudolf Laban's "Festkultur"', *Dance Research: The Journal of the Society For Dance Research* 17 (1999), 73–96.

Kidel, Mark, *Beyond the Classroom: Dartington's Experiments in Education*, Devon, 1990.

Kikuchi, Yuko, 'The Myth of Yanagi's Originality: The Formation of *Mingei* Theory in its Social and Historical Context', *Journal of Design History* 7 (1994), 247–66.

Kimble, Gregory A., and Michael Wertheimer (eds.), *Portraits of Pioneers in Psychology*, New York and London, 1998.

King, Laura, 'Future Citizens: Cultural and Political Conceptions of Children in Britain, 1930–1950s', *Twentieth Century British History* 27 (2016), 389–411.

King, Richard, *Orientalism and Religion: Postcolonial Theory, India, and the 'Mystic East'*, London, 1999.

King, Walter, 'The Lost Worlds of Dartington Hall', *Totnes Review* 2 (2007), 50–9.

Kirke, Alice, 'Education in Interwar Rural England: Community, Schooling, and Voluntarism', unpublished PhD thesis, University College London, 2016.

Kitchener, Richard F., 'Bertrand Russell's Flirtation with Behaviorism', *Behavior and Philosophy* 32 (2004), 275–91.

Kitto, Pat, *Dartington in Conisbrough*, London, 2010.

Klingensmith, Daniel, *One Valley and a Thousand: Dams, Nationalism, and Development*, Oxford, 2007.

Koven, Seth, *Slumming: Sexual and Social Politics in Victorian London*, Princeton, 2004.

'The "Sticky Sediment" of Daily Life: Radical Domesticity, Revolutionary Christianity, and the Problem of Wealth in Britain from the 1880s to the 1930s', *Representations* 120 (2012), 39–82.

The Match Girl and the Heiress, Oxford, 2015.

Kowol, Kit, 'An Experiment in Conservative Modernity: Interwar Conservatism and Henry Ford's English Farms', *Journal of British Studies* 55 (2016), 781–805.

Kripal, Jeffrey J., *Esalen: America and the Religion of No Religion*, Chicago, 2007.

Kripalani, Krishna, *Rabindranath Tagore: A Biography*, London, 1962.

Kumar, Krishan, 'Ideology and Sociology: Reflections on Karl Mannheim's "Ideology and Utopia"', *Journal of Political Ideologies* 11 (2006), 169–81.

Lambert, Royston, 'What Dartington Will Do', *New Society* 13 (1969), 159–61.

Lash, Joseph P., *Eleanor and Franklin*, London, 1972.

Lattin, Don, *Distilled Spirits*, Berkeley; Los Angeles, 2012.

Lawrence, Christopher and Anna-K. Mayer (eds.), *Regenerating England: Science, Medicine and Culture in Interwar Britain*, Amsterdam, 2000.

Lawrence, Christopher and George Weisz (eds.), *Greater Than the Parts: Holism in Biomedicine, 1920–1950*, New York, 1998.

Lawrence, Jon, 'The Transformation of British Public Politics after the First World War', *Past and Present* 190 (2006), 185–216.

Lawson, Max, 'N.F.S. Grundtvig', *Prospects: The Quarterly Review of Comparative Education* 23 (1993), 613–23.

Lee, Jonathan M., 'A Year Made in Dartington', 2011, www.jonathanmlee.net/2016/05/01/a-year-made-in-dartington-dartington-hall-trust/.

Lee, Lesley Fox, 'The Dalton Plan and the Loyal, Capable Intelligent Citizen', *History of Education* 29 (2000), 129–38.

LeMahieu, D. L., *A Culture for Democracy: Mass Communication and the Cultivated Mind in Britain Between the Wars*, Oxford, 1988.

Leventhal, F. M., '"The Best for the Most": CEMA and State Sponsorship of the Arts in Wartime, 1939–1945', *Twentieth Century British History* 1 (1990), 289–317.

'"A Tonic to the Nation": The Festival of Britain, 1951', *Albion: A Quarterly Journal Concerned With British Studies* 27 (1995), 445–53.

Levitas, Ruth, *Utopia and Method: The Imaginary Reconstitution of Society*, Basingstoke, 2013.

Levy, David W., *Herbert Croly of the New Republic: The Life and Thought of an American Progressive*, Princeton and Guildford, 1985.

Light, Alison, *Forever England: Femininity, Literature and Conservatism Between the Wars*, London, 1991.

Mrs Woolf and the Servants: The Hidden Heart of Domestic Service, London, 2007.

Limond, David, 'From a Position of Educational Prominence to One of Almost Total Obscurity? Royston James Lambert and Dartington Hall School', *Journal of Historical Biography* 12 (2012), 60–88.

Lineman, Denis, 'Regional Survey and the Economic Geographies of Britain 1930–1939', *Transactions of the Institute of British Geographers* 28 (2003), 96–122.

Loane, Edward, 'William Temple and the World Council of Churches: Church Unity "Lite"', in *William Temple and Church Unity: The Politics and Practice of Ecumenical Theology*, New York, 2016, 153–77.

Lofton, Kathryn, 'Considering the Neoliberal in American Religion', in Jan Stievermann, Philip Goff and Detlef Junker (eds.), *Religion and the Marketplace in the United States*, Oxford and New York, 2015, 269–88.

Long, Vicky, 'Industrial Homes, Domestic Factories: The Convergence of Public and Private Space in Interwar Britain', *Journal of British Studies* 50 (2011), 434–64.

Longhurst, Noel, 'Twinned with Narnia? The Postcapitalist Possibilities of a Countercultural Place', unpublished PhD, University of Liverpool, 2010.

'The Emergence of an Alternative Milieu: Conceptualising the Nature of Alternative Places', *Environment and Planning* 45 (2013), 2100–19.

Loorbach, Derk, Flor Avelina, Alex Haxeltine, Julia M. Wittmay, Tim O'Riordan, Paul Weaver and René Kemp, 'The Economic Crisis as a Game Changer? Exploring the Role of Social Construction in Sustainability Transitions', *Ecology and Society* 21 (2016), doi:10.5751/ES-08761-210415.

Lovelock, James, *Gaia: The Practical Science of Planetary Medicine*, [n.p.], 1991.

Luckin, Bill, *Questions of Power: Electricity and Environment in Inter-War Britain*, New York, 1990.

MacCarthy, Fiona, *Eric Gill*, London, 1989.

William Morris: A Life for Our Time, London, 2015.

MacClancy, Jeremy, 'Mass Observation, Surrealism, Social Anthropology: A Present-Day Assessment', *New Formations* 44 (2001), 90–9.

MacDonald, Claire, 'Desire Paths: John Cage's Transatlantic Crossing', *PAJ: A Journal of Performance and Art* 34 (2012), 35–46.

Madge, Pauline, 'Design, Ecology, Technology: A Historiographical Review', *Journal of Design History* 6 (1993), 149–66.

Madison, James H., 'John D. Rockefeller's General Education Board and the Rural School Problem in the Midwest, 1900–1930', *History of Education Quarterly* 24 (1984), 181–99.

Maloney, C. J., *Back to the Land: Arthurdale, FDR's New Deal, and the Costs of Economic Planning*, Hoboken, NJ, 2011.

Mandler, Peter, 'Politics and the English Landscape Since the First World War', *Huntingdon Library Quarterly* 55 (1992), 459–76.

The Fall and Rise of the Stately Home, New Haven, CT and London, 1997.

'Against Englishness: English Culture and the Limits to Rural Nostalgia, 1850–1940', *Transactions of the Historical Society* 7 (1997), 155–75.

Marks, Steven G., 'Abstract Art and the Regeneration of Mankind', *New England Review* 24 (2003), 53–79.

Martin, D. E., 'Dickinson, Goldsworthy Lowes (1862–1932)', *Oxford Dictionary of National Biography*, Oxford University Press, www.oxforddnb.com/view/article/32815.

Martin, Jay, *The Education of John Dewey, A Biography*, New York, 2002.

Marwick, Arthur, 'Middle Opinion in the 1930s: Planning, Progress and Political Agreement', *English Historical Review* 79 (1964), 285–98.

Marx, Leo, *The Machine in the Garden: Technology and the Pastoral Ideal in America*, Oxford, 1999 [1964].

Massey, Doreen, 'Places and their Pasts', *History Workshop Journal* 39 (1995), 182–92.

Mathieson, Margaret, 'English Progressive Educators and the Creative Child', *British Journal of Educational Studies* 38 (1990), 365–80.

Matless, David, 'Definitions of England, 1928–89: Preservation, Modernism and the Nature of the Nation', *Built Environment* 16 (1990), 179–91.

'Nature, the Modern and the Mystic: Tales from Early Twentieth Century Geography', *Transactions of the Institute of British Geographers* 16 (1991), 272–86.

'Regional Surveys and Local Knowledges: The Geographical Imagination in Britain 1918–1939', *Transactions of the Institute of British Geographers* 17 (1993), 464–80.

Landscape and Englishness, London, 1998.

'Topographic Culture: Nikolaus Pevsner and the Buildings of England', *History Workshop Journal* 54 (2002), 73–99.

Mayer, F. Stephan, *Transforming Psychological Worldviews to Confront Climate Change: A Clearer Vision, A Different Path*, California, 2018.

McCarthy, Helen, *The British People and the League of Nations: Democracy, Citizenship and Internationalism, c.1918–45*, [n.p.], 2013.

McCarthy, Kathleen, D., 'From Government to Grass-Roots Reform: The Ford Foundation's Population Programmes in South Asia, 1959–1981', *Voluntas: International Journal of Voluntary and Non-Profit Organisations* 6 (1995), 292–316.

McGovern, Charles, F., *Sold American: Consumption and Citizenship, 1890–1945*, Chapel Hill, 2006.

McKibbin, Ross, *Classes and Cultures: England 1918–1951*, Oxford, 1998.

Meckier, Jerome, 'Mysticism or Misty Schism? Huxley Studies Since World War II', *The British Studies Monitor* 5 (1974), 165–77.

Meller, Helen E., *Towns, Plans, and Society in Modern Britain*, Cambridge, 1997.

Menard, Louis, *The Metaphysical Club*, New York, 2001.

Mendelsohn, Everett and Helga Nowotny (eds.), *Nineteen Eighty-Four: Science Between Utopia and Dystopia*, Dordrecht and Boston, 1984.

Meredith, Anne, 'From Ideals to Reality: The Women's Smallholding Colony at Lingfield, 1920–1939', *Agricultural History Review* 54 (2006), 105–21.

Mingay, G. E., *A Social History of the English Countryside*, London, 1990.

Minihan, Janet, *The Nationalization of Culture: The Development of State Subsidies to the Arts in Great Britain*, New York, 1977.

Minion, Mark, 'The Fabian Society and Europe During the 1940s: The Search For a "Socialist Foreign Policy"', *European History Quarterly* 30 (2000), 237–70.

Misukiewicz, Claude, 'Lewis L. Lorwin and the Promise of Planning: Class, Collectivism, and Empire in US Economic Planning Debates, 1931–1941', unpublished PhD, Georgia State University, 2015.

Mitter, Partha, 'Decentering Modernism: Art History and Avant-Garde Art from the Periphery', *The Art Bulletin* 90 (2008), 531–48.

Monroe, John Warne, *Laboratories of Faith: Mesmerism, Spiritualism, and Occultism in Modern France*, Ithaca, NY and London, 2008.

'Surface Tensions: Empire, Parisian Modernism, and "Authenticity" in African Sculptures, 1917–1939', *American Historical Review* 117 (2012), 445–75.

Morefield, Jeanne, *Covenants Without Swords: Idealist Liberalism and the Spirit of Empire*, Princeton, 2005.

Morgan, Sue, '"The Word Made Flesh": Women, Religion and Sexual Cultures', *Women, Gender and Religious Cultures in Britain, 1800–1940*, (eds) Sue Morgan and Jacqueline de Vries, New York, 2010, 159–87.

'"Sex and Common-Sense": Maude Royden, Religion, and Modern Sexuality', *Journal of British Studies* 52 (2013), 153–78.

Morris, Jeremy, 'The Strange Death of Christian Britain: Another Look at the Secularization Debate', *The Historical Journal* 46 (2003), 963–76.

'Secularization and Religious Experience: Arguments in the Historiography of Modern British Religion', *The Historical Journal* 55 (2012), 195–219.

Morris-Suzuki, Tessa, 'Beyond Utopia: New Villages and Living Politics in Modern Japan and Across Frontiers', *History Workshop Journal* 85 (2018), 47–71.

Mukherjee, Sumita, 'The Reception Given to Sadhu Sundar Singh, the Itinerant Indian Christian "Mystic", in Interwar Britain', Interwar Britain, *Immigrants & Minorities* 35 (2017), 21–39.

Neaman, Elliot Y., *A Dubious Past: Ernst Jünger and the Politics of Literature After Nazism*, Berkeley, CA and London, 1999.

Neima, Anna, 'Dartington Hall and the Quest for "Life in its Completeness", 1925–45', *History Workshop Journal* 88 (2019), 111–33.

'The Politics of Community Drama in Interwar England', *Twentieth Century British History* 31 (2020), 170–96.

The Utopians: Six Attempts to Build the Perfect Society, London, 2021.

Nelson, Adam R., *Education and Democracy: The Meaning of Alexander Meiklejohn, 1872–1964*, Wisconsin, 2001.

Neuman, Johanna, *Gilded Suffragists: The New York Socialites Who Fought for Women's Right to Vote*, New York, 2017.

Nicholas, Larraine, *Dancing in Utopia: Dartington Hall and Its Dancers*, Alton, Hampshire, 2007.

Nicholson, Virginia, *Among the Bohemians: Experiments in Living 1900–1939*, London, 2003.

Nurser, Canon John, 'The "Ecumenical Movement" Churches, "Global Orders", and Human Rights: 1938–1948', *Human Rights Quarterly* 25 (2003), 841–81.

Nuttall, Jeremy *Psychological Socialism: The Labour Party and Qualities of Mind and Character, 1931 to the Present*, Manchester, 2006.

Overy, Richard, *The Morbid Age: Britain Between the Wars*, London, 2009.

Owen, Alex, *The Darkened Room: Women, Power and Spiritualism in Late Victorian England*, London, 1989.

'Occultism and the "Modern" Self in *Fin-de-Siècle* Britain', in Martin Daunton and Bernhard Rieger (eds.), *Meanings of Modernity: Britain from the Late-Victorian Era to World War II*, Oxford, 2001, 71–96.

The Place of Enchantment: British Occultism and the Culture of the Modern, Chicago and London, 2004.

'The "Religious Sense" in a Post-War Secular Age', *Past and Present* 1 (2006), 159–77.

Parascandola, John, 'Organismic and Holistic Concepts in the Thought of L. J. Henderson', *Journal of the History of Biology* 4 (1971), 63–113.

Parker, David H., '"The Talent at Its Command": The First World War and the Vocational Aspect of Education, 1914–39', *History of Education Quarterly* 35 (1995), 237–59.

Parker, Martin, George Cheney, Valérie Fournier and Chris Land (eds.), *The Routledge Companion to Alternative Organization*, London and New York, 2014.

Parmar, Inderjeet, 'Foundation Networks and America Hegemony', *European Journal of American Studies* 7 (2012), 2–25.

Pedersen, Susan and Peter Mandler (eds.), *After the Victorians: Private Conscience and Public Duty in Modern Britain: Essays in Memory of John Clive*, London and New York, 1994.

Perry, Roland, *Last of the Cold War Spies: The Life of Michael Straight, the Only American in Britain's Cambridge Spy Ring*, Cambridge, MA, 2005.

Peters Scott, J., '"Every Farmer Should Be Awakened": Liberty Hyde Bailey's Vision of Agricultural Extension Work', *Agricultural History* 80 (2006), 190–219.

Pfeiffer, John R., Review of Mark Kidel's *Beyond the Classroom*, *Utopian Studies* 2 (1991), 204–7.

Phillips, Anne, *Holistic Education: Learning from Schumacher College*, Totnes, 2008.

Phillips, Paul T., 'One World, One Faith: The Quest for Unity in Julian Huxley's Religion of Evolutionary Humanism', *Journal of the History of Ideas* 268 (2007), 613–33.

Pinder, John (ed.), *Fifty Years of Political and Economic Planning: Looking Forward 1931–1981*, London, 1981.

Ponsonby, Julia, 'From Farm to Feast', 2009, www.resurgence.org/magazine/article2824-from-farm-to-feast.html.

Ponzio, Alessio, *Shaping the New Man: Youth Training Regimes in Fascist Italy and Nazi Germany*, Madison, 2015.

Prasad, Ram Chandra, 'The Organisation Pattern of the River Valley Projects in India: A Study of the Board vis-à-vis the Public Corporation', *The Indian Journal of Political Science* 22 (1961), 214–25.

Preston-Dunlop, Valerie, *Rudolf Laban: An Extraordinary Life*, London, 1998.

Prochaska, Frank, *Women and Philanthropy in Nineteenth-Century England*, Oxford, 1980.
  The Voluntary Impulse: Philanthropy in Modern Britain, London, 1998.
  Christianity and Social Service in Modern Britain: The Disinherited Spirit, Oxford and New York, 2006.

Pugh, Martin, 'Astor, Nancy Witcher, Viscountess Astor (1879–1964)', *Oxford Dictionary of National Biography*, Oxford University Press, www.oxforddnb.com/view/article/30489.

Punch, Maurice, *Progressive Retreat: A Sociological Study of Dartington Hall School and Some of Its Former Pupils*, Cambridge, 1977.

Quayum, Mohammad A., 'Imagining "One World": Rabindranath Tagore's Critique of Nationalism', *Interdisciplinary Literary Studies* 7 (2006), 33–52.

Raeburn, J. R. and J. O. Jones, *The History of the International Association of Agricultural Economists: Towards Rural Welfare Worldwide*, Aldershot, 1990.

Rauchway, Eric, 'A Gentlemen's Club in a Woman's Sphere: How Dorothy Whitney Straight Created *The New Republic*', *Journal of Women's History* 11 (1999), 60–85.
  The Refuge of Affections: Family and American Reform Politics, 1900–1920, New York, 2001.

Ree, Harry, *Educator Extraordinary: The Life and Achievements of Henry Morris, 1889–1961*, London, 1973.

Reed, Christopher, 'Sublimation and Eccentricity in the Art of Mark Tobey: Seattle at Midcentury', in *Japanese Aesthetics and Western Masculinities*, New York, 2017, 201–90.

Renwick, Chris, *Lost Biological Roots: A History of Futures Past*, Basingstoke, 2012.

Richards, Sam, *Dartington College of Arts: Learning by Doing. A Biography of a College*, Totnes, 2015.

Ritschel, Daniel, 'A Corporatist Economy in Britain? Capitalist Planning For Industrial Self-Government in the 1930s', *The English Historical Review* 106 (1991), 41–65.

The Politics of Planning: The Debate on Economic Planning in Britain in the 1930s, Oxford, 1997.

Robb, David, 'Brahmins from Abroad: English Expatriates and Spiritual Consciousness in Modern America', *American Studies* 26 (1985), 45–60.

Robertson, Roland, 'Glocalization: Time-Space and Homogeneity-Heterogeneity', in Mike Featherstone, Scott Lash and Roland Robertson (eds.), *Global Modernities*, London, 1995, 25–44.

Robbins, Sarah Ruffing, 'Sustaining Gendered Philanthropy through Transatlantic Friendship: Jane Addams, Henrietta Barnett, and Writing for Reciprocal Mentoring', in Frank Q. Christianson and Leslee Thorne-Murphy (eds.) *Philanthropic Discourse in Anglo-American Literature, 1850–1920*, Bloomington, IN, 2017, 211–35.

Robinson, Emily, *The Language of Progressive Politics in Modern Britain*, London, 2017.

Robinson, Emily with Camilla Schofield, Florence Sutcliffe-Braithwaite and Natalie Thomlinson, 'Telling Stories about Post-war Britain: Popular Individualism and the "Crisis" of the 1970s', *Twentieth Century British History* 28 (2017), 268–304.

Robinson, Sandra and Alastair Niven (eds.), *Discourses of Empire and Commonwealth*, Leiden, 2016.

Rodgers, Daniel T., *Atlantic Crossings: Social Politics in a Progressive Age*, Cambridge, 1998.

Rogan, Tim, *The Moral Economists: R.H. Tawney, Karl Polanyi, E.P. Thompson and the Critique of Capitalism*, Oxford and London, 2017.

Roper, Michael, 'Between Manliness and Masculinity: The "War Generation" and the Psychology of Fear in Britain, 1914–1950', *Journal of British Studies* 44 (2005), 343–62.

Rose, Nikolas, *The Psychological Complex: Psychology, Politics and Society in England, 1869–1939*, London, 1985.

Inventing Ourselves: Psychology, Power and Personhood, Cambridge and New York, 1996.

Rose, Sonya, *Which People's War? National Identity and Citizenship in Britain 1939–1945*, Oxford, 2003.

Rosenberg, Emily, 'Missions to the World: Philanthropy Abroad', in Lawrence J. Friedman and Mark D. MacGarvie (eds.), *Charity, Philanthropy and Civility in American History*, Cambridge, 2003, 241–57.

Ross, Katherine and Gardens Advisory Committee, *Dartington Hall Gardens: Historical Report*, [n.p.], 2016.

Ross, Dorothy (ed.), *The Origins of American Social Sciences*, Cambridge, 1991.

Ross, Dorothy *Modernist Impulses in the Human Sciences 1870–1930*, Baltimore, 1994.

Runciman, David, *Pluralism and the Personality of the State*, Cambridge, 1997.

Rutkoff, Peter M. and William B. Scott, *New School: A History of the New School for Social Research*, New York, 1986.

Sackley, Nicole, 'The Village as Cold War Site: Experts, Development, and the History of Rural Reconstruction', *Journal of Global History* 6 (2011), 481–504.

'Village Models: Etawah, India, and the Making and Remaking of Development in the Early Cold War', *Diplomatic History* 37 (2013), 749–78.

Saler, Michael T., *The Avant-Garde in Interwar England: Medieval Modernism and the London Underground*, New York; Oxford, 1999.

'"Clap If You Believe in Sherlock Holmes": Mass Culture and the Re-enchantment of Modernity, c. 1890–c. 1940', *The Historical Journal* 46 (2003), 599–622.

As If: Modern Enchantment and the Literary Prehistory of Virtual Reality, Oxford, 2012.

Sandel, Michael, *Democracy's Discontent: America in Search of a Public Philosophy*, London, 1996.

Satia, Priya, 'Byron, Gandhi and the Thompsons: The Making of British Social History and Unmaking of Indian History', *History Workshop Journal* 18 (2016), 135–70.

Savage, Mike, *Identities and Social Change in Britain Since 1940: The Politics of Method*, Oxford, 2010.

Savage, Mike with Gaynor Bagnall and Brian Longhurst, *Globalisation and Belonging*, London, 2005.

Schumacher, E. F., *Small is Beautiful: A Study of Economics as If People Mattered*, London, 1973.

Selleck, R. J. W., *The New Education, 1870–1914*, London, 1968.

English Primary Education and the Progressives, 1914–1939, London, 1972.

Sengupta, Santosh Chandra (ed.), *Rabindranath Tagore: Homage from Visva-Bharati*, Santiniketan, 1962.

Sharp, Martin, *Michael Chekhov: The Dartington Years*, DVD, Palomino Films, 2002.

Shaw, Jane, *Octavia, Daughter of God: The Story of a Female Messiah and her Followers*, London, 2011.

Sheail, John, *Rural Conservation in Interwar Britain*, Oxford, 1981.

Sherington, G. E., 'The 1918 Education Act: Origins, Aims and Development', *British Journal of Educational Studies* 24 (1976), 66–85.

Short, Brian, *Battle of the Fields: Rural Community and Authority in Britain during the Second World War*, Woodbridge, 2014.

Shoshkes, Ellen, 'Jaqueline Tyrwhitt: A Founding Mother of Modern Urban Design', *Planning Perspectives* 21 (2006), 179–97.

'Tyrwhitt, (Mary) Jaqueline (1905–1983)', *Oxford Dictionary of National Biography*, Oxford University Press, www.oxforddnb.com/view/article/106752.

Sidnell, Michael, *Dances of Death: The Group Theatre of London in the Thirties*, London, 1984.

Silver, Harold, *Education, Change, and the Policy Process*, London, 1990.

Sinfield, Alan, *Literature, Politics, and Culture in Postwar Britain*, Berkeley; Los Angeles, 1989.

Singerman, David Roth, 'Keynesian Eugenics and the Goodness of the World', *Journal of British Studies* 55 (2016), 538–65.

Sinha, Subir, 'Lineages of the Developmental State: Transnationality and Village India, 1900–1965', *Comparative Studies in Society and History* 50 (2008), 57–90.

Sluga, Glenda, *Internationalism in the Age of Nationalism*, Philadelphia, 2013.

Sluga, Glenda and Patricia Clavin, *Internationalisms, a Twentieth-Century History*, Cambridge, 2017.

Smiles, Sam (ed.), *Going Modern and Being British: Art, Architecture and Design in Devon c. 1910–1960*, Exeter, 1998.

Smith, Joanna, '"Work Collectively and Live Individually": The Bata Housing Estate at East Tilbury', *Twentieth Century Architecture* 9 (2008), 52–68.

Smith, Roger, 'Biology and Human Values: C.S. Sherrington, Julian Huxley and the Vision of Progress', *Past and Present* 178 (2003), 210–42.

Smith, Mark C., *Social Science in the Crucible*, Durham and London, 1994.

Snell, Reginald, *From the Bare Stem: Making Dorothy Elmhirst's Garden at Dartington Hall*, Devon, 1989.

Snowman, Daniel, *The Hitler Emigrés: The Cultural Impact on Britain of Refugees from Nazism*, London, 2002.

Spalding, Frances, *John Piper, Myfanwy Piper: Lives in Art*, Oxford, 2009.

Stansky, Peter, *On or About December 1910: Early Bloomsbury and Its Intimate World*, Cambridge, MA, 1996.

Stansky, Peter and William Abrahams, *Journey to the Frontier: Julian Bell and John Cornford: Their Lives and the 1930s*, London, 1966.

Stanton, Bernard F., *Agricultural Economics at Cornell: A History, 1900–1990*, Ithaca, NY, 2001.

Stapledon, Olaf, *Odd John: A Story Between Jest and Earnest*, London, 1935.

Stapleton, Julia, 'Localism Versus Centralism in the Webbs' Political Thought', *History of Political Thought* 12 (1991), 147–65.

   Group Rights, [n.p.], 1995.

   'Historiographical Review: Political Thought, Elites, and the State in Modern Britain', *The Historical Journal* 24 (1999), 251–68.

   Political Intellectuals and Public Identities in Britain Since 1850, Manchester, 2001.

   'Resisting the Centre at the Extremes: "English" Liberalism in the Political Thought of Interwar Britain', *The British Journal of Politics & International Relations* 1 (1999), 270–92.

Stears, Marc, 'Guild Socialism and Ideological Diversity on the British Left, 1914–1926', *Journal of Political Ideologies* 3 (1998), 289–305.

   Progressives, Pluralists, and the Problems of the State: Ideologies of Reform in the United States and Britain, 1909–1926, Oxford, 2006.

Demanding Democracy, Princeton and Oxford, 2010.

'Guild Socialism', in Mark Bevir (ed.), *Modern Pluralism: Anglo-American Debates Since 1880*, Cambridge, 2012, 40–59.

Out of the Ordinary: How Everyday Life Inspired a Nation and How it Can Again, Cambridge, MA, 2021.

Steedman, Carolyn, *Dust*, Manchester, 2001.

Stegges, Tracy L., *School, Society, and State: A New Education to Govern Modern America, 1890–1940*, Chicago, 2012.

Stephenson, Andrew, 'Strategies of Situation: British Modernism and the Slump, c.1929–1934', *Oxford Art Journal* 14 (1991), 30–51.

Stewart, W. A. C. and W. P. McCann, *The Educational Innovators, vol. 2: Progressive Schools 1881–1967*, London, 1968.

Progressives and Radicals in English Education, 1750–1970, London, 1972.

'Progressive Education – Past, Present and Future', *British Journal of Educational Studies* 2 (1979), 103–10.

Stoler, Ann Laura, 'Colonial Archives and the Arts of Governance: On the Content in the Form', in Francis X. Blouin and William Rosenberg (eds.) *Archives, Documentation, and Institutions of Social Memory: Essays from the Sawyer Seminar*, Ann Arbor, MI, 2006, 267–79.

Stolliday, Ivor, 'Dartington's Money', unpublished note, 2007 [access by courtesy of the author].

Stott, Martin, *Spilling the Beans*, London, 1986.

Straight, Michael, *After Long Silence*, London, 1983.

Suri, Jeremi, 'The Rise and Fall of the International Counterculture, 1960–1975', *American Historical Review* 114 (2009), 45–68.

Susman, Warren, *Culture as History: The Transformation of American Society in the Twentieth Century*, New York, 1973.

Sutcliffe, Steven J., *Children of the New Age: A History of Spiritual Practices*, London, 2003.

Swanberg, W. A., *Whitney Father, Whitney Heiress*, New York, 1980.

Sykes, Marjorie and Jehangir P. Patel, *Gandhi, His Gift of the Fight*, Rasulia, 1987.

Symons, Julian, *The Thirties: A Dream Revolved*, London, 2001 [1960].

Taylor Allen, Ann, *The Transatlantic Kindergarten: Education and the Woman's Movement in Germany and the United States*, New York, 2017.

Taylor, Paul Beekman, *Gurdjieff and Orage: Brothers in Elysium*, York Beach, ME, 2001.

Thomas, Matthew, *Anarchist Ideas and Counter-Cultures in Britain, 1880–1914*, Aldershot, 2005.

Thomas, Zoë, *Women Art Workers and the Arts and Crafts Movement*, Manchester, 2020.

Thomson, Mathew, *Psychological Subjects: Identity, Culture and Health in Twentieth-Century Britain*, Oxford, 2006.

Lost Freedom: The Landscape of the Child and the British Post-War Settlement, Oxford, 2013.

Tichelar, Michael, 'The Scott Report and the Labour Party: The Protection of the Countryside During the Second World War', *Rural History* 15 (2004), 167–87.

Tingley, Donald F., 'Ellen Van Volkenburg, Maurice Browne and the Chicago Little Theatre', *Illinois Historical Journal* 80 (1987), 130–46.

Tisdall, Laura, 'The Psychologist, the Psychoanalyst and the "Extraordinary Child" in Postwar British Science Fiction', *Medical Humanities Special Issue, 'Science Fiction and the Medical Humanities'* 43 (2016), 4–9.

'Teachers, Teaching Practice and Conceptions of Childhood in England and Wales, 1931–1967', unpublished PhD, University of Cambridge, 2014.

A Progressive Education? How Childhood Changed in Mid-Twentieth-Century English and Welsh Schools, Manchester, 2019.

Titmuss, Christopher, *Freedom of the Spirit*, London, 1991.

Tonn, Joan C., *Mary P. Follett: Creating Democracy, Transforming Management*, New Haven, CT and London, 2003.

Tooze, Adam, 'A Small Village in the Age of Extremes: The Häusern Experiment', unpublished paper, 2014, 1–29.

Trahair, Richard, *Behavior, Technology, and Organizational Development: Eric Trist and the Tavistock Institute*, New Brunswick, 2015.

Turner, Fred, *The Democratic Surround: Multimedia and American Liberalism from World War II to the Psychedelic Sixties*, Chicago and London, 2013.

Twigg, Julia, 'The Vegetarian Movement in England 1847–1981', unpublished PhD, London School of Economics, 1981.

Upchurch, Anna, 'John Maynard Keynes, the Bloomsbury Group and the Origins of the Arts Council Movement', *International Journal of Cultural Policy* 10 (2004), 203–17.

'"Missing" From Policy History: The Dartington Hall Arts Enquiry, 1941–1947', *International Journal of Cultural Policy* 19 (2012), 610–22.

The Origins of the Arts Council Movement: Philanthropy and Policy, London, 2016.

Ussishkin, Daniel, 'The "Will to Work": Industrial Management and the Question of Conduct in Inter-War Britain', in Laura Beers and Geraint Thomas (eds.), *Brave New World: Imperial and Democratic Nation-Building in Britain Between the Wars*, London, 2011, 91–108.

Van der Veer, Peter, 'Spirituality in Modern Society,' *Social Research* 76 (2009), 1097–120.

Van Volkenburg Browne, Ellen and Edward Nordhoff Beck (eds.), *Miss Aunt Nellie: The Autobiography of Nellie C. Cornish*, Seattle, 1964.

Vaninskaya, Anna, *William Morris and the Idea of Community: Romance, History and Propaganda, 1880–1914*, Edinburgh, 2010.

Vernon, James, *Modern Britain, 1750 to the Present*, Cambridge; New York, 2017.

Vertinsky, Patricia, *Disciplining Bodies in the Gymnasium: Memory, Monument, Modernism*, London, 2004.

'Schooling the Dance: From Dance Under the Swastika to Movement Education in the British School', *Journal of Sport History* 31 (2004), 273–95.

'Movement Practices and Fascist Infections: From Dance Under the Swastika To Movement Education in the British Primary School', in Jennifer Hargreaves and Patricia Vertinsky (eds.), *Physical Culture, Power, and the Body*, London and New York, 2007, 25–51.

'Physique as Destiny: William H. Sheldon, Barbara Honeyman Heath and the Struggle for Hegemony in the Science of Somatotyping', *Criminal Behaviour and Mental Health* 24 (2007), 291–316.

Veysey, Laurence R., *The Communal Experience: Anarchist and Mystical Communities in Twentieth-Century America*, Chicago and London, 1973.

Vincent, Andrew, 'Classic Liberalism and Its Crisis of Identity, *History of Political Thought*, 11 (1990), 143–61.

Vincent, Matthew, 'The Rich Column: Modern Means to Finance an Old Country Estate', 30 November 2018, *Financial Times*, www.ft.com/content/eefd5280-cc7f-11e8-8d0b-a6539b949662.

Vinen, Richard, *A History in Fragments: Europe in the Twentieth Century*, London, 2000.

Wade Martins, Susanna, 'Smallholdings in Norfolk, 1890–1950: A Social and Farming Experiment', *The Agricultural History Review* 54 (2006), 304–30.

Walker, Andrew, 'The "Uncertainty of Our Climate": Mary Kelly and the Rural Theatre', in Kristin Bluemel and Michael McCluskey (eds.), *Rural Modernity in Britain: A Critical Intervention*, Edinburgh, 2018, 121–34.

Wallis, Mick, 'Kelly, Mary Elfreda (1888–1951)', *Oxford Dictionary of National Biography*, www.oxforddnb.com/view/article/69833?docPos=1.

'Unlocking the Secret Soul: Mary Kelly, Pioneer of Village Theatre', *New Theatre Quarterly* 16 (2000), 347–58.

Wallmeier, Philip, 'Exit as Critique: Communes and Intentional Communities in the 1960s and Today', *Historical Social Research* 42 (2017), 147–71.

Ward, Stephen V., 'A Pioneer "Global Intelligence Corps"? The Internationalization of Planning Practice, 1890–1939', *The Town Planning Review* 76 (2005), 119–41.

Weight, Richard, 'State, Intelligentsia and the Promotion of National Culture in Britain, 1939–45', *Historical Research* 69 (1996), 83–101.

Weight, Richard and Abigail Beach (eds.), *The Right to Belong: Citizenship and National Identity in Britain, 1930–1960*, London, 1998.

Webb, James, *Harmonious Circle: The Lives and Works of G.I. Gurdjieff, P.D. Ouspensky and Their Followers*, London, 1980.

Westbrook, Robert B., *John Dewey and American Democracy*, Ithaca, NY, 1991.

Whetham, Edith H., *The Agrarian History of England and Wales, vol. 8: 1914–39*, Cambridge, 1978.

Agricultural Economists in Britain 1900–1940, Oxford, 1981.

Whiting, R. C., 'Political and Economic Planning (*act.* 1931–1978)', *Oxford Dictionary of National Biography*, Oxford University Press, www.oxforddnb.com/view/theme/95962.

Wiebe, Heather, 'Benjamin Britten, the "National Faith", and the Animation of History in 1950s England', *Representations* 93 (2006), 76–105.

Williams, Anthea, 'Elmhirst, Leonard Knight (1893–1974)', rev. *Oxford Dictionary of National Biography*, Oxford University Press, www.oxforddnb.com/view/article/31072.

Williams, John Alexander, *Turning to Nature in Germany: Hiking, Nudism, and Conservation 1900–1940*, Stanford, 2007.

Williams, Raymond, *Culture and Society*, London, 2017 [1958].

The Country and the City, London, 2017 [1973].

Winter, Jay, *Dreams of Peace and Freedom: Utopian Moments in the Twentieth Century*, New Haven, CT and London, 2006.

Winters, Elmer A., 'Man and His Changing Society: The Textbooks of Harold Rugg', *History of Education Quarterly* 7 (1967), 493–514.

Wollaeger, Mark, *Modernism, Media and Propaganda: British Narrative From 1900 to 1945*, Princeton, 2006.

Wooldridge, Adrian, *Measuring the Mind: Education and Psychology in England, c. 1860–1990*, Cambridge, 1994.

'The English State and Educational Theory', in S. J. D. Green and R. C. Whiting (eds.), *The Boundaries of the State in Modern Britain*, Cambridge, 1996, 231–58.

Worley, Matthew, 'What Was the New Party? Sir Oswald Mosley and Associated Responses to the "Crisis", 1931–1932', *History* 92 (2007), 39–63.

Wright, Patrick, *The Village That Died for England: The Strange Story of Tyneham*, London, 1995.

Yang, Jiling, 'In Search of Martha Root: An American Baha'i Feminist and Peace Advocate in the Early Twentieth Century', unpublished PhD thesis, Georgia State University, 2005.

Young, Michael, *Small Man: Big World*, London, 1949.

The Chipped White Cups of Dover: A Discussion of the Possibility of a New Progressive Party, London, 1960.

The Elmhirsts of Dartington: The Creation of a Utopian Community, London, 1982.

Zablocki, Benjamin, *Alienation and Charisma*, New York, 1980.

Index

For EU product safety concerns, contact us at Calle de José Abascal, 56–1°,
28003 Madrid, Spain or eugpsr@cambridge.org.

www.ingramcontent.com/pod-product-compliance
Ingram Content Group UK Ltd.
Pitfield, Milton Keynes, MK11 3LW, UK
UKHW020359140625
459647UK00020B/2549